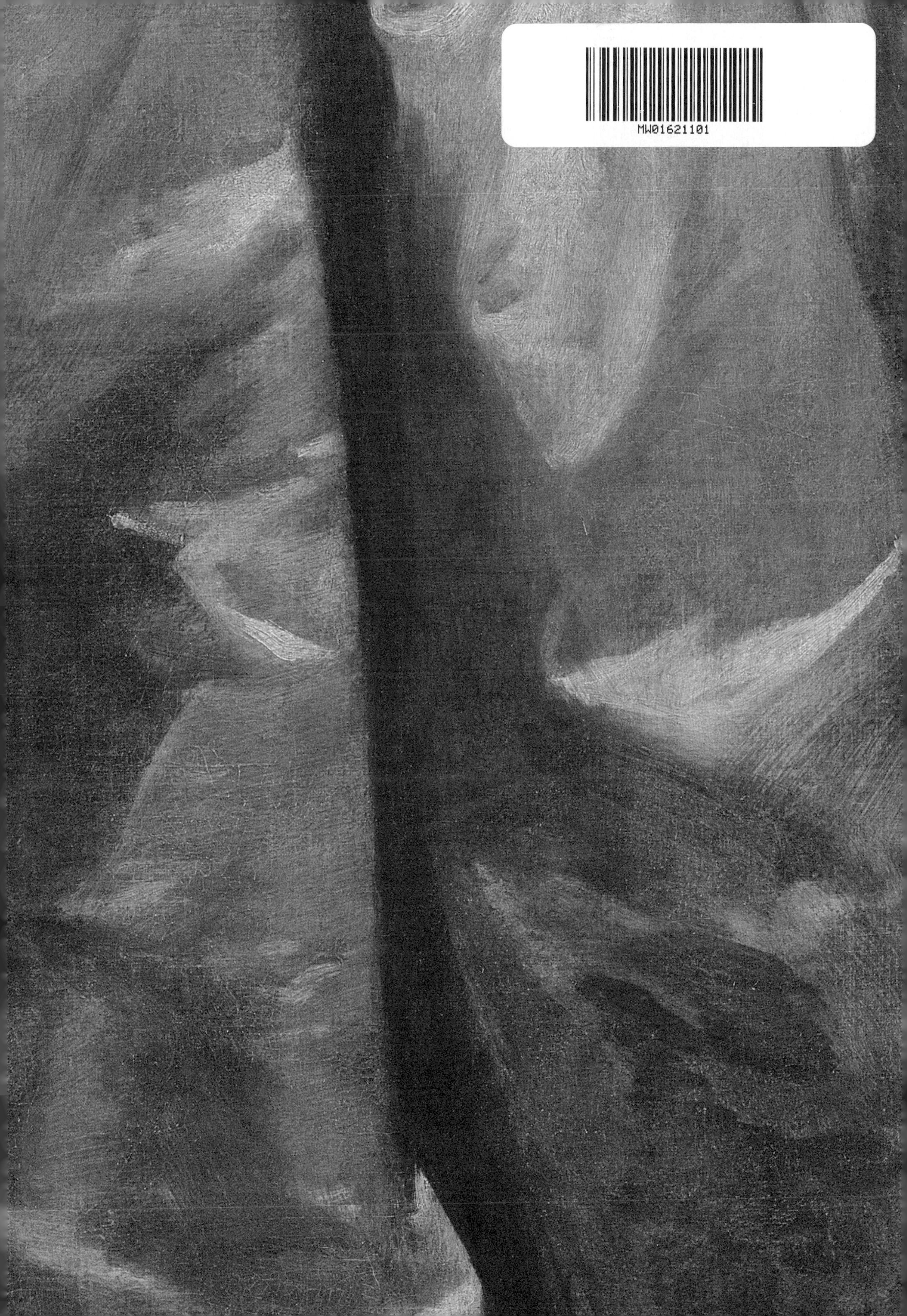
MW01621101

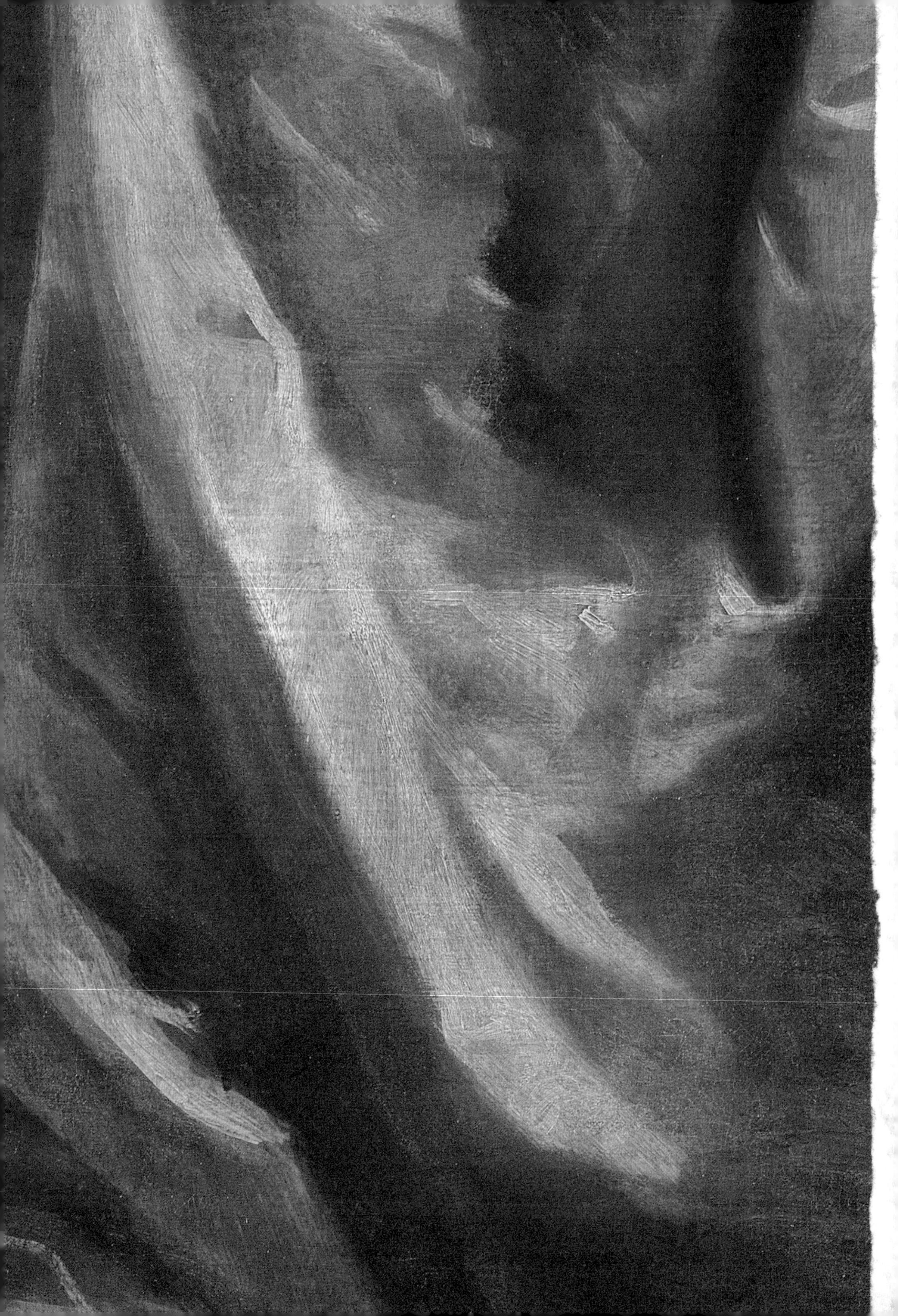

VAN DYCK
AND THE MAKING OF ENGLISH PORTRAITURE

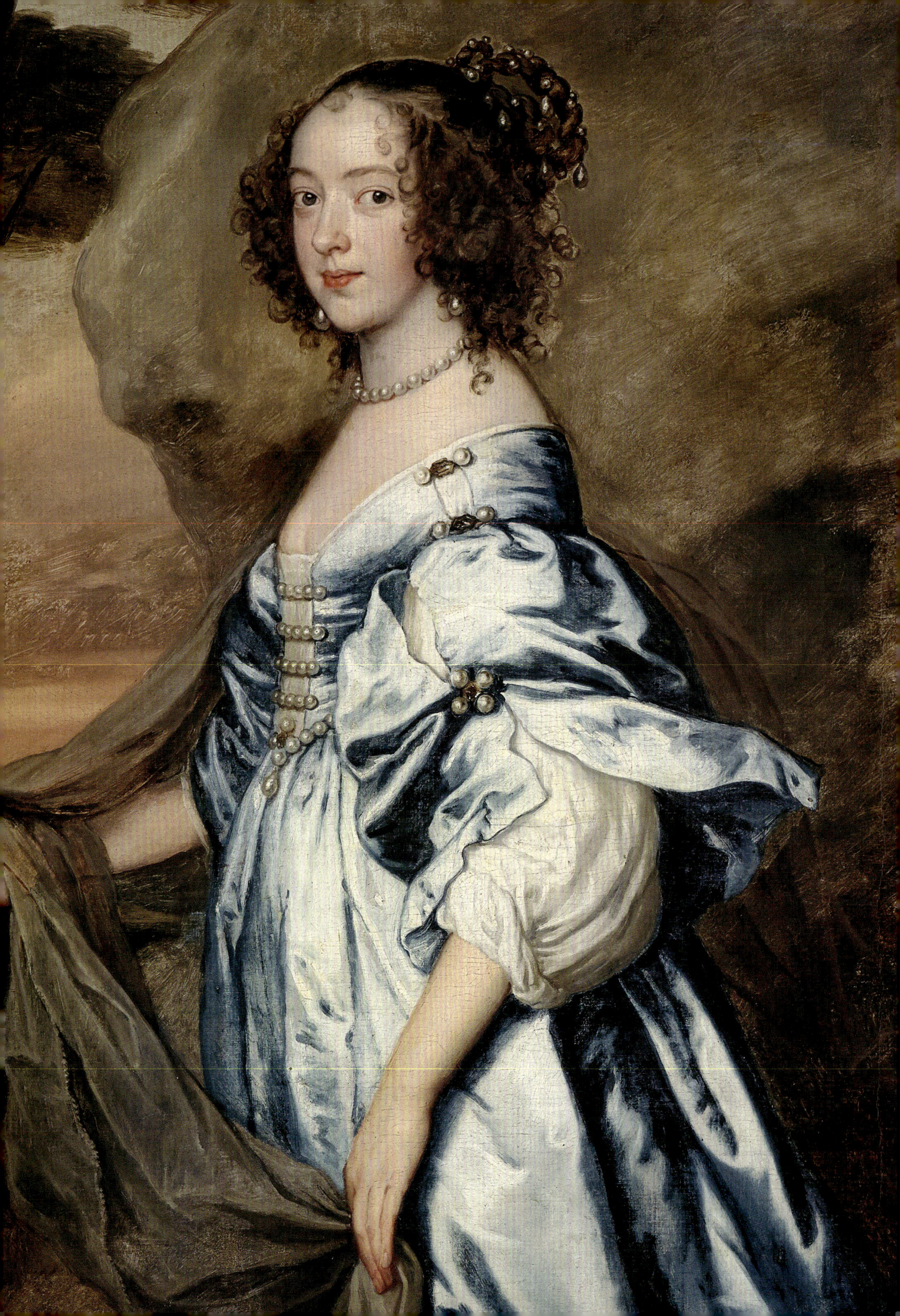

ADAM EAKER

VAN DYCK
and the Making of English Portraiture

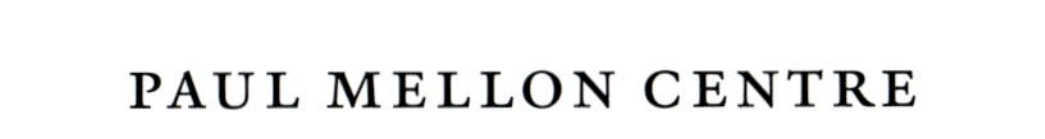

PAUL MELLON CENTRE
FOR STUDIES IN BRITISH ART

Distributed by Yale University Press
New Haven and London

First published in 2022 by the
Paul Mellon Centre for Studies in British Art
16 Bedford Square · London WC1B 3JA
paul-mellon-centre.ac.uk

ISBN 978-1-913107-34-5 HB

Library of Congress Control Number: 2022937498

British Library Cataloguing-in-Publication Data
A catalogue record for this book is available from the British Library

Designed by Dalrymple
Typeset in Mark van Bronkhorst's Verdigris
Origination by Evergreen Colour Management Ltd
Printed in China through
World Print Ltd

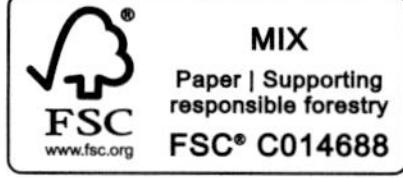

Endpapers Anthony van Dyck, *Lucy Hay, Countess of Carlisle*, 1637, private collection [detail of fig. 11]

Frontispiece Anthony van Dyck, *Lady Anne Carey*, ca. 1636, New York, Frick Collection [detail of fig. 9]

[CONTENTS]

TO MY PARENTS

Acknowledgments

The origins of this book lie in a hot Munich afternoon some fifteen years ago, when I made my first visit to the Alte Pinakothek as a young art history student. I had come in search of masterpieces encountered in a survey course on art of the Northern Renaissance, but it was the room of paintings by Van Dyck that stopped me in my tracks. His history paintings conveyed a deep unease and a psychological violence far subtler than anything I had seen in the work of his contemporaries. I made a note to read everything about him that I could.

A few years later, I began the PhD program at Columbia University intending to write a dissertation on the art of nineteenth-century Denmark. That I ended up a scholar of baroque painting owes a very great deal to the teaching, encouragement, and example of my adviser, David Freedberg, who taught a seminar on Rubens that first year. Aaron Hyman and I became friends in that Rubens seminar and have been discussing the artist and art history ever since. He read a full draft of this book and gave it both the rigorous feedback and a vote of confidence that made all the difference.

When I was a very young painter, Emily Trespas introduced me to the studio as a place of transformation and refuge. That she died before I could give her a copy of this book is a deep sorrow to me. I became an art historian as a result of Emily's encouragement and undergraduate courses at Yale with Anne Dunlop, David Joselit, Jacqueline Jung, and Christopher Wood; my sophomore year, Chris recommended that I read an essay he had written about the early modern studio, and my scholarly fate was sealed. Allison Stielau used to let me walk her back to her apartment so we could continue discussing Chris's lectures, and she has now been an essential interlocutor and reader for fully half of my life.

My engagement with British art meanwhile has grown from seeds planted early on by Tim Barringer, Matthew Hargraves, Martin Postle, the late Charles Ryskamp, and the peerless staff and collections of the Yale Center for British Art. At the start of my work on Van Dyck, the Belgian American Educational Foundation generously funded a year of research in Antwerp, where I was co-hosted by the Rubenianum and the University of Antwerp's department of history. At those institutions, I would like to thank Guido Marnef and Véronique Van de Kerkhof for their logistical support. In Belgium, I had the privilege of interacting with a scholarly community remarkably free of chauvinism about its cultural patrimony. In particular, I am grateful to the late Arnout Balis, Nico Van Hout, Koen Jonckheere, Bert Schepers, Hans Vlieghe, and, especially, Bert Watteeuw and Katlijne Van der Stighelen. One memorable Antwerp afternoon, Nora De Poorter took a red pen to my project proposal, and I remain thankful for her skepticism and generosity.

No project on Van Dyck would be possible without the vast enterprise of cataloguing undertaken by Susan Barnes, Nora De Poorter, Horst Vey, and Sir Oliver Millar, or the many generations of researchers whose archival discoveries fill the pages of this book. The international community of Van Dyck scholars has been unfailingly welcoming to a project that sought to counter many long-held beliefs about the artist. I have benefitted greatly from exchanges with Susan Barnes, Kristin Belkin, Elizabeth Honig, Emilie Gordenker, Friso Lammertse, Anne-Marie Logan, Alejandro Vergara, Sir Christopher White, and Jeremy Wood. Mirjam Neumeister invited me back to Munich to lecture on Van Dyck when she curated her own landmark exhibition on the artist. Within the small world of scholarship on sixteenth- and seventeenth-century English art, I owe many debts to Tabitha Barber, Tarnya Cooper, Jessica David, Diana Dethloff, Susan Foister, Elizabeth Goldring, Erin Griffey, Catharine MacLeod, Hilary Maddicott, David Taylor, and, especially, Edward Town. Coffee with the generous and learned Karen Hearn has been a repeated pleasure on visits to London.

My writing of the book's opening chapters coincided with the opportunity to co-curate an exhibition on Van Dyck's portraits at the Frick Collection. The two projects are more adjacent than overlapping, but fragments of my catalogue entries are woven sporadically into this text. I am deeply grateful to the Frick Collection for its abundant support of my work on Van Dyck, and to the Andrew W. Mellon Foundation, which funded the Anne. L. Poulet Curatorial Fellowship that I held. My co-curator for the exhibition, Stijn Alsteens, has been a model of rigor and a constant source of insight into Van Dyck's working method. Van Dyck-themed road trips through England with Stijn, Bert Watteeuw, Lieneke Nijkamp, Allison Stielau, and Christian Thiemann have been a highlight of my research, and I am thankful to the owners and keepers of country houses who made their holdings accessible to me. I particularly thank Kate Heard for showing me the Countess of Carnarvon's one surviving painting, in storage at Windsor Castle. Brigid von Preussen and Jamie Castell have been the most generous of hosts in both London and Oxford, as well as delightful conversation partners about the eighteenth century. I gave what became the first chapter of this book as a paper at a conference on British portraiture at the Huntington Library and Art Museum in 2015, an immensely fruitful few days that I will always view as a scholarly turning point. Portions of the first two chapters were first published in *Art History*, vol. 41 (September 2018), and I am grateful to the Association for Art History for granting me permission to reproduce that material here.

I especially thank Mark Hallett for his repeated encouragement that I submit a manuscript to the Paul Mellon Centre for Studies in British Art, and Emily Lees and Tom Powell for the consummate professionalism with which they shepherded the book through review and publication. In collaboration with Emily, Robert Dalrymple designed a book even more beautiful than I could ever have imagined. The two anonymous reviewers for the PMC provided invaluable suggestions and critique that I have attempted to honor throughout these pages. Hilary Becker secured images permissions with her characteristic good humor and professionalism. Nancy Marten brought her gimlet eye to the copy-editing, saving me from many mistakes. Any errors or infelicities that remain are naturally my own.

No one could ask for a better colleague or mentor than Maryan Ainsworth, whose wise counsel and friendship have been a mainstay of my professional life. Two further Met colleagues, Joe Scheier-Dolberg and Niv Allon, read early drafts of the introduction and offered both encouragement and bracing critique. At a later stage, Holly Shaffer offered her own insightful response to this section of the manuscript. As chairs of the Met's department of European painting, Keith Christiansen and Stephan Wolohojian were unstintingly supportive of a project that lay outside my immediate curatorial duties. With the support of Michael Gallagher, Dorothy Mahon undertook a year-long conservation treatment of Richard Cosway's *Marianne Dorothy Harland* at my request, resulting in the beautifully cleaned painting now visible in these pages. During the same period, Stephen Lloyd gave me a warm welcome to the study of Richard and Maria Cosway, to which he has contributed so much.

During the different stages of writing this book, I had the immense privilege of open stack access at three of the world's greatest art history libraries: the Rubenianum in Antwerp, the Frick Art Reference Library, and the Thomas J. Watson Library at the Metropolitan Museum of Art. My debts to their staff, and to that of Butler and Avery Libraries at Columbia University, go far beyond late fees, particularly in the face of library closures imposed by COVID-19.

In the midst of the pandemic, Noah Eaker and Jessica Sindler let me turn their apartment into my writing studio. Others who have provided companionship, conversation, or assistance at critical junctures during the long gestation of this project include Zainab Bahrani, Andrea Bayer, Rebecca Ben-Atar, Sam Bibby, Diane Bodart, Shira Brisman, Michael Cole, Michele Frederick, Cordula Grewe, Caitlin Henningsen, Anne Higonnet, Max Hollein, Michael Gallagher, Meredith Gamer, Alexandra Libby, Michaelyn Mitchell, Martin Moeller-Pisani, Uta Neidhardt, David Pollack, David Pullins, Xavier Salomon, Katherine Stirling, Matthias Ubl, Jill Wickenheisser, Jonny Yarker, Julie Zeftel, and Marina van Zuylen.

That the final chapter of this book was written to the sound of the flute owes everything to my husband, Brandon Patrick George, who sets an example of discipline and devotion every day of our life together.

This book is dedicated to my parents, Lynn Hamilton and Mark Eaker, who have never once discouraged me from traveling down the rabbit hole.

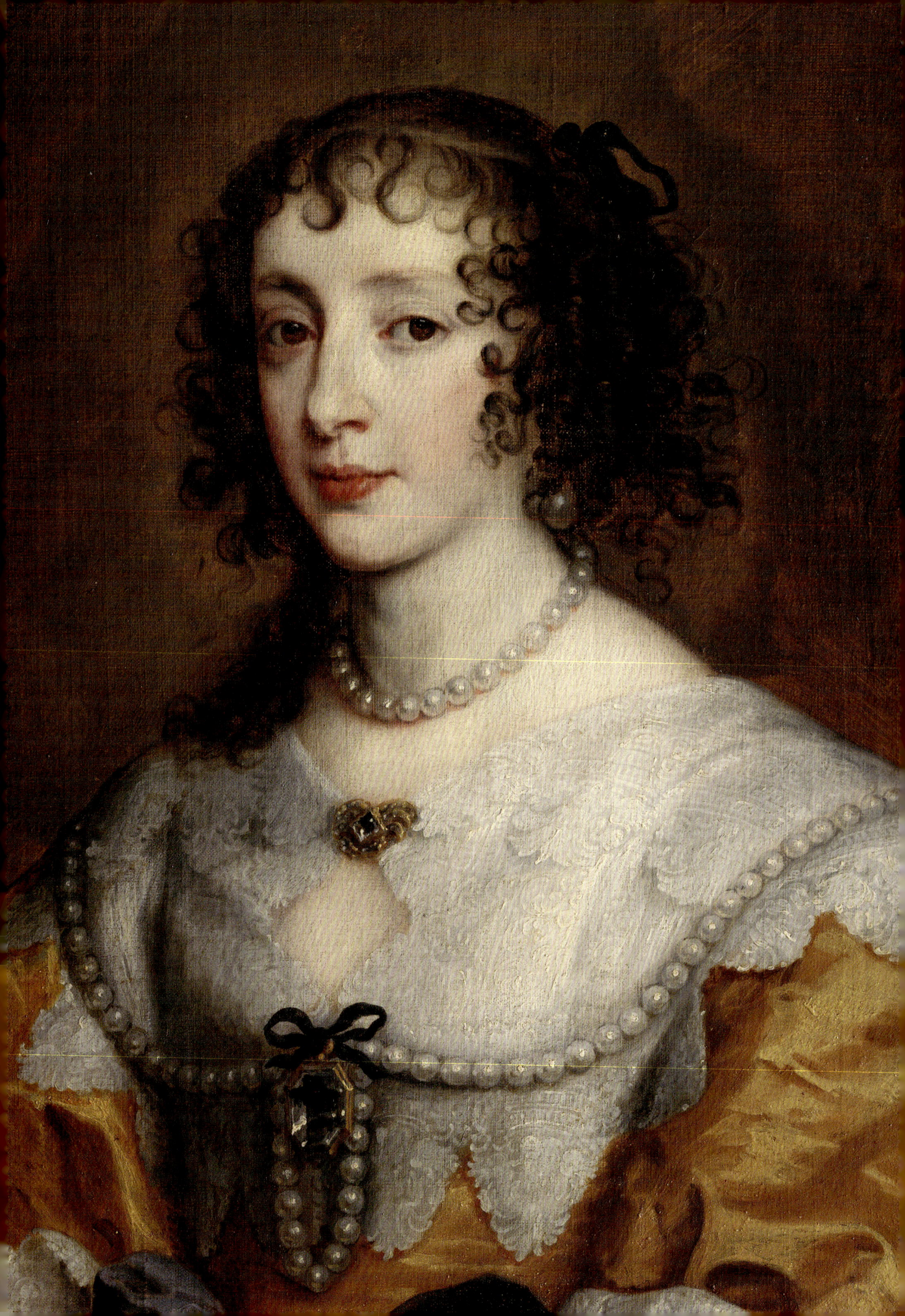

[INTRODUCTION]

Studio Scenes

In the opening pages of his *Anecdotes of Painting in England*, first published in 1762, Horace Walpole pondered the possibility of an English history of art. Contrasting his own production with the systematic narratives of Italian and French writers, Walpole argued that the uneven and belated achievements of English painting meant its history could only ever be a collection of "particularities" and "curious trifles."[1] Another problem facing the chronicler of art in England was the foreignness of its key practitioners. Where Giorgio Vasari celebrated Tuscan identity by tracing a lineage from Giotto to Michelangelo, Walpole was forced to concede that his native country "has very rarely given birth to a genius in [painting]. Flanders and Holland have sent us the greatest men that we can boast."[2] Recounting fragmentary incidents from the lives of foreigners, Walpole constantly undercut the claims of a patriotic master narrative.

Like Walpole's, this book provides a new account of painting in early modern England, taking its point of departure from the art and legacy of one foreign-born painter, Anthony van Dyck. Through his public persona as a courtier, figure of fashion, and object of erotic fascination, Van Dyck transformed the professional identities available to English artists, and a self-consciously Van Dyckian lineage of painters can be traced from his lifetime to the end of the eighteenth century and beyond. Van Dyck's role in the elevation of painting as a fine art in England is hardly news to art historians;[3] seventeenth- and eighteenth-century painters and art theorists made clear their debt to him as they sought to articulate the origins of an "English school."[4] But rather than accord Van Dyck an unproblematic status as a founding father, I argue that he and his emulators were a perpetual source of unease and ambivalence on the part of patrons, critics, and artistic rivals. By centering his artistic practice on the portrait sitting, Van Dyck transformed the perception of painters within English culture and offended guardians of traditional hierarchies. Equally disturbing was the close association between Van Dyck's art and female portraiture – and the prominence of women artists among his followers. Feminine, foreign, addicted to luxury, the Van Dyckian painter became increasingly beleaguered in the face of an academic organization of art and the emergence of an explicitly patriotic art criticism. Recovering the

Detail of Anthony van Dyck, *Queen Henrietta Maria*, 1636 [see fig. 12]

history of English art before these developments, this book provides an alternative perspective on its genealogies and historical self-consciousness.

Taking a page from Walpole, mine is an anecdotal history to the extent that I read the transmission, embellishment, and recycling of artistic anecdotes as a major symptom of a culture's relationship to its artists. My account of Van Dyck's legacy builds upon a series of close readings of artworks and texts ranging from poems and plays to early biographies, art theory, and studio gossip. Through these texts, I excavate a vernacular discourse on early modern English art centered on the socially and sexually fraught encounter of the portrait sitting. Van Dyck's portraits emerged from a display of verbal acuity – the artist's famous conversation during his portrait sittings. He quickly inspired a conflicted response from poets and playwrights, who seized on the painter as a figure of foreign luxury, or imagined him as the third term in erotic triangles of portraitist, female sitter, and male patron. Texts and images defined the Van Dyckian painter in opposition to a series of foils: the model, the mistress, the patron, the slave. Such binaries reflected the hierarchical gradations of court life, within which Van Dyck and his heirs were consummate operators. But they also indicated the studio's status as an arena for contesting relations of power.[5]

Van Dyck died in 1641, on the eve of one of the greatest traumas of English history, the Civil War. Because of his close association with the court and patronage of Charles I, Van Dyck's paintings rapidly acquired a prelapsarian quality and a political potency that is an essential part of their legacy. During the Restoration, artists and writers embraced the emulation of Van Dyck as a form of historical reparation, bridging over the caesurae of civil war, regicide, and interregnum. Modern art historians, by contrast, have tended to reinforce the sense of rupture between Van Dyck and England's putative "discovery of painting" in the late seventeenth century, treating the artist's achievement as a foreign graft that largely failed to bear native fruit.[6] Unlike standard histories of English art that begin with the Restoration or Glorious Revolution before focusing on the developments of the Georgian period, my account stresses self-conscious continuities within artistic practice from the 1630s to the end of the eighteenth century.[7] Many of the constitutive features of the early modern English art world, such as the London "season," the centrality of portraiture to artistic ambition, and the work of aristocratic women as cultural arbiters, date to the Caroline period and went hand-in-hand with Van Dyck's English triumph. Over the course of the eighteenth century, however, an increase in cultural chauvinism, the marginalization of court patronage, and a diminished historical memory of the Civil War meant that Van Dyckian emulation shifted from being a powerful artistic identity to a superannuated pose.

Even before Van Dyck's arrival in England, the centrality of portraiture to local artistic culture created a particularly receptive climate for the orchestration of spectacular sittings. Such sittings were partly a legacy of miniaturists like Nicholas Hilliard, who distinguished their practice of "limning" from that of ordinary painting because it required delicacy of touch, familiarity with costly materials, and proper comportment before elite sitters.[8] In his treatise on limning, Hilliard recalled "the wourds also and reasoning of her Majestie [Elizabeth I], when first I came in her highnes presence to drawe," and how the queen questioned him during her sitting on the subject of shading in portraiture.[9] Befitting a treatise that consistently emphasizes the limner's need to assert his own gentility, Hilliard's anecdote establishes both his own expertise and his physical proximity to the most majestic of sitters. Part of Van Dyck's achievement was to translate the self-ennobling claims of English limners to full-scale painting on canvas.

Van Dyck's working method fascinated his earliest biographers, who turned to his sitters for information about his portrait practice. From Sir Kenelm Digby, for example, Giovanni Pietro Bellori acquired the following description:

> *Concerning his mode of painting, he was in the habit of executing his work straight off* [alla prima]*; and when he was making portraits, he would begin them in the morning early, and without interrupting his work he would keep those lords to dine with him; even if they were important personages and great ladies, they went there gladly, as if for recreation, attracted by the variety of entertainments. After dinner he would return to the work, or else he might have painted two in one day, finishing them later with some retouching.*[10]

For his part, Roger de Piles spoke to the banker and collector Everhard Jabach, who had thrice sat to Van Dyck, obtaining an even more detailed account:

> *The painter gave the day and hour to the persons whom he had to paint, and never worked more than an hour at a time on a portrait, whether it be to sketch it out or to finish it; and when his clock told him that the hour was up, he would rise and bow to the person to indicate that that was enough for one day, and would make an appointment for another day and another hour: after which his valet came to clean his brushes and prepare another palette, while he received the next person to whom he had given an appointment. He worked thus at several portraits during the same day with extraordinary swiftness.*[11]

These descriptions of Van Dyck in the studio emphasize his mastery and control, with the artist's portraits representing the output of a nearly industrialized process that unfolds according to strict choreography. But they also have contributed to the perception that Van Dyck's artistry was tainted by an unseemly commercialism and a dependence upon the labor of others.

Van Dyck' s working method allowed him to display his own lordly way of life. As recounted by Bellori, "He rivaled the magnificence of Parrhasius, keeping servants, carriages, horses, players, musicians, and jesters, and with these entertainments he played host to all the great personages, knights and ladies, who came daily to have their portraits painted at his house."[12] Bellori's account deftly summarizes the features by which we can recognize the Van Dyckian studio in its many subsequent incarnations. For painters who followed Van Dyck's example, the studio was a site of luxurious consumption, of aristocratic recreation, and of the artist's demonstrative munificence. Within this paradigm of art-making, the painter no longer positioned himself within the household of his patron, but instead occupied his own princely establishment: in other words, the studio.

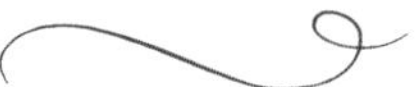

ANTHONY VAN DYCK WAS BORN IN ANTWERP IN 1599 INTO A FAMILY OF mercers. The sparse documentation for his early life indicates an unsettled childhood following his mother's death and his father's insolvency.[13] After an apprenticeship with Hendrick van Balen, Van Dyck registered as a master with Antwerp's Guild of St. Luke on February 11, 1618. Nevertheless, sources refer to Van Dyck as a student or assistant in Rubens's workshop for several years after this date.[14] Among the most intriguing of these sources is a description of a portrait sitting that he witnessed as a young man in Rubens's studio. In a letter dated to 1620, Francesco Vercellini, an Italian member of the household of the Earl and Countess of Arundel, described a visit that Lady Arundel made to Peter Paul Rubens's house in Antwerp, where she sat for a portrait by the master:

> *On my arrival in this city, I at once presented the letter of your Excellency to Signor Rubens the painter, which he received with a joyful countenance. But after having read it, he displayed yet more pleasure, and made me this reply: Although I have refused to paint the portraits of many princes and gentlemen ... yet I cannot refuse the Earl the honour he does me in commanding* [one from] *me, holding him for one of the four evangelists, and a supporter of our art ... Signor Rubens has promised my lady not to take the portrait of any person whatever, except such as are ordered by your Excellency. Van Dyck is still with Signor Rubens, and his works are hardly less esteemed than those of his master.*[15]

Vercellini vividly recounts the courtly negotiation that attended portrait sittings and that Van Dyck observed as a young man in Rubens's workshop. Portrait sittings entailed the intrusion into the studio of an outsider whose authority rivaled or eclipsed the artist's.[16] Lady Arundel's visit to Rubens recast the painter as a vassal in a hierarchical chain in which he occupied at best a middling position. This encounter resulted in a portrait that was not the fruit of solitary invention, but rather a testimony to the artist's relationship to a social superior.

Vercellini's account, destined for his employer, describes the sitting in terms intended to flatter the patron and to reinforce feudal distinctions. Rubens's finished portrait of Lady Arundel provides its own staging of hierarchical difference, a tableau that unfolds before a heraldic banner held aside like a theatrical curtain by one of the countess's attendants [fig. 1].[17] Through the inclusion of this banner, Rubens naturalized an archaic feature of portraiture, the coat of arms, and made it the backdrop for a scene of unquestioned inequality. The central and only seated figure, Lady Arundel, appears with an entourage that condenses a whole noble household of people and animals. The countess's attendants function

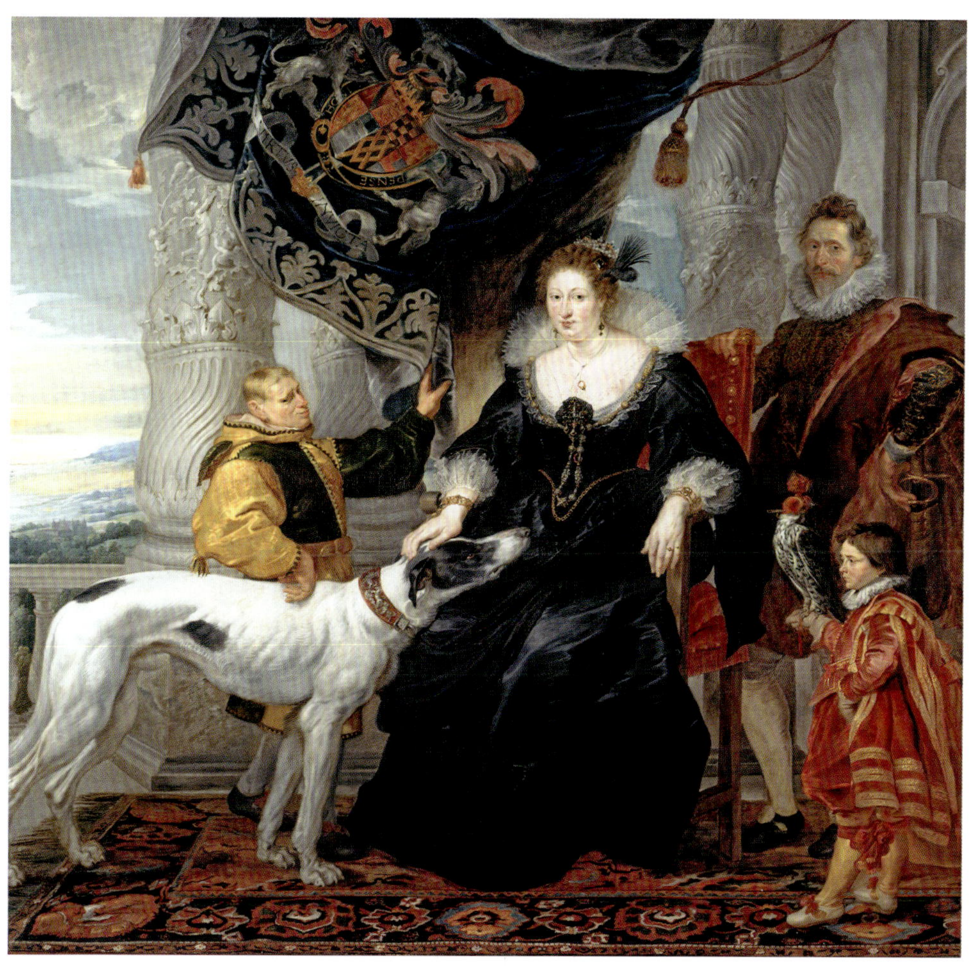

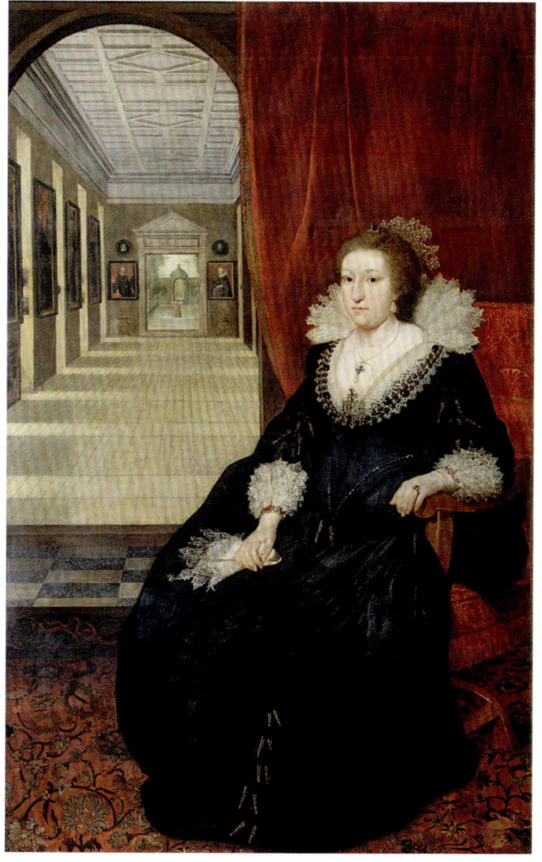

1 Peter Paul Rubens, *Aletheia Talbot, Countess of Arundel, with Her Entourage*, 1620, oil on canvas, 259 × 267 cm, Munich, Alte Pinakothek

2 Daniel Mytens, *Aletheia Talbot, Countess of Arundel*, ca. 1618, oil on canvas, 207 × 127 cm, London, National Portrait Gallery within Rubens's portrait as foils, establishing binaries between the dominant and servile, female and male, beautiful and deformed. Like many early modern aristocrats, Lady Arundel seems to have had a particular investment in retainers who would offer a striking visual contrast to her own body.[18] In other portraits, metapictorial passages provided another kind of foil or framing device. In Daniel Mytens's painting of the countess, for example, she appears at the end of a long gallery of ancestral portraits, the terminus of a celebrated lineage [fig. 2].[19] Here, dynastic portraiture supplants heraldry, showing how either might testify to noble descent.[20] Both Rubens and Mytens imagined their sitter as a pedigreed collector of persons and things. Within these depictions, the relationship between the countess and her portraitist is kept scrupulously offstage.

The social stratifications of the noble household, so explicitly staged by Rubens's portrait and later reenacted by the jesters and musicians of Van Dyck's studio, represented a fixed hierarchy that many early modern artists sought to avoid. Over the course of the seventeenth century, the tact required by the portrait sitting struck an increasing number of artists and art theorists as a form of self-abasement. In the words of Joanna Woodall, a "hostile, dualist conception of portraiture" emerged in art theory, mapping onto portrait sittings the conflict between a painter's ambitions and a sitter's vanity.[21] Rubens's own ambivalence toward the genre is apparent from his claim to have "refused to paint the portraits of many princes and gentlemen," as though his portrait of Lady Arundel were a special concession. Later in the century, Guido Reni's biographer Malvasia reported that when "summoned to France to paint the portrait of that king with the offer of a thousand doubloons and another thousand for provisions for the journey, [the artist] replied that he was not a painter of portraits."[22]

Within this context, Van Dyck's choice to specialize in portraiture has troubled most commentators on his art since the seventeenth century. Bellori, for example, explained Van Dyck's career as a portraitist in terms of a thwarted education in Rubens's studio. According to the biographer: "As Rubens became aware that his pupil [Van Dyck] was proceeding to usurp the credit for his colors and would shortly jeopardize his reputation, being a very shrewd man, he took his opportunity from some portraits that Anthony painted and, acclaiming them with the highest praises, proposed him in his stead to anyone who came to request portraits, in order to keep him from figures [*per rimuoverlo dalle figure*]."[23] Bellori placed the blame for Van Dyck's squandered talents on his master's sly withholding of access to "figures," to be understood here broadly as commissions for history paintings and the life study they entailed.[24] Building on this origin story, subsequent scholars have seen Van Dyck's focus on portraits as symptomatic of an intellectual deficit or vulgar commercialism.[25] In the 2004 catalogue raisonné, for example, Nora De Poorter wrote, "The goal he had probably set himself – to become a successful history painter like Rubens and the celebrated Italians – was overly ambitious. Instead, he found a path [portraiture] that was perfectly suited to his exceptional talent."[26] Time and again, Rubensian history painting has provided the metric by which Van Dyck's career is assessed and found wanting. Yet as this book shows, Van Dyck built his career around portraiture in self-aware contradistinction to Rubens. He saw portraits and portrait sittings as an arena for self-assertion. In doing so, he created a paradigm of artistic subjectivity that generations of painters would follow.

Shortly after Lady Arundel's visit to Antwerp, Van Dyck traveled to England, where he enjoyed the patronage of the Arundels and the future Duke of Buckingham.[27] His self-presentation as a young aristocrat – not a working painter – is already apparent in a self-portrait he painted while at the English court [fig. 3]. Here, Van Dyck calls attention to the idleness of his hands and the studied nonchalance of his pose, echoed in the demonstratively loose brushwork of the lace that spills from his collar.[28] After some four months in England, Van Dyck briefly returned to Antwerp before traveling in Lady Arundel's entourage to Italy, where he would spend the next six years.

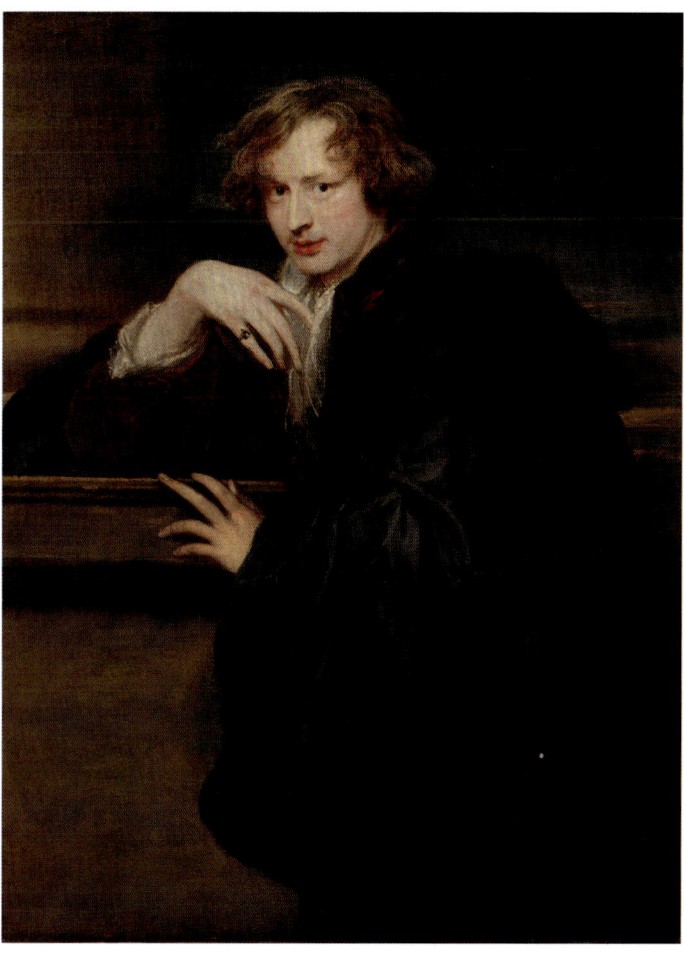

3 Anthony van Dyck, *Self-Portrait*, ca. 1620–21, oil on canvas, 119.7 × 87.9 cm, New York, Metropolitan Museum of Art

Although Van Dyck's Italian portraits largely lie outside the scope of this study, his art historical encounters as he traveled up and down the length of the peninsula laid the groundwork for the subsequent innovations of his second English sojourn, when he was intermittently resident in London from 1632 until his death in 1641. Van Dyck's Italian travels, when he accompanied Lady Arundel, conversed with Sofonisba Anguissola, and sketched the portraits of Titian and Raphael, were formative for the model of artistic subjecthood that he would soon bring with him to England. Van Dyck's confident self-presentation in Italy, both in person and in his self-portraits, allowed the young artist to combine his cultivation of high patronage and his development as a portraitist with his abiding interest in the language of clothes. Bellori avidly described the young Flemish artist's appearance: "resplendent in rich attire of suits and court dress ... in addition to his fine clothes, he adorned his head with plumes and hatbands, wore gold chains crossed on his chest, and kept a retinue of servants."[29] Emulating aristocratic comportment and dress, Van Dyck turned himself into a kind of living portrait, an image of the fashionable and aristocratic elegance with which he would make his name.

In a pattern that will recur throughout this book, Van Dyck's sartorial display soon incurred the derision of his fellow artists:

> *By imitating the pomp of Zeuxis,* [Van Dyck] *drew all eyes to himself: this, which should have been seen by the Flemish painters living in Rome as a credit to them, aroused resentment against him and very great hatred: for these men, who were used to a merry convivial life at that time, had a tradition, when one of them was newly arrived in Rome, of inviting him to supper with them at the tavern and giving him a nickname ... Anthony refused these bacchanals; and they, taking his reserve for disdain, condemned him as an ambitious man, denouncing both his pride and his art.*[30]

This masculine contempt has persisted in responses to the artist into our own era, with writers time and again implying that the elegant Van Dyck was something more than a painter – but also something less than a man.

Unlike most previous commentators, I treat Van Dyck's (frequently hostile) literary reception not as evidence of his actual personality, but rather as part of a broader cultural field that engaged with portraiture and portrait sittings.[31] Van Dyck, "imitating the pomp of Zeuxis," modeled his behavior on classical topoi as he played the role of the famous artist before his sitters and rivals.[32] The sources discussed here attest to a widespread interest in the mechanics of portrait sittings – how long did they last? Where did they take place? How many were necessary for an accurate likeness? Writers often broached such questions through the example of Van Dyck; more than a century after his death, English artists were still discussing his sittings, collecting his drawings, and painting self-portraits in costumes and poses derived from his work.

Throughout this book, I use the term "Van Dyckian painter" to refer to a paradigm of artistic identity embraced by many ambitious artists in seventeenth- and eighteenth-century England. I define painters as Van Dyckian through such traits as the centrality of portraiture to their oeuvres and the personal charisma that was instrumental to their success. These Van Dyckian painters transformed their studios into cultural attractions and made swiftness and fluency signature features of their paintings' facture. Their work contains explicit citation of Van Dyck's paintings, and they usually trained themselves through copying his portraits. Early biographies of Van Dyckian painters praise their parallel accomplishments in the arts of conversation, music, or literature, and their social elevation through either literal ennoblement or aristocratic friendships. All of the Van Dyckian painters at the heart of this book shared a commitment to self-portraiture and to collecting the work of other painters.

Critically, my definition of the Van Dyckian painter does not limit itself to questions of style or pictorial citation. Most of the painters discussed here borrowed poses from Van Dyck's portraits and strove to rival his bravura rendering of flesh and fabric. But they also emulated Van Dyck in the way they spoke to clients, the friendships they cultivated, and the homes they kept. These painters' clientele appreciated not only their finished products but also the pleasure of observing the artistic process during portrait sittings. The trace of the master's hand, even in works that entailed heavy workshop participation, bestowed a measurable economic value. Very early in their histories, many Van Dyck portraits left dynastic collections to circulate on the open market, where they were often more esteemed for Van Dyck's authorship than for their sitters' identities. As Jonathan Richardson the Elder wrote in 1715, "This Nation [England] is many Thousands of Pounds the richer *for Van-Dyck's* Hand ... which is as current Money as Gold in most parts of *Europe*."[33] In our own day, Van Dyck's paintings, largely ignored by academic art historians, are almost exclusively the object of connoisseurial attention closely allied with the interests of the market.[34] Museums (and curators) who dedicate exhibitions to his work run the risk of too close an alliance with a donor class that would see itself reflected in images of inherited authority.[35]

As figures of both courtliness and commercialism, of retrograde politics and suspect sexuality, Van Dyckian painters make a poor fit within teleological narratives of modernity. As but one example of the discomfort they continue to inspire, I cite Thomas Crow's recent apologia for his inclusion of Thomas Lawrence, a Van Dyckian painter par excellence, in an account of art in post-Napoleonic Europe:

> *The artists who have been figuring most prominently in this book add up to a roll call of the indisputable greats of the period: David, Goya, Canova, Gros, Géricault, Ingres. But Lawrence? From shortly after his death in 1830 until relatively recently, Lawrence has been saddled with a reputation as a facile virtuoso and superficial flatterer of his largely aristocratic clientele. Even with some recent historical rehabilitation, few would place him in the company just listed.*[36]

The qualities Crow cites as mitigating against Lawrence's greatness – facile virtuosity and flattery "of his largely aristocratic clientele" – are also defining traits of the Van Dyckian painter. My book does not attempt to rescue Van Dyck and his emulators for modernism, but it does argue that their reception embodies a powerful and recurring paradigm within the historiography of Western art. As the concluding discussion of John Singer Sargent suggests, the figure of the society portraitist – defined by financial success, perceived effeminacy, and critical deprecation – continues to challenge our understanding of what it means to be an "indisputable great" today.

In my recovery of the Van Dyckian model of art-making, I interpret portraiture both as a finished product and as a process made visible in the ritual of the sitting and in the preparatory works that emerged from the studio.[37] The circulation of these preparatory works as aesthetic objects in their own right is itself an important chapter in the history of Van Dyck's reception and would be decisive for the subsequent course of English painting. Artists who copied Van Dyck's works or acquired his drawings claimed their places in an artistic lineage that had little to do with the patrimony, centered on history painting, mapped out by Continental writers. Instead, this alternate genealogy emphasized the comportment of the portraitist in the context of the sitting and offered a rare opening to female practitioners. The "making of English portraiture" in this book's title refers both to the process of painting and to the formation of a national canon that remains the subject of intense ambivalence today.

Fellow artists' emulation of Van Dyck was a form of interpretation that entailed identifying and appropriating the most salient aspects of his achievement. Read in this light, a historical account of Van Dyckian emulation can serve as a corrective to previous psycho-biographical attempts to explain the artist's career. These attempts extend back to Bellori's claim that Rubens deliberately thwarted Van Dyck's development as a history painter, but they have found their most telling modern formulation in an essay published in 1950 by the prominent curator Wilhelm Valentiner.[38] Riddled with errors and dubious surmises, Valentiner's interpretation of "Van Dyck's character" has had a surprisingly long afterlife in the literature on the artist, in spite of archival discoveries refuting many of its most basic assertions.[39] Valentiner adduced his evidence from the artist's self-portraits and from seventeenth- and eighteenth-century biographies read not as literary texts but as statements of fact. For example, Valentiner provides the following interpretation of Van Dyck's early self-portrait painted at the English court [fig. 4]:

> *The young artist appears extremely handsome, his features finely drawn, his eyes dark, observant, intense yet coquettish, his brown curly hair carefully groomed, yet falling nonchalantly upon his forehead. His mouth, with indefinite outlines, is not very sensuous, his long, straight sharply-pointed nose expressive of an inexhaustible, penetrating curiosity about life and people, which he preserved to the end of his days. The skin is pale; the elongated fingers are white and boneless … The gestures are more like those of a young society woman than of a painter.*[40]

4 Anthony van Dyck, *Self-Portrait* [detail of fig. 3]

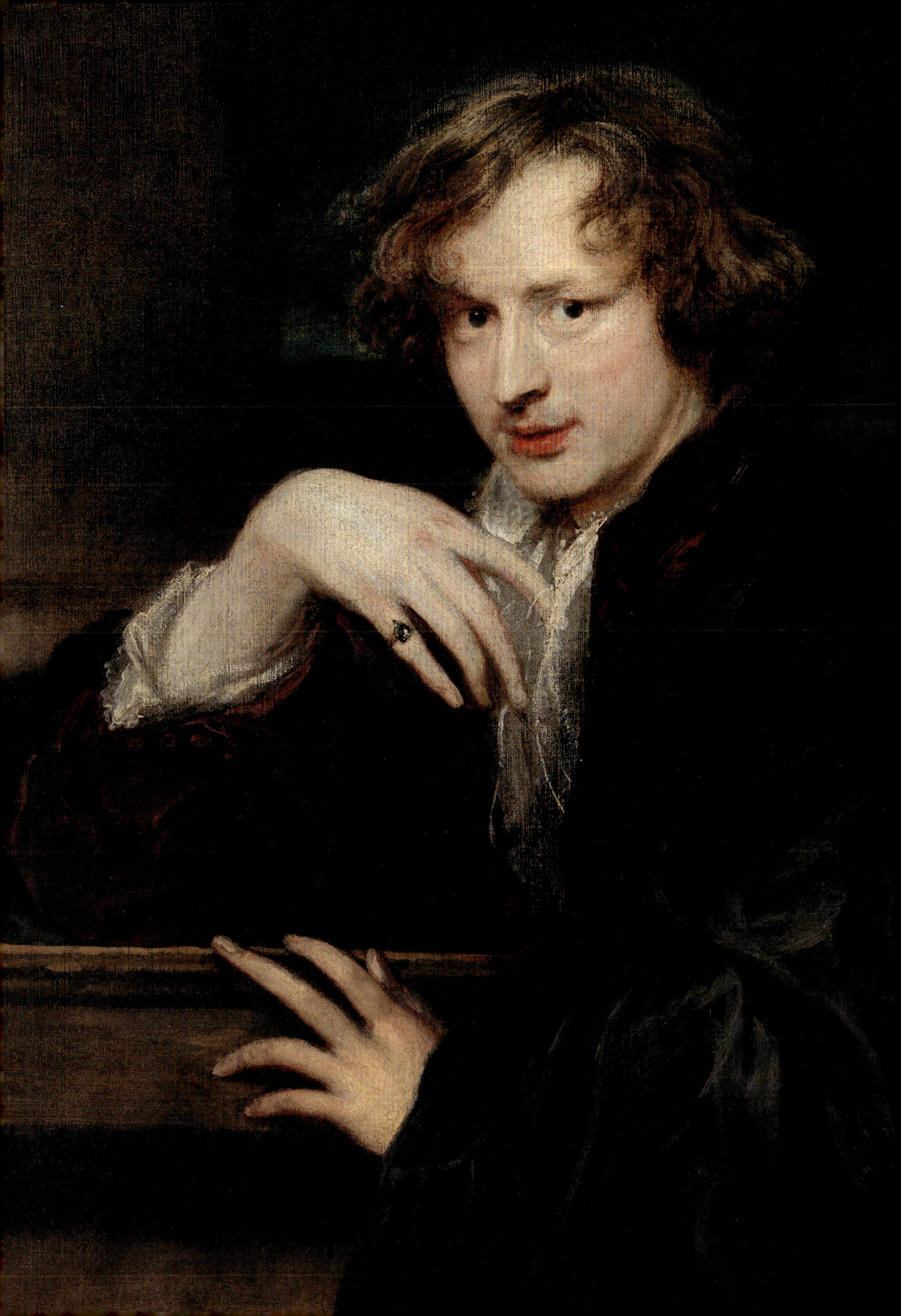

For Valentiner, this "coquettish," "carefully groomed," "indefinite," and "boneless" apparition expressed symptoms of moral weakness. Scornful of Van Dyck's successful courtly career, Valentiner declared himself "repelled" by Van Dyck's "sycophantic" self-portrait with a sunflower,[41] gleefully recounted anecdotes of the artist's stinginess or truculence, and finally arrived, like so many commentators before and since, at an unfavorable comparison with Rubens: "Van Dyck had neither the strength of character nor the intelligence of Rubens. Vanity – a fault unknown to the latter – is a sign of limited mentality. Beyond being a great painter he was little more than a man of wealth, pampered by courts and women, having to do only with persons of high rank and getting into trouble even with them because of his greediness."[42]

Although we might like to dismiss it as a mere curiosity, Valentiner's essay continues to color discussions of Van Dyck, and particularly of his decision to concentrate on portraiture. As this book reveals, Valentiner's critique of Van Dyck extended a profound discomfort with the artist's perceived transgressions that dates back to the 1630s. Moreover, Valentiner's gendered language echoes throughout many of the most prominent writers on Van Dyck of the past seventy years, whether in Julius Held's assertion that Van Dyck was "one of the most feminine of all painters,"[43] or Zirka Filipczak's contention that "figures by Van Dyck lack physical vigor; they rarely hold objects or other persons firmly," thus bespeaking "a socio-psychological relationship of dependence" between the painter and his patrons.[44] As recently as 2021, Christopher White has evoked the "ostentatious posturing" of the New York self-portrait, with its "almost feminine, pristine white fingers."[45]

These gendered readings of Van Dyck's art do contain a significant, albeit unwitting, grain of truth about his reception: from his own lifetime down to the twenty-first century, Van Dyck's art and public persona have both been coded as female. Van Dyck's reception as "one of the most feminine of all painters" has a great deal to do with the genre in which he worked and its traditional association with female practitioners. As Vasari remarked of Sofonisba Anguissola, "If women know so well how to make [i.e., gestate] living men, what marvel is it that those who wish are also so well able to make them in painting?"[46] Yet such an association between portrait-painting and maternity was a double-edged sword, reducing women's art-making to a "passive, bodily production" that aligned with contemporary notions of *ritrarre* (roughly, portrayal) as the antithesis of inventive and emulative art.[47] Limits on women's artistic education meant that the genres most associated with *ritrarre* – portraits, still lifes, and copies of other masters – were often the only genres open to them. Conversely, these genres became feminized even when their practitioners were male. Early modern Italian art writing mapped such dichotomies as *disegno* versus *colore* onto a male–female binary.[48] Gendered criticism also inflected writing about different "national" schools of painting. Ever since Michelangelo supposedly declared that Flemish painting "will appeal to women, especially very old and young women and also to monks and nuns and to certain noblemen who have no sense of true harmony," Northern European art had served critics as a feminine counterexample to the masculine achievements of Italian, particularly Florentine and Roman, painters.[49] As this book shows, such gendered binaries would later resurface in the articulation of a self-consciously English (and masculine) national school in the eighteenth century, grounded in the repudiation of Van Dyck and his emulators.

Critics have also consistently contrasted Rubens and Van Dyck in male and female terms, often understating key parallels between their careers.[50] In making his home at Blackfriars into a theater for spectacular portrait sittings, Van Dyck certainly had the older artist in mind. A famous account of a visit to Rubens's studio by the young doctor Otto Sperling in 1621 reveals the artist's studied performance of his own virtuosity and erudition. Sperling asserts that Rubens, "all the while pursuing his labors, was having Tacitus read aloud to him while he dictated a letter. We kept quiet for fear of disturbing him; but he, addressing us, without interrupting his work and still following the reading and continuing to dictate his letter, responded to our questions as though to give us proof of his powerful faculties." Rubens had a servant conduct Sperling and his companions "through his magnificent mansion ... showing us the antiquities and Greek and Roman statues that he possesses in considerable number." Finally, they arrived at the studio itself:

> *We also saw a vast windowless room, which nonetheless lets in the daylight through a large opening in the center of the ceiling. There a good number of young painters were gathered, each one occupied with a different work for which Signor Rubens had furnished a chalk sketch, touched here and there with paint. The youths were to complete these pictures in paint, until at last Signor Rubens would bring them to perfection ... This all is called Rubens's work, through which this man has assembled enormous wealth and has been honored by kings and princes with great gifts and many jewels.*[51]

Sperling showed himself to be highly attuned to the performative aspects of Rubens's practice, describing how the artist's demonstrative verbal facility and collecting reinforced his virtuosic painting.[52] As the perceptive doctor realized, it was the staging of the artist himself as a work of art that allowed him to appropriate the labors of his young assistants through the alchemy of a few final touches.

Van Dyck had himself been one of those young men in the windowless room. His mature studio practice emulated Rubens in its commodification of the finishing touch and dependence upon the collaboration of many assistants. But he broke with Rubens in making his studio primarily a place for the painting of portraits. Sperling's visit to Rubens's palazzo was incidental, the excursion of a curious traveler. By contrast, almost everyone who sought out Van Dyck's home in Blackfriars did so in order to sit for a portrait. Van Dyck's breach with Rubens consisted in opening up his art to the sitter's active participation.

My account of Van Dyck's legacy builds on the rich body of scholarship that has examined the performative portrait practices of eighteenth-century artists such as Angelica Kauffman and Joshua Reynolds by showing the extent to which they continued the innovations of seventeenth-century artists and Van Dyck in particular.[53] Indeed, tracing the reception of Van Dyck's sittings on the part of artists like Peter Lely, Mary Beale, or Richard and Maria Cosway bestows a historical specificity on the oft-repeated claim that Van Dyck founded an English school of portraiture. A recognition of the sitting's centrality to early modern artistic culture provides a point of departure for new interpretations of paintings by Van Dyck and other artists, as well as of major ekphrastic texts in English literature. At the same time, this book admittedly charts just *one* strand of Van Dyck's reception, centered on elite painters working in London. The broader diffusion of his legacy to provincial centers or colonial territories, particularly as facilitated by reproductive prints, lies beyond the scope of my study.[54]

The novelty of this book's approach stems in part from disparities of periodization in the study of early modern visual and literary culture in England. As noted previously, the rich and varied literature on Georgian painting rarely makes explicit connections to earlier English art. Moreover, there is a striking contrast between the methodological approaches to English literature of the sixteenth and seventeenth centuries (among the most prestigious objects of study in the Anglophone world) and those applied to the frequently deprecated visual arts of the same period. Scholarly attention to gender, homoeroticism, and the historical contingency of sexual identity within early modern English literature has been foundational to the field of queer theory writ large.[55] By contrast, the study of English art before Hogarth remains largely defined by archival, connoisseurial, and technical approaches.[56] These have been invaluable in establishing individual bodies of work and charting the structures of an early modern English art world.[57] But, with a few notable exceptions primarily in the work of literary scholars and of art historians working in North America or Germany, English visual arts before the eighteenth century have rarely been the subject of analysis informed by critical theory.[58] Building on the foundation of hard-won documentation for a frequently deprecated and marginalized chapter of art history, this book attempts an admittedly belated application of queer and feminist approaches to early modern English painting.[59]

To say that I provide a queer reading of Van Dyck and his followers is not intended as speculation about the actual sexual practices of historical individuals; indeed, I agree with Eve Kosofsky Sedgwick that "the sexual context of the [early modern] period is too far irrecoverable for us to be able to disentangle boasts, confessions, undertones, overtones, jokes, the unthinkable, the taken-for-granted, the unmentionable-but-often-done-anyway."[60] (Furthermore, it will be seen that early sources attributed to Van Dyck both an effeminate comportment and a problematic *hetero*sexuality due to the superior rank of the women he pursued.) At the same time, I take to heart Sharon Marcus's cautionary words that defining queerness as simply "the multiple ways that sexual practice, sexual fantasy, and sexual identity fail to line up consistently ... expresses an important insight about the complexity of sexuality, but it also describes a state experienced by everyone. If everyone is queer, then no one is – and while this is exactly the point queer theorists want to make, reducing the term's pejorative sting by universalizing the meaning of queer also depletes its explanatory power."[61]

In what follows, my attention is focused on a particular kind of "gender trouble," whether in the case of men, like Van Dyck and Richard Cosway, perceived as effeminate, or women, like Mary Beale and Maria Cosway, who transgressed upon the male territory of art-making and publicity. In discussing male and female artists together, I aim both to propose an alternative narrative of English art in which the achievements of women are central, but also to excavate long-neglected alliances and complicities between male and female cultural actors. I furthermore draw on scholarship that uses psychoanalytic and structuralist models to understand the erotic and creative configurations available within a given cultural context or historical moment. As I have already indicated, the love triangle is a key structure for my analysis, reflecting as it does intersections between the portrait sitting and early modern fears of (and fascination with) cuckoldry. Scholars such as Marcia Pointon and Angela Rosenthal have mapped out the tense triangular dynamics enacted in portrait studios of the eighteenth century; as this study shows, these structures already pervaded literary responses to Van Dyck's art in the 1630s.[62]

My emphasis on the anecdote likewise draws inspiration from both contemporary queer theory and early modern forms of queer selfhood enacted by figures like Horace Walpole. The telling anecdote has, of course, become a defining, even clichéd, rhetorical practice of New Historicism.[63] But "deep gossip," to borrow a phrase of Allen Ginsberg's productively harnessed by Henry Abelove, can also provide "an indispensable resource for those who are in any sense or measure disempowered," particularly those whose gendered performance subverts social expectations and norms.[64] For example, by dispatching scabrous insider intelligence to far-flung correspondents, Walpole initiated them into his own mode of "queer complicity."[65] In their letters, Walpole and his correspondents shaped a "counterpublic" operating in sly opposition to the mainstream.[66] This book likewise maps the early modern English art world as a sequence of such counterpublics, constructed, regulated, and undermined by the formal and informal discourse of both artists and connoisseurs.

Even in texts intended for publication, Walpole positioned himself more as an intimate raconteur than a high-minded authority. The *Anecdotes of Painting in England* reworked materials gathered by the engraver and antiquarian George Vertue, which allowed Walpole to adopt the guise of the ironic, aristocratic editor, forever apologizing for the patriotic boosterism of his socially inferior informant. Indeed, in his dedication to Lady Hervey, Walpole presented himself as the suave intermediary who "made [Vertue] tolerable company" to the dedicatee.[67] Through this deployment of Vertue as an authorial foil, Walpole undercut any straightforward reading of his own text.[68]

Dealing in anecdotes, Walpole constantly questioned their truth value. A telling example appears in his life of another foreign-born founding figure of English art, Hans Holbein the Younger. According to the story, "one day as Holbein was privately drawing some lady's picture for the king, a great lord forced himself into the chamber." Outraged, the artist threw the earl down a flight of stairs. When the battered earl lodged a complaint with Henry VIII, the king defended the artist, declaring, "You have not to do with Holbein, but with me; I tell you, of seven peasants I can make as many lords, but not one Holbein." Walpole concludes that "Henry's behavior is certainly the most probable part of the story."[69]

Like a painting, an anecdote has a provenance. Walpole traced his story back to Holbein's acquaintances in Basel, via Karel van Mander's 1604 *Schilderboeck* and verses by the Cavalier poet Richard Lovelace, characteristically described by Walpole as "not worth repeating."[70] Dismissed by both Walpole and modern Holbein scholarship as a fiction, this anecdote is nonetheless revealing about the fraught nature of the sitting and the exceptional status of court artists in early modern England.[71] It contains many tropes that will become familiar over the course of this book: the artist's provocative seclusion with a female sitter; the intrusion of a male beholder into the sitting, establishing a triangular relationship rife with social and erotic tensions; and the sovereign's recognition of the artist's exceptional gifts, enabling a transgression of class boundaries permitted to no other subject.

Again, I do not take the many anecdotes retailed by early modern artistic biographers as statements of fact or windows into artists' souls. Rather, they provide indications of how early audiences understood artists' achievements and, in particular, their sense of the cultural stakes of the portrait sitting. Making a roughly chronological progress across some hundred and fifty years, this book documents the canonization of seventeenth-century artists by eighteenth-century emulators and critics. As such, it contributes both to the study of Van Dyck and to the historiography of English art more generally.

The first two chapters explore Van Dyck's literary reception in 1630s London, where his portrait sittings became a new feature of fashionable life, widely discussed in poetry and plays. The theatrical metaphor of the scene of the sitting connects Van Dyck's practice with the concerns of contemporary "city comedy" and its fixation on feminine consumption, social mobility, and foreign luxury. A focus on the sitting not only provides a context for Van Dyck's portraits, but also helps account for the appearance of the paintings themselves. Certain features – beautifully painted hands and faces that are clearly demarcated in their facture from the rest of the painting, brilliant highlights that skitter across the surface of draperies – characterize portraits of Van Dyck's maturity because they were the aspects of the painting that called attention to the master's finishing touch. Van Dyck's bravura performance as a painter of faces, typically without the mediation of a detailed preparatory drawing, provided the sitting with its *pièce de résistance*.[72] Other aspects of the portrait – backdrop, pose, drapery

– could be stereotyped and farmed out to studio assistants because they were made outside of the context of the sitting. Indeed, Van Dyckian practice can be understood to enrich the finished work through the experience of the sitting, the charisma of the artist, and the virtuosity of visible brushwork. The collecting and circulation of preparatory or unfinished pieces, practices that gathered speed in the decades immediately following Van Dyck's death, reveal a fascination with the famous artist's touch among the most sophisticated English collectors, who sought to distinguish themselves in an art market dominated by seriality and workshop production.

The third chapter moves beyond Van Dyck's own lifetime to discuss his legacy for a group of women artists including Joan Carlile and Anne Killigrew. By emphasizing gentility, social performance, and high patronage, the Van Dyckian model of an artistic career represented an alternative to the emulation of classical antiquity within an exclusively male academic setting. Van Dyck's self-fashioning as a princely painter contributed to the rise of genteel practitioners of both sexes. In the cultural climate of the Interregnum and Restoration, Van Dyckian women artists, often closely associated with royal patronage, became figures of fascination to contemporary writers attempting to make sense of the tumultuous decades following the collapse of the Caroline monarchy. As well as exploring images of the woman artist at work, this chapter reads ekphrastic poetry by and about women painters to reveal the important role that they played in the formation of Van Dyck's status as an object of emulation.

The final two chapters examine the shifting fortunes of the Van Dyckian painter in the eighteenth century, beginning with an account of highly contrasting responses to Van Dyck by two Augustan art writers, Lord Shaftesbury and Jonathan Richardson the Elder. I then discuss William Hogarth's ambivalent relationship to the artist, revealing that his own status as the founder of a distinctly English school rested on a repudiation of the Van Dyckian paradigm. That this paradigm did not simply die out is shown by the subsequent account of the art and careers of the married painters Maria and Richard Cosway. Patronized at the highest levels of society, the Cosways were intensely visible figures whose fashionable lives often overshadowed their actual artistic production. In self-portraits, they embraced an old master pose that entailed explicit citations of Rubens and Van Dyck. Like these earlier painters, the Cosways transformed their studio into a luxurious residence housing a celebrated collection. But the Cosways' courtly affiliation in an art world that had been transformed by public exhibition spaces, a competitive market, and nationalist criticism made them the target of vitriolic attacks from which their reputations have never recovered. In particular, Maria Cosway's identity as a famous woman artist crystallized the misogyny that had long animated anti-Van Dyckian critiques. Placed alongside the responses of other eighteenth-century artists to Van Dyck's precedent, the Cosways offer a cautionary tale about the Van Dyckian painter's eventual marginalization within narratives of English art.

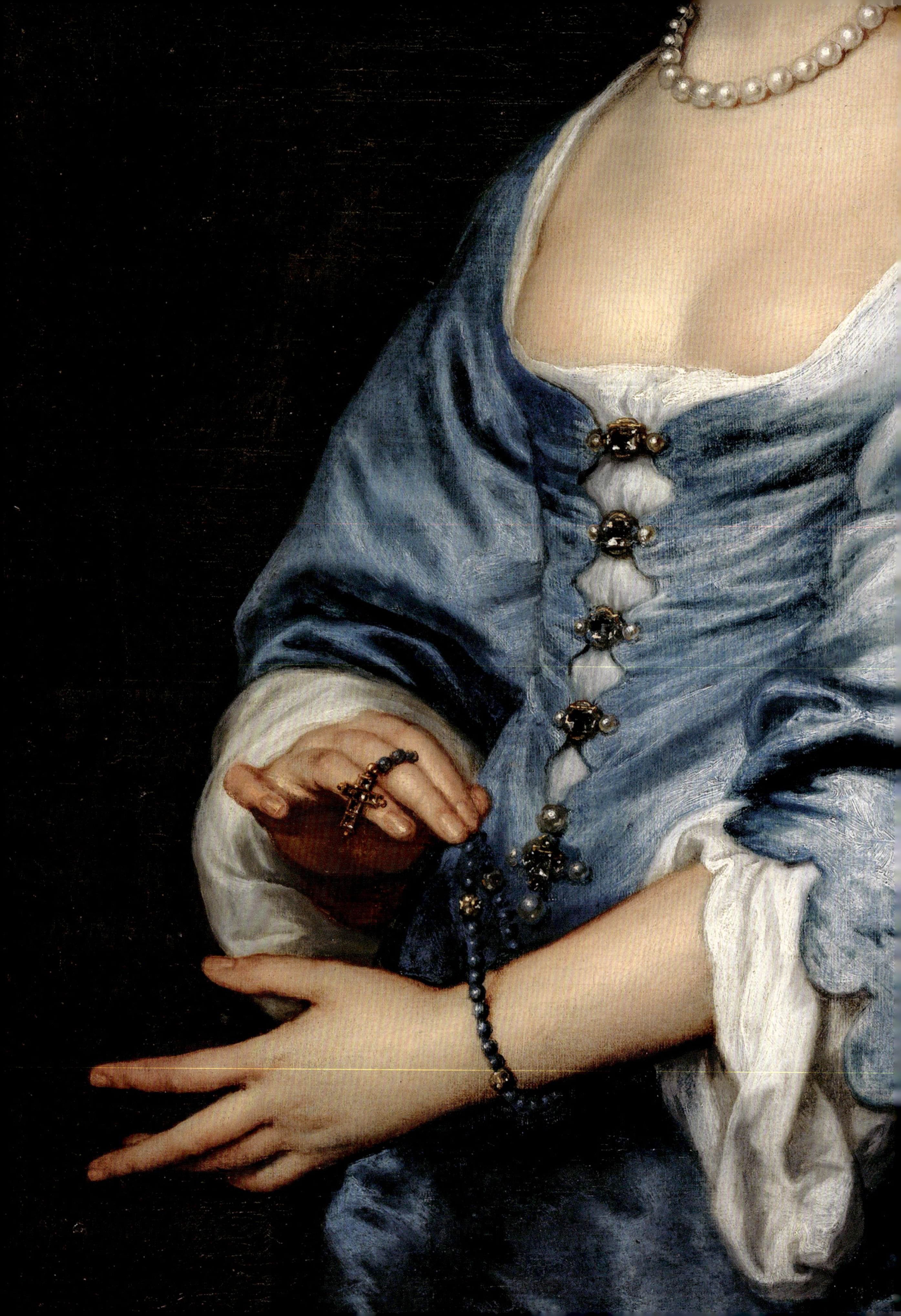

[CHAPTER ONE]

The Scene of the Sitting

On the twentieth of April 1672, Peter Lely paid a call on the painter Mary Beale.[1] As recorded in the diary of her husband, Charles, Lely first praised Beale's copy in miniature of a family portrait by Van Dyck as the best imitation he had ever seen of that artist. A discussion of Van Dyck's portraits ensued, and in particular of the legendary speed at which he worked. When Charles Beale expressed his surprise that Van Dyck was able to capture a perfect likeness in a single day, Lely countered with the following anecdote about Van Dyck's portrait of the musician and painter Nicholas Lanier, which he claimed had required a full week of concentrated labor:

> *Mr Laniere himself told me, he satt seaven entire dayes for it to S^{r}. Anto. & that he painted upon it of all those seaven dayes both morning & afternoon. & only intermitted the time they were at dinner. and he said likewise that tho Mr Laniere sat so often & so long for his picture, y^{t} he was not permitted so much as once to see it. till he* [Van Dyck] *had pfectly finisht ye face to his own satisfaction – This was the picture wch being showd to King Charles ye first caused him to give order that V. Dyck should be sent for over into England.*[2]

Lanier's portrait, recorded in the inventory of Charles I's collection at Whitehall and subsequently acquired by the sitter himself in 1649, is now in Vienna; a preparatory drawing for the painting survives in Edinburgh [figs. 5 and 6].[3] Together, drawing, painting, and Lely's anecdote allow for an unusually thorough reconstruction of the making of one of Van Dyck's most celebrated portraits.

Lely told his story, and Charles Beale wrote it down in his diary, because Mary Beale was an artist with a deep interest in portrait sittings. Early in her career, Beale internalized Van Dyck's legacy by making copies of his portraits, like the miniature of the Porter family that Lely admired, but Beale also sought to observe the workings of portrait sittings first-hand. Shortly after Lely's visit recounted above, she and her husband arranged to have their friend John Tillotson sit for Lely, paying the artist in both cash and pigments so that Mary Beale could study his technique. In his notebook, Charles Beale recorded the sittings that he and his wife witnessed in Lely's studio. For example, on June 5, 1672: "Dr Tillotson sat about 3 houres to Mr Lely for him to lay in a dead Colour of his picture for me. he

Detail of Anthony van Dyck, *Mary, Lady van Dyck*, ca. 1640 [see fig. 17]

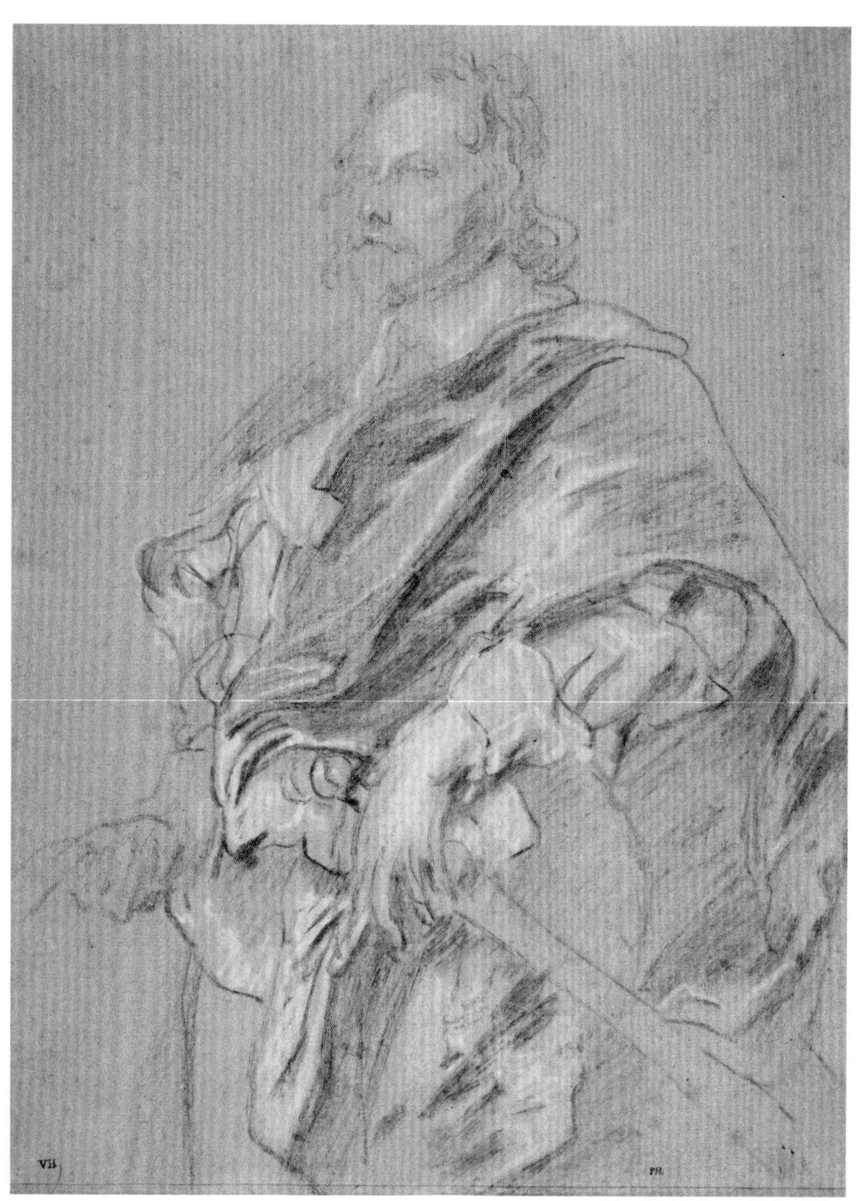

5 Anthony van Dyck, *Nicholas Lanier*, ca. 1628, black chalk, heightened with white, on blue paper, 39.4 × 28.8 cm, Edinburgh, National Galleries of Scotland

6 Anthony van Dyck, *Nicholas Lanier*, ca. 1628, oil on canvas, 111 × 87.6 cm, Vienna, Kunsthistorisches Museum

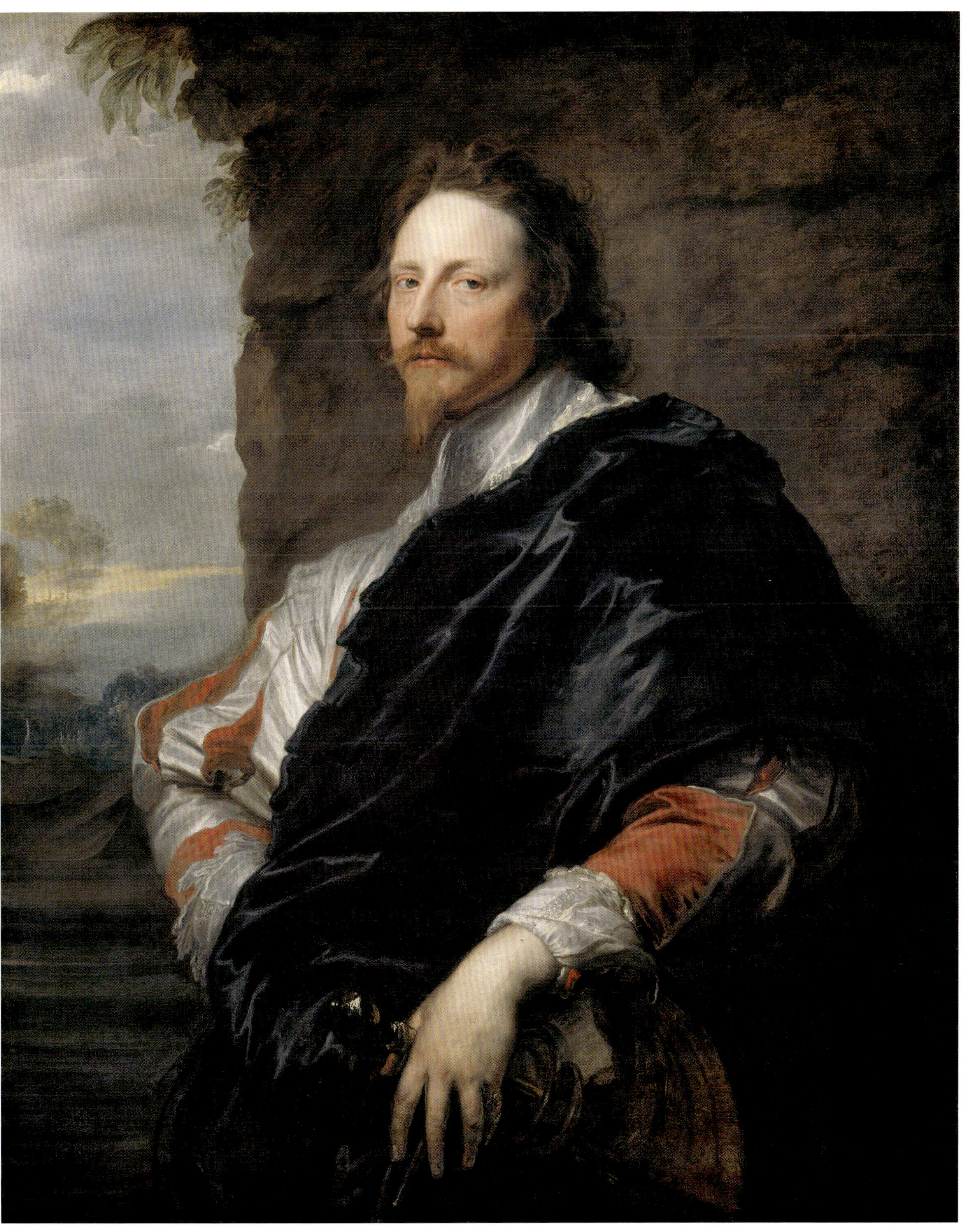

apprehending the colour of the Cloth upon which he painted was too light. before he began to lay on the flesh colour he glazed the whole place where the face & haire were drawn in colour over thin with cullens [Cologne] earth & a little bonn [bone] black (as he told us) made very thin with varnish."[4] In his capacity as Mary Beale's business manager and the chronicler of her studio, Charles would make equally detailed notes on the progress of her own portraits across a series of sittings.[5]

For Mary Beale, as for Van Dyck and Lely before her, the sitting was a critical site for the transmission of artistic knowledge and the cultivation of social relations between painters and sitters. Many sources, ranging from diaries like Charles Beale's to love poems and plays, allow us to reconstruct seventeenth-century portrait sittings with a level of detail absent from any earlier period. Within these texts, certain themes surface again and again – most prominently, the dissemination of artistic expertise and the artist's demonstration of his or her own gentility. But there was also a dark side to the portrait sitting, expressed in recurrent triangular rivalries between painter, sitter, and a jealous observer of their intimacy. The potentially fraught nature of the sitting can even be gleaned from Lely's changing behaviour toward the Beales as he made progress on their friend's portrait: "1 Aug. 1672 Dr Tillotson sat to Mr Lely about 3 houres ... his manner in the painting of this picture this time especially seemd strangely different both to my self and my dearest heart ... this wee thought was a more conceiled misterious scanty way of painting then [*sic*] the way he used formerly, wch wee both thought was a farr more open & free & much more was to be observed and gaind from the seeing him paint then."[6] When it gradually dawned on Lely that Beale was not simply an admiring amateur but also a professional rival, he began to guard his professional secrets from her. As in this example, what would initially seem to be a dyad of portraitist and sitter is often revealed in early modern sources to have in fact been a triangle, with all of the jealousy and rivalry that structure implies.

The following two chapters explore a body of early modern English literary sources that focus on the portrait sitting. These range from the technical writings of artists to poems and plays that present portrait sittings as part of a new culture of urban luxury and feminine consumption. Interpreting the sitting as a "scene" emphasizes its status as a choreographed and performative cultural practice.[7] In both reality and in their literary reception, Van Dyck's sittings entailed the encounter between two figures of fashion, the princely painter and the female aristocrat, at a moment when both were surfacing in contemporary literature as cultural arbiters (and perceived agents of sexual transgression). The texts and images surveyed here reveal the deeply ambivalent reaction that both portraitists and their sitters might inspire.

— *The Queen in the Studio* —

The partial survival of Charles Beale's notebooks makes his wife's portrait practice one of the best documented for the entire seventeenth century. However, the interest that the Beales showed in portrait sittings was by no means unique among their contemporaries. Just as Lanier described his sittings with Van Dyck to Lely, who passed the account on to Charles and Mary Beale, others who sat to Van Dyck served as informants for his earliest biographers. Although the descriptions of Van Dyck's working method by Bellori and de Piles cited in this book's introduction differ in their timelines from Lely's anecdote, these accounts all emphasize Van Dyck's control of the sitting. It is Van Dyck who performs the role of gracious host and entertains sitters at his residence, whereas another, lesser painter might travel to his clientele. Moreover, the artist determines the length of the sitting, elaborating a carefully scripted choreography to which each session adheres. In the case of Lanier, Van Dyck's self-assurance even extended to denying his sitter a glimpse of his own portrait until it was finished to the artist's satisfaction. It is hardly surprising that such tales would appeal to figures like Bellori, de Piles, or Lely, who all, whether through writing or painting, contributed to an idea of the painter as a gentleman practitioner of a liberal art.[8]

The widespread fascination with portrait sittings in the second half of the seventeenth century is inextricable from the pan-European reception of Van Dyck. It was through his example, arguably more than that of any other artist, that writers thought about portrait sittings. The gifts of portraits that Charles I and Henrietta Maria made to foreign courts cemented the fame of Van Dyck's English portraits abroad and excited curiosity about his working method and public persona. For example, when Van Dyck's likeness of Charles I in three positions was dispatched to Rome as the basis for a sculpture by Bernini, the painting was exhibited at the Pantheon [fig. 7].[9] It subsequently entered Bernini's personal collection and may have been the inspiration for his own celebrated method of taking a portrait by observing a sitter from a variety of angles as he or she continued to speak and move naturally.[10] During the English Civil War, exiled royalists arrived on the Continent with more portraits in tow and served as informants for writers like Bellori, further diffusing knowledge of Van Dyck's portrait sittings.

On the basis of Sir Kenelm Digby's account, Bellori described sitting for Van Dyck as a *sollazzo*, a recreation, and archival documentation confirms that even Charles I traveled to Van Dyck's home to sit for the painter and see his collection, going so far as to have a causeway purpose-built so that the royal barge might dock at the artist's house.[11] Early modern court ceremonial enacted status through access to ever more secluded spaces of royal intimacy. But rather than having Van Dyck traverse these spaces to reach the king, Charles I traveled to the painter.[12]

The king may have been inspired to this act of condescension by his mother-in-law, Maria de' Medici, whose portrait by Van Dyck played an important role in cementing the artist's ties to the English royal family. Banished by her son from France, Maria fled to the Spanish Netherlands in 1631. Maria's flight created a diplomatically precarious situation for France's northern neighbors. On the one hand, as the queen dowager of France and mother-in-law of the kings of Spain and England, she retained her elevated rank; on the other, her son's open enmity made her a burdensome and controversial guest. Despite this, Maria received

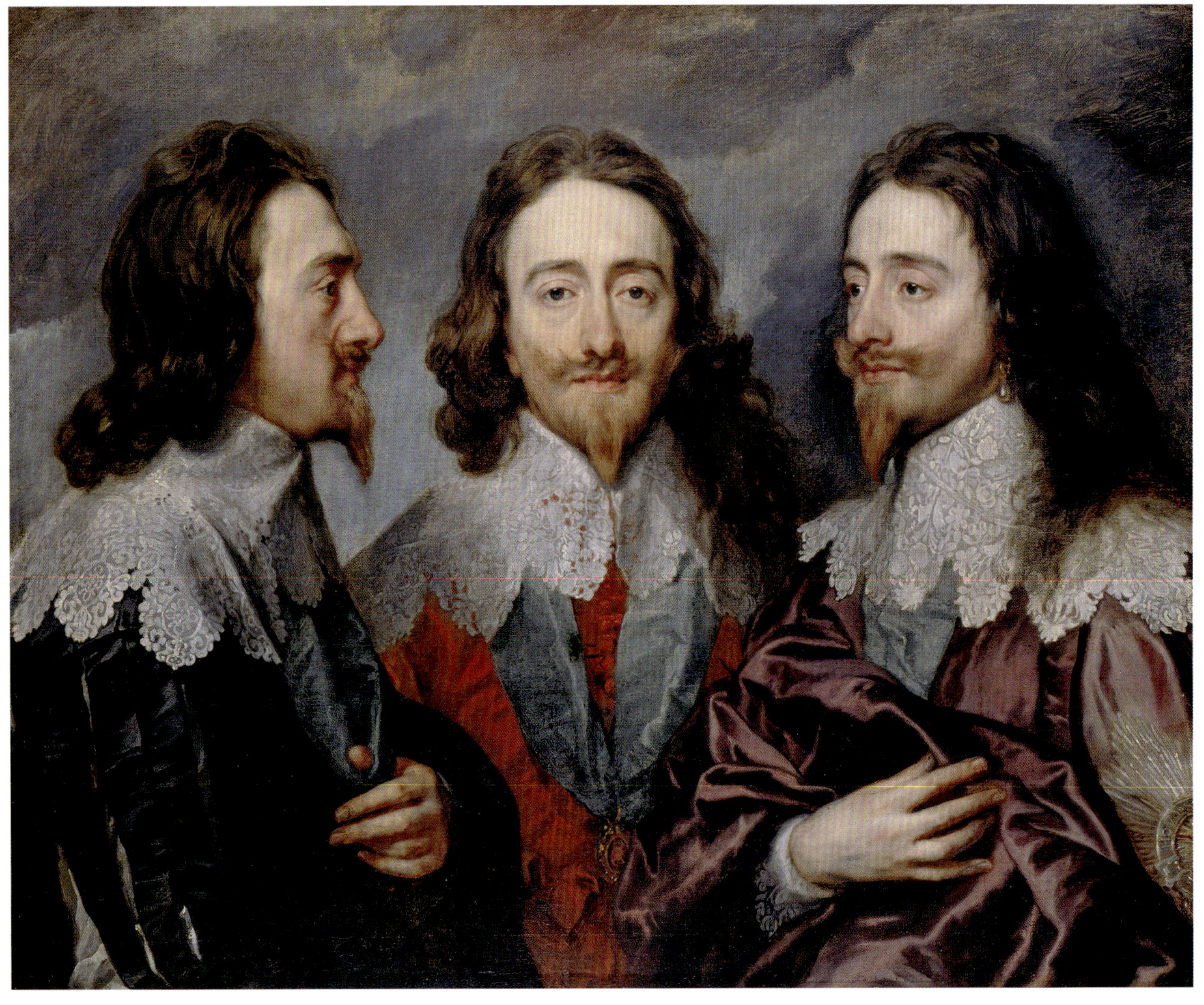

7 Anthony van Dyck, *Charles I*, 1635–36, oil on canvas, 84.4 × 99.4 cm, Royal Collection

a lavish reception upon her arrival in the Low Countries.[13] Archduchess Isabel Clara Eugenia, Governor of the Spanish Netherlands, met her on the outskirts of Mons and then accompanied her to Brussels. From September 4 to October 16, 1631, the burghers of Antwerp hosted the queen and archduchess in their city. Here, Maria lodged at an abbey and was entertained with processions, sermons, and theatricals.

The most detailed account of the queen in Antwerp comes from her court historiographer, Jean Puget de la Serre, whose *Histoire curieuse* of the queen's voyage to the Low Countries was published in Antwerp the following year.[14] In his description of Maria's visit to Antwerp, Puget de la Serre lingers on her encounter with the city's two most famous painters. In the words of her historian, "The queen was curious to see all the rich and beautiful pictures in the house of Monsieur Rubens." Puget de la Serre characterized Rubens as "a man whose industry, though rare and marvelous, is the least of his qualities: his judgment in matters of state, and his wit and his comportment lift him so high above the profession he practices that the fruits of his prudence are as admirable as those of his brush." Puget de la Serre reveals a prejudice against Rubens's profession at the same time as he argues that the artist has transcended it. Such ennoblement stems from royal favor, as when "Her Majesty obtained great contentment from contemplating the animated marvels of [Rubens's] paintings."

Puget de la Serre follows his fulsome praise for Rubens with a comparison between him and Van Dyck that intriguingly elevates the latter over his erstwhile master, due to his unsurpassed practice of portraiture. Indeed, the chronicler argues that "Monsieur Van Dyck has carried off the prize over all the other great painters, who with their overly bold hands have dared to portray the queen; for, without lying, art has never yet known how to represent majesty enthroned as he has done in his new portrait." Comparing Van Dyck favorably to Apelles, Puget de la Serre notes: "Her Majesty did him the honor of visiting his home, where she saw in the salon his Titian cabinet, which is to say, all of the masterpieces by that great master," a master whom, the writer implies, Van Dyck is well on his way to surpassing.[15]

For all of his formulaic praise, Puget de la Serre offers an important insight into early perceptions of Rubens and Van Dyck, and particularly into the role that the studio visit played in the establishment of both artists' fame. The writer's admiration for the two painters extends beyond their actual production to their important art collections, which Puget de la Serre cites as the major enticement for the queen to visit their homes. Indeed, in his praise of Rubens, the courtier is openly dismissive of the manual practice of art. In their self-portraits, Rubens and Van Dyck promoted a similar image of the court artist, in which comportment effaces occupation.

Puget de la Serre's account offers a courtly counterweight to critical voices such as Bellori, who wrote at a greater temporal and geographic remove from Van Dyck's career. Like Bellori, Puget de la Serre compares Van Dyck to Titian, and like Bellori he views portraiture as the genre in which Van Dyck made his greatest mark. But in Puget de la Serre's view, these were precisely the traits that allowed Van Dyck to surpass even Rubens, whereas subsequent critics would relegate him – with his orientation toward Venice over Rome and toward portraiture over history painting – to a permanent second place. Puget de la Serre's courtly criteria allow us to make better sense of artistic choices that frustrated academicians.

As already noted, in his description of Van Dyck's collection, Puget de la Serre dwells on the prominence of Titian (he does not name any of the artists whose works Rubens owned). The *Histoire curieuse* thus offers us further evidence of the way that early modern artists could structure their receptions by furnishing homes and studios with carefully chosen works of art. In this case, Van Dyck's collecting

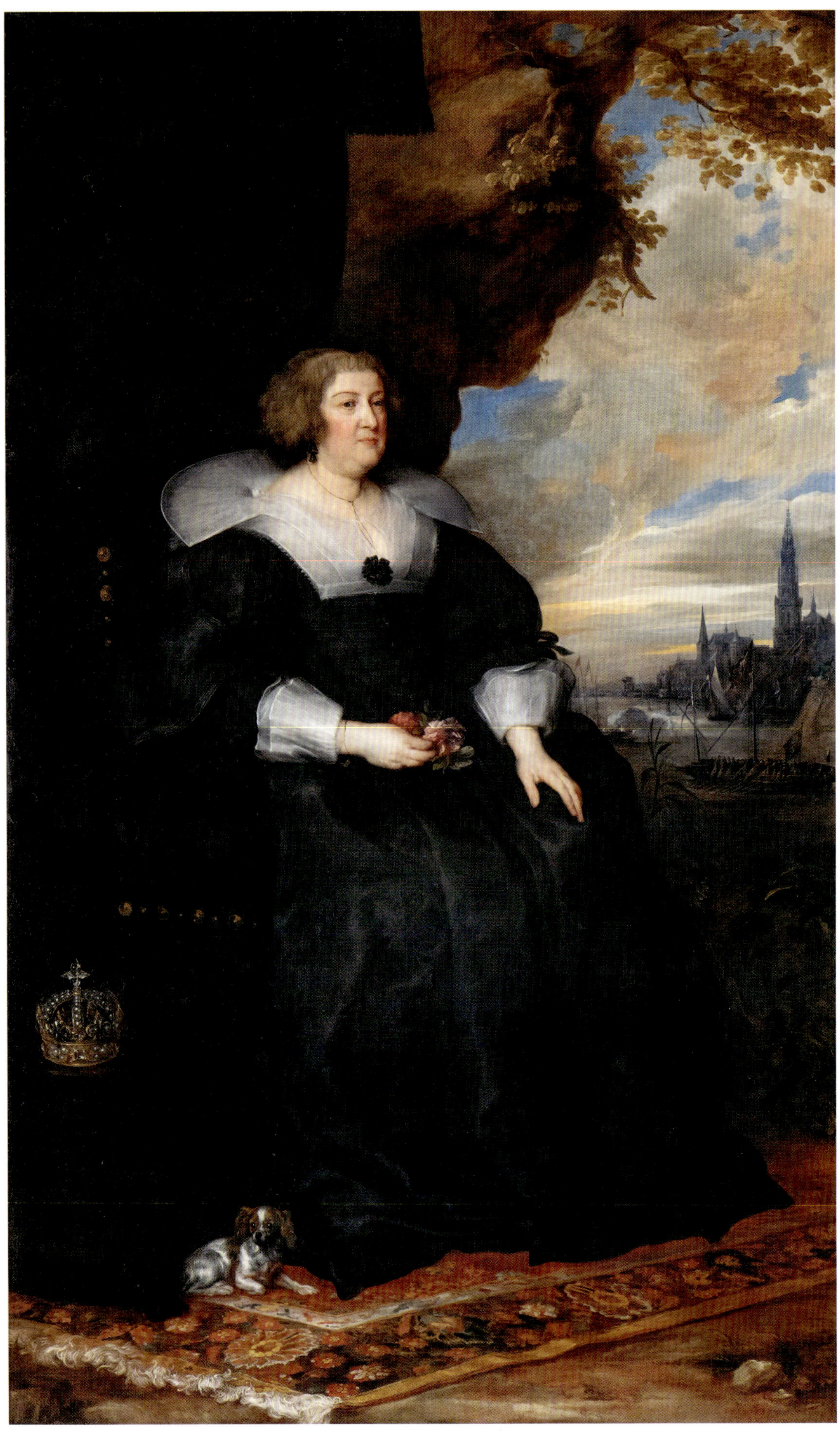

and display of Titian's works helped to ensure that he would be seen as Titian's rightful heir, allowing the artist to bypass his debt to Rubens and emerge from the constriction of being merely the second most famous painter in Antwerp.[16] Subsequent generations of painters would similarly declare their status as Van Dyck's heirs through the display of his work in their home studios or, like Mary Beale, by making copies they could show to visitors.

Because it was Van Dyck and not Rubens who painted the queen's portrait on the occasion of her visit to Antwerp, his work receives more attention and higher praise in Puget de la Serre's history. From Puget de la Serre's perspective, it was Van Dyck's practice of portraiture, embodied in his image of the queen, that allowed him to emerge from Rubens's shadow and claim "the prize over all the other great painters." From this vantage point, the honor bestowed by the queen consisted in Van Dyck's exclusive access to her person in the context of the sitting. This intimacy contrasts with the exclusion of other painters who, according to Puget de la Serre, strained for the merest glimpse of Maria in her quarters at the abbey. As he recounts, "I once again noticed the ruse of a great number of painters, who under the pretext of watching the queen dine, pilfered with a subtle brush all the features of her face."[17] This anecdote, however spurious, gives a vivid sense of how physical proximity to royalty translated into prestige and status at early modern courts. The fact that Maria herself traveled to Van Dyck's and Rubens's homes, a phenomenon that would be duplicated in Van Dyck's relations with Charles I, conferred upon them both an exalted status as artist favorites.

For all of Puget de la Serre's praise, Van Dyck's portrait of Maria is ultimately a conservative image, betraying little of the innovation that would soon mark the artist's work for Maria's daughter and son-in-law [fig. 8].[18] Posed against a background that combines vague pastoral foliage with a meticulous portrayal of Antwerp's monuments, Van Dyck's queen is herself an uneasy mixture of realism and bombast. But Van Dyck does distinguish his portrait through the inclusion of the Antwerp skyline, based upon a drawing that still survives today.[19] Through this local topography, Van Dyck insisted upon the occasional nature of his portrait in the sense of commemorating a specific event: Maria's visit to Antwerp (and, implicitly, the artist's own home). Van Dyck's portrait, local rhetoricians' poems praising the queen, and Puget de la Serre's *Histoire curieuse* all served to publicize the favor Maria had bestowed on the city and to highlight the achievements of Antwerp's most talented citizens. Multiplication of the portrait in both painted and printed copies further served to link Van Dyck's fame with that of his sitter. By the end of the 1630s, versions of this painting were in the royal collections in both The Hague and London.[20]

8 Anthony van Dyck, *Maria de' Medici*, 1631, oil on canvas, 225 × 140 cm, Bordeaux, Musée des Beaux-Arts

— *"Ready to be drawne"* —

Maria de' Medici's favor naturally played an important role in promoting Van Dyck at her daughter's court. In London, the appeal of visits to Van Dyck's studio as a form of entertainment may also have been reinforced by the proximity of his house to the Blackfriars theater. Such an association becomes apparent in a letter from the late winter of 1636, in which Prince Charles Louis of the Palatine reported to his mother on the progress of a portrait of Charles I: "The King sate jesterday at van Dykes ... his howse is closse by blake Friers where the Queene saw Lodwik Carliles second part of Arviragus of [*sic*] Felicia acted, which is hugely liked of everyone."[21] Contemporary theater, meanwhile, parodied the association between fashionable life and sittings with foreign painters like Van Dyck.[22] In James Shirley's *The Lady of Pleasure*, the title character, already lampooned for spending a fortune on "gaudy furniture and pictures, / Of this Italian Master, and that Dutchman,"[23] is called offstage to sit for her portrait by "the Belgicke gentleman."[24] As Shirley's reference to the "Belgicke gentleman" indicates, Van Dyck's portrait sittings inspired poets and playwrights almost from the moment of his arrival in London.[25]

The Lady of Pleasure, licensed for performance in 1635, is a prominent example of the English theatrical genre known to scholars as "city comedy." Such plays responded to a new type of urban resident defined by (frequently superficial) refinement and ostentatious consumption.[26] City comedies took the effortlessly aristocratic bodies of Van Dyck's portraits and demystified them as the products of lessons, shopping, and expensive clothes. Like contemporary "high-life" genre painting in the Netherlands, city comedies documented and questioned the self-fashioning of urban elites as they strove to acquire the outward signs of aristocratic civility. In common with such paintings, these comedies frequently focused on women, whose appetites of various kinds lead them beyond the confines of the domestic sphere.[27]

The main character of *The Lady of Pleasure*, Aretina Bornwell, convinces her husband, a country squire, to sell his estate and embrace a life of extravagance in London. At the same time, she attempts to instruct her bookish nephew in the ways of fashion, bringing about his transformation into a libidinous fop. Aretina's behavior is contrasted with that of Celestina, a clever and wealthy widow with a variety of suitors (one with the tellingly ridiculous name of Hairecut). By the end of the play, a series of mortifications, including her husband's pursuit of Celestina, has compelled Aretina's moral reform and return to country life. In his choice of subject, Shirley drew on the contemporary controversy around the emergence of the London "season" and the migration of the landed gentry to the capital, giving him the opportunity to parody various fashionable types.[28]

The allusion to Van Dyck as "the Belgicke gentleman" who paints Aretina's portrait (but never appears onstage) underscores his close association with female aristocratic portraiture. Within a few years of Van Dyck's arrival in London, the court poet Sir John Suckling compared a gathering of fashionable beauties to "a gallerie hung with *Titians* or *Vandikes* hand."[29] Van Dyck's portraits of two of Suckling's cousins, Lady Anne Carey and Frances, Lady Buckhurst, demonstrate how he repeated successful prototypes in his English portraits to create a distinctive image of aristocratic femininity [figs. 9 and 10].[30] Both women appear full-length and in three-quarter profile, striding to the left through identical Arcadian landscapes. There is no evidence that these closely related women, who likely knew each other's portraits, resented their generic resemblance to one another. Such assimilation to a fashionable type was, after all, what one paid for when sitting for Van Dyck. Thumbing through a catalogue of Van Dyck's English portraits evokes a nearly endless enfilade of such paintings, much like Suckling's imagined "gallerie." Being portrayed in this manner became a hallmark of the modishness parodied in contemporary drama.

In *The Lady of Pleasure*, Aretina lists having her portrait painted as one of the leisure activities that constitute "A Ladies morning worke." Such women "rise, make fine, / sit for our picture, and tis time to dine."[31] While they parodied new-fangled fashions, city comedies also flattered the insider knowledge of their audience by alluding to real-life figures from the court.[32] Indeed, the characters of Aretina and Celestina may both allude to Lucy Hay, Countess of Carlisle, whose coterie of admirers offered an alternative to the court life centered around Henrietta Maria.[33] Van Dyck was closely associated with both Lady Carlisle and her lover, Viscount Wentworth, the future Earl of Strafford, and supplied them with portraits to exchange as gifts.[34] On February 20, 1637, Sir Beverley Newcomen reported to Wentworth that Lady Carlisle "setts very Constantly [to Van Dyck] ... though it be could [cold]; and frosty wether."[35] The portrait these chilly sittings produced reveals the qualities that indelibly linked Van Dyck with feminine luxury in Caroline London [fig. 11]. His sitter glances provocatively at the viewer as she strides across a threshold between exterior and interior space, draped in shimmering fabric. An independent female portrait commissioned to commemorate an extramarital relationship, Van Dyck's image of the countess embodies both the threat and the attraction of the empowered and urbanized "new women" of the Caroline period.[36]

While Aretina represents the folly of a country squire's wife in headlong pursuit of urban pleasure, Celestina provides a more positive image of the witty and accomplished salonnière. In the words of one admirer:

> ... *my conversation*
> *Nere knew so elegant and brave a soule,*
> *With most incomparable flesh and bloud,*
> *So spirited, so Courtly speakes the Languages,*
> *Sings, Dances, playes o'th Lute to admiration,*
> *Is faire and paints not, games too, keeps a table,*
> *And talkes most witty Satyre ...*[37]

Alongside these traits, Celestina is an avid consumer of new luxuries. Indeed, she is first seen in the play berating her steward about the quality of her tapestries,

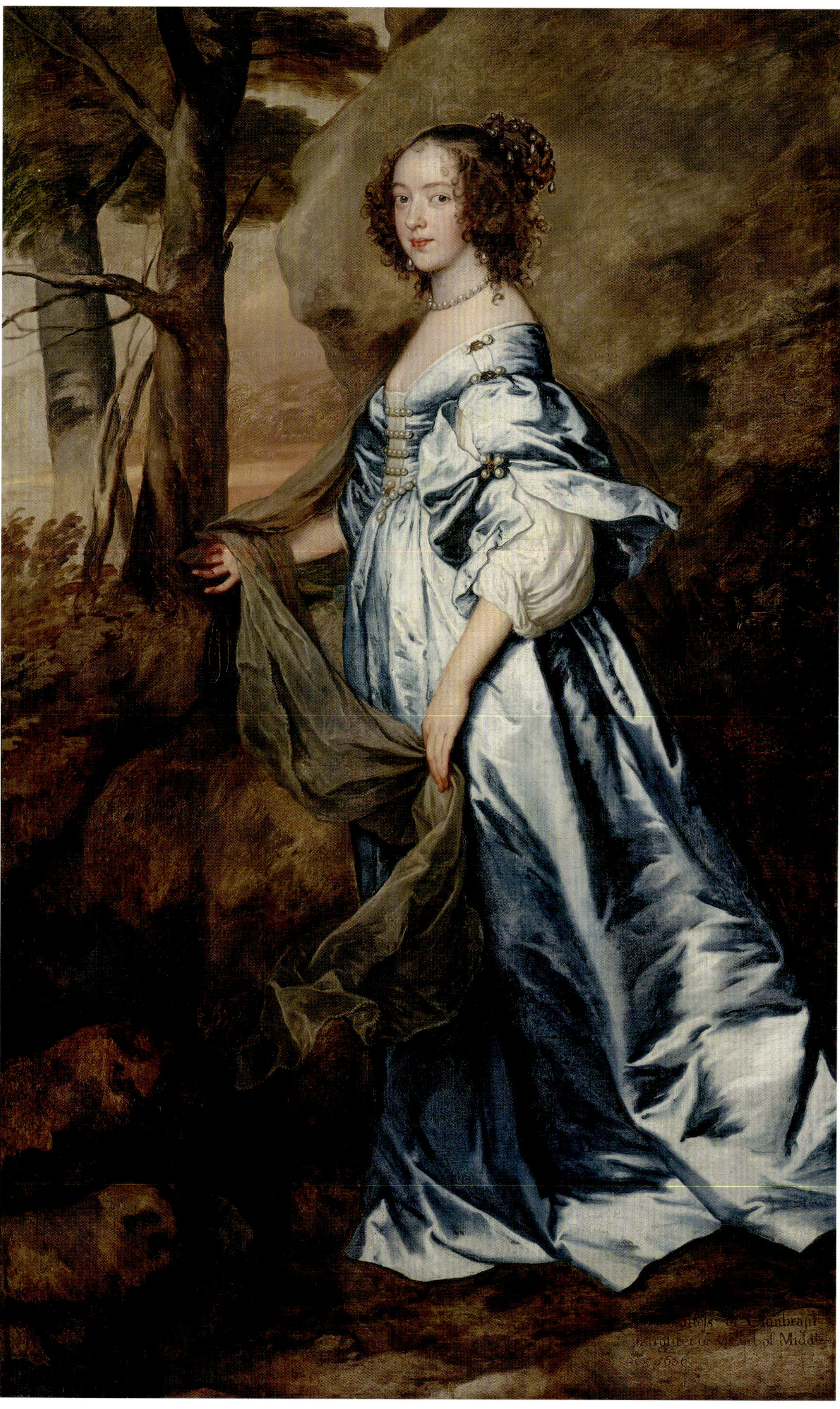

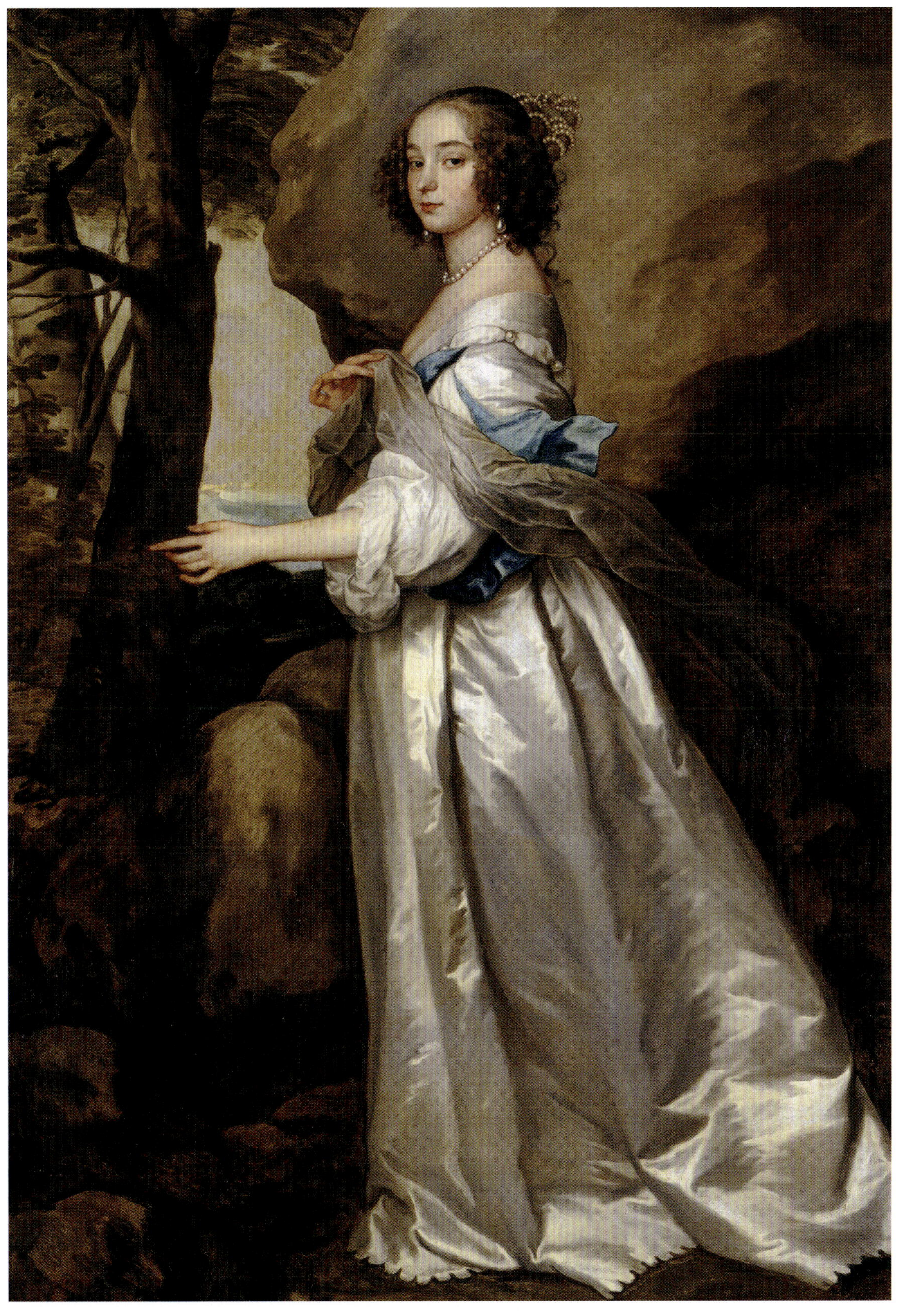

9 Anthony van Dyck, *Lady Anne Carey, later Viscountess Claneboye and Countess of Clanbrassil*, ca. 1636, oil on canvas, 211.1 × 127. 6 cm, New York, Frick Collection

10 Anthony van Dyck, *Frances, Lady Buckhurst, later Countess of Dorset*, ca. 1637, oil on canvas, 187 × 128 cm, Sevenoaks, Knole, Sackville Collection

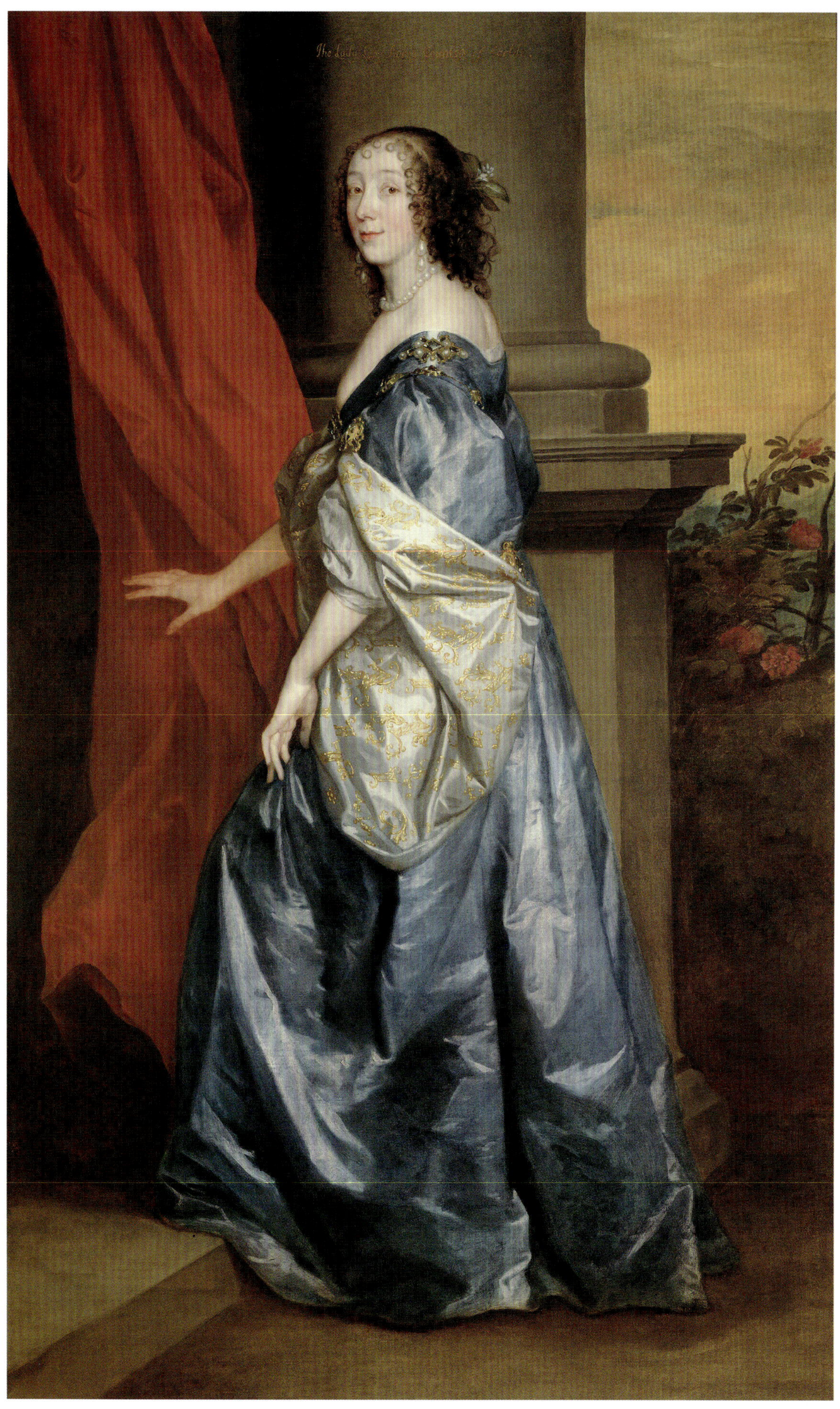

carriage, and sedan chair (the latter two notably means of transportation that allowed upper-class women to circulate around London). Chided by the steward for the rumors her lavish spending has inspired, Celestina retorts:

Must I be limited to please your honour?
Or for the vulgar breath confine my pleasures?
I will pursue 'em in what shapes I fancie,
… my entertainements shall
Be oftner, and more rich; who shall controule me?

Celestina presents consumption and magnificence as tools of a transgressive female autonomy. Giving voice to social ambition, she declares her intention to "Be hospitable then, and spare no cost / That may engage all generous report … till the Court envie" her establishment. Under Celestina's patronage, her house in the Strand will become "the Academy of wits, who shall / Exalt with rich Sacke, and Sturgeon, / Write Panegryicks of my feasts, and praise / The method of my wittie superfluities."[38] Celestina's salon, defined by a generous table and artful conversation, recalls the early descriptions of Van Dyck's studio, such as Bellori's assertion that the painter kept "servants, carriages, horses, players, musicians, and jesters" and provided "the most sumptuous repasts" for his aristocratic visitors.[39] Eventually, Shirley reveals Celestina's profligacy as a canny strategy to enhance her value on the marriage market. Early commentators similarly understood Van Dyck's munificence as an important feature of his artistic self-promotion.

In depicting the transformation of Aretina's nephew from scholar to fop, *The Lady of Pleasure* underscores the artificial nature of the fashionable poses that appear so natural in Van Dyck's portraits. As a shaper of the luxurious body, Van Dyck resembled not only the hostesses of fashionable salons, but also the dancing masters and hairdressers, often foreign-born, who were such frequent theatrical figures of fun. City comedies "mock the quest for new forms of cultural legitimation and social mobility, turning a critical eye on unskilled members of city or country who attempt to master the refinements of emerging town culture and an equally critical eye on the instructors – often imposters – who teach them."[40] At his princely studio, Van Dyck occupied a socially and sexually ambiguous position, somewhere between society lady and dancing master.

Van Dyck posed a further threat to social convention in England through his Catholic faith and his association with prominent Catholic figures at court, most notably the queen herself.[41] Shirley included an allusion to this highly controversial facet of fashionable life by having Aretina's steward remark that when her portrait is finished, "she will be hang'd / next the French Cardinall in the dining room."[42] In Aretina's town house, the display of portraits serves to reveal

11 Anthony van Dyck, *Lucy Hay, Countess of Carlisle*, 1637, oil on canvas, 218.4 × 130.8 cm, private collection, courtesy of the Trustees of the Rt Hon Olive Countess of Fitzwilliam's Chattels settlement by permission of Lady Juliet Tadgell fashionable Catholic sympathies, while the wordplay on "hanging" provides a fleeting image of misogynist and anti-Catholic violence. Henrietta Maria not only sought to appoint Van Dyck's brother as one of her chaplains but also commissioned portraits for the artist that served as gifts for the queen's influential coreligionists abroad.[43] Among his finest portraits of the queen is the half-length commissioned as a gift for Francesco Barberini, Cardinal Protector of England and Scotland [fig. 12]. Here, the pregnant queen cradles her arms in front of her abdomen, resulting in "a portrait with obvious resonance for the papacy, to which she promised to raise her children as Catholics and vowed to serve the Catholic cause."[44] As the author of such an image, Van Dyck was inevitably associated with the menacing cosmopolitanism and religious irregularities of the queen's court.

But Van Dyck represented more to Caroline writers than a popish foreigner beckoning women to sit for their portraits offstage.[45] Van Dyck's portraits of the queen or Lady Carlisle took their place alongside poetic tributes to these influential women, and both paintings and poems can be understood as competing bids for patronage.[46] Perceiving in the foreign artist an unsettling rival, early literary commentators on Van Dyck's art were quick to eroticize the exchange between portraitist and sitter. For example, in a tribute to the painter's portrait of his beloved, Dorothy Sidney, the poet Edmund Waller playfully asked Van Dyck:

Why thou couldst not at one assay
The face to aftertimes convey,
Which this admires. Was it thy wit
To make her oft before thee sit?
Confess, and we'll forgive thee this;
For who would not repeat that bliss?
And frequent sight of such a dame
Buy with the hazard of his fame?[47]

Waller's conceit depends on the idea that Van Dyck's "fame" derived from his ability to capture a likeness "at one assay," to work with the "extraordinary swiftness" admired by Roger de Piles. According to Waller, Van Dyck's repeated sittings with the poet's muse not only threatened his reputation for speed, but also recast the portrait sitting as a form of seduction, in which Van Dyck exploited his control over the artistic process to obtain the "bliss" of studying a beautiful woman.[48] Because Dorothy Sidney was not Waller's actual mistress but rather the object of unrequited admiration, Van Dyck's sittings with her acquired an additional edge. Taking the sitting as the premise for a conventional tribute to a painter, Waller nonetheless shared with Lely, Bellori, and de Piles an understanding of the sitting as an enactment of the artist's mastery over his model.

With even greater ambivalence than Waller, Ben Jonson recognized the sitting's potential for triangulated desire between painter, poet, and beautiful sitter. The third section of Jonson's poetic cycle *Eupheme*, a tribute to the recently deceased Venetia Digby, opens by describing the famous court beauty as "sitting and ready

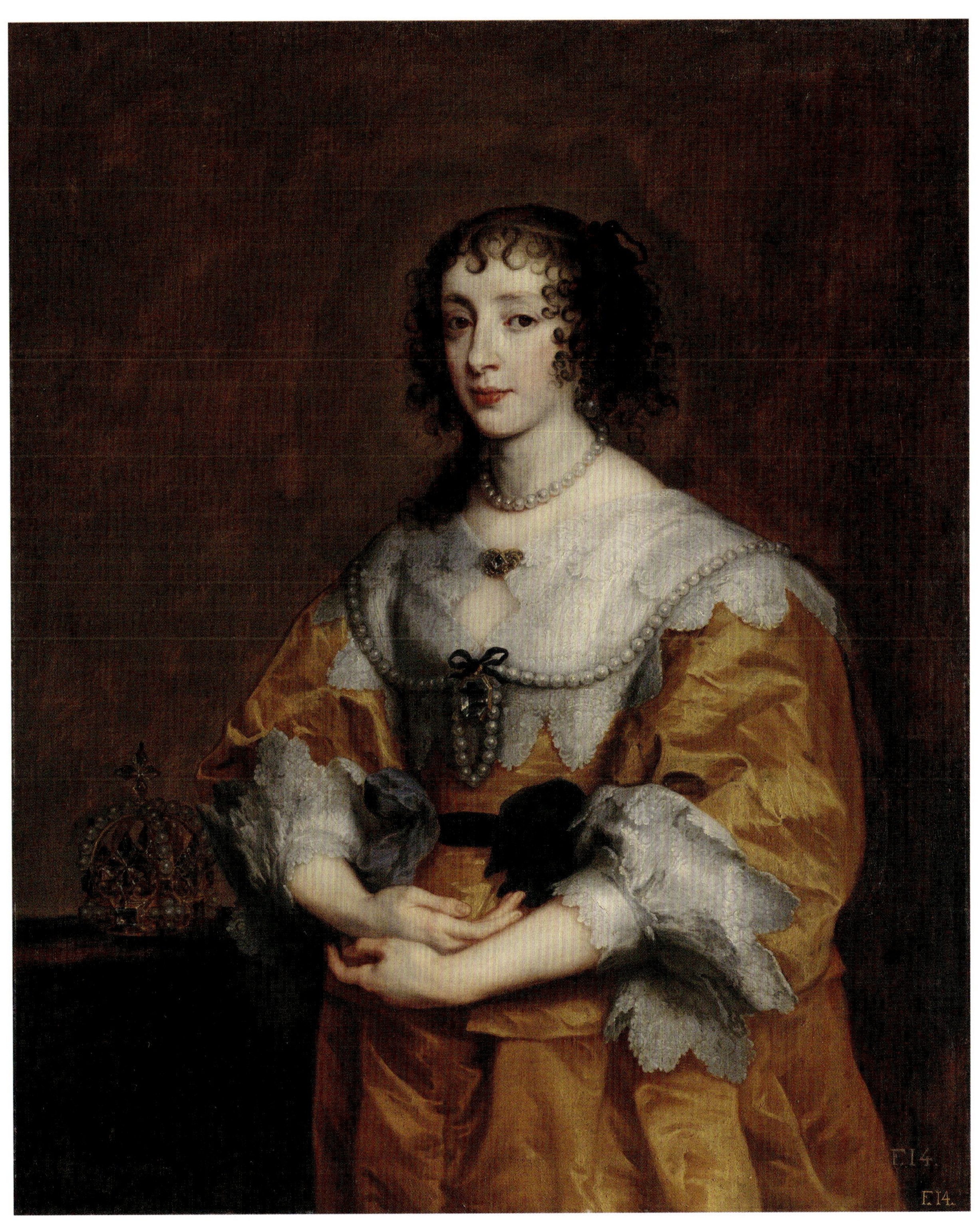

12 Anthony van Dyck, *Queen Henrietta Maria*, 1636, oil on canvas, 105.7 × 84.5 cm, New York, Metropolitan Museum of Art to be drawne," that is, awaiting the arrival of her portraitist. In a nod to Venetia's beauty, Jonson dismisses the "Velvets, Silkes, and Lawne" that disguise her enticing limbs. Having thus beguiled the reader with a mental image of Venetia clothed in "nought ... but the ayre," Jonson moves on to an exposition of his own poetic gifts. He *will* after all allow something to be "interpos'd" between Venetia's beauty and "the Painters view": not clothes to disguise it, but rather poetic "fancie" to assist the painter. Jonson opposes his fancy – what we might otherwise term invention – with the painter's "hand," a tool that can function only with the guidance of the poet.[49] With this synecdoche, he emphasizes the visual artist's status as a manual, not intellectual, laborer. Indeed, in the following section of *Eupheme*, Jonson summarily dismisses his imagined portraitist with the lines:

Painter, yo' are come, but may be gone,
Now I have better thought thereon.
...
Beside, your hand will never hit,
To draw a thing that cannot sit.[50]

Like Venetia's velvets, silks, and lawn, Jonson considers painted representation to be ultimately superfluous, and he likens the portraitist's work to a kind of cosmetic deception, or "falshood fayre," of which true beauty has no need.[51]

The unnamed painter of *Eupheme* is a straw man, enlisted in a rehearsal of tropes about the portrayal of beautiful women that had been current in European literature since Petrarch wrote his poems on Simone Martini's portrait of Laura.[52] The subgenre of "instructions to a painter" meanwhile extended back to the lyrics of the Greek anthology.[53] Yet Jonson's evocation of his richly dressed sitter awaiting the arrival of her portraitist has a contemporary specificity that many poems in this tradition lack. And unlike most of those earlier lyrics, which engage with fictional works of art, Jonson's *Eupheme* is also an agonistic response to a very real portrait that Anthony van Dyck had painted of Venetia Digby.

A famous beauty married to the courtier and natural philosopher Sir Kenelm Digby (who would later inform Bellori about Van Dyck's studio practice), Venetia died suddenly in her sleep on May 1, 1633, at the age of thirty-two.[54] In a letter to his brother, Sir Kenelm described Venetia's premature death and posthumous portrayal by Van Dyck: "When we came in, wee found her almost cold and stiffe; yet her blood was not so setteled but that our rubbing of her face brought a little seeming color into her pale cheeks, which continued there till she was folded up in her last sheete, and Sir Anthony Van Dike hath expressed [this] excellently well in his picture."[55] Van Dyck's portrait of Venetia reflects the anomalous circumstances of the deathbed sitting in its unusual composition [fig. 13].[56] In the upper corners of the painting, bed curtains part to reveal a close-up image of the deceased, framed in the manner of a proscenium. Despite its poor condition, the portrait still conveys a powerful oscillation between the appearance of sleep and indications of death. In one disturbingly naturalistic detail, Venetia's left eyelid

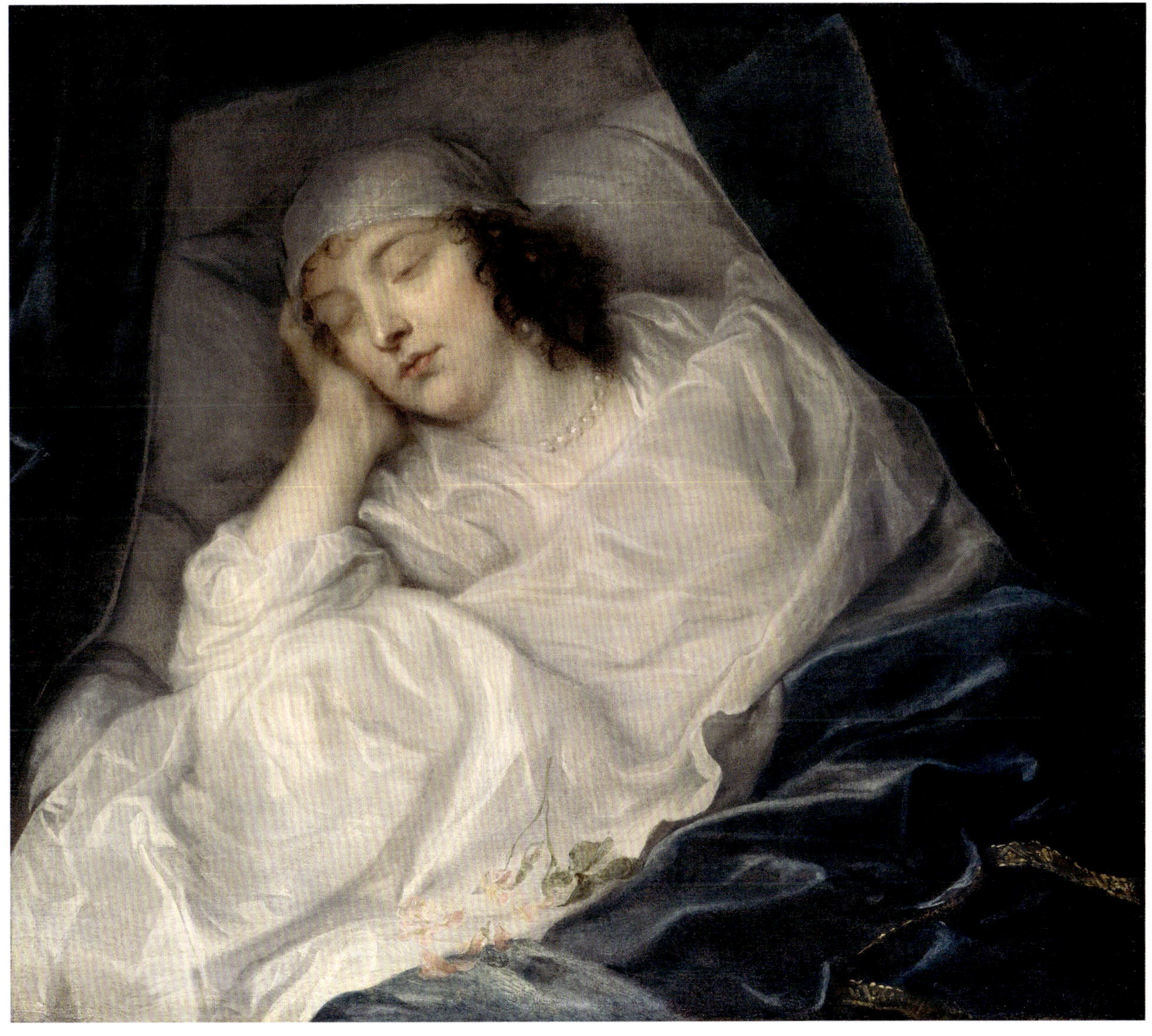

13 Anthony van Dyck, *Venetia, Lady Digby, on Her Deathbed*, 1633, oil on canvas, 74.3 × 81.8 cm, London, Dulwich Picture Gallery

lifts slightly to reveal the eye underneath, while the right lid is firmly shut. Dark locks of hair spill out of her nightcap, and her cheeks are indeed flushed with the "little seeming color" Sir Kenelm described. Venetia's gesture of cradling her head in one hand seems to assert her liveliness even as it mimics – with a traditional signifier of melancholy – the affective state inspired by her posthumous portrait.

Sir Kenelm left behind a striking description of his own ritualized interactions with the painting he called his "onely constant companion." According to the widower, Venetia's portrait "standeth all day over against my chaire and table where I sitt writing or reading or thinking, God knoweth, litle to the purpose; and att night when I goe into my chamber I sett it close by my beds side, and by the faint light of a candle, me thinks I see her dead indeed."[57] The painting took pride of place within a proliferating corpus of memorials – casts of Venetia's limbs, a lavish tomb, and literary tributes.[58] In this context, it embodied Sir Kenelm's primarily non-aesthetic relationship to portraiture, which functioned for him more as a relic of his lost beloved than as an object of connoisseurial scrutiny. But rather than diminishing Van Dyck's contribution, this talismanic relationship to the portrait recast the deathbed sitting as a quasi-sacred rite.

Digby was one of Ben Jonson's major patrons, and the poet wrote his *Eupheme* cycle as much in honor of Venetia's widower as of Venetia herself.[59] Yet in their writings, Jonson and Digby display very different attitudes toward portraiture. Although meditating on her death, Jonson imagines Venetia sitting in fashionable attire for an anonymous portraitist who cannot hope to capture her essence. Digby, by contrast, describes a postmortem examination in which Van Dyck produced a haunting stand-in for his lost wife, a painting that is both a "shadow" and a "Master peece," "so like [Venetia], that [those] who saw her before she was putt in her coffin will sweare it is she."[60] When Jonson contended that a painter's "hand will never hit, / To draw a thing that cannot sit," he was arguing against just such a belief in portraiture's power to serve as a surrogate for a missing person. Lyrics by writers such as Donne or Carew frequently opposed the greater accuracy of "the image in the lover's heart" to that produced by the painter.[61] In the *Eupheme* poems, Jonson mapped the traditional rivalry between poets and painters onto a love triangle that curiously eclipsed Venetia's widower and took the portrait sitting as its arena of combat.

Jonson's treatment of the painter in his cycle dispensed with the flattery of Waller's ode on the portrait of Dorothy Sidney. Extending Venetia's apotheosis, which he declared could never have adequate visual presentation, in line after line of verse, he served up a bold denigration of painting's commemorative capacities. Perhaps in response to the elaborate allegorical vision in *Eupheme* and the professional threat it implied, Van Dyck soon supplemented Venetia's deathbed likeness with a painting that compensated for the first portrait's muteness with an overabundance of literary signifiers [fig. 14].[62] This second, allegorical portrait now survives in two versions.[63] Here Venetia appears in the guise of Prudence, a serpent wrapped around one hand, while the other rests on a pair of doves. She places her foot upon a slumbering Cupid, his torch extinguished, while the two-faced figure of Fraud is bound and huddled beside her. A trio of putti crown Venetia with laurels. Bellori, who saw one version of this painting when Sir Kenelm was in exile in Rome, recorded that it bore an inscription from Juvenal: "Nullum numen abest si sit Prudentia" (No divinity is absent if Prudence be present).[64]

Bellori's description of the allegorical portrait of Venetia is the longest ekphrastic passage in his life of Van Dyck, occurring within an account of Sir Kenelm's friendship with the artist. According to Bellori, "As this gentleman was praised among the foremost subjects of the realm for his worthy qualities and learning,

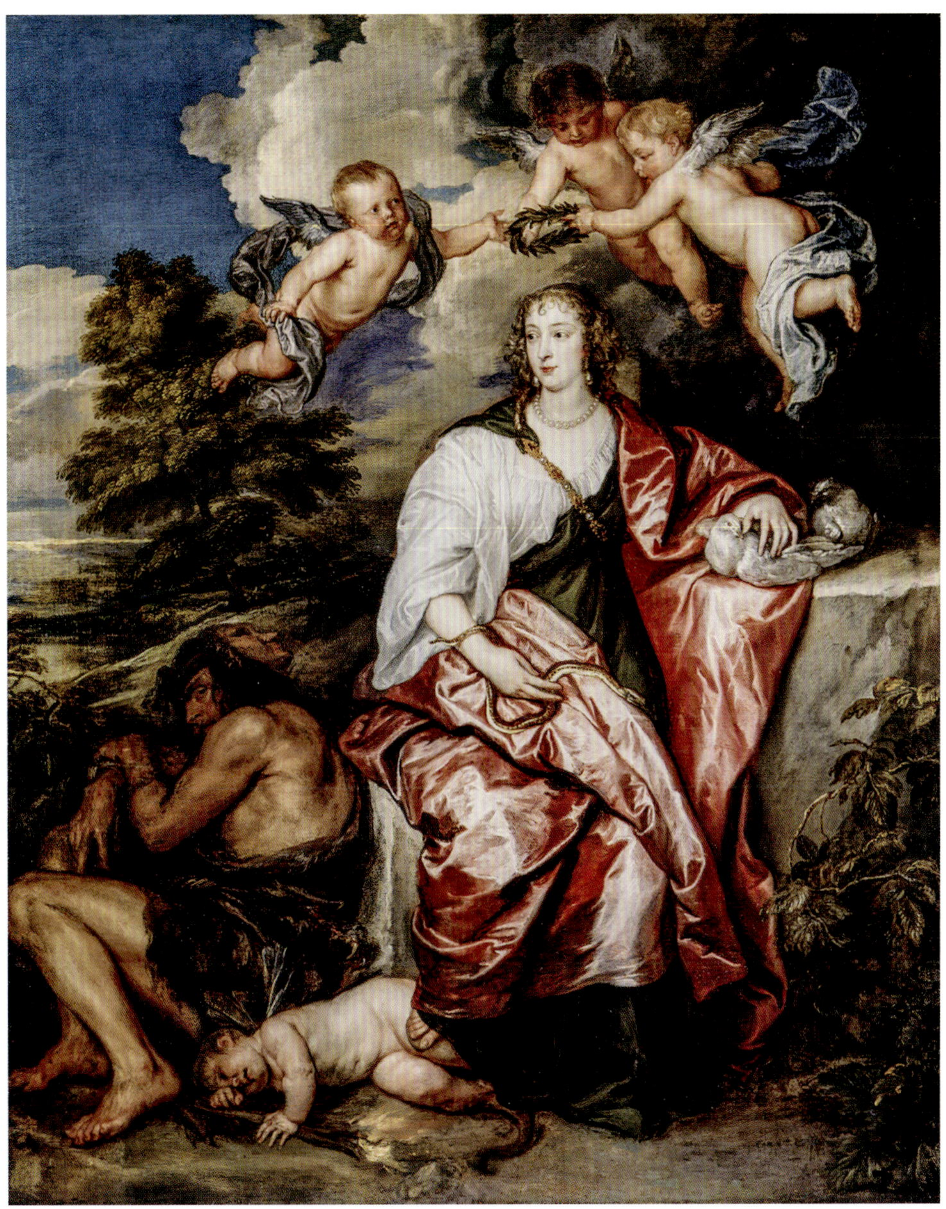

14 Anthony van Dyck, *Venetia, Lady Digby*, 1633, oil on canvas, 100.9 × 80 cm, London, National Portrait Gallery

Van Dyck entrusted all his fortunes to him, in a mutual relationship of sympathy and goodwill."[65] The description of Van Dyck's friendship with Sir Kenelm introduces a list of the works that he painted for this patron, including the portrait of Venetia. This catalog concludes with Bellori's own assertion of intimacy with Sir Kenelm, when he declares, "This knight, while staying in Rome … as resident agent of the queen of England, informed me [*mi diede contezza*] of all that happened to Van Dyck after he went to the court of London."[66] Roger de Piles would use similar language in identifying the source for his knowledge of Van Dyck's sittings as the banker Everhard Jabach.[67] The seemingly banal sentence performs important work for Bellori's text, establishing the authoritative source of his account while also positioning him within the same elite circles of patronage as Van Dyck himself. Indeed, Van Dyck's triumph as a courtier, his ability to present himself as a work of art in his own right, was as much a source of fascination for Bellori as the artist's paintings.[68]

Bellori attributes to Sir Kenelm himself the idea of depicting Venetia *in forma della Prudenza*. He then describes Venetia's rich costume of "a white gown with a colored veil and a jeweled baldric," as well as the elaborate collection of allegorical signifiers that surrounds her before shifting agency back to the painter, noting that "Van Dyck was so pleased with this invention that he painted another one on a smaller scale," likely the version today in London's National Portrait Gallery.[69] For a writer of Bellori's ambition and aesthetic program, the allegorical likeness offers more to describe, more figures to name and allusions to decipher than Van Dyck's other portraits. Out of all his paintings, it lends itself the most to ekphrasis.

The allegorical figure that serves as a header to Bellori's life of Van Dyck, a depiction of *Imitatio sapiens* trampling the monkey of mimesis as she regards herself in a mirror, alludes to an ideal of portraiture that transcends the genre's limitations through the exercise of judgment and invention.[70] Formally, the engraving seems inspired by Venetia's portrait, in which a female allegorical figure also tramples a bestial embodiment of vice. Bellori expands upon the ideal of portraiture embodied in this engraving in his discussion of the portraits of Carlo Maratta [fig. 15]. Here, Bellori explicitly connects the younger artist to Van Dyck through Maratta's English patrons, one of whom, the Duke of Buckingham, "wished to take him to England and promote him in the favor of the good king Charles [11], in whose name he too was summoned to court, where Rubens and Van Dyck had gone earlier with much honor."[71]

Bellori dwells on two groups of Maratta's portraits in particular – those of English patrons and "portraits of friends and persons whom he found congenial, which he made gladly," including Bellori himself.[72] Through this catalog of Maratta's portraits, Bellori elaborates two discrete portrait systems, one an economy of friendship, where portraits are made "gladly," and one an economy of cash and prestige, wherein Maratta "was stimulated by the prices and the liberality of those gentlemen who sought after him."[73] It is within this latter category that Bellori again reaches descriptive heights in a passage on the pendant portraits, now lost, of the Earl and Countess of Melfort. The writer evokes the earl's regalia, declaring that "there is no lack of vivacity in the ornaments of his costume and in the arrangement of the figure and face, which looks straight out as though he is speaking to someone," a clear allusion to Bernini's precepts for portraiture. Maratta showed both figures within an architectural setting, with the countess "strolling for pleasure in a gallery." The combined effect of expression, accoutrements, costume and setting meant that, for Bellori, the paintings were not "mere portraits, but they may take their place among compositions of figures."[74] In this passage, Bellori traces a trajectory by which portraiture may vie with history painting, with requirements that are both internal and external to the work itself. The most ambitious portraits must exhibit a degree of variety and detail that can sustain extended ekphrasis. But such portraits will also be ennobled by their sitters, becoming indices of patronage and proximity to great lords and ladies. This is the ideal of portraiture that Bellori perceived Van Dyck to have approached most closely in his portrait of Venetia as Prudence. But Bellori also saw how anomalous this work was for Van Dyck, expressing one particular patron's literary culture more than the artist's own ambitions for portraiture.

In the various written and painted memorials to Venetia, amorous rivalry provided an allegory for artists' and writers' professional jockeying for their patron's

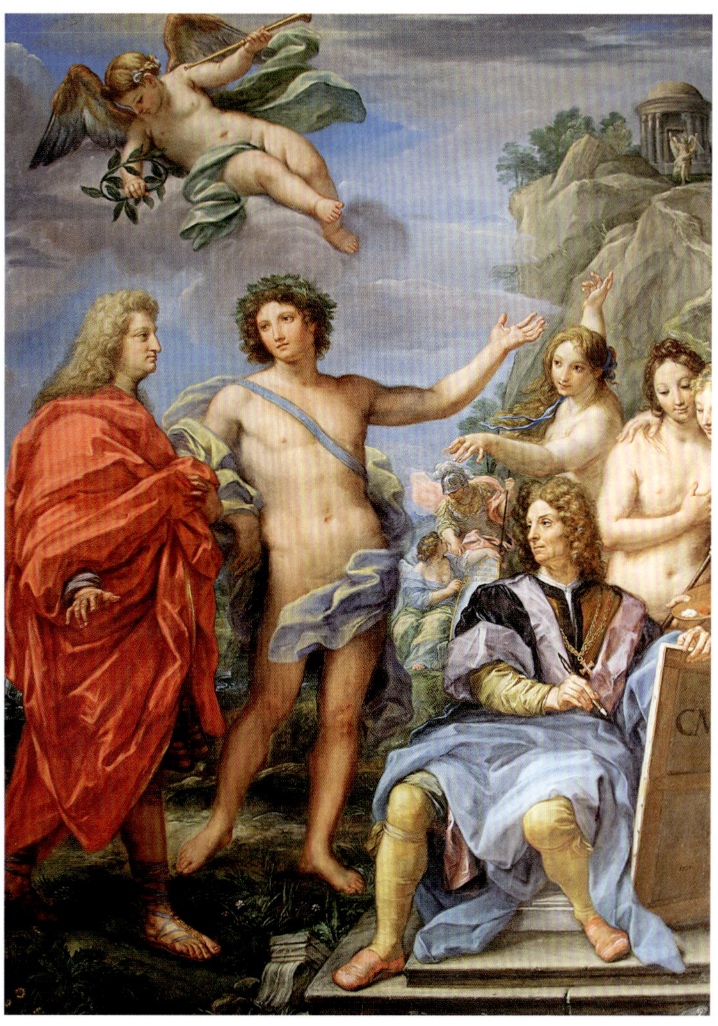

15 Carlo Maratta, *Self-Portrait with Marchese Niccolò Pallavicini*, 1705, oil on canvas, 299.7 × 212 cm, Stourhead (Wiltshire)

favor. Even before his wife's death, Sir Kenelm's own writings had made portraits a focus for sexual rivalry. In the prose romance known as the *Loose Fantasies* that he composed as a *roman à clef* based upon his courtship of Venetia, the character Stelliana mistakenly believes Kenelm's alter ego Theagenes to have died abroad and in her grief becomes the mistress of Mardontius, just as Venetia was said to have done with the Earl of Dorset. Mardontius marks his triumph by displaying Stelliana's portrait "as a glorious trophy of her conquered affections."[75] When Stelliana and Theagenes are finally reunited, she refuses to marry him until he can recover this portrait, asserting that "she would never suffer that one man should possess her, and another such a gage of a former, though half constrained, affection."[76] This episode, apparently based on a real dispute over Venetia's likeness, concretizes the triangular structure of the Petrarchan tradition, although its protagonists lack the rival identities of poet and painter.[77]

Love triangles revolving around portraits had a clear classical precedent in the tale of Apelles and Campaspe. According to Pliny, Alexander the Great was so taken with Apelles' portrait of Alexander's mistress Campaspe that he bestowed his concubine upon the painter.[78] The competitive passions enacted in such tales recall the triangulated structure of desire first outlined by René Girard, and then given important feminist and queer revisions by Eve Kosofsky Sedgwick and Nancy Vickers, among others.[79] Such a structure reveals the narrative of cuckoldry, so integral to early modern fictions of the sitting, as an important site for the negotiation of men's rivalrous desire to emulate and possess one another, as enacted through the medium of a woman's body. More recently, Christiane Hille has argued that the "triumph of painting" achieved by Rubens and Van Dyck in England rested upon a foundation of homoerotic bodily display and same-sex rivalry at the Jacobean court.[80] Of course, the competition aroused by the triangle of sitter, painter, and observer did not necessarily have to be sexual, as when Lely worked to guard his professional secrets from Mary Beale, a female painter whose gender gave its own complicated inflection to her practice and reception.[81] But writers like Waller and Jonson worried that male painters' emulation of gentlemen might extend to appropriating the pose of the lover. In the theatricalized studios where artists played the role of aristocrats, they performed for a double audience of both desirable female sitters and ambivalent male patrons.

The dramatic potential of the sitting was not lost on playwrights, as when John Lyly took the story of Apelles and Campaspe as the subject of a play, printed in 1584, that was the earliest English theatrical representation of a painter.[82] But even as Rubens and Van Dyck enjoyed unprecedented triumphs at the English court, such dramatic depictions of painters became paradoxically ever more denigrating.[83] In 1600, the boy players of St. Paul's staged a romantic comedy by an unknown author, entitled *The Wisdom of Doctor Dodypoll*, whose opening scene depicts a portrait sitting. In an ambiguous assertion of painting's nobility, the play's painter is eventually revealed to be an earl in disguise who takes advantage of the sitting to achieve clandestine proximity to his beloved.[84] But by 1640, when

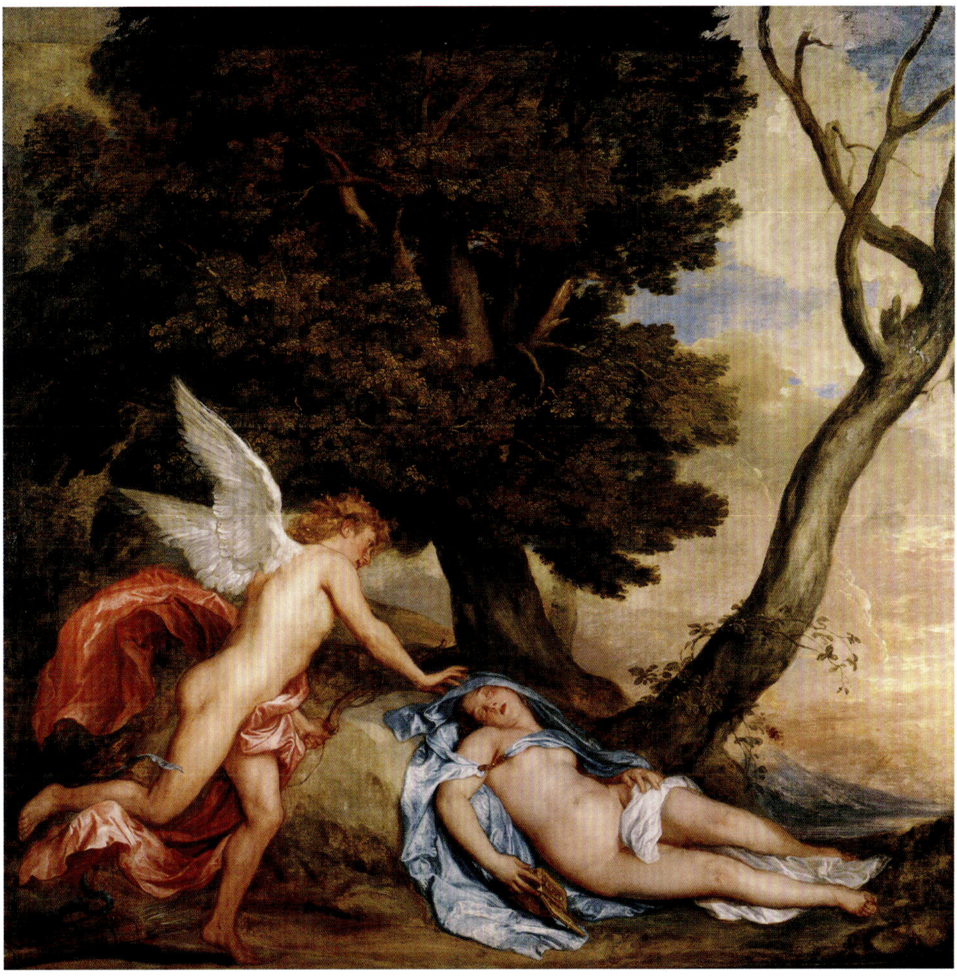

16 Anthony van Dyck, *Cupid and Psyche*, ca. 1638, oil on canvas, 199.4 × 191.8 cm, Royal Collection

Van Dyck's career was at its height, a more representative depiction was Dainty, a pickpocket who poses as a painter in Richard Brome's *The Court Beggar*. Brome gives voice to his audience's anxiety about the abundant nudity in the Continental paintings then being imported by Charles I and his courtiers.[85] In the play, a chambermaid who aspires to model for such works declares: "I have heard that Limners or Picture-drawers, doe covet to have the fairest and best featur'd wives, (or if not wives, Mistresses) that they can possibly purchace, to draw naked Pictures by … whom they make to sit or stand naked in all the severall postures, and to lie as many ways to helpe their art in drawing, who knows how I may set his fancy a worke?"[86] Royal commissions like Van Dyck's *Cupid and Psyche* combined sensual nudity with claims of neo-Platonic transcendence [fig. 16].[87] Brome's chambermaid vividly punctured such pretensions by insisting on sexual transgression as a foundational practice of art.

The erotic possibilities of the sitting also colored further instances of English playwrights responding to Van Dyck's success. In Shirley's *The Ball*, first performed in 1632, the character Freshwater teases Lady Rosamond for having her portrait painted by an Englishman, recommending instead that she "trust ... your face with the Dutch." Writing at a time of heightened tension between the native Painter-Stainers Company and the foreign-born artists in court service,[88] Shirley cast the allurements of "outlandish" painters in distinctly erotic terms, with Freshwater counselling Lady Rosamond to seek out a painter

that can please the ladies every way;
You shall not sit with him all day for shadows.
He has regalios, and can present you with
Suckets of fourteen-pence a pound, Canary
Prunellas, Venice glasses, Parmesan
Sugars, Bologna sausages, all from Antwerp ...

In the face of this enticing litany, Rosamond responds:

I have heard of him by – a noble lady
Told me the t'other day, that sitting for
Her picture, she was stifled with a strange
Perfume of horns.[89]

This exchange's graphic language of "sausages" and "horns" makes explicit the fear of cuckoldry that is so characteristic of literary depictions of portrait sittings. Shirley shared with Waller and Jonson an understanding of the portrait sitting as the site for an exciting but socially destabilizing erotic triangle between mistress, lover, and painter. In the work of these writers, only one member of the triangle – the poet/lover – has a voice, while painter and mistress are equally mute.

The perception that Van Dyck's seductiveness might violate social boundaries also colored contemporary gossip about the painter. A 1636 letter from Lord Conway to Lord Wentworth reveals both Van Dyck's intimacy with his aristocratic clientele and the discomfort that his flirtations with well-born women inspired: "You were so often with Sir *Anthony Vandike*, that you could not but know his Gallantries for the Love of [Lady Stanhope]; but he is come off with a *Coglioneria*, for he disputed with her about the Price of her Picture, and sent her Word, that if she would not give the Price he demanded, he would sell it to another that would give more."[90] Conway's anecdote neutralizes the threat of the knighted painter and his pretentions to Lady Stanhope's hand by reducing him to a greedy tradesman whose "Gallantries" devolve into farce. Aristocratic men's gossip here serves a socially conservative function, putting the painter back in his place.

In fact, Van Dyck did eventually marry the daughter of a Scottish earl, Lady Mary Ruthven. Twentieth-century commentators interested in Van Dyck's "character" distinguished his belated turn to family life from the vigorous domestic activity of Rubens.[91] Given the brevity of his marriage, it is not surprising that

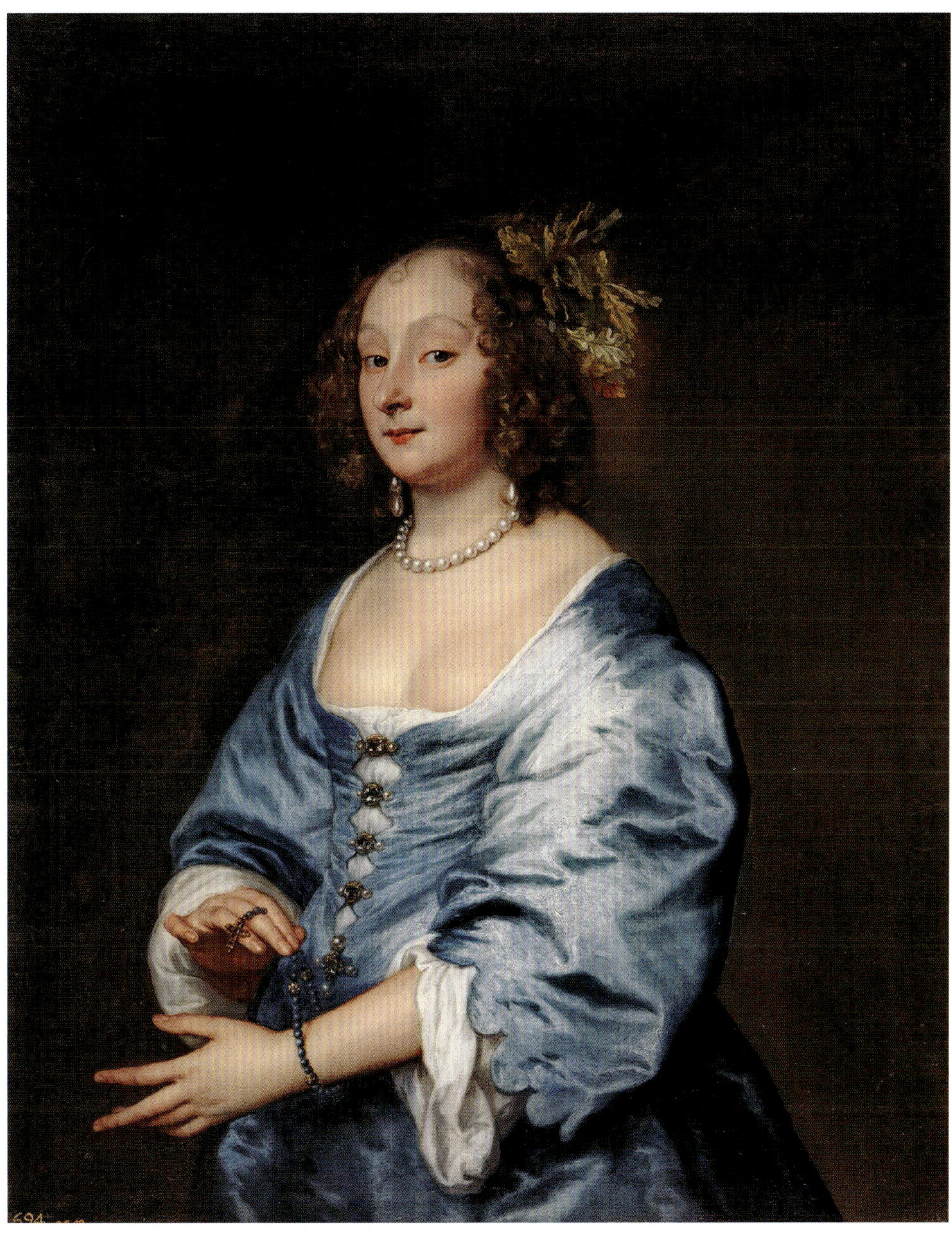

17 Anthony van Dyck, *Mary, Lady van Dyck*, ca. 1640, oil on canvas, 104 × 81 cm, Madrid, Museo del Prado

only one portrait of Van Dyck's wife survives [fig. 17].[92] Yet just like Rubens's own marital portraits, Van Dyck's portrait of his wife is a sensuously painted, entirely autograph work. Lady Mary wears stylized and informal "morning dress" that exposes a great deal of pearlescent skin, while Van Dyck's vivid brushwork captures the shimmering folds in the blue fabric. The sitter's tapered fingers call attention to her refinement, but also to the proscribed Catholic faith that she shared with her husband, emblematized in the crucifix that she displays. A cluster of oak leaves bound in her hair may symbolize constancy; William Sanderson, an early writer on the painting, identified the leaves as the "*Embleme*, *Strong* and *lasting*. So was she."[93]

In *Graphice*, his 1658 treatise on painting, Sanderson used Lady Mary's likeness for an object lesson in the genteel ekphrasis of women's portraits. Sanderson advised women to display their own portraits to advantage, not hung "like an offender in Chaines ... to be seen a far off" but rather exhibited so as to invite close scrutiny and praise.[94] Illustrating the difficulties that portraits posed to the emergent class of lay connoisseurs, Sanderson aimed to "teach the Gallant by [example] how to ascribe due praise to a deserving person and so in sooth with modesty and truth, to commend both portrait and sitter."[95] Sanderson picked up on a tradition that conflated artists' wives with their painted representations, describing the painting as "*Vandick*'s rare Mistresse, and his Masterpiece."[96] As in other such texts, an assertion that the sitter's beauty is unembellished coexists uneasily with praise of the painter's talent; as Sanderson declared, Lady Mary "needed not of his *Art* to help her forward."[97]

After Van Dyck's death, Abraham Cowley addressed an elegy to his widow that provides an interesting counterpoint to the *paragone* between painting and poetry staged by Jonson and other poets during Van Dyck's lifetime. [98] Cowley begins by proclaiming a grief-induced aphasia that levels the distinction between verbal and non-verbal art forms:

> *... Poetry must become*
> *An art, like painting here, an art that's dumb.*
> *Let's all our solemn grief in silence keep,*
> *Like some sad picture which he made to weep,*
> *Or those who saw't, for none his works could view,*
> *Unmov'd with the same passions which he drew.*

Cowley understands the affective power of Van Dyck's paintings to be a key factor in their verisimilitude. Analogizing the relationship between sitter and portrait to that between identical twins, Cowley claims that "Nature herself, amaz'd, does doubting stand / Which is her own, and which the painter's hand." The equivalence between sitter and representation provides a model for the equality Cowley claims between Van Dyck's artistry and the painter's own character: "Nor was his life less perfect than his art." Restaging the queer competitiveness of both court and studio, Cowley says, "Most other men, set next to him in view, / Appear'd more shadows than the men he drew."

Van Dyck's marriage to Lady Mary, an alliance that further cemented his assimilation to the aristocracy, provided Cowley with a concluding image of the harmony between the artist's life, work, and sexuality. Positing a seamless unanimity between spouses – "Your joys and griefs were wont the same to be" – Cowley equates Van Dyck's portrait of his wife with the artist's begetting of a daughter in her mother's image:

No wonder death mov'd not his gen'rous mind,
You, and a new-born you, he left behind.
Ev'n Fate express'd his love to his dear wife,
And let him end your picture with his life.

Cowley's depiction of Van Dyck as a contented husband and father had little impact on a historiographic tradition that preferred to see the painter as profligate, enervated, and sexually ambiguous. Likewise, the portrait of Lady Mary that fascinated early writers like Cowley and Sanderson as a triumphal merger of art and private life soon disappeared from view in England. Likely seized by creditors from Van Dyck's estate, the painting appears in a Spanish royal inventory of the mid-eighteenth century as the "portrait of a princess wearing a rosary on her wrist."[99] Its sitter's true identity lost, the Madrid painting remained little known until the end of the nineteenth century.

Van Dyck's marriage may have mitigated the threat his sexuality posed to aristocratic men. Prior to this, however, he had a far more unconventional relationship with the courtesan Margaret Lemon. Despite being a figure of fascination in the Van Dyck literature, almost nothing is known with certainty about her life.[100] Recently, Hilary Maddicott has made a convincing argument that Lemon was the "famous Curtizan" who committed suicide in Oxford in 1643 following the death of her lover in the Battle of Alton.[101] This same "knowne strumpet" was said "to walke the streets in mans apparel, and hath been maintained in the height of glory and excesse."[102] Lemon's appearance *en travesti*, recorded in a portrait miniature by Samuel Cooper [fig. 18], shows how the promotional strategies of courtesans might overlap with those of painters, recalling the young Van Dyck's self-display on the streets of Rome "resplendent in rich attire" and followed by "a retinue of servants."[103] Lemon's relationship with Van Dyck, documented in the portraits he produced of her, may have been as much a creative as an erotic collaboration. In one such painting, Lemon adopts the pose of the *Venus pudica*, as mediated by Titian's painting of a woman in a fur wrap, then in the collection of Charles I [fig. 19]. Van Dyck probably painted Lemon in this guise for the king himself.[104] The work advertised Lemon's beauty and sexual availability at the same time as it promoted Van Dyck's status as Titian's heir. Depicting his model/mistress in a state of provocative undress, Van Dyck reinforced the popular image of his studio as the erotic playground of a latter-day Apelles and Campaspe. Even more than his association with society ladies of dubious reputations, Van Dyck's images of Lemon linked him indissolubly to the figure of the "lady of pleasure," understood as both a woman of independent appetites and a courtesan.

An oft-cited but much later anecdote has Margaret Lemon threatening to bite off Van Dyck's finger in a fit of jealousy toward his female sitters.[105] Mid-seventeenth-century gossip, meanwhile, placed Van Dyck and Margaret Lemon in a further love triangle, one in which Van Dyck himself played the role of cuckold.

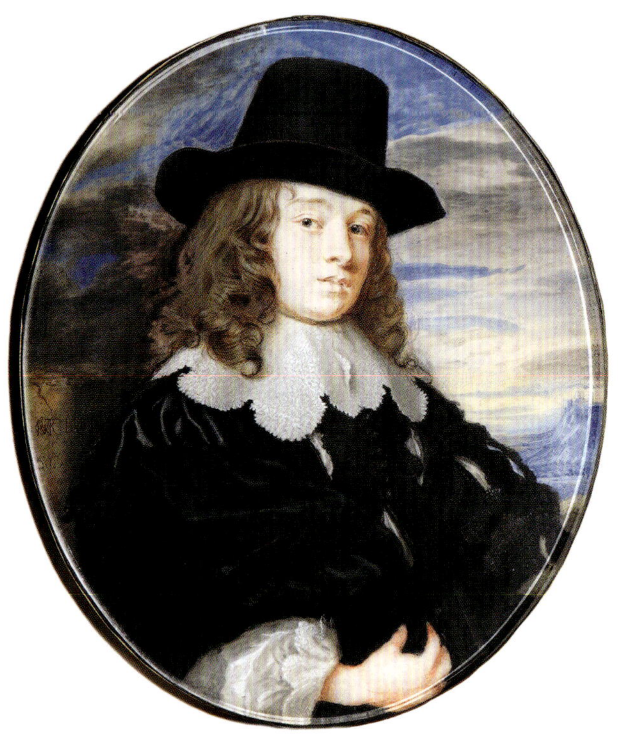

18 Samuel Cooper, *Margaret Lemon*, ca. 1635, watercolor on vellum, 12 × 9.8 cm, Paris, Fondation Custodia

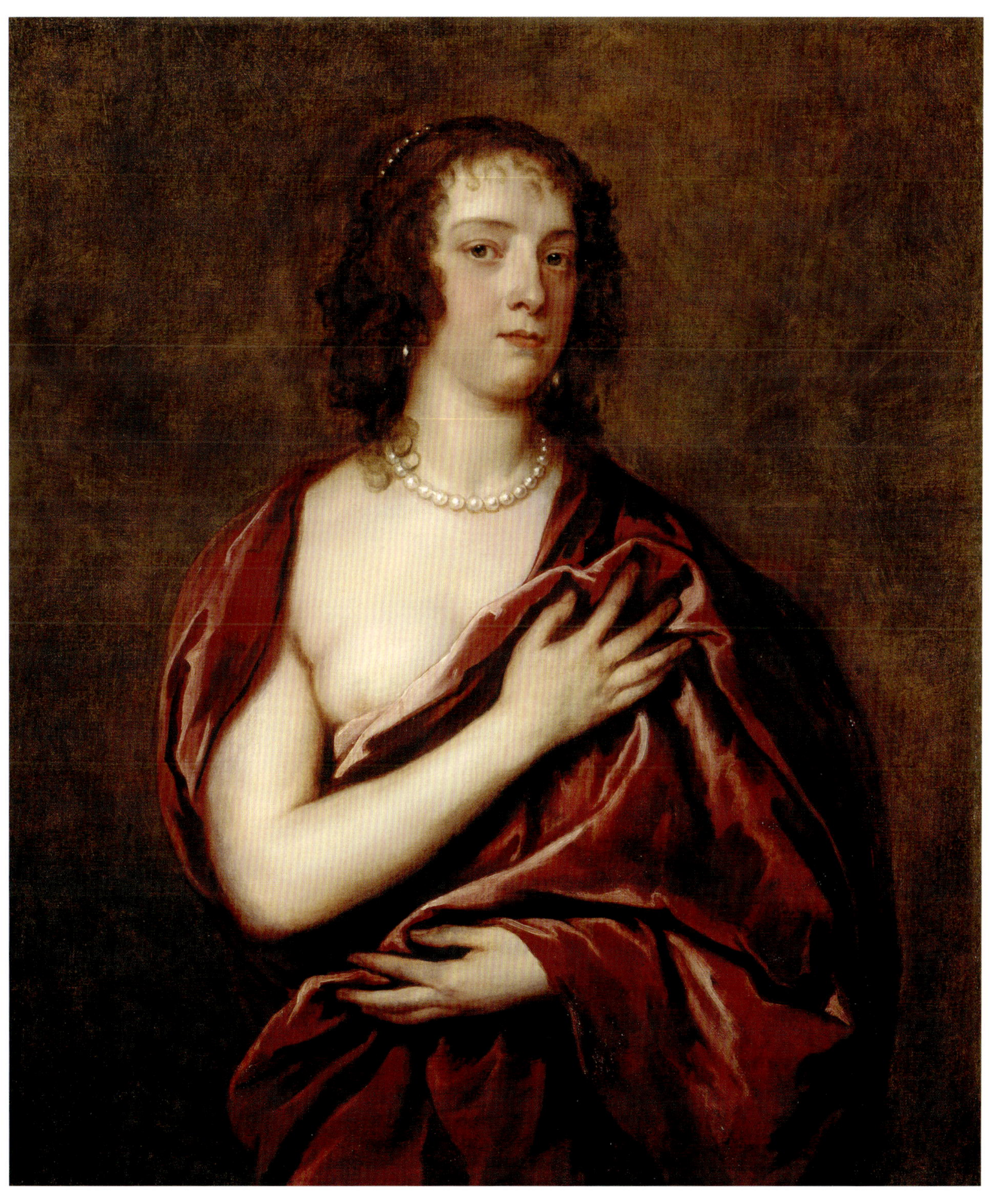

19 Anthony van Dyck, *Margaret Lemon*, ca. 1638, oil on canvas, 93.3 × 77.8 cm, Royal Collection

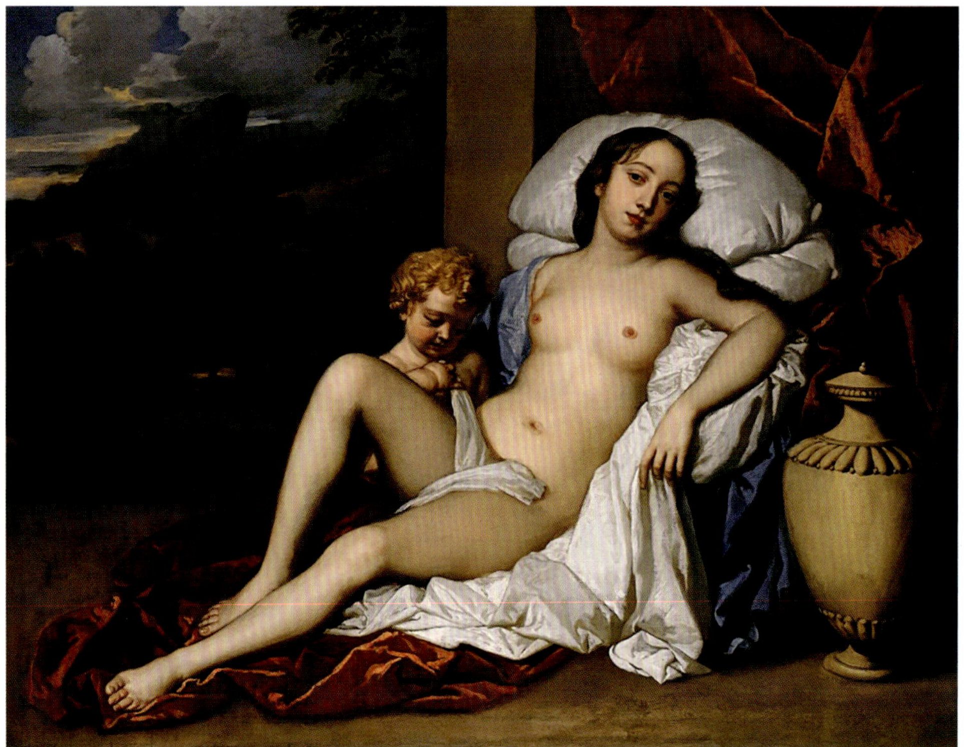

20 Sir Peter Lely, *Nell Gwyn as Venus*, ca. 1670, oil on canvas, 123.8 × 156.8 cm, private collection (courtesy of Sotheby's)

Around 1652, Richard Symonds remarked in his miscellaneous biographical notes on Van Dyck, "'Twas wondered by some that knew him that … he would keepe a mistres of his in his house Mrs Leman & Suffer Porter to keep her company."[106] Maddicott has identified Van Dyck's rival with Giles Porter, the younger brother of Van Dyck's friend and patron Sir Endymion Porter.[107] It was this same Porter whose death in the Civil War prompted Lemon's suicide in 1643. Like Lord Conway's mention of Van Dyck's "*Coglioneria*," Symonds's anecdote calls attention to Van Dyck's dubious status as a gentleman: the same man whose avarice spoiled his courtship of Lady Stanhope is seen here to tolerate his mistress's attentions to another man. Both bits of gossip, whatever their basis in fact, add further evidence about the role that Van Dyck's (perceived) sexuality played in his public persona.

The association between Van Dyck and meretricious beauty becomes even clearer in Thomas Killigrew's play *Thomaso*, written while the author was in exile in Madrid.[108] In one scene, a group of men gather to examine the portrait of a courtesan hung outside her home to advertise her services:

> PEDRO. *'Tis an Excellent Picture, whose hand can it be?*
>
> CARLO. Van Dikes, *and 'tis well done.*
>
> JOHAN. *He was a great Master, and a Civil Pencil.*

> CARLO. *Why, do you think he has flatter'd her?*
>
> PEDRO. *By Saint* Iago, *he cannot; Observe her without prejudice; Is there one Grace, one beauty more then* [sic] *she set before his Eyes? And softness, such as pencils cannot reach; That smile, there's a grace and sweetness in it* Titian *could never have catch'd.*[109]

Killigrew's play reveals the extent to which Van Dyck's reputation had become fixed within a few years of his death. In addition to reinforcing the association between Van Dyck and female beauty, particularly that of courtesans, Killigrew, like so many other writers, relates Van Dyck's achievement to Titian's. But even as he praises Van Dyck's talent and "Civil Pencil," Killigrew captures the ambivalence surrounding the artistic merit of portraits of beautiful women. Either such portraits were acts of flattery or they were artless, merely recording – but failing to capture entirely – a beauty that preceded their art. When she rewrote Killigrew's play for the Restoration stage as *The Rover*, Aphra Behn cut the explicit reference to Van Dyck but further heightened the association between the traffic in women and the circulation of portraits, an association that brings the work of the portraitist uncomfortably close to that of the pimp.[110]

In this same climate of Restoration permissiveness, Charles II and Lely conspired in a real-life revision of Pliny's tale of Apelles and Campaspe that took the form of a provocative depiction of the king's mistress Nell Gwyn as Venus [fig. 20].[111] According to George Vertue, "this picture was painted at the express command of K. Charles 2d nay he came to Sr Peter Lillys house to see it painted when she was naked on purpose."[112] In the painting, Cupid serves as a surrogate for the voyeuristic king, peering between "Venus's" legs as he lifts the drapery nestled there. Meanwhile, the courtesan's frank gaze implicates the beholder in a further triangular relationship with the figures in the painting. Gwyn's pose looks back to celebrated works of Venetian painting through the medium of Van Dyck's *Cupid and Psyche*. After the king's execution, Lely had himself acquired Van Dyck's painting, but Charles II assiduously reclaimed it and much of the rest of his father's collection upon the Restoration.[113] Built upon a traffic in paintings and bodies between court and studio, Gwyn's portrait acknowledges the privileged access of the artist while affirming the royal beholder's ultimate possession of both sitter and painting. The king's visit to the studio is no longer an act of royal condescension to a favored painter, but rather a reclamation of his *droit du seigneur*, enacted through the portrait sitting.

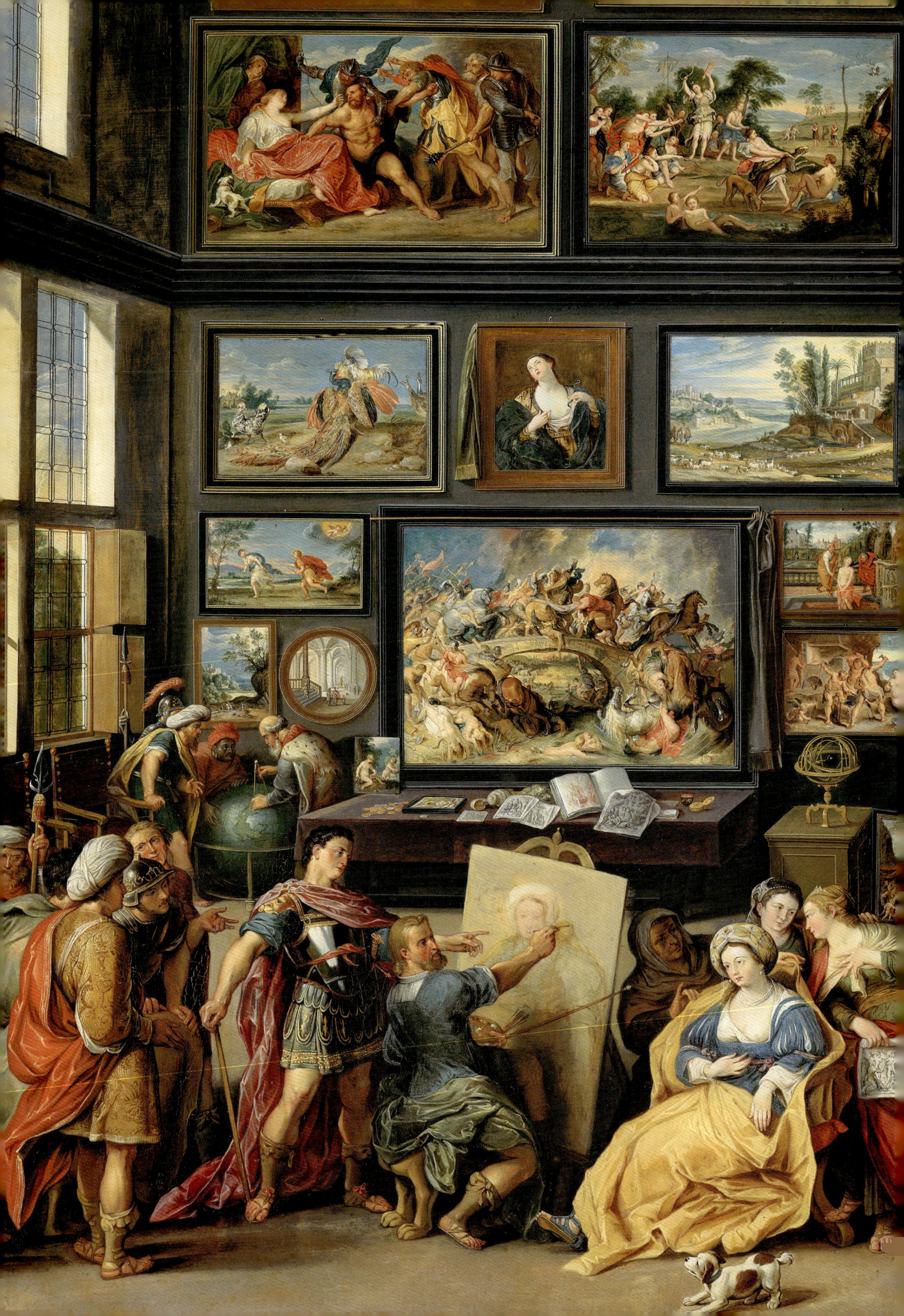

[CHAPTER TWO]

Impudent Painters

IN HIS 1710 TREATISE ON PAINTING, THE *GROOT SCHILDERBOEK*, GÉRARD de Lairesse honored Van Dyck as "the first [painter] who carried the modern manner so high as to gain it the name of art."[1] However retrograde the Van Dyckian mode may appear today, de Lairesse's praise alerts us to the fact that, for decades after his death, Van Dyck figured as the embodiment of a particular kind of artistic modernity. In the seventeenth and eighteenth centuries, modern painting was above all fashionable painting, attentive to the mutability of taste in a world addicted to variety and consumption. In de Lairesse's words, "Things antique are always the same, but the mode continually changing; its very name implies mutability, since nothing is more inconstant than what depends on fashion; which alters not only annually, but even daily in those who mimic the court."[2] Like the fops of city comedy, painters who documented fleeting fashions exposed themselves to ridicule, modish one day and superannuated the next.[3] Yet within the inherently inferior category of the modern, de Lairesse could single out certain practitioners as exemplary. Notable among these was Van Dyck, "never enough to be commended, [who] gained excellence in [the] antique as well as the modern manner, by strictly following the ... three graces in both."[4] Laudable modernity, in de Lairesse's account, was idealist modernity, recognizing that "modern painting can ... not be accounted art, when nature is simply followed; but when nature is corrected and improved by a judicious master ... the painting must then be noble and perfect."[5]

Beyond the exercise of idealizing judiciousness, modern painting might also attest to the gentility and fashionableness of the painter. De Lairesse reinforced the identification of painters with their work by arguing that it would be easier "for a citizen to play a citizen's part than any other; and for a painter to keep to the management of what he daily meets with ... Thus Rubens and Van Dyk [*sic*], by daily conversing with the great at court, were fixing their thoughts on what is sublime and lofty in ... art."[6] De Lairesse placed these artists within a tradition, going back to Karel van Mander's life of Pieter Bruegel, that read painters as ethnographers or participant-observers of a given social class.[7] But whereas earlier writers applied this paradigm primarily to the painters of peasant life, de Lairesse made it socially versatile, applicable to both courtly and urban settings.

Detail of Guillam van Haecht, *Apelles Painting Campaspe*, ca. 1630 [see fig. 29]

The praiseworthy modern artist assimilated himself into the life of the court and mirrored its values in his art. Indeed, Van Dyck's success among the English aristocracy derived from not only his extraordinary talent but also his personal charisma. The most famous description of this quality appears in a letter from 1637, addressed to Van Dyck by William Cavendish, Earl (later Duke) of Newcastle:

> *Noble S^r^,*
> *The favors off my freindes you have so transmitted unto mee as the longer I looke on them, the more I think them Nature & nott Arte. Itt is nott my Error alone, iff Itt bee a disease Itt is Epidemicall, for sutch power hath your hande on the Eyes of Man-kinde. Nexte the Blessinge off your Coumpanye, & Sweetnes off Conversation, The Greateste happiness weare to bee an Argus or all over butt one eye, so Itt, or theye, weare Ever fixed upon that which wee must Cale yours. Whatt wants In Judge-mente I can suplye with admiration, Ande scape the title off Ignorante since I have the Luck to bee astonish'de In the righte Place, Ande the happiness to bee Pationatly Your Moste Humble Servant,*
> *W. Newcastle*[8]

In his letter, Newcastle imagines a complete bodily surrender to the power of painting, a becoming "all over but one eye" fixed forever on the sight of Van Dyck's portraits. Newcastle's voice is emphatically not that of a connoisseur, but rather one whose visceral response to painting compensates for "wants in judgment." Yet even this pleasure is subordinated to the "the blessing of [Van Dyck's] company, & sweetness of conversation." Praising the artist for his portraits of Newcastle's friends, the earl makes clear that Van Dyck's comportment has elevated him to that elite company.

Poets asserting the superiority of their medium reveled in painting's muteness. By contrast, partisans of Van Dyck's art saw the painter's eloquence as an essential supplement to the experience of his portraits. Rubens recorded his erudition and tact in hundreds of letters, but Van Dyck's conversation has left very few archival traces. His portraits, however, reveal Van Dyck's investment in disposing figures in configurations that both add a narrative element to portraiture and emphasize its social embeddedness, making friendship as well as servitude visible. In Van Dyck's hands, portraiture became a means of staging relations of power that could be both infinitely subtle and brutally dehumanizing. This paradox becomes clear in a parallel examination of two seemingly disparate kinds of portrait – those depicting pairs of friends and those depicting a white sitter flanked by an attendant of color.

— *Double Portraits* —

The triangular relationship between lover, mistress, and painter that is so central for the European tradition exists in tension with another triangle: that implied by the so-called friendship portrait. Such likenesses put the affective relationship of two sitters on show for a third party outside the frame.[9] Friendship portraits posit the beholder as a third term, who may be subject to the painted gaze of one

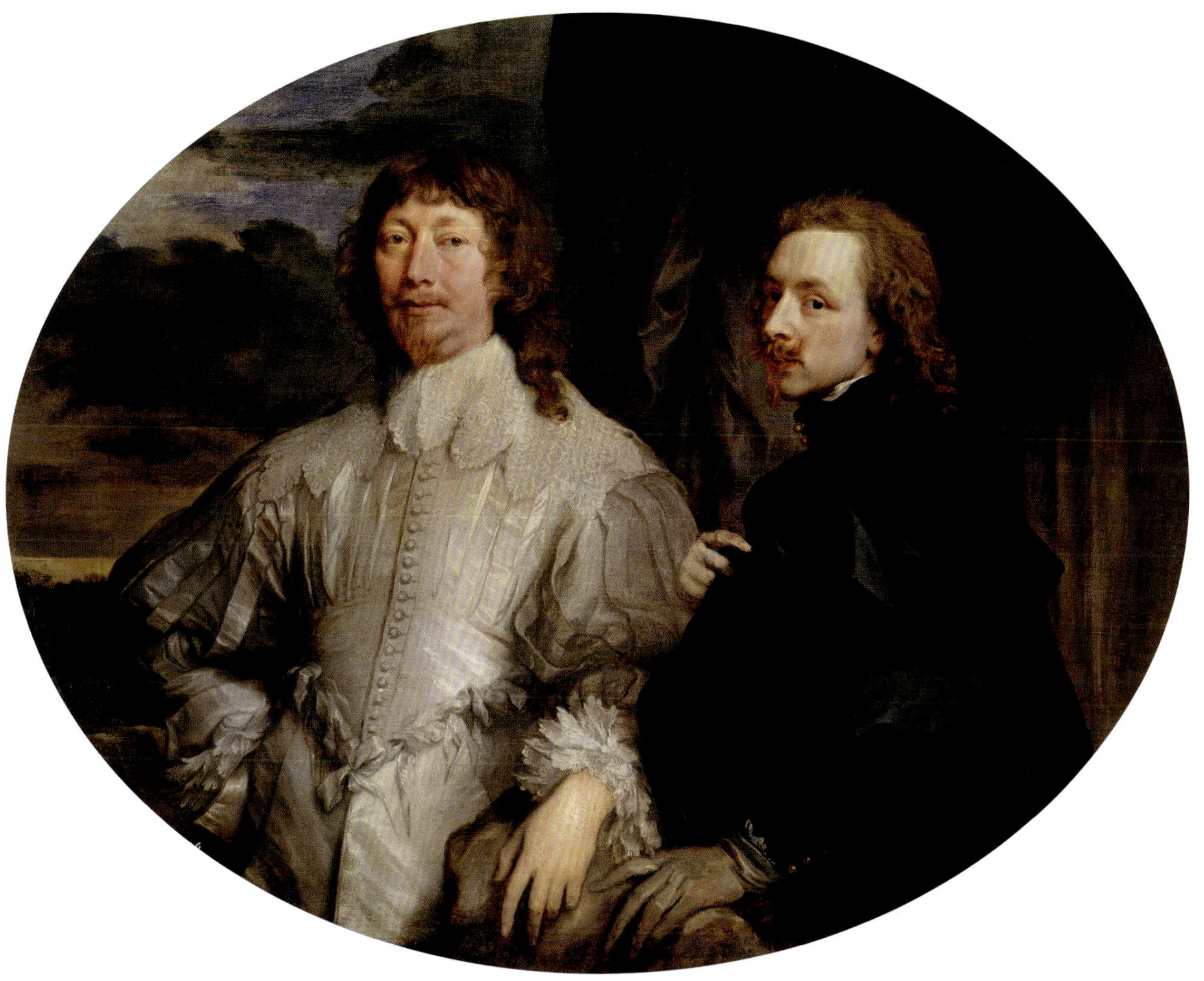

21 Anthony van Dyck, *Self-Portrait with Endymion Porter*, ca. 1632–33, oil on canvas, 110 × 114 cm, Madrid, Museo del Prado

or more of the sitters, but whose precise relationship to them remains nonetheless opaque. Are we, in looking at such a double portrait, cast in the role of another friend who relates to the sitters on equal footing? Or do we rather play the part of a rival, forced to look upon a dynamic of intimate patronage from which we are excluded?

We might profitably direct these questions toward Van Dyck's self-portrait with the English courtier Endymion Porter [fig. 21].[10] The two men appear side by side, both looking out at the beholder, although Van Dyck poses in such a way that he appears to be momentarily distracted as he turns toward his friend. Their physical intimacy is heightened by the disruptive detail of Van Dyck's gloved index finger, extended to almost, but not quite, graze Porter's bare knuckle. In this portrait, Van Dyck's posture, his placement in the traditionally female heraldic sinister (that is, beholder's right) of the painting, and his more muted attire all establish him in a deferential relationship to Porter.[11] At the same time, the artist appears almost to have slipped out from behind the easel to insinuate himself into his patron's portrait.[12] Viewed in this light, Van Dyck's double portrait can be said to commemorate the studio encounter between patron and painter. It is as close as Van Dyck ever came to depicting a portrait sitting.

Scholars often trace the origins of the conversation piece, perhaps the most significant innovation of eighteenth-century English art, to Dutch genre painting.[13] But these group images, which combine a keen investigation of body language and material culture with the portrayal of identifiable individuals, also owe a debt to the friendship portraits of the seventeenth century. Such paintings expanded the purview of portraiture by making their sitters' identities explicitly contingent, relational, and socially situated. In his lives of Van Dyck and Maratta, Bellori indicated portraiture's potential to approach the stature of history painting through iconographic density and a complex arrangement of figures, as in Van Dyck's allegorical portrait of Venetia Digby as Prudence [see fig. 13]. But while that portrait remained anomalous within his oeuvre, Van Dyck's friendship portraits proved the more lasting achievement, developing portraiture's ability to function as a map of social and affective relationships.

In another such portrait, Van Dyck depicted Thomas Killigrew and a man usually identified as his brother-in-law, William, Lord Crofts [fig. 22].[14] Like that of Venetia Digby, this painting has its origins in a man's grief for his wife, but now the widower and his brother-in-law are the subjects rather than the departed woman herself. The painting claims for the two men the status of chief mourners, dressed in elegantly disheveled black and displaying the late Mrs. Killigrew's rings and cross. Even more than in his self-portrait with Endymion Porter, Van Dyck's double portrait of Killigrew and Crofts draws its power from the tension of triangular dynamics. Formally, there is the inverted triangle plotted by the men's two heads and the drawing of two female figures that dangles from Killigrew's hand. As this drawing, perhaps a sketch for a funerary monument, makes clear, shared relationships to women mediate the affective tie between the two men, even beyond the grave. The men's gazes provide a further triangle that implicates the viewer. Crofts looks at his brother-in-law, but Killigrew looks out at us, languidly, skeptically, or mournfully. The blank page in Croft's hands, a striking vacuum at the center of the image, rebuffs intimacy or insight. The painter draws the viewer into a dynamic of intimacy that ultimately proves elusive.

The power dynamics of friendship portraits, where heraldic convention might place a social superior on the viewer's left or twist a subordinate's body toward his interlocutor, are relatively subtle. Such paintings promote intimacy while acknowledging gradations of social difference. Something else entirely happens in another type of Van Dyck double portrait – those that place an elite white sitter alongside a non-white attendant figure. Van Dyckian portraiture mobilized racial hierarchies as a bald statement of the fixed and violent power relations that

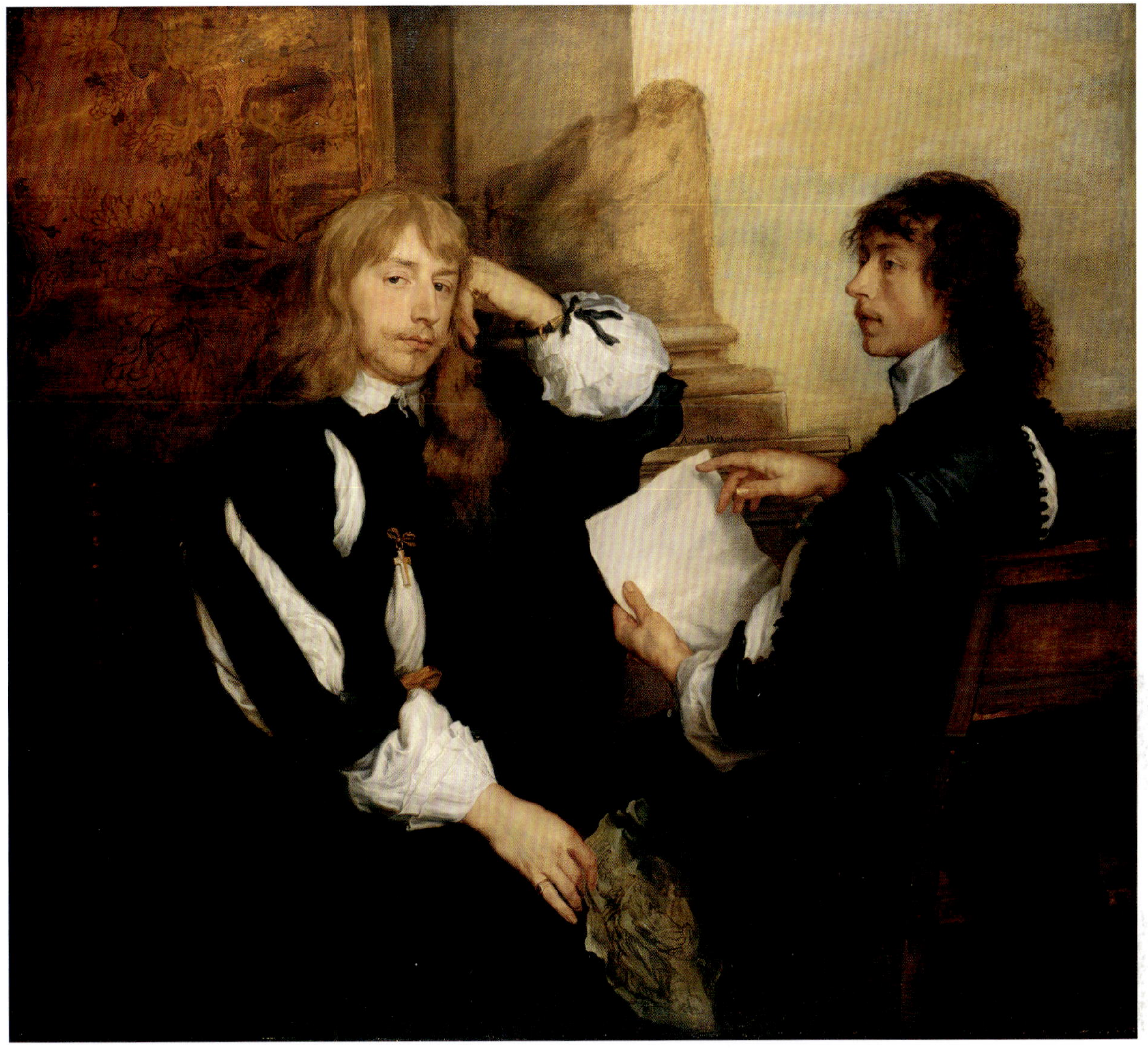

22 Anthony van Dyck, *Thomas Killigrew and William, Lord Crofts (?)*, 1638, oil on canvas, 132.7 × 143.5 cm, Royal Collection

defined the courtly subject.[15] His portraits of white sitters flanked by attendants of color replace the friendship portrait's productive ambiguities with rigid binaries of complexion and class that look back to images of the feudal household, such as Rubens's portrait of Lady Arundel with her dog and dwarfs. Such portraits naturalized an emergent trans-Atlantic slave trade and constituted the white enslaver as the paragon of aristocratic self-possession through his or her ownership of another human being.[16]

Kim Hall has called the Black figures who appear in early modern portraits "meta-objects, symbols for the accumulation of profitable foreign goods during

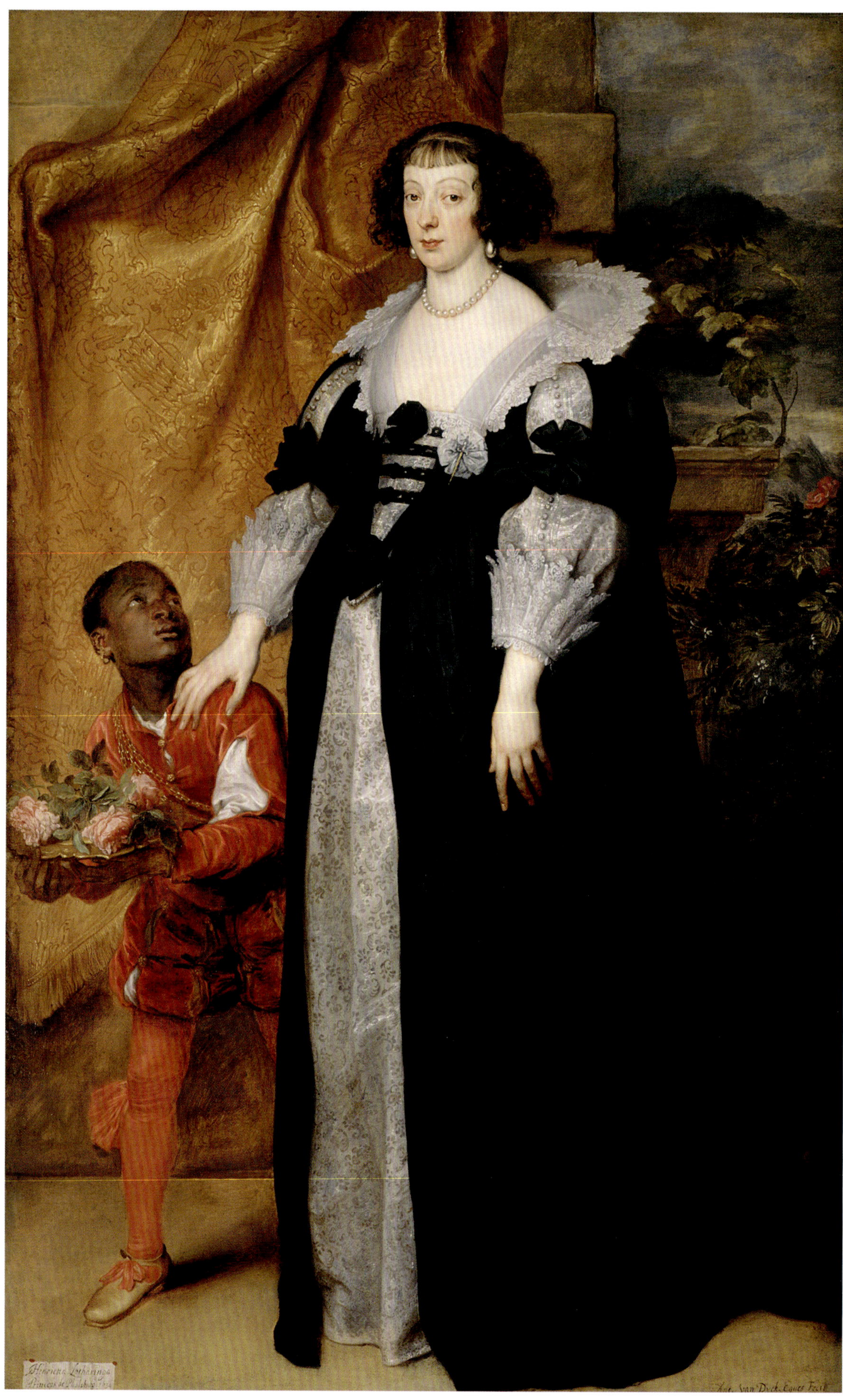

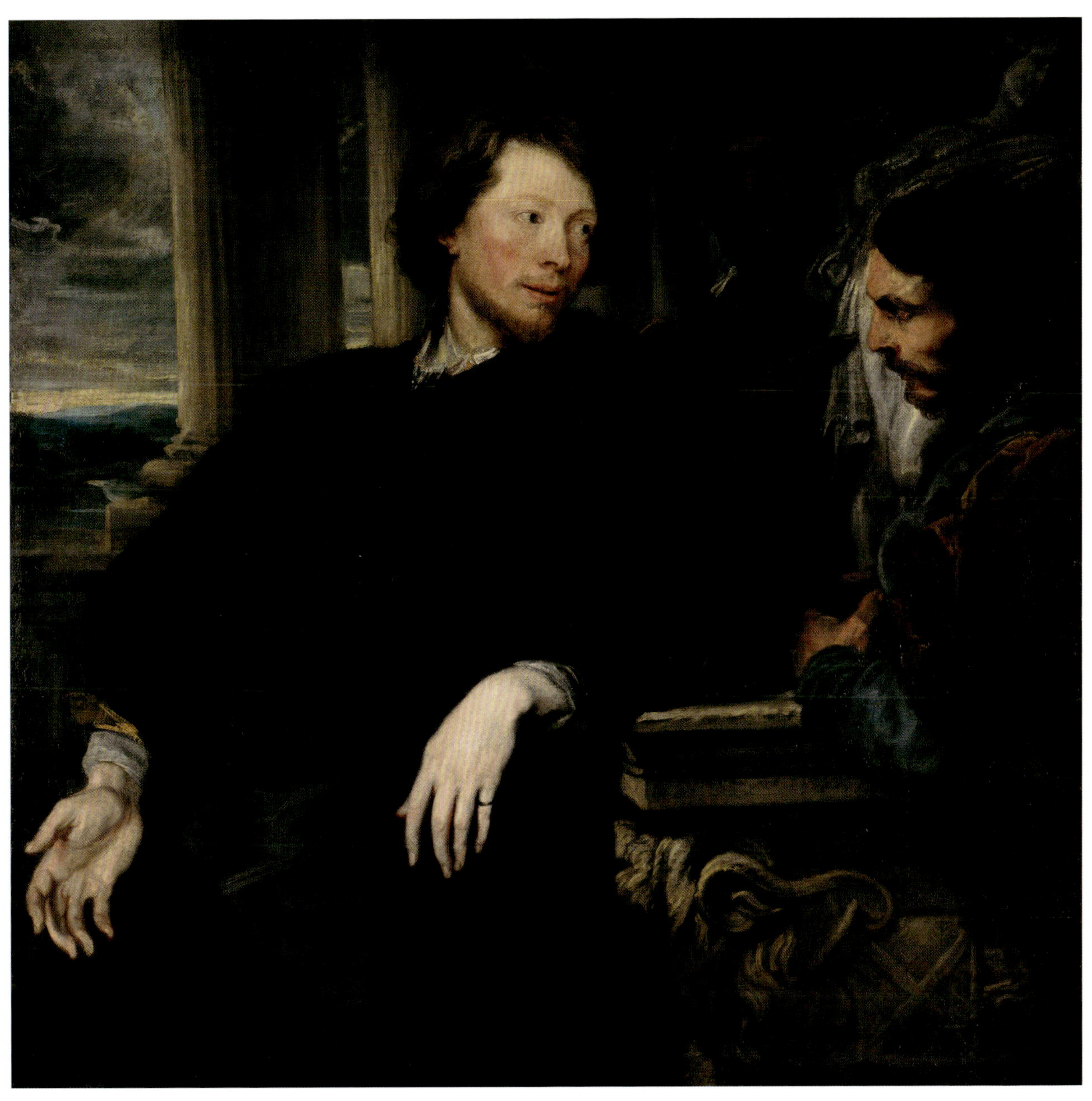

23 Anthony van Dyck, *Princess Henrietta of Lorraine, Attended by a Page*, 1634, oil on canvas, 213.4 × 127 cm, London, Iveagh Bequest, Kenwood House

24 Anthony van Dyck, *Portrait of George Gage with Two Men*, ca. 1622–23, oil on canvas, 115 × 113.5 cm, London, National Gallery this era."[17] As such, the attendant embodies the luxury so characteristic of Van Dyckian portraiture, becoming one further item in the list of delicacies by which the consuming woman is enticed into the studio. In Van Dyck's portrait of Henrietta of Lorraine attended by a Black page, we again encounter a triangular structure built around unreciprocated gazes [fig. 23].[18] Crouching as he proffers a basket of roses, the page looks up at his mistress. Her gaze, by contrast, goes out impassively to the beholder. In one sense, the depiction of the page is the more convincing portrait, in that it savors of animation and life study. But this is a naturalism put to the purpose of reducing its object to a mere foil. Everything in the painting proclaims that only the denatured aristocrat, stoic to the point of impenetrability, possesses subjecthood here. Endymion Porter made a gift of this portrait to Charles I shortly after it was painted in Brussels. The artist's conceit of depicting the princess, in the words of the Whitehall inventory, "with a Blackamoure by" likely appealed to the king both as a citation of Titian and a staging of absolute difference between rulers and ruled.[19]

In other portraits, Van Dyck recruited non-white figures for an experimental narrativization of portraiture that played with the conceits of genre painting. In one of his first depictions of an English sitter, he showed the art dealer George Gage scrutinizing a work of classical sculpture presented by two men [fig. 24].[20] One of these figures, standing in the background, is dark-skinned. He, alone of the three men, looks out at the viewer as he extends a finger to the sculpted female body. With his gaze and his gesture, he places the beholder in the position of buyer, on a par with Gage as an appraising connoisseur. But this man's Blackness also serves a demonstrative function, highlighting or even constituting the whiteness of both marble sculpture and English connoisseur. At the same time, his sardonic and engaging look enacts a mild subversion of the portrait's claims about gentility and self-possession, a subversion that would disappear in the more formulaic portraits of later years.

A decade later, Van Dyck used another pointing finger to take this blurring of portraiture and narrative painting even further, in a full-length image of William Feilding, 1st Earl of Denbigh [fig. 25].[21] Denbigh had previously made a tour of Persia and India, visiting the Mughal court. Van Dyck presents him as an intrepid traveler, armed with a gun as he strides forward with unusual animation. Both his costume and the landscape convey a fanciful Indo-European hybridity, juxtaposing a snow-capped mountain with a palm tree and a lace collar with striped silk pajamas. A turbaned young man draws Feilding's attention to the parrot up in the tree. His stature, complexion, and posture all secure his role as a deferential accessory. Well before the establishment of British imperialism in Asia, the Van Dyckian mode had articulated the basic dynamic through which relations of colonial subjugation would take visual form in portraiture.[22]

25 Anthony van Dyck, *William Feilding, 1st Earl of Denbigh, with an Attendant*, ca. 1633–34, oil on canvas, 247.5 × 148.5 cm, London, National Gallery

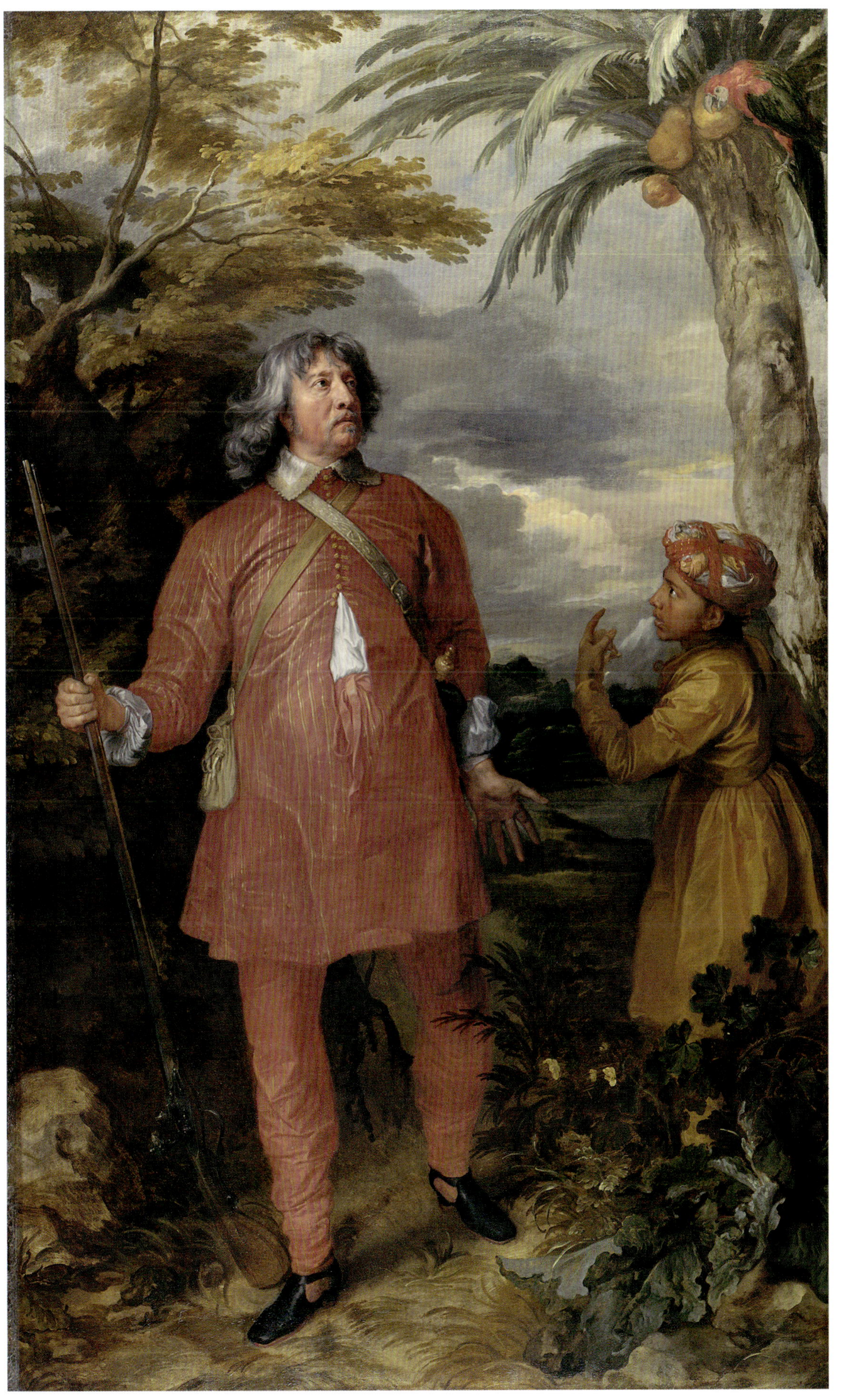

— *Discours d'un peintre flamand* —

In eighteenth-century biographies of Van Dyck, tales of his effrontery and violation of class boundaries multiplied, much to the fascination of those who have attempted psycho-biographical readings of his work. But these later anecdotes, written down decades after Van Dyck's death, primarily demonstrate the general perception that portrait sittings were socially fraught situations and that Van Dyck's conduct within them was exemplary. Introducing one such episode in a life of the artist published in 1729, the Dutch writer Jacob Campo Weyerman declared that Van Dyck should serve as "a model for other great masters, who often let themselves be treated like lackeys by gilded donkeys."[23] In Weyerman's tale, Van Dyck is summoned to paint the bishop of Ghent, but has an angry confrontation with his condescending sitter, with the artist going so far as to suggest that the bishop fetch his equipment from an anteroom. Weyerman follows up on this tale with a series of quips that Van Dyck is said to have exchanged with his royal patrons in England, flattering the queen's hands because he expects "an extraordinary reward" from them, and sympathizing with the cash-strapped king since "an artist who keeps an open table for his friends and an open purse for his mistresses, as I do, is now and then not unacquainted with the bottom of his cashbox."[24] These tales may bear no relation to Van Dyck's actual conversation during portrait sittings, but they speak volumes about his early reception. For writers like Weyerman, Van Dyck's familiarity and boldness with his social superiors, even to the point of insolence, defined his public persona; he demonstrated that familiarity primarily in the context of the portrait sitting.

Weyerman tells another story about a royal portrait that illuminates the fine line between one artist's witty nonchalance and another's boorish faux pas. Writing about Godefridus Schalcken's portrait of *William III by Candlelight*, Weyermann describes it as "a night-light piece, life-size but not from life" that depicts the king "holding a light[ed] candle without either candle-holder or candlestick [with] the candle grease dripping down the king's fingers" [fig. 26].[25] Weyerman dismissed the painting as a "stupid" and "impudent" embarrassment to Dutch painters, because it revealed a lack of knowledge about courtly protocol.[26] Decades later, Horace Walpole elaborated this criticism into an imagined sitting between the painter and king, claiming that Schalcken

> *once drew king William, but as the piece was to be by candle-light, he gave his majesty the candle to hold, till the tallow ran down upon his fingers. As if to justify this ill-breeding, he drew his own picture in the same situation. Delicacy was no part of his character*

26 Godefridus Schalcken, *King William III by Candlelight*, ca. 1695, oil on canvas, 74.9 × 62.2 cm, Atcham, Attingham Park (National Trust)

27 Godefridus Schalcken, *James Stuart, Duke of Lennox and Richmond, by Candlelight*, ca. 1695 oil on canvas, 94.6 × 144.8 cm, New York, Leiden Collection

28 Godefridus Schalcken, *Self-Portrait*, 1695, oil on canvas, 92.3 × 81 cm, Florence, Uffizi

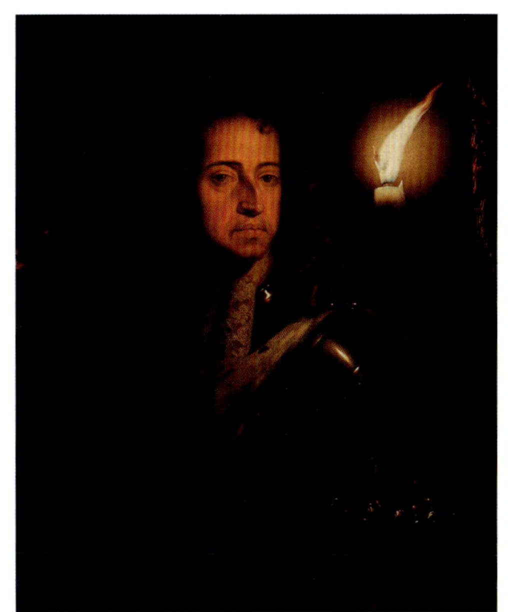

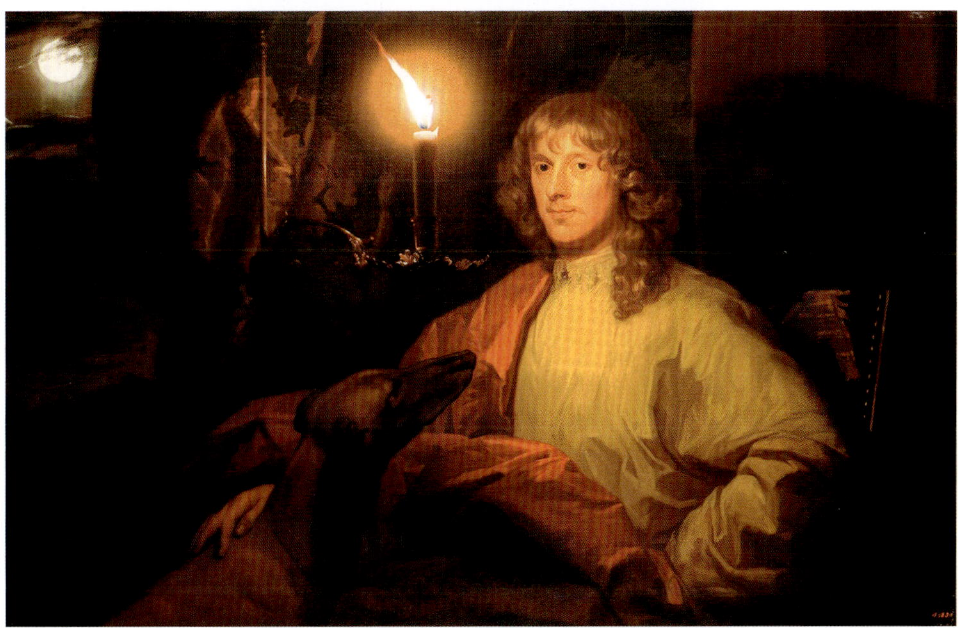

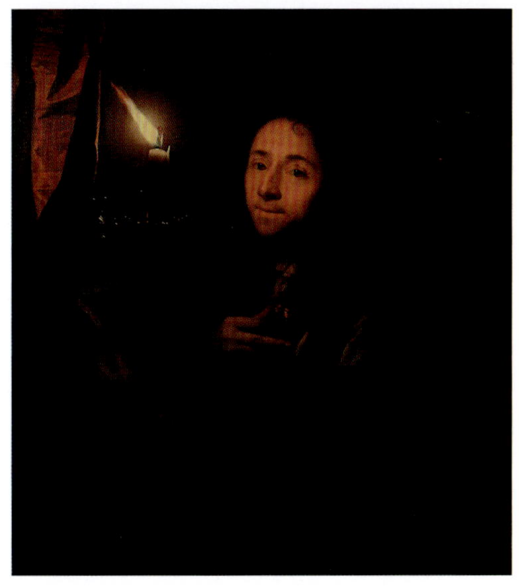

> *– having drawn a lady who was marked with the small-pox but had handsome hands, she asked him, when the face was finished, if she must not sit for her hands. – "No," replied Schalken* [sic], *"I always draw them from my house-maid."*[27]

Both Weyerman and Walpole present Schalcken as an antitype of the Van Dyckian painter, marked by gaucheness and indelicacy.[28] Yet his request to the king to hold the candle during the sitting recalls Van Dyck's reported conduct before the bishop of Ghent, illustrating how easily the boldness of the genius might shade into impudence. Likewise, Schalcken's use of a maidservant as a hand model was a practice attributed to Van Dyck by Roger de Piles. But Van Dyck's success required the effacement of such studio shortcuts within the flattering finished product, much as his wittiness and virtuosity justified the liberties attributed to him in studio anecdotes.

In his own paintings, Schalcken playfully looked to Van Dyck's legacy, particularly as he sought to attract English aristocratic patronage following his move to London in 1692. For example, he recast Van Dyck's portrait of James Stuart, Duke of Lennox and Richmond, as yet another candlelit scene [fig. 27].[29] Like Mary Beale, Schalcken copied Van Dyck to demonstrate his internalization of the most prestigious tradition within English aristocratic portraiture. At the same time, he mapped onto this prototype his own signature effects of illumination, giving his sitter an uncanny, even spectral quality, like a revenant from the Caroline past. When it came time for Schalcken to paint a self-portrait for the collection of Cosimo III of Tuscany, he naturally depicted himself in the old-fashioned slashed doublet and twisted pose of Van Dyck's own self-portrait with Endymion Porter [fig. 28].[30] But rather than placing the patron within the painting, as Van Dyck had done, Schalcken directs his gesture of deference outward, toward a princely recipient in another corner of Europe.

A Van Dyckian painter had to pull off boldness without crossing the line into Schalcken's impudence. High-wire acts of verbal acuity recur as a frequent attribute in early modern artists' biographies. In his life of Rubens, for example, de Piles recounts that "Queen Maria de' Medici took such pleasure in his conversation that throughout the time he worked on the two cycles of painting that he made in Paris … Her Majesty was constantly behind him, charmed equally by hearing him speak and watching him paint."[31] Antonio Palomino meanwhile compared the visits of Philip IV to Velázquez with those that Alexander the Great made to Apelles.[32] Velázquez, of course, depicted one such royal studio visit in *Las Meninas*, the greatest of all monuments to the intimacy between artists and royal sitters. As Palomino's comparison indicates, writers on princely studio visits were reworking another foundational anecdote from the *Natural History*. According to Pliny, in addition to artistic skill,

> [Apelles] *also possessed great courtesy of manners, which made him more agreeable to Alexander the Great, who frequently visited his studio … but in the studio Alexander used to talk a great deal about painting without any real knowledge of it, and Apelles*

would politely advise him to drop the subject, saying that the boys engaged in grinding the colours were laughing at him: so much power did his authority exercise over a King who was otherwise of an irascible temper.[33]

Pliny's tale was well known in Van Dyck's day and the subject of many works of art, among them a depiction by the Flemish painter Guillam van Haecht [fig. 29].[34] Van Haecht transposed Pliny's anecdote to a fictional Antwerp gallery, blurring the lines between the collection and the studio. In the painting, Alexander gestures over Apelles' shoulder as the artist paints Campaspe, so that the composition unites the two famous anecdotes about the relationship between artist and king. The point of Van Haecht's painting, and of the anecdote itself, is that within the studio the artist's knowledge gives *him* the ultimate authority.[35]

For a select audience of artists and connoisseurs, such tales provided satisfying evidence of the transcendence of social hierarchies that artistic mastery might allow. But for royalists determined to defend the sacred claims of absolutist monarchy following Charles I's execution, the king's Alexander-like patronage coexisted uneasily with the princely elevation of painters like Van Dyck. In his martyr's life of the king, Richard Perrinchief rewrote the Alexander and Apelles story to vest supreme expertise in the king's own person:

He was well skilled in things of Antiquity, could judge of Meddals whether they had the number of years they pretended unto; His Libraries and Cabinets were full of those things on which length of Time put the Value of Rarities. In painting He had so excellent a Fancy, that He would supply the defect of Art in the Workman, and suddenly draw those Lines, give those Airs and Lights, which Experience and practice had not taught the Painter … He delighted to talk with all kind of Artists.[36]

Making artistic skill into a princely attribute implicitly raised the status of other artists. But Perrinchief was swift to deny any equivalence between prince and painter by attributing to Charles an innate and sovereign skill that no "Experience and practice" could equal.[37]

Perrinchief noted Charles's enjoyment of artistic shop talk, and portrait sittings in general afforded a welcome opportunity for artists to demonstrate their expertise not only in painting but in polite conversation as well. As one character in Shirley's *The Lady of Pleasure* observes, "Sitting's but / A Melancholy exercise without / Some company to discourse."[38] On the level of practice, artistic treatises offered suggestions to painters about the importance of conversation for banishing the tedium of posing for one's portrait. For example, Nicholas Hilliard counselled that "*Discret* talke or reading, quiet merth or musike ofendeth not, but shortneth the time, and quickneth the sperit both in the drawer, and he which is

OVERLEAF

29 Guillam van Haecht, *Apelles Painting Campaspe*, ca. 1630, oil on panel, 104.9 × 148.7 cm, The Hague, Mauritshuis

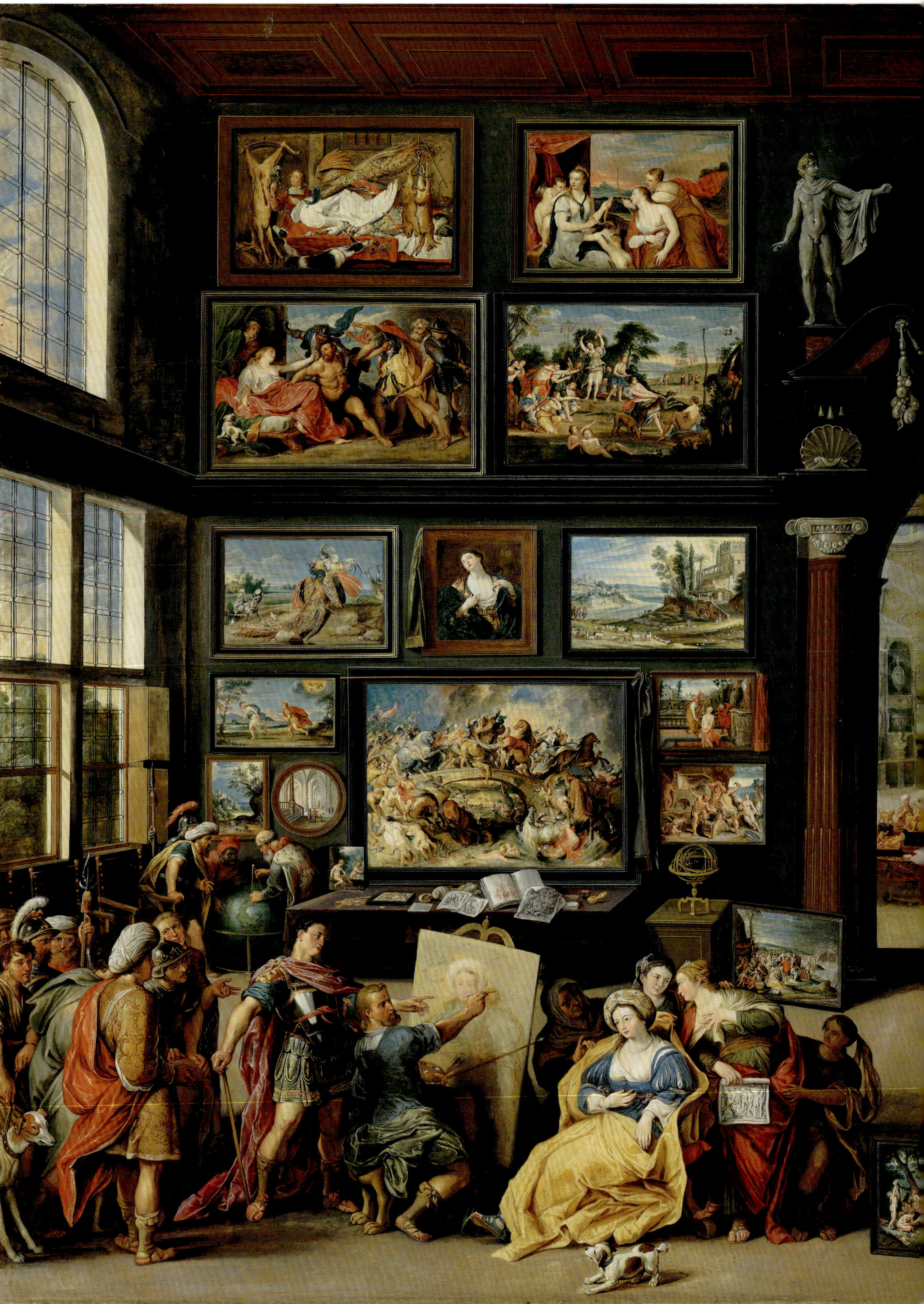

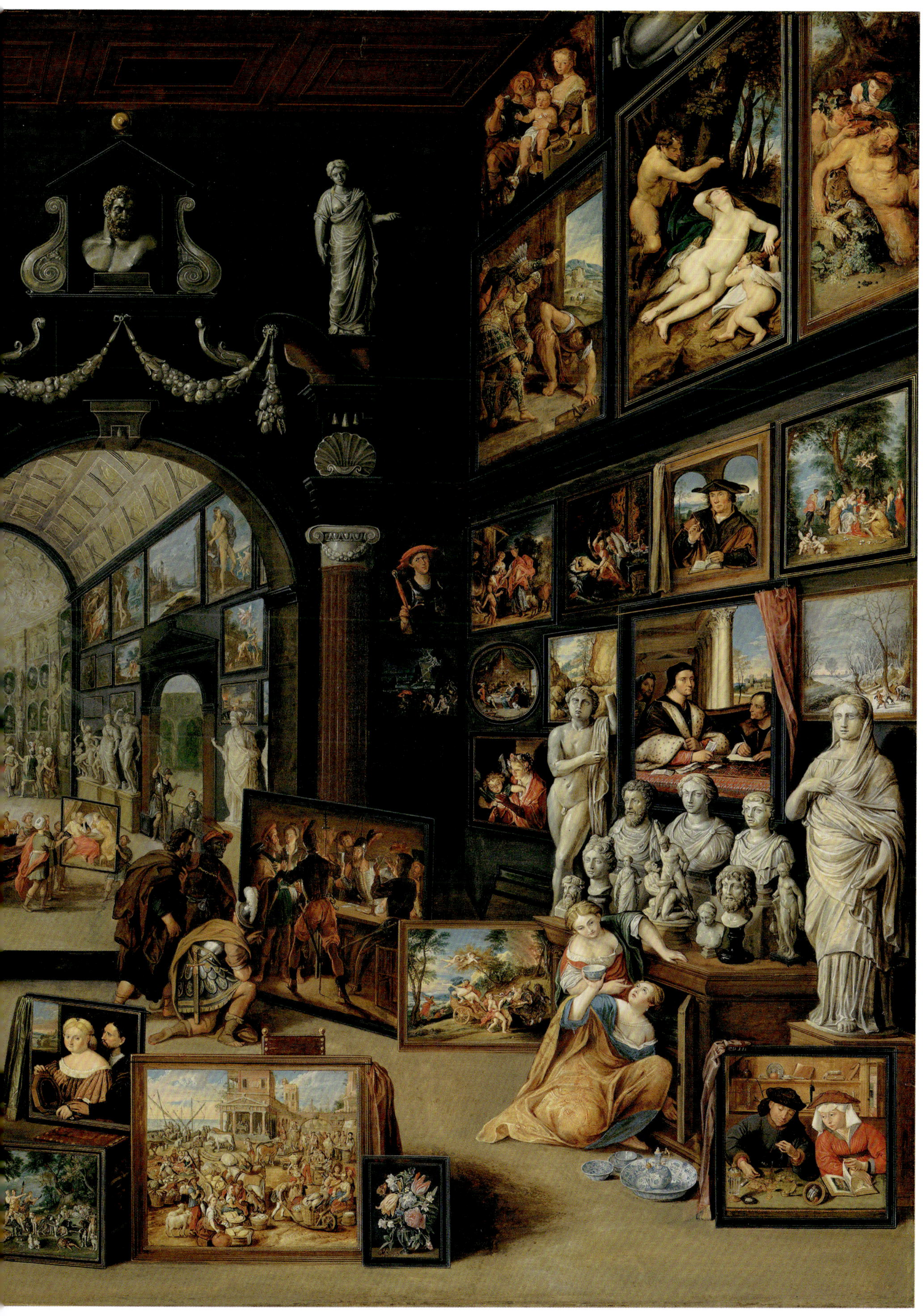

drawne."[39] For the painter Edward Norgate, with whom Van Dyck lodged upon his arrival in England, engaging a sitter in conversation was also a means of obtaining the most natural likeness; he advised that during the "sitting you shall doe well to bend your observations upon what conduces most to the Likenes ... and to this purpose the party sitting is by occasion of Discourse to be sometimes in motion, and to regard you with a freindly [*sic*] merry and Joviall aspect, where in you must bee ready and suddaine, to catch and steal your observations."[40] Conversation thus provides a cover for the portraitist's scrutiny of his subject, with observation occurring on the sly.

Portrait sittings naturally awakened curiosity on the part of sitters about the mechanics of taking a likeness, and courtiers as well as painters took advantage of this opportunity to entertain an immobilized prince. As John Evelyn noted with complacency in a diary entry from January 10, 1662: "Being call'd into his Majesties Closet, when Mr. Cooper (the rare limmer) was crayoning of his face & head ... I had the honour to hold the Candle whilst it was doing ... during which his Majestie was pleased to discourse with me about severall things relating to Painting & Graving &c."[41] During another of Charles II's sittings with Samuel Cooper shortly after the Restoration, Thomas Hobbes took advantage of the opportunity to reintroduce himself to the king, who "was diverted by Mr. Hobbes's pleasant discourse" and soon rewarded him with a pension.[42]

The aspects of the artistic process that a sitter actually witnessed in the studio would have contributed to his or her own curiosity. De Piles, drawing upon Everhard Jabach's account, noted the speed with which Van Dyck worked, and Bellori, relying upon Digby, described his method as *alla prima*. The surviving evidence of Van Dyck's unfinished paintings confirms that he usually painted sitters without the mediation of a detailed drawing of their faces. Instead, Van Dyck would roughly mark out a pose with anchoring lines in brown paint, proceeding to capture the sitters' face directly from life. This procedure often resulted in halo-like pentiments demarcating the border between the area of Van Dyck's own autograph contribution and that of his workshop assistants. For example, in the portrait of an unknown woman now in Louisville, the highly finished painting of the face contrasts with the areas of bare canvas encompassing the sitter like a shawl [fig. 30].[43] The conjuring up of such a countenance without the mediation of drawing must indeed have been a mesmerizing performance.[44]

Van Dyck's own conversation during the sitting probably more closely resembled Evelyn's technical discourse than the piquant repartee ascribed to the artist by early biographers. A variety of sources attest that many seventeenth-century English aristocrats and men of learning, far from disparaging the manual aspects of art-making, were fascinated by artisanal trade secrets.[45] In his commonplace book from the 1640s, Thomas Marshall recorded Van Dyck's own assertion that "Most art lovers are so little aware of what the work of art they see really consists of, that they find it difficult to point out a real master among hundreds."[46] Perhaps as a result, Van Dyck's recorded discussions of art with English patrons

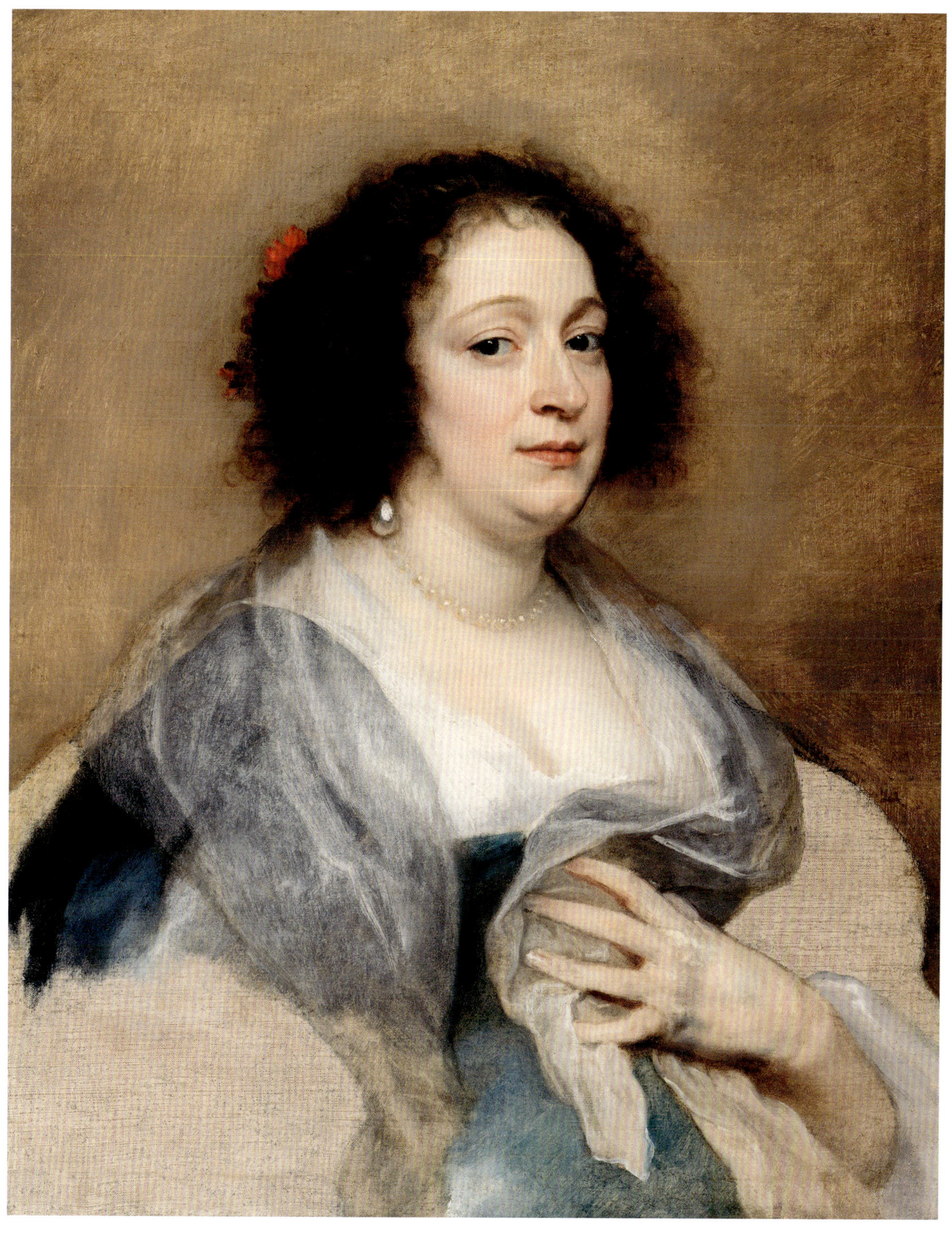

30 Anthony van Dyck, *Portrait of a Woman*, ca. 1640, oil on canvas, 75.9 × 59.1 cm, Louisville, Speed Museum of Art and friends seem to have been particularly focused on imparting knowledge of its technical aspects. George Vertue claimed that Van Dyck hosted weekly gatherings "for the Virtuosi of London" at his home; otherwise uncorroborated, this assertion can be placed alongside further evidence for Van Dyck's participation in learned exchanges about art prior to the rise of formal academies in England.[47]

In one manuscript, compiled over several decades, the French doctor Theodore Turquet de Mayerne made notes on the techniques and materials of painting.[48] De Mayerne, who served as physician to three English monarchs in turn, had access to such court painters as Daniel Mytens, Rubens, and Van Dyck himself. His notes give an insight into the kind of artistic conversation that was carried on in English aristocratic circles during the years Van Dyck spent in London. For example, a typical entry reads:

> *(Discourse of a Flemish painter at My Lord Newport's, 16 Sept. 1633)*
> *His ordinary varnish for pictures – is made with turpentine balsam very white, spirits of turpentine very clear, & Mastic. It is very liquid and very beautiful.*[49]

De Mayerne's *Discours d'un peintre flamand* recalls the trade secrets that Lely passed on to Mary Beale or the "many good discourses" on portraiture that Sofonisba Anguissola shared with Van Dyck when he drew her portrait as a young man in Palermo.[50] In his manuscript, de Mayerne reveals a number of insights gleaned from Van Dyck, whom he termed a "most excellent painter."[51] Van Dyck recounted to de Mayerne his experimental use of fish glue or isinglass as a primer and his preference for orpiment as "the most beautiful yellow one can imagine."[52] The two men discussed the "very excellent green" in the paintings of Orazio Gentileschi, then also resident in London, with Van Dyck speculating that the Italian artist used an herbal preparation to obtain this effect.[53] De Mayerne's notes have been mined by conservators seeking to reconstruct Van Dyck's technique, but in their blend of practical insight, flattery, and aesthetic appraisal, they also offer us the most important surviving record of Van Dyck's celebrated conversational art.[54]

— *Picturing the Sitting* —

By the time Lely told his anecdote about Van Dyck and Lanier to the Beales, portrait sittings had become a part of court spectacle under Charles II.[55] George Vertue, who transcribed Charles Beale's diaries, also recorded a story about the young Godfrey Kneller outshining Lely as the two worked simultaneously on portraits of the king before an audience of courtiers.[56] Such a tale, with its echo of ancient stories of artistic competition, gains plausibility in the light of a diary entry written by Samuel Pepys on July 15, 1664, where he notes seeing the famous beauty Frances Stewart "having her picture" painted at Whitehall, with "the King and twenty more I think, standing by all the while."[57]

The noted impiety of Restoration court portraits, for which royal mistresses posed not just as Venus but also as saints or even the Virgin Mary, reveals a sophisticated familiarity with the studio and a wry acknowledgment that the depiction of saints had always depended on the recruitment of profane models.[58] Even in less libertine circles, a man's accompaniment of a woman to her portrait sitting was an important marker of intimacy, as when Evelyn escorted Margaret Blagge to Matthew Dixon's studio for the painting he had commissioned of her.[59] Familiarity with artists' studios extended across the ranks of society. In 1664, a candidate for the position of lady's maid in Pepys's household sought to impress the diarist by bringing him to the studio of Jacob Huysmans, where he admired "as good pictures I think as ever I saw."[60] Travelers to London numbered artists' studios among the city's attractions. Prince Cosimo of Tuscany, for example, visited Samuel Cooper's home in 1669, much as he had previously sought out Rembrandt in Amsterdam.[61]

Letters dispatched from London in the summer of 1663 by the Dutch polymath Christiaan Huygens richly document the appeal of artists' studios to cultured and inquisitive tourists. On June 23, Huygens wrote to his brother Constantijn that he had "been to see the painter Lilly [Lely]" and asked him how he fabricated the pastels he used in portrait drawings, obtaining the artist's promise to supply the recipe.[62] On the 29th, Huygens noted that he had seen a selection of Nicholas Lanier's collection of drawings, but had not yet obtained Lely's recipe, because, when he revisited the studio, "there was a Lady sitting."[63] Finally, on July 13, Huygens was able to provide his brother with a minute description of Lely's pastels and papers, switching from French to Dutch to record the technical details, and appending as well an English-language list, perhaps in Lely's own hand, of all the requisite pigments.[64] Christiaan's brother Constantijn made his own notes on artistic lore; his diary entry for March 2, 1690, for example, records a visit to a certain "Mrs Remy" whose "husband [Remigius van Leemput] was a painter in the time of Van Dyck, about whom she had much to tell, including how he kept and maintained Mrs. Lemon for a long time in his house."[65] Technical insights and salacious gossip might both serve as studio souvenirs.

Just as the seventeenth century saw a surge in literary records of the portrait sitting and studio life, it also witnessed an exponential increase in the collection and preservation of preparatory works for portraits. Such drawings and oil sketches were particularly coveted by artists who sought inspiration for their own portraits. Van Dyck's sketch of Nicholas Lanier, for example, passed through the collections of no fewer than three painters: Prosper Henry Lankrink, Joseph van Aken, and Allan Ramsay (and Lankrink likely acquired it from Lely himself, whom he served as a landscape painter).[66] Meanwhile, the portrait of the Porter family that Mary Beale copied appears to have been a touchstone for English artists; two of Van Dyck's surviving preparatory drawings for the portrait bear the collection stamps of Lankrink and Jonathan Richardson Senior and Junior.[67] As Christiaan Huygens recorded, Lanier himself formed the first significant collection of drawings in England, a practice in which he was emulated by Lely.[68] In their circulation among artists and art writers, drawings and anecdotes reinforced

Van Dyck's standing and the fascination of his sittings in late seventeenth- and eighteenth-century England. Tracing such provenances reveals a historically self-conscious and self-referential tradition within early modern English painting.

Mary Beale seized upon the interest in preparatory works when she painted a self-portrait in which she displays an unfinished canvas depicting her two sons, while her palette hangs from a peg in the background [fig. 31].[69] Such an image figuratively invited viewers into Beale's "paynting roome" and put her working method on view.[70] On the Continent, genre scenes, meanwhile, took portrait sittings as a subject of art. In his print *The Noble Painter* of 1642, Abraham Bosse depicted an artist in a studio richly decorated with books, sculptures, and paintings [fig. 32]. He sits before an easel that bears the portrait of an aristocratic sitter, who stands alongside him to demonstrate the accuracy of the likeness. Placing a portrait at the heart of its depiction of artistic ennoblement, Bosse's engraving validates portraiture as the path to self-advancement.[71]

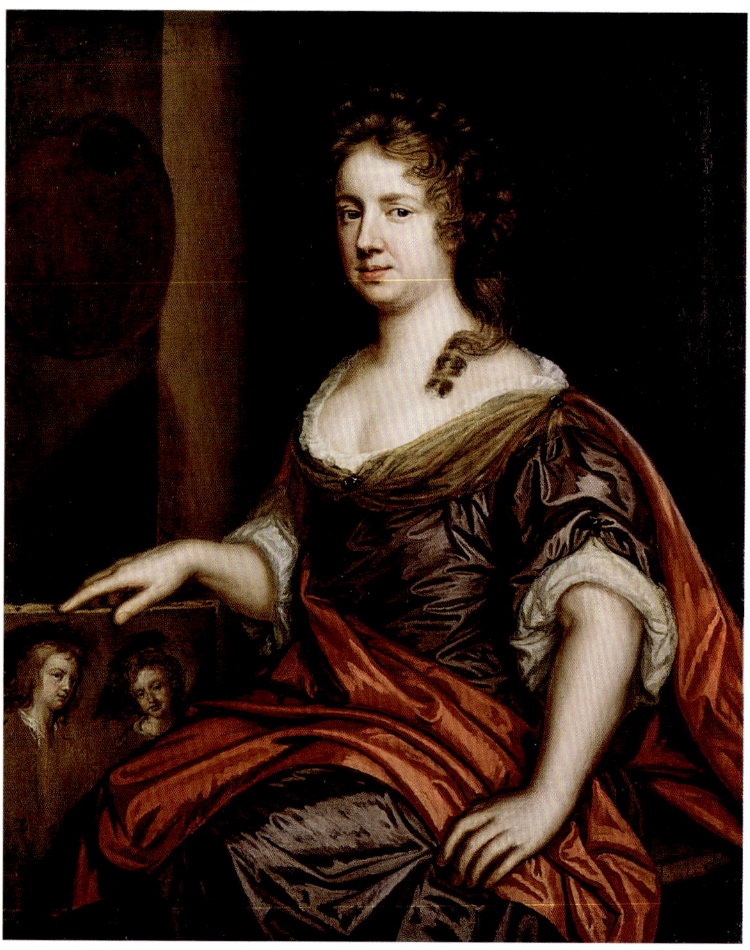

31 Mary Beale, *Self-Portrait*, 1665, oil on canvas, 109.2 × 87.6 cm, London, National Portrait Gallery

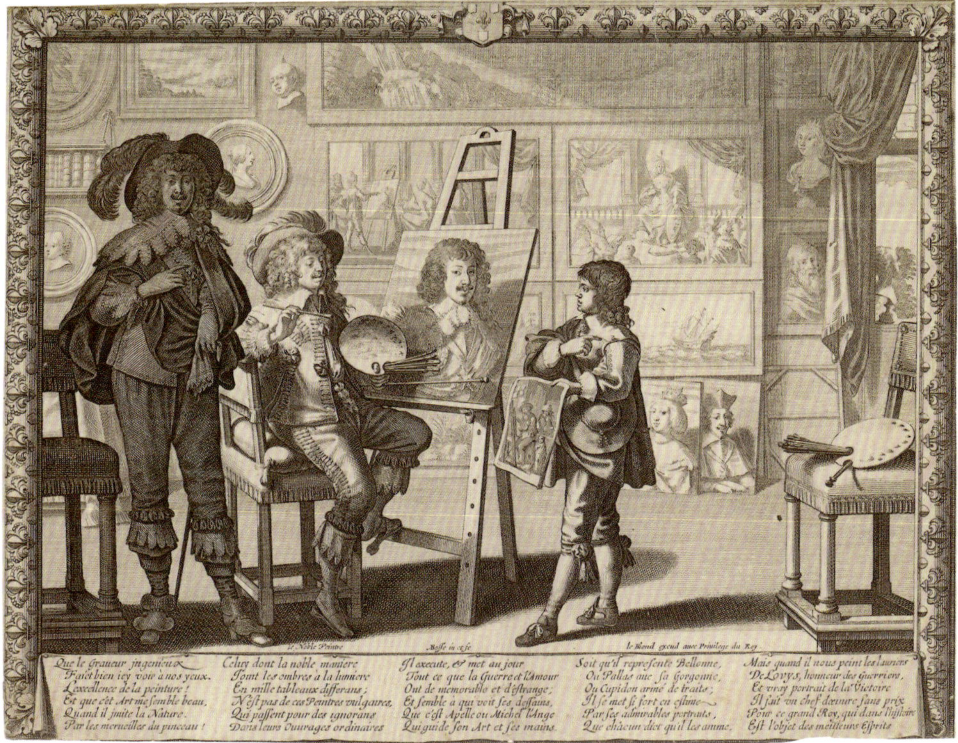

32 Abraham Bosse, *Le Noble Peintre*, 1642, etching, first state, 25.7 × 32.8 cm, New York, Metropolitan Museum of Art

Genre paintings depicting studio visits affirmed the status of the sophisticated connoisseurs whom their painters aimed to attract.[72] But they also explored the erotics of the portrait sitting, particularly when they depicted artists entertaining female sitters in the studio. One such painting, by Frans van Mieris the Elder, shows a seated artist engaging a female sitter in conversation [fig. 33].[73] Her back to us, we can still glimpse her face in the unfinished portrait that appears to meet our gaze. In the background, a maid enters bearing a drink on a tray. Like the woman in the portrait, she looks out at the viewer. Distinguished from both portraitist and sitter by her gaze and class, she triangulates and ironizes their interaction. The plaster cast of Cupid hanging from the ceiling likewise emphasizes the erotic tensions of the scene. A historiographic tradition, dating back to the eighteenth century, that identifies the sitter as Van Mieris's wife may represent an attempt to defuse the more transgressive scenario of an artist seducing his socially superior client.

Genre paintings depicting portrait sittings, as well as portraits that self-referentially stage their own making, proliferated in the decades after Van Dyck's death and may have fueled curiosity about his studio practice. Indeed, one of the most important seventeenth-century depictions of a portrait sitting was commissioned by Everhard Jabach, Van Dyck's patron and Roger de Piles's informant for the

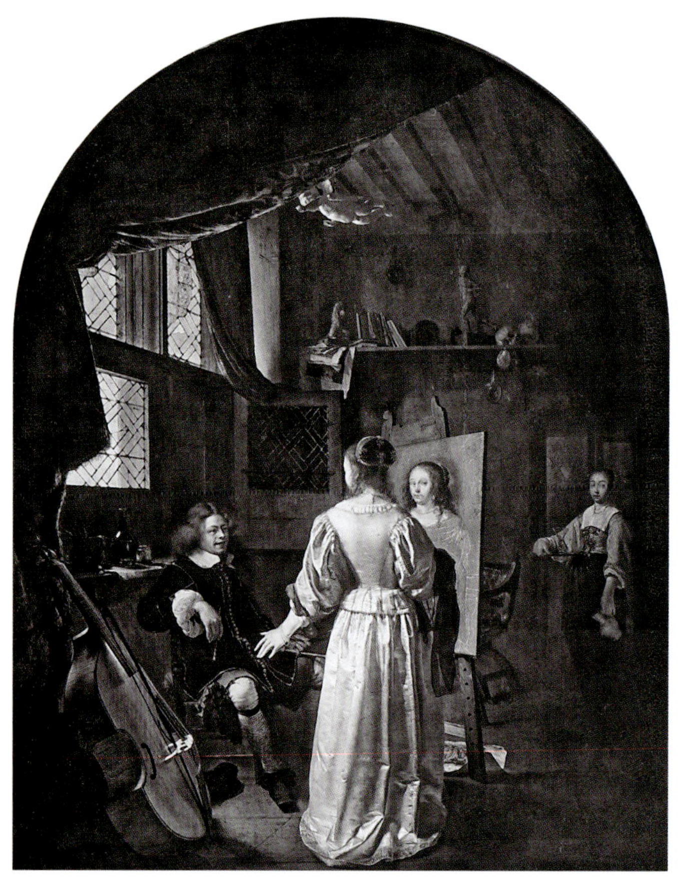

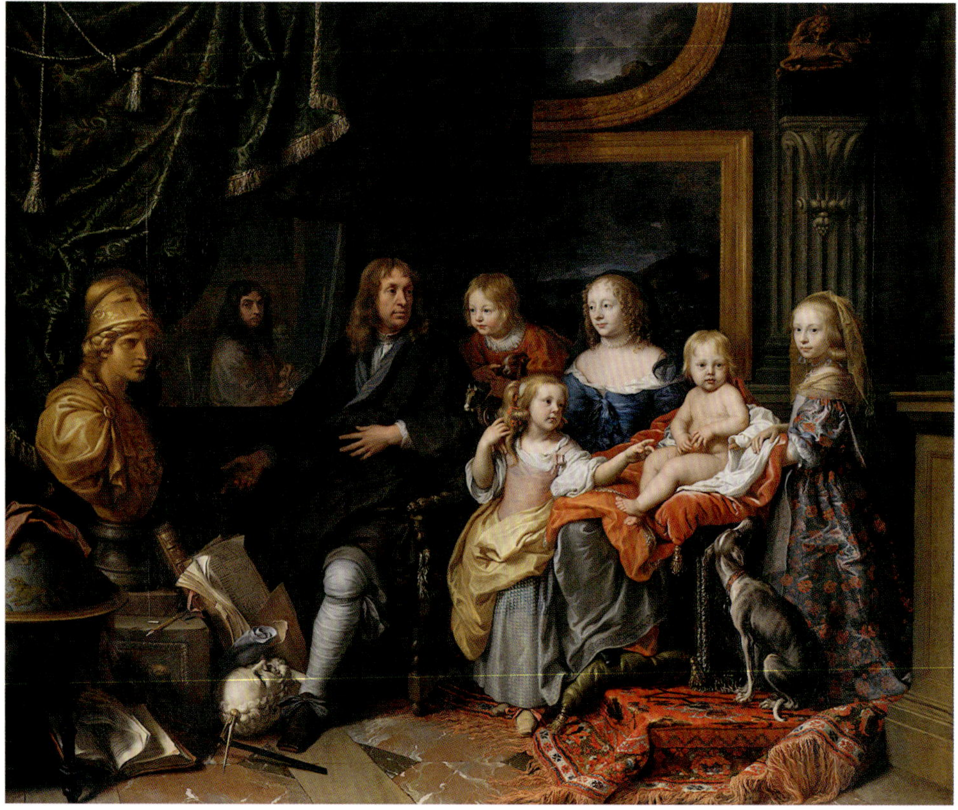

33 Frans van Mieris the Elder, *Studio Scene*, ca. 1656, oil on panel, 59.5 × 46 cm, formerly Dresden, Gemäldegalerie

34 Charles Le Brun, *The Jabach Family*, ca. 1660, oil on canvas, 280 × 328 cm, New York, Metropolitan Museum of Art artist's working method. The Cologne-born banker amassed an important art collection that was eventually expropriated by Louis XIV; he not only sat three times to Van Dyck, but also to Lely and many other painters.[74] Some twenty years after Van Dyck painted him, Jabach commissioned a massive family portrait from Charles Le Brun that was surely indebted to his experience of Van Dyck's London studio [fig. 34]. Two versions of this portrait, which was subsequently admired by Joshua Reynolds and Johann Wolfgang von Goethe, were executed in short succession.[75] Reynolds recognized the portrait's indebtedness to Van Dyck when he wrote, "The heads themselves are equal to the best of Vandick; but there is a heaviness over the picture, which Vandick never had, and this is its only defect."[76]

In Le Brun's painting, the Jabach family appears in an interior that recalls the richly furnished studio of Bosse's noble painter. But this space is more likely to be Jabach's own *studiolo*, filled with his paintings, books, sculptures, celestial globe, and mathematical instruments. One scholar has interpreted the painting as the depiction of the wife and children's exceptional visit to this space of masculine learning,[77] but they are not the only interlopers on the scene. In a mirror on the rear wall, we catch a glimpse of the artist himself, sitting at his easel as he dips his brush into a bit of white paint on his palette. Le Brun's pointed stare seems directed out of the canvas at us, the viewers of the painting, in a similar conceit to the reflection in Velázquez's *Las Meninas*. But in fact, Le Brun is looking at the Jabach family, and we are looking not only at their portrait, but also at their portrait sitting.

Van Dyck never took the step of depicting his own sittings, and for this reason he has not featured in discussions that celebrate the "self-awareness" of baroque painting.[78] Ironically, the romanticism that mythologizes such figures as Rembrandt while dismissing Van Dyck as a sycophant rests on a foundation of the latter's *mise-en-scène* of the portrait in the theater of the studio. No scholar has done more to illuminate the ways that seventeenth-century painting draws upon the life of the studio than Svetlana Alpers, particularly in her work on Rembrandt.[79] Yet Van Dyck figures only briefly in her account, and then merely as the embodiment of a "smooth" style of painting contrasted with Rembrandt's "rough" performances. Alpers declares: "It was the smooth style associated with Van Dyck, rather than the rough one, that was perceived as appropriate to the court ... Instead of appealing to a knowing and imaginative courtier, the rough style was seen as passé and, in the case of Rembrandt at least, as being tainted with the marks of the studio."[80] Such a binary may have operated for art theorists, but it scarcely accounts for the performative qualities of Van Dyck's actual practice (or the frequent occurrence of visible brushwork in his portraits). And the "knowing and imaginative courtier" whom Alpers imagines rejecting the "marks of the studio" is precisely the sort of person, like Sir Kenelm Digby or Everhard Jabach, who would have sought out Van Dyck's house at Blackfriars to watch him paint and then, decades later, given a detailed account of his experience to Bellori or de Piles. However much he may have departed from his precedent visually, Rembrandt was looking squarely to Van Dyck and London when he made his studio into the realm of a princely painter.[81]

The ease with which Van Dyck has been dismissed from most accounts of serious baroque painting stems in part from his willingness to serve a large, rich, and frequently unsophisticated clientele. If de Mayerne's notes represent one type of vernacular artistic discourse in seventeenth-century England, grounded in curiosity and learned exchange, then the testimony of another of Van Dyck's sitters gives insight into a very different response to his art. In the autumn of 1639, Eleanor, Countess of Sussex, exchanged a series of letters with her friends Sir Edmund Verney and his son Ralph. Sir Edmund had commissioned the countess's portrait by Van Dyck, an expense she considered "money ill bestowde."[82] Nevertheless, in her letters, the countess provided specific instructions for her portrayal by the artist: "Put Sr Vandyke in remembrance to do my picture wel. I have sene sables with the clasp of them set with dimons [diamonds] – if thos that I am picturdc in wher don so I think it would look very wel in the pictuer. If Sr Vandyke thinke it would do well I pray desire him to do all the clawes so." As the countess understood, one responsibility of the portraitist was the reproduction of contemporary fashion, de Lairesse's hallmark of modern painting. This extended to fictionalizing the actual clothing in which his sitter appeared.

The countess did not limit her directives to sables and diamonds. In another letter, she wrote, "I am glade you have prefalede [prevailed] with Sr Vandike to make my picture lener, for truly it was to[o] fat ... I see you will make him trimme it for my advantage every way." In the end, however, the portrait failed to please. When the countess learned that the Verneys had employed a copyist to duplicate the portrait, she wrote, "I wish [it] coulde be mended in the fase, for itt is very ugly ... it cannot bee worse then itt is." The countess's ultimate attitude to the portrait was one of querulous, self-deprecating resignation, declaring that the "ill favourede" portrait "makes me quite out of love with myselfe," although she conceded that "truly I thinke itt is lyke the originale."

The late nineteenth-century editor of the Verney letters saw in them "good proof that Vandyke did not flatter his sitters, as he has been often accused of doing."[83] In more recent years, one partisan of the artist has cited the countess's portrait in his retort to a critic's comparison of Van Dyck to Andy Warhol.[84] Indeed, the Countess of Sussex represents one nightmare scenario for those who would celebrate portraitists as truthtellers and penetrating judges of character. That an artist as gifted as Van Dyck should busy himself with the embellishment of sables or the thinness of a countess's face would seem to confirm every fear that artists and academicians had about the lucrative occupation of portraiture. The notion that Van Dyck instead displeased the countess with an honest portrayal has allowed his admirers to claim for him something of the probity so frequently projected onto Rembrandt. Indeed, the equation of ugliness with a form of ethical practice recently led one critic to make the dizzying claim that Rembrandt expressed his antipathy to the slave trade by intentionally depicting two patrons as "rich non-entities."[85]

Compared with this romanticism, the Countess of Sussex's approach to portraiture is instructively level-headed. She understood her portrait as a marker of her friendship with the Verneys. She wanted to look her best in it. Such a desire on the part of a patron, so often excoriated in art history, particularly when it comes to female sitters, has been a given for most of European portraiture. That Van Dyck failed to please his sitter in this particular instance tells us more about Lady Sussex's sense of humor as expressed in letters to friends than it does about his artistic practice or intentions. Certainly, both Van Dyck and Rembrandt were portraitists who achieved success by assimilating their sitters to a signature style. Within each artist's body of work, any one portrait is more likely to resemble another portrait of the same date than it is to reveal profound truths about an individual sitter.

Two defining features of Van Dyck's mature portrait practice – seriality and (at least the perception of) flattery – have excluded him from the modern canons of artistic genius and independence that embrace such figures as Rembrandt. Ironically, his contemporaries and near contemporaries perceived him to be a man who asserted his authority to the point of arrogance, denying Nicholas Lanier a glimpse of his own portrait, ordering the bishop of Ghent to fetch his brushes and paints, or making Lady Sussex appear fatter than she liked. Oscillating between impudence and sycophancy, the Van Dyck of historiography is almost always measured in terms of his relationships to social superiors or as the foil to other, better painters. He is the antitype of artistic independence.

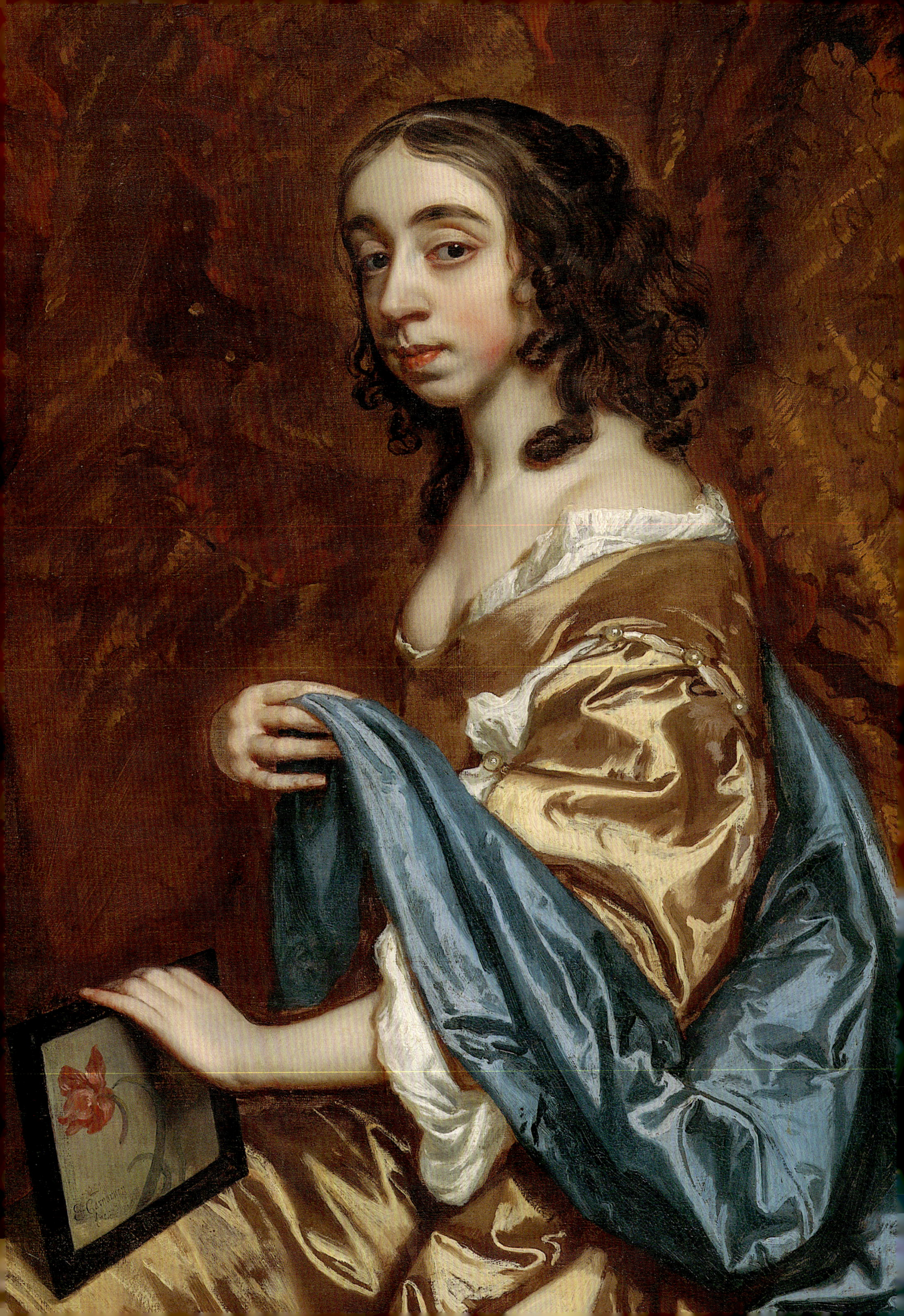

[CHAPTER THREE]

Artists and Gentlewomen

IN THE "ESSAY TOWARDS AN ENGLISH SCHOOL OF PAINTERS" THAT HE appended to a translation of Roger de Piles's *The Art of Painting* in 1706, Bainbrigg Buckeridge indicated the degree to which Van Dyck had come to figure as the standard of excellence for English painters in the decades following his death.[1] For example, Buckeridge reports that the miniaturist Samuel Cooper "was commonly stil'd the *Van-Dyck* in *little*, equalling that Master in his beautiful Colouring, and agreeable Airs of a Face."[2] Having described Cooper's pan-European fame and major works, Buckeridge declares, "That which brought Mr. *Cooper* to this Excellency, was his Living in the time of *Van-Dyck*, many of whose Pictures he copy'd, and which made him imitate his *Stile*."[3] But as Buckeridge makes clear, copying Van Dyck extended beyond emulating the master's style to reproducing his social success as well.[4] Cooper, for example, combined "his Abilities in Painting" with "his great Skill in Music, especially the *Lute*, wherein he was reckon'd a Master. He was many Years abroad and Personally acquainted with most of the great Men in *Holland* and *France*, as well as those of his own Country."[5]

This model of "Excellency," combining Van Dyck's manner and his social graces, is familiar from any number of English artists' lives of the seventeenth and eighteenth centuries. What has gone largely unnoticed, however, is the opportunity that Van Dyck's example offered to women painters. By emphasizing gentility, social performance, and high patronage, the Van Dyckian model represented an alternative to one focused on rivaling classical antiquity or commanding stupendous prices. For example, Buckeridge describes Mary Beale as "an *English* Gentlewoman" who

> *had great numbers of Persons of good Rank* [that] *sat to her, especially the greatest part of the dignify'd Clergy of her time, an Acquaintance she got by her Husband, who was much in favour with that Robe. She was little inferiour to any of her Contemporaries, either for Colouring, Strength, Force of Life, insomuch that Sir* Peter [Lely] *was greatly taken with her Performances, as he would often acknowledge. She work'd with a wonderful Body of Colours, was exceedingly Industrious and her Pictures are much after the* Italian *Manner, which she learnt by having copy'd several of the great Masters of that Country, whose Pictures she borrow'd out of Sir* Peter's *Collection.*[6]

Detail of Peter Lely, *Mary Capel and Her Sister Elizabeth*, ca. 1657 [see fig. 43]

Although Buckeridge does not praise Beale as effusively as Samuel Cooper, he describes her success, like the miniaturist's, as socially embedded and rooted in conscious imitation. In fact, Buckeridge applies nearly identical aesthetic criteria to both artists. Cooper's art is notable for Van Dyckian "beautiful Colouring ... Strength ... soft and tender Liveliness," Beale's for "Colouring, Strength, [and] Force of Life," qualities that even the eminent Sir Peter repeatedly acknowledged. According to Buckeridge, both Cooper and Beale distinguished themselves through their self-positioning vis-à-vis an artistic mentor at the same time as they cultivated acquaintances in the upper ranks of society.

In the second half of the seventeenth century, a number of women artists achieved renown by operating in this Van Dyckian mode. Some of these women announced their debt to Van Dyck through copying his works or including pictorial citations within their original compositions. For others, emulation consisted more in their self-presentation as genteel practitioners making gifts of their "performances" to a courtly audience. This chapter explores literary and visual (self-) depictions of these women painters to chart a feminine line of descent for Van Dyck within English art. At the same time, it offers new readings of major ekphrastic texts from English literature of the seventeenth century to reveal a widespread cultural investment in the figure of the woman artist.

— *Pittora de natura* —

Van Dyck's reputation as a painter whose gentility informed both his life and his art was a critical factor in his ability to serve as a model for women artists. Gentility, sociability, and participation in a gift economy offered women artists a form of cover for ambitions that might otherwise have compromised their reputations.[7] But these qualities had also been essential to male artists like Rubens or Van Dyck who sought to escape the status of tradesmen. In the case of these artists, personal refinement and friendship mitigated highly commercial enterprises. For women artists, however, similar professional strategies have sometimes misled later commentators into underestimating the ambition of their practice. But rather than operating on the margins of the contemporary art world, women artists in the seventeenth century were figures of fascination, even if that fascination sometimes reduced them to the status of allegorical signifiers.

In his discussion of the modern manner, cited above, Gérard de Lairesse praised Van Dyck alongside the genre painter Frans van Mieris.[8] The latter was a painter of elegant modern subjects and fashions, attentive to the textures and rites of luxurious living. But de Lairesse singled out what he considered an anomalous work in Van Mieris's oeuvre, an allegorical portrait "representing the art of painting ... its hair, head-attire, dress, and furniture so very beautiful and truly *antique*, that I never saw the like done by any other *modern* master" [fig. 35].[9] This small exquisite work on copper depicts the art of painting as embodied by the artist's wife, presented in the role of a woman painter.[10] Bearing the allegorical attributes prescribed by Cesare Ripa, she has the recognizable presence of a real woman, and adopts the self-caressing gesture, with fingers lifted to her golden chain, that is a staple of the Van Dyckian repertoire. Describing this painting as the one work that allowed Van Mieris to transcend the limitations of the modern manner, de Lairesse reveals something of the symbolic weight that male artists and art writers placed on the figure of the woman artist as an allegory of art itself. And, as Van Dyck's example shows, male artists might become feminized in art literature when they worked in genres traditionally associated with female practitioners.

Matrilineal genealogies are a striking feature of Van Dyck's earliest historiography. Bellori claimed that Van Dyck inherited his artistic talent from his mother, a gifted embroiderer, implying that a parallel existed between her son's production and women's artistry.[11] The contemporary Flemish writer Cornelis de Bie gives even more detail, describing "a wondrously beautiful chimney cloth" that Van Dyck's mother embroidered with the story of Susanna and the Elders, the subject of one of Van Dyck's greatest early history paintings.[12] In fact, Van Dyck's grandmothers, both successful businesswomen, were important early influences on him; each had art collections, and one, Cornelia Pruystinck, had an import business for fashionable accessories. His other grandmother, Lynken Cuypers, specified in her will that her grandchildren should choose among her "nine best paintings" when they came of age.[13] This bequest was the foundation of Van Dyck's celebrated art collection.

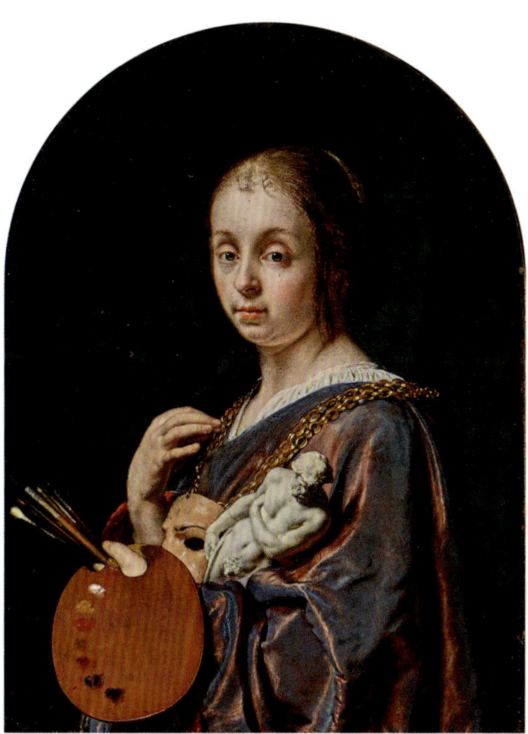

35 Frans van Mieris the Elder, *Pictura*, 1661, oil on copper, 12.7 × 8.9 cm, Los Angeles, J. Paul Getty Museum

Beyond these family connections, Van Dyck affiliated himself with a female predecessor when he sought an alternative professional model to Rubens. The longest prose passage in Van Dyck's *Italian Sketchbook*, indeed the longest to survive from his hand, describes his encounter in Palermo on July 12, 1624 with the nonagenarian painter Sofonisba Anguissola:

> *At ninety-six she still has all her memory and a most ready mind ... While I was making her portrait she alerted me to various things: not to put the light too high, so that the shadows wouldn't become too deep in the lines of old age, and much other good talk, as well as recounting a part of her life, through which it was clear that she was a born painter and a miraculous one and that the greatest pain she had is that she can no longer paint, having lost her sight; her hand was still steady without the slightest tremor.*[14]

Van Dyck's handwritten description of this portrait sitting frames a quick sketch of Anguissola, bracing herself against the arms of a chair as she leans forward, as though toward an interlocutor [fig. 36]. Van Dyck also painted a finished portrait of the artist on canvas, now in the Sackville collection at Knole. The abraded condition of the latter impedes an appreciation of its original quality, and it is unclear from Van Dyck's text whether this is the *ritratto* he prepared in Anguissola's presence, or whether the portrait he refers to was simply the rough drawing from the sketchbook, worked up into a finished painting at a later date.[15] The meeting between the two painters has long been known as an art historical curiosity, but little attention has been paid to the fact that this passage is Van Dyck's most extensive surviving statement on the work and career of another artist, as well as his only first-person description of a portrait sitting. Besides her advice on lighting, Van Dyck unfortunately did not record the *molti altri buoni discorsi* that Anguissola shared with him. Still, it is clear that the painter's technical knowledge and the story of her life so impressed Van Dyck that he declared her a *pittora de natura*, a born painter like himself.

Anguissola, the daughter of minor Cremonese aristocrats, had a career shaped by the constraints, as well as opportunities, of both her gender and her social station.[16] Indeed, the rise of the "gentleman artist" may be as much of a meaningful context for Anguissola's career as that of the *virtuosa*.[17] After a childhood in which her father actively promoted his daughter's accomplishments through gift-giving, correspondence, and visits to local courts, Anguissola obtained a position as lady-in-waiting to Isabel of Valois, the young bride of Philip II. Anguissola's beauty, comportment, and technical knowledge (conveyed in drawing lessons to the queen) contributed as much to her court career as did her finished portraits.[18] The financial arrangements made for the artist reflected the variety of her services: she received a salary and pension in her capacity as a lady-in-waiting, but was never paid for any individual works of art, which were always proffered as "gifts" to her patrons.[19] In return, Anguissola obtained sumptuous gifts of clothing; her early biographer Pietro Paolo de Ribera recounts that the queen "once gave her a dress richly adorned with gold of great value, and once a necklace of jewels and pearl

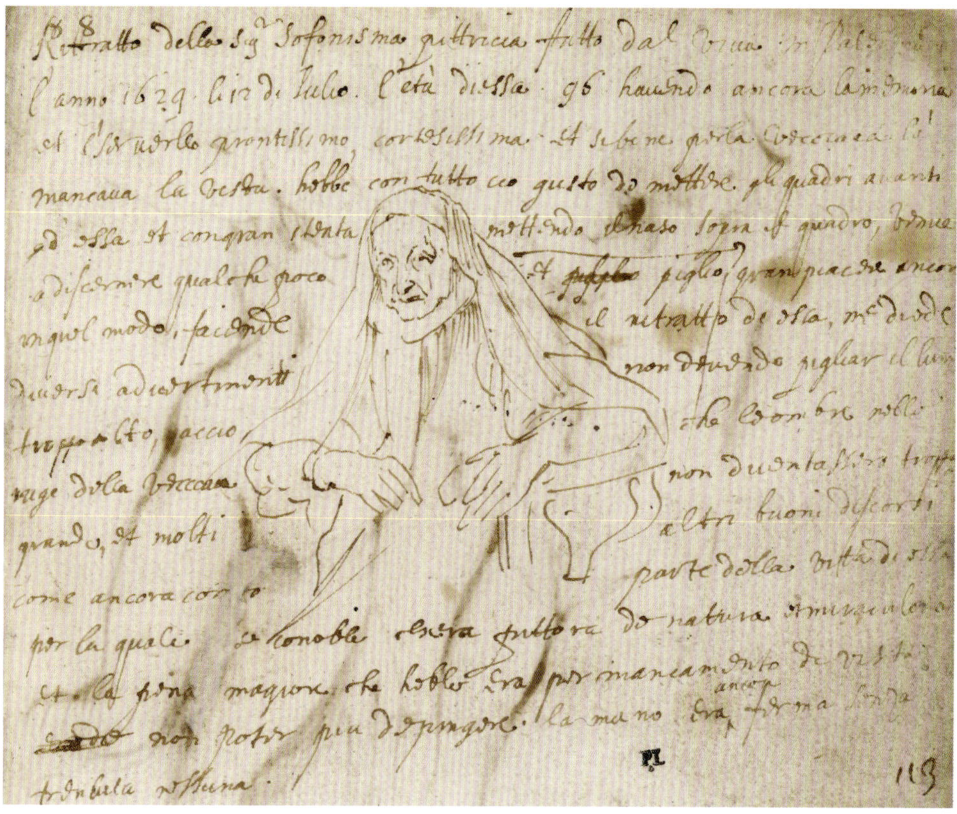

36 Anthony van Dyck, *The Italian Sketchbook*, fol. 110, 1624, pen and ink, 19.9 × 15.8 cm, London, British Museum

pendants, and other royal objects such that she found herself richly dressed and adorned," and these gifts soon made their way into her self-portraits.[20] When Van Dyck later portrayed himself with the gold chain bestowed upon him by a royal patron, he had Anguissola's example to draw upon. Her career, centered on portraiture, royal favor, and participation in a gift economy, contained critical seeds of the Van Dyckian paradigm.

The link between Van Dyck and the cultural archetype of the artistic gentlewoman becomes clear if we return to Bainbrigg Buckeridge's sketch of the English school. Here we find a further striking instance of a Van Dyckian woman artist in his brief life of Joan Carlile, introduced as "an *English* Gentlewoman, Contemporary with *Van-Dyck*." According to Buckeridge, Carlile "copy'd the *Italian* Masters so admirably well, that she was much in favour with King *Charles* I. who became her Patron, and presented her and Sir *Anthony Van-Dyck* with as much *Ultra-marine* at one time, as cost him above 500 *l*."[21] Much has been made of Carlile's status as England's first documented "professional woman painter," based on her short-lived attempt to establish a studio in Covent Garden in the 1650s.[22] But such a move appears only to have been necessary after Carlile was forced by the Civil War out of the economy of royal patronage described by Buckeridge. Rather than positioning Carlile as the founding mother of a recognizably modern lineage of "professional artists," we should place her in the context of other women, such as Susanna Horenbout or Esther Inglis, who since the early Tudor period had made gifts of their artistic productions to curry royal favor.[23]

Buckeridge's brief life of Carlile makes clear that he viewed the artist's attainment of Charles I's patronage as her signature achievement. The gift of precious ultramarine to *both* Carlile and Van Dyck lends them a striking equivalence in the eyes of the monarch. It also recalls the gifts of pigment that the Beales made to Lely so that Mary Beale might watch him paint. Like Beale, Carlile participated in exchanges of technical insights among artists and virtuosi: for example, passing along notes on painting she had obtained from Nicholas Lanier to the court doctor Turquet de Mayerne.[24] Carlile's will directed that her pictures should be sold to pay her debts, but added a codicil specifying bequests of individual paintings to her daughter, to "her deare freind Mrs. Herman," and to the "worthy Mrs. Colt."[25] She understood her work to have value within both an art market and a gift economy.

Carlile's surviving paintings are group portraits and individual images of women in a strikingly Van Dyckian mode. Using a pattern, she made repeated variations of the same composition, depicting a woman in white satin striding across a woodland landscape [fig. 37]. In both their general composition and specific motifs, like the splayed fingers gathering stiff folds of cloth, these paintings reveal Carlile's close study of Van Dyck. Carlile's individual portraits, with only slight adjustments from sitter to sitter, are in essence identical "performances" repeated for different patrons. They adopt a defining trait of Van Dyck's later English practice, the repetition of stock poses, at the same time that they position Carlile as Van Dyck's follower, a self-affiliation that was still clear to Buckeridge several decades after Carlile's death.

Meanwhile, Carlile's two surviving group portraits speak to her patronage relationships. For example, the hunting party now at Lamport Hall commemorates her husband's keepership of the royal deer park at Richmond and the Carliles' friendship with Sir Justinian Isham [fig. 38]. If, as most scholars agree, the woman on the far left is Carlile's self-portrait, then this image resembles Van Dyck's friendship portrait with Sir Endymion Porter in effacing any signs of the artist's craft at the same time that it places her on a level of near parity with her patron. Like other women artists discussed in this chapter, Joan Carlile espoused explicitly Royalist politics, even amidst the dangers of the Interregnum. Carlile's husband Lodowick also used his talents to cultivate royal favor, serving as a groom of the privy chamber while writing plays with such titles as *The Deserving Favourite*.[26] Indeed, it was Lodowick's play *Arviragus and Philicia* that Prince Charles Louis of the Palatine described as "hugely liked of everyone" in his letter about Charles I sitting to Van Dyck at his house in Blackfriars.[27]

Lodowick Carlile's preface to the *The Deserving Favourite*, first published in 1629, adopts a stylized reluctance about the marketplace that is typical for courtly

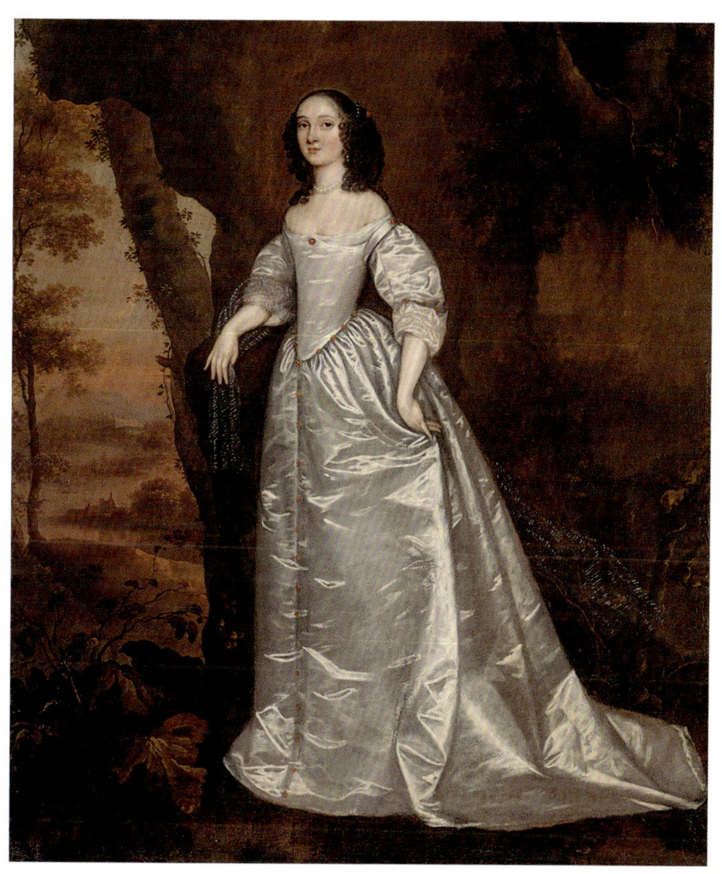

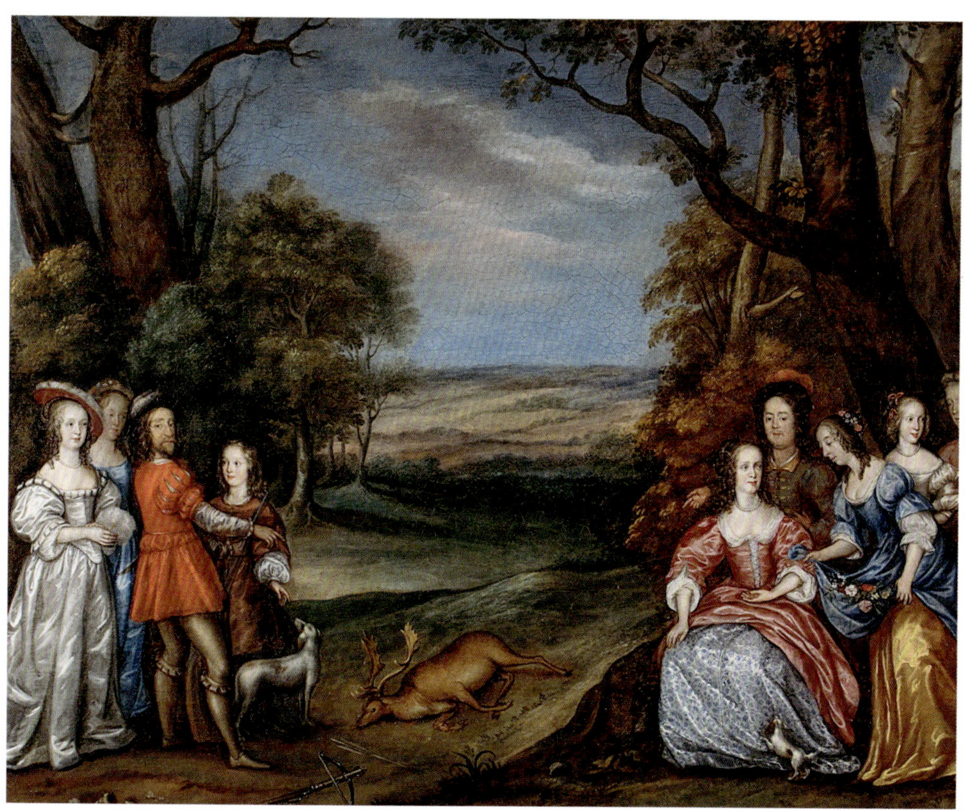

37 Joan Carlile, *Portrait of a Woman*, oil on canvas, 110.7 × 90 cm, ca. 1650, London, Tate

38 Joan Carlile, *The Stag Hunt*, ca. 1650, oil on canvas, 61 × 74 cm, Lamport Hall (Northamptonshire)

performers. Dedicating the work to two gentlemen of the bedchamber, Thomas Carey and William Murray (whose wife and daughters appear in Joan Carlile's portraits), the author asserts that "this Play, which ... at first was not design'd to travel so farre as the common Stage, is now prest for a greater journey, almost without my knowledge."[28] The "Printers Epigrammaticall Epistle" that follows the preface reinforces Carlile's modest pose, declaring, "Unknowne to th'Author this faire Courtly Piece / Was drawne to th'*Presse*." According to his printer, Carlile "Stoopes not for drosse; his *profit* was his *pleasure*."[29] However artificial, these claims that Lodowick Carlile worked for his own pleasure – that he was, in other words, an amateur – provide an important context for courtly artists, and especially women artists whose work many art historians have marginalized as "amateur" in a negative sense. As the dedication indicates, even when courtly performers did venture into the marketplace (or print), they were careful to cloak their actions in a rhetoric of reluctance or even coercion.

In asserting that they performed for pleasure, the courtiers who made gifts of their plays and paintings aspired to resemble the princes they served. In the seventeenth century, members of royal houses increasingly expressed their superiority through feats of artistic accomplishment – dancing in masques, turning ivory on lathes, or even painting portraits.[30] Indeed, royal panegyrists claimed that monarchs effortlessly surpassed professionals, as in Perrinchief's tribute to Charles I quoted in the previous chapter. While early commentators viewed Van Dyck as adopting the airs of a potentate – in Buckeridge's words, "few Princes were more visited, or better serv'd"[31] – princely practitioners of the seventeenth century increasingly posed as artists. When these royal painters were women, they further complicated the relationship between art, gender, and gentility.

— *"Princess Löysa Drawing": Exile and Ekphrasis in the 1640s* —

Shortly after Van Dyck's death in 1641, the economy of favor inhabited by courtiers like the Carliles collapsed, with the court's retreat to Oxford followed by the Civil War, the king's beheading, and years of Royalist exile. In this situation of crisis, Royalist artists and writers were forced to refashion the encomia they dedicated to a dynasty in exile.[32] While the Carliles maintained a low profile at Richmond, many Royalists traveled abroad, and their encounters with Continental modes of writing and picturing had a profound impact on the development of English art following the Restoration. In the literature of exiled Royalism, close readings of royal portraiture become statements of allegiance and meditations on the nature of monarchy. Replacing the ambivalence of the texts discussed in the previous chapters with a more reverential tone, these texts represent an important shift in English writing about portraiture.

One Royalist exile, the poet and soldier Richard Lovelace, found himself in The Hague sometime in the mid-1640s. Having spent time in prison for his defiance of Parliament, Lovelace traveled abroad, perhaps to throw in his lot with foreign armies or to recruit other soldiers to the cause of Charles I. The exact date and purpose of his visit to the Netherlands remain unknown, the primary evidence being one of Lovelace's own poems, first published in 1649 under the title "Princess Löysa Drawing."[33] Like the poems discussed in the previous chapters that make a conceit of the portrait sitting, "Princess Löysa Drawing" concerns the poet's observation of an artist at work. Beginning with the words "I saw," Lovelace introduces a sequence of mythological scenes, eventually revealed to be the subjects of paintings by Princess Louise Hollandine of the Palatinate, a painter whom Lovelace praises as "a little Diety [*sic*], / Minerva in Epitomy."

The daughter of the so-called Winter King and Queen of Bohemia, Frederick v of the Palatinate and Elizabeth Stuart, Louise Hollandine was born in 1622. Her second name reflected her parents' gratitude for the sanctuary they found in the Netherlands after Catholic forces had driven them from Prague. Like all of her siblings, Louise Hollandine received an extensive education, including instruction in painting from her mother's favorite portraitist, Gerard van Honthorst. Even after she horrified her relations by converting to Catholicism and eventually becoming abbess of a French monastery, Louise Hollandine remained a dedicated painter.[34]

Lovelace's poem makes Venus the surrogate for his own beholding of the princess's works, telling us that the goddess initially mistook Louise Hollandine for her son Cupid (an intriguing moment of gender confusion that establishes the princess as an androgynous creator). Venus realizes her mistake when she recognizes the artist's skill in reversing the havoc that Cupid has wrought, reuniting the lovers he famously tore asunder:

But viewing then whereas she made
Not a distrest, but lively shade
Of Eccho, whom he had betrayd,
Now wanton, and ith' coole oth' Sunne
With her delight a hunting gone;
And thousands more, whom he had slaine,
To live, and love, belov'd againe ...

Amazed at Louise Hollandine's handiwork, Venus exclaims, "Ah this is true Divinity!" Lovelace then embarks on the central ekphrastic litany of the poem, unfolding a sequence of anti-Ovidian scenes. Before Venus's eyes, the painter provides revisionist happy endings for Syrinx, Ariadne, Daphne, and other tragic figures of classical myth.

The poem's final tableau rewrites Venus's own tragic love story, courtesy of the princess's reconciliatory art. Unlike the many works where Adonis resists Venus's entreaties, Lovelace tells us that in Louise Hollandine's painting,

... *Adonis* [kneeled] *fresh as spring,*
Gaye as his youth, now offering
Her selfe those joyes with voice and hand,

Which first he could not understand.
Transfixed Venus stood amas'd,
Full of the Boye and Love, she gaz'd;
And in imbraces seemed more
Sencelesse and cold, then he before.

Awakening from her amorous stupefaction, Venus returns her attention to Cupid, all of whose malicious work she has just seen undone:

Uselesse Childe! In vaine (said she)
You beare that fond Artillerie:
See heere a Pow'r above the slow
Weake execution of thy bow.
So said, she riv'd the Wood in two,
Unedged all his Arrowes too,
And with the string their feathers bound
To that part whence we have our wound.
See, see! the darts by which we burn'd
Are bright Loÿsa's pencills turn'd;
With which she now enliveth more
Beauties, then they destroy'd before.

The poem thus concludes by providing an origin story for Louise Hollandine's art. According to Lovelace, she derives her power from Cupid's disarmament, with his arrows refashioned as her benevolent brushes, the phallus as weapon reworked as the tool of a woman artist.

Lovelace's "Princess Löysa Drawing" builds upon a larger practice of ekphrastic writing in Cavalier poetry. The description of portraits provided court poets with panegyric opportunities: in praising a portrait, they could also praise its sitter. At the same time, the evocation of a portraitist's skill, particularly in the case of Van Dyck and Lely, served as an analogy for the poet's own vivid descriptive power in words.[35] A famous instance is Lovelace's poem on Lely's portrait of Charles I and the Duke of York, an ekphrasis that pays tribute to the embattled king by praising his likeness [fig. 39].[36] Lovelace here describes a remarkable assimilation between royal and artistic power, praising Lely for channeling the majesty of his sitters, "as if thou didst inherit / For that time all their greatnesse, and didst draw / With those brave eyes your Royall Sitters saw."[37] "Princess Löysa Drawing" builds on these equivalences of portrait and sitter, portraitist and poet, with the further complication that it praises a royal subject who is herself a working portraitist.

Lovelace's description of Louise Hollandine's artistry departs from his encomium to Lely in that no social gulf separates the portraitist from her sitters. Instead, these "sitters" are themselves mythological beings, while Lovelace elevates Louise Hollandine to the status of a "little Diety." In according her a

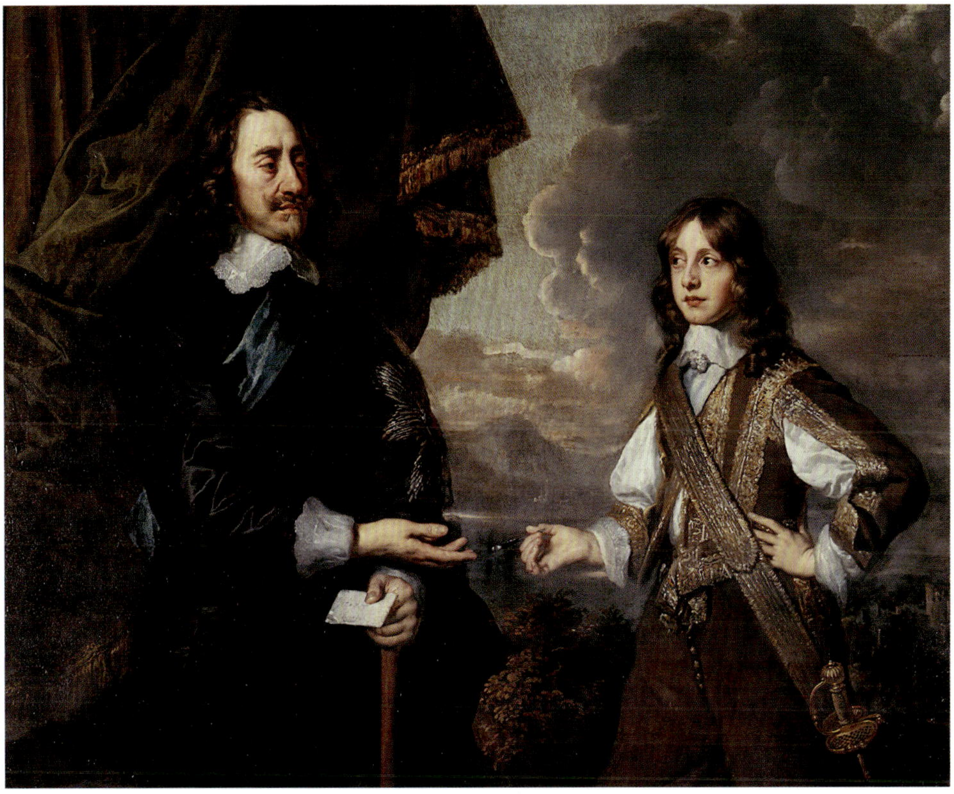

39 Peter Lely, *Charles I and the Duke of York*, 1647, oil on canvas, 126.4 × 146.7 cm, Brentford, Syon House, Duke of Northumberland

semi-divine status, Lovelace recalls the performances of Louise Hollandine's female Stuart relatives in court masques.[38] In a masque, the chaos and vice of the anti-masquers were reversed in the masque proper, when royal ladies entered to restore the forces of virtue and Platonic love. Louise Hollandine similarly undoes Cupid's mischief in Lovelace's poem. The princess's grandmother, Anne of Denmark, pioneered this mode of royal female performance, in which the subjugation of Eros was often explicit.[39] One masque, for example, presented to her by the young pupils of Ladies Hall in 1617, took "Cupid's banishment" as its subject, with a bacchanalian anti-masque succeeded by the triumph of Diana and her nymphs.[40] Elizabeth of Bohemia, Louise Hollandine's mother, had brought the Stuart masque with her to The Hague, much to the horror of local Calvinist preachers. Cupid featured prominently in the ballet written for Elizabeth in 1624 by Constantijn Huygens, in which Cupid steals fire from the queen's eyes to forge the arrows with which he tames the nations of the world.[41] In both her masquing and in the allegorical portraits she commissioned from Honthorst, Elizabeth of Bohemia presented herself as a heroine whose moral triumph compensated for her worldly losses and anticipated the eventual restoration of her dynasty.[42] While Lovelace's ekphrasis of Louise Hollandine's paintings does not make explicit

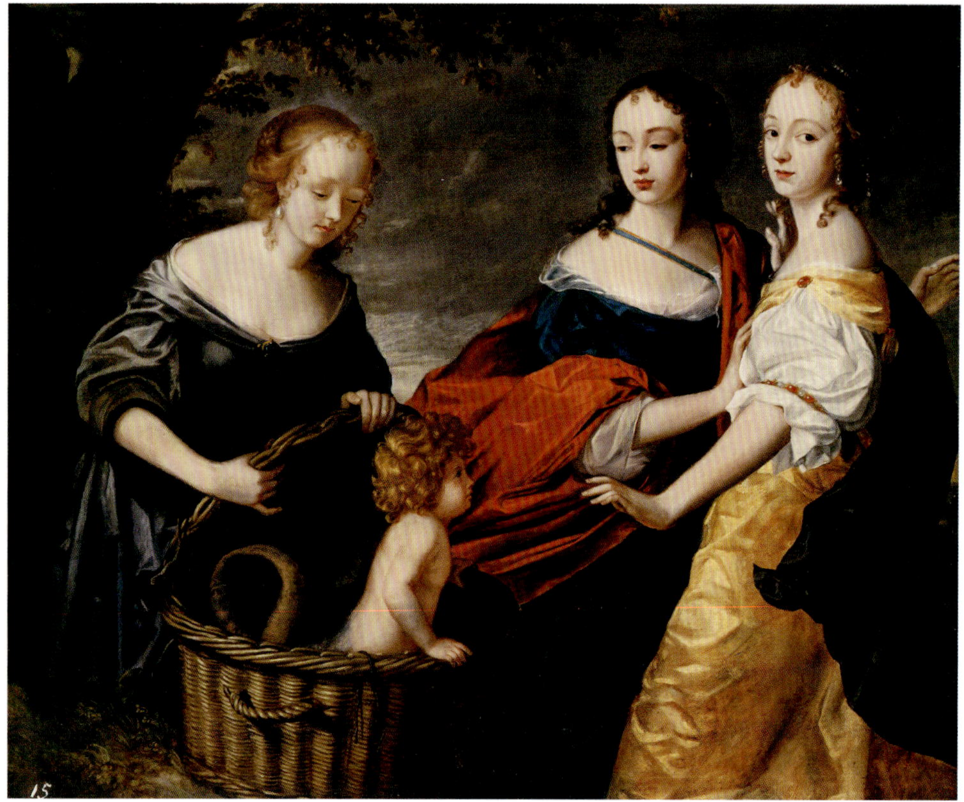

40 Princess Louise Hollandine of the Palatinate, *Allegorical Portrait of Three Ladies and a Child as the Finding of Erichthonius*, n.d., oil on canvas, 132.7 × 157.5 cm, private collection

the political upheavals that brought the exiled poet and princess together in The Hague, its depiction of a royal woman's artistic performance as a pacifying force aligns with Stuart ideology.[43]

Louise Hollandine's documented practice as an artist provided Lovelace with his point of departure, but the images he describes bear little resemblance to her surviving works, which consist mostly of portraits, some in historiated guise, of her royal relations [fig. 40]. Although documentary sources do refer to history paintings by the princess, the Ovidian repertoire of scenes that Lovelace attributes to Louise Hollandine's "pencils" is likely culled not from her actual art but from the same mythological stock that populated court spectacles and the allegorical portraits of Honthorst. The poem's final lines, declaring that Louise Hollandine "enliveth more / Beauties, then [Cupid] destroy'd before" comes the closest of any part of the poem to describing her actual artistic practice as a portraitist, primarily of other women. By describing Louise Hollandine in this way, Lovelace was also able to pay a compliment to her extended family, which provided most of her sitters.

As the description of a woman artist at work, Lovelace's poem finds parallels in contemporary allegories of painting, in which a female figure often embodies the art of painting itself, as in the painting by Frans van Mieris that so impressed Gérard de Lairesse. Within Charles I's collection, Louise Hollandine's paintings, presented as gifts to her uncle, kept company with Artemisia Gentileschi's *Allegory of Painting*, likely a self-portrait that drew on the symbolic language of Cesare Ripa to fashion the image of a woman artist at work.[44] Closer to home, Louise Hollandine's teacher, Honthorst, made two paintings in which women appear at work on male portraits, proposing complex pictorial games of object and subject.

Early modern male artists' depictions of women painters defy any straightforward reading as realistic portrayals of female colleagues. Instead, the use of female figures to allegorize abstract concepts, in this case painting itself, may undercut the agency of the women depicted. At the same time, the fact that Honthorst is known to have had many female students, Louise Hollandine among them, provides an important context for his two enigmatic portrayals of women artists. One of these women can be identified as Honthorst's student Margareta de Roodere, whose portrait in the act of painting her father functioned as a signifier of filial piety.[45] In the other of these paintings, now in Sacramento, Honthorst depicted a young woman at work on what may be the artist's own self-portrait [fig. 41].[46]

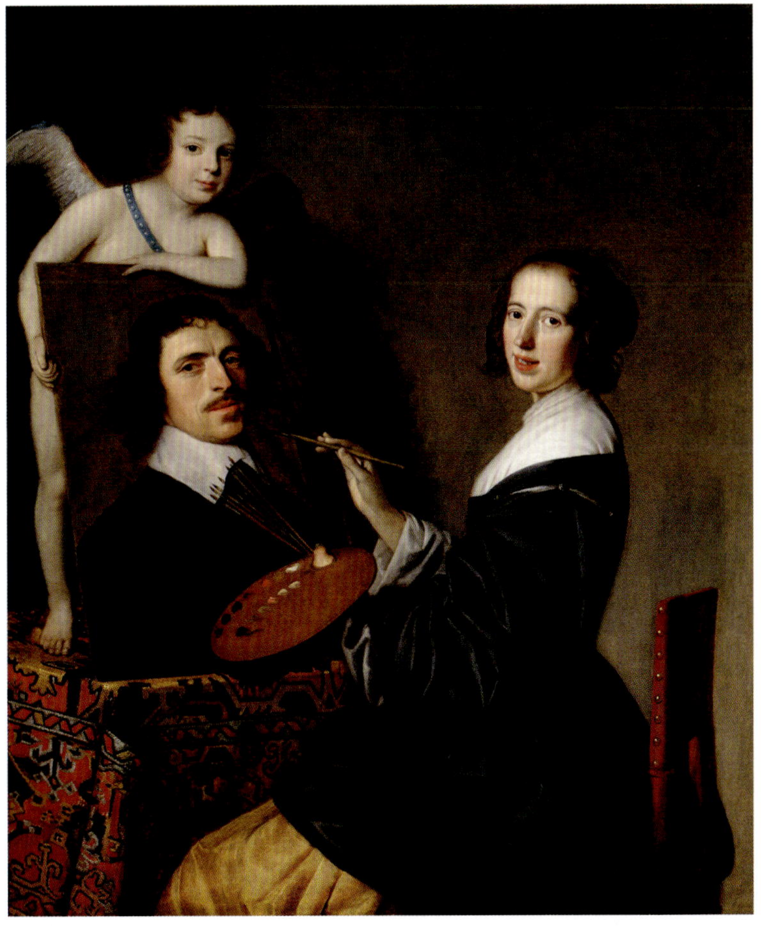

41 Gerard van Honthorst, *Allegory of Painting*, 1648, oil on canvas, 138 × 113 cm, Sacramento, Crocker Museum

Unlike some allegorical depictions of women artists, Honthorst's painting contains realistic details such as the woman's maulstick and carefully arranged skirts. But contrasting with this everyday depiction of the artist is the figure of Cupid, who functions as a kind of living easel, holding up the man's portrait and presenting it to the viewer. Unlike in Lovelace's poem, where the princess and Cupid work at cross-purposes and painting is opposed to amorous mischief-making, Honthorst's woman painter appears to collaborate with Cupid in taking the man's likeness. Using realism to domesticate conventional allegories of Pictura as a woman artist, Honthorst seems to forswear agency in the creation of his own self-portrait. Instead, he places himself in the position of both beholder and artist's model.

Allegorical depictions of women artists may have informed Lovelace's tribute to Louise Hollandine, but as a poet he was also engaging in a rivalry with the visual arts he purported to praise. The swift medium of poetry allowed Lovelace to conjure scenes of mythological revisionism that could never exist in an actual painting. Likewise, his use of dialogue recalls the dramatic medium of the masque more than it does actual painting. Here, as in ekphrastic writing since antiquity, description serves less to evoke actual works of art than to provide opportunities for epideixis and rhetorical display.[47] But unlike the Caroline poets cited in the previous chapters, who often used ekphrasis to assert superiority over artistic rivals, Lovelace was an avidly cosmopolitan admirer of the visual arts.

In another poem to Peter Lely, Lovelace lamented the "transalpine barbarous Neglect" of painting in England, "this un-understanding land."[48] Here, Lovelace again puts a painter in relation to Venus and Cupid, but this time the male artist himself fashions these deities:

Your beauteous Pallet first defin'd Loves Queen,
And made her in her heav'nly colours seen;
You strung the Bow of the Bandite her Son,
And tipp'd his Arrowes with Religion.[49]

Lovelace further eroticizes male artistic creation as a kind of transgressive paternity and revels in the seductive potential of the portrait sitting, asking Lely: "what Princesse not / But comes to you to have her self begot?" Going a step further, Lovelace casts the practice of portraiture as a form of Adam-like self-propagation: "As when first man was kneaded, from his side / Is born to's hand a ready made up Bride." Declaring that Lely's "Skill doth an'mate the prolifick flood, / And thy red Oyl assimilates to blood," Lovelace extends to the artist's materials the potency of bodily fluids.

This fantasy of art-making as a form of erotic self-gratification recurs in a poem by the miniaturist Thomas Flatman, a friend of Charles and Mary Beale.[50] In the Pindaric ode "The Review," published with his collected poems in 1674, Flatman describes his own practice of painting in terms that reveal his familiarity with earlier ekphrastic lyrics.[51] Flatman's autobiographical poem charts his passage from innocence to experience, as erotic disappointment prompts artistic creation:

To extricate my self from Love
Which I could ill obey, but worse command,
I took my Pencils in my hand,
With that Artillery for Conquest strove,
Like wise Pygmalion then did I
My self design my Deity;
Made my own Saint, made my own Shrine:
If she did frown, one dash could make her smile,
All bickerings one easie stroak could reconcile …

Flatman's poem provides a fantasy of total, Pygmalion-like control over the erotic object, the powerless "Deity" whose every affective deviation the male artist's "stroak" can correct.[52] In the end, though, it is the artist's own ungoverned emotional life that destroys his self-begotten mistress:

… on a day, but then I knew not why,
A tear faln from my eye,
Wash'd out my Saint, my Shrine, my Deity:
Prophetique chance; the lines are gone,
And I must mourn o're what I doted on …

For Flatman, the onanistic seductions of art-making prove ultimately sterile, reduced to an early developmental stage in his journey to self-knowledge and religion.

The rhetoric of generation that appears in Lovelace's poem to Lely or Flatman's autobiography in verse might also be applied to women's art, their creativity analogized (as in Mary Beale's self-portrait) to maternity. But Lovelace was careful to avoid such associations in his description of the unmarried Louise Hollandine. Despite his scenes of erotic union, Lovelace emphasizes here not seduction but reconciliation, the replacement of love's torment and fatal consequences with a sequence of happy endings. The contented marriage between Charles I and Henrietta Maria had served in court masques as a wishful model for the relationship between the king and his subjects.[53] At a moment of that relationship's brutal rupture, Lovelace presented the art of Charles's niece as a force of Royalist restoration.

Masquing and portraiture both asserted royal continuity in the face of the Stuart dynasty's material losses and geographic displacement.[54] "Princess Löysa Drawing," in which an exiled poet describes an exiled princess's art as a work of mythopoetic reparation, offers one model for thinking through Royalist cultural performance in the wake of the English Civil War. In this light, Lovelace's ekphrasis serves not as a documentary source for the princess's paintings, but rather as testimony to the ideological significance her artistry may have had for an audience of banished courtiers.

Other contemporary accounts of Louise Hollandine's work provide a useful measure of Lovelace's deviation from faithful description. For example, Abraham van der Doort's inventory of the collection of Charles I, compiled at the end of the 1630s, contains the following entries for two paintings that Louise Hollandine had given to her uncle: "Item the Picture don upon the right lighte of a ffaulkner at length wth a ffaulcon on his left fist, and staffe in his right Arme a ffaulkcon bágg hanging on his back a sword by his side – in a Landscept, a white dog by, wc^h was sent from the hage by Sr Robt Anstrother to you Ma^ty for a token from your Neece being in a square frame wth Iseing Glass over it" and "Item sent more by the Princes Louesa your Ma^ts Nee a Landscept peece wherein the – Angell is Conducting Tobias with a fish under his Arme, the Angell being in red – and white habbitt a little dog following – wch Picture beinge wthout a glasse in a black. frame p^rsented also to yor Ma^ty"[55] Van der Doort's description of Louise Hollandine's paintings reveals a different set of priorities from Lovelace's poem. He offers a straightforward enumeration of their subject matter, but also records their authorship, provenance, framing, and place of display within the palace. By contrast, Lovelace treats the paintings as completely dematerialized mythological tableaux, enacted by speaking performers rather than glimpsed within the stasis of a frame.

In 1649, the same year that Lovelace published his poem about Louise Hollandine, the Royalist cause reached its nadir in the execution of Charles I, which took place on a scaffold outside of the Banqueting House at Whitehall, the erstwhile site of Stuart masquing. Soon, the Commonwealth set about dispersing the king's art collection, including the two paintings he had received from his niece. Making Van der Doort's inventory seem expansive by comparison, the sales catalogue describes the princess's paintings merely as "A Falconer in Lymbing," which sold for ten shillings, and "Tobyas & ye Angell in Water Colo^r done by the Kings Neece," which brought 2 pounds, six shillings.[56] With the brutal demystification of monarchy constituted by the king's beheading and the stripping of his palaces, the stakes of royal performance had never been higher.

— *"Painted by herself": Accomplishment and Restoration* —

For both artists and aristocrats of the Interregnum, Van Dyck's portraits provided a repertoire of motifs with which to assert continuities with the culture of the fallen Caroline court. In his portraits from the 1650s, Peter Lely emphasized his status as Van Dyck's heir, catering to aristocrats who had experienced war, sequestration, imprisonment, and the violent deaths of kin. In his portrait of the Capel sisters, for example, he responded to Van Dyck's innovative double portraits of women, images closely associated with Henrietta Maria's ladies-in-waiting [figs. 42 and 43].[57] The Capel sisters, Mary and Elizabeth, were the daughters of the Royalist commander Arthur, Lord Capel, who was beheaded the same year as Charles I. In 1648, Mary Capel married Henry Seymour, Lord Beauchamp, who died in 1654 after confinement in the Tower.[58] Lely's portrait most likely commemorates her second marriage, in 1657, to the future first Duke of Beaufort.

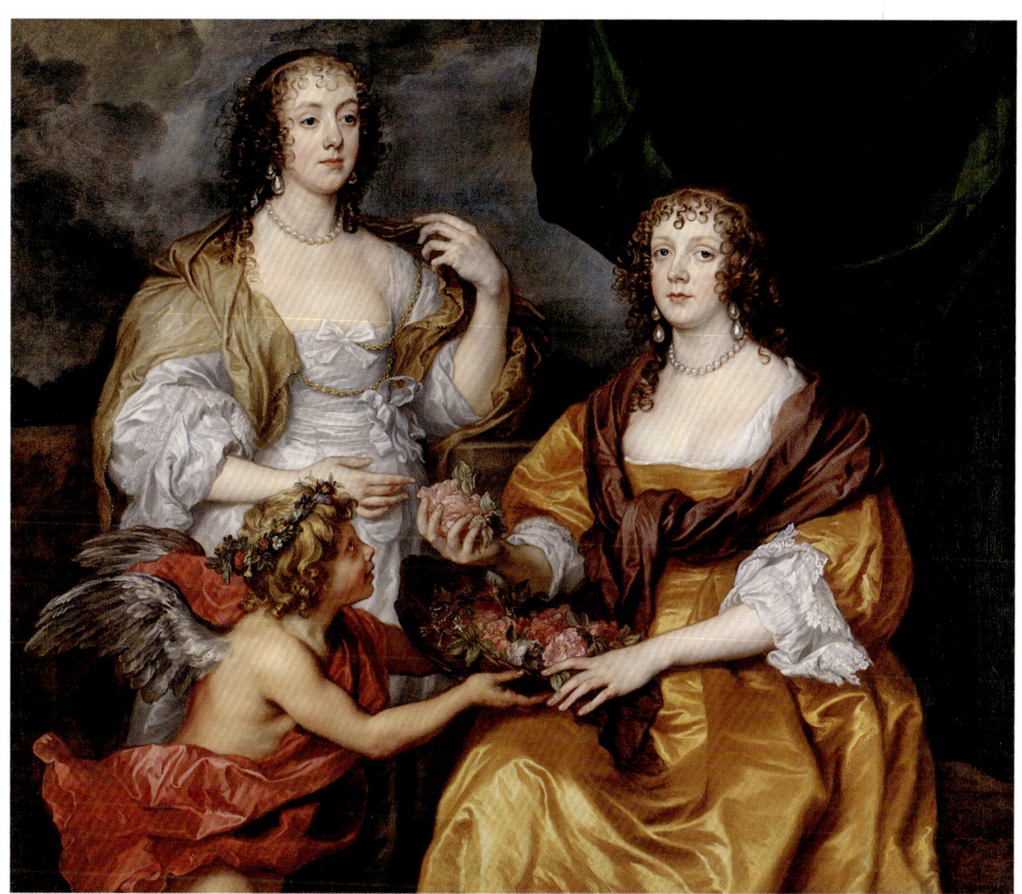

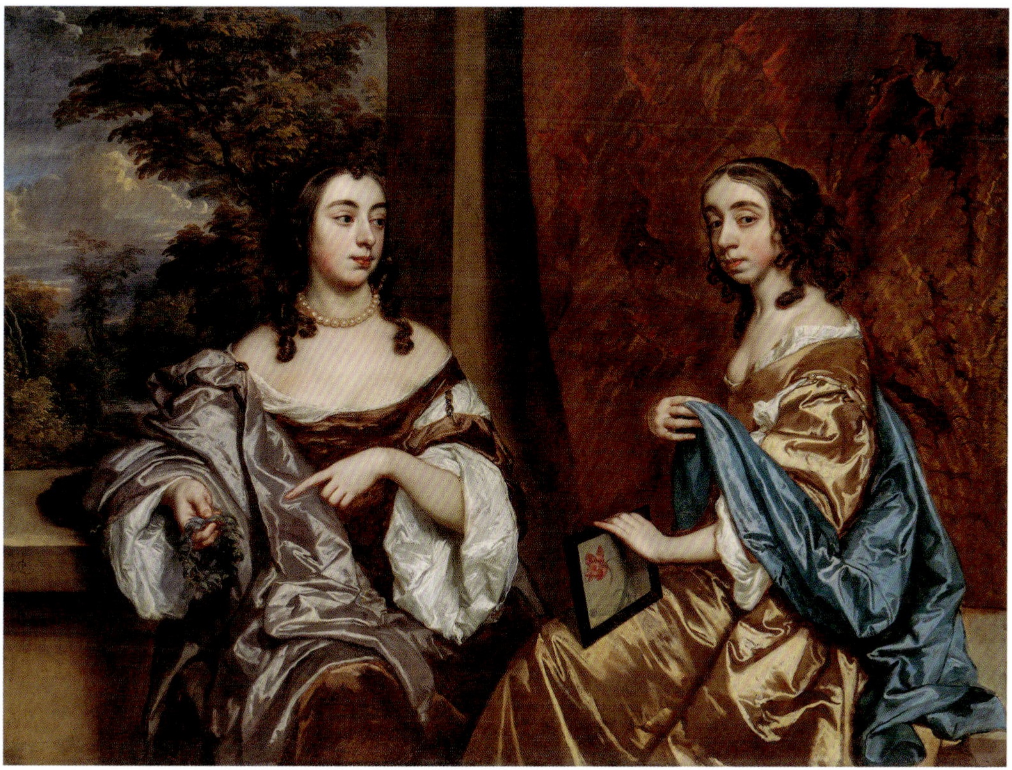

42 Anthony van Dyck, *Lady Elizabeth Thimbelby and Dorothy, Viscountess Andover*, ca. 1637, oil on canvas, 132.1 × 149 cm, London, National Gallery

43 Peter Lely, *Mary Capel, Later Duchess of Beaufort, and Her Sister Elizabeth, Countess of Carnarvon*, ca. 1657, oil on canvas, 130.2 × 170.2 cm, New York, Metropolitan Museum of Art

Holding a loosely painted wreath that may be myrtle, symbolic of marriage, Mary appears with her sister, the Countess of Carnarvon.[59]

Lady Carnarvon holds a small painting of a tulip in her lap. The signature *E Carnarvon / fecit*, beneath a countess's coronet, leaves no doubt as to the painting's authorship – in fact, it is a much more assertive signature than Lely's own, incised in the parapet at left. With her extended index finger, Mary seems to be calling her sister's attention to the myrtle wreath: in other words, to matrimony. But Elizabeth ignores her sister's gesture as she peers out at the viewer, tilting her painting to make it visible and rupturing the fictive cohesiveness of the painting to address the beholder. The triangular structure that Lely inherited from Van Dyck's double portraits, with their positioning of the beholder in an ambiguous relationship to the pair depicted, serves here to mediate between two models of aristocratic womanhood. Both Mary and Elizabeth appear apart from their husbands, with their tie of blood kinship providing the painting's principle object of commemoration (in fact, the painting was part of a series of portraits of the Capel siblings). With her wreath and averted gaze, Mary represents the more conventional image of an aristocratic bride. Elizabeth, by contrast, is confrontational in her address to the beholder, displaying her own artistic performance in a way that recalls Honthorst's depictions of women painters.

At least one of the Countess of Carnarvon's paintings survives today, a gouache of flowers in a vase [fig. 44].[60] Both of the Capel sisters participated in botany and horticulture, whether in the form of flower painting or botanical research and patronage.[61] Flower painting was one manifestation of a broader culture of female accomplishment in the Restoration period, as genteel parents began to invest, both financially and emotionally, in their daughters' acquisition of skills in the visual arts.[62] Another portrait by Lely depicts a young woman, as yet unidentified, holding a brush and a man's miniature portrait in her hand [fig. 45].[63] The table beside her supports a crumpled drawing, a bookrest, and other artistic implements. As in his portrait of the Countess of Carnarvon, Lely depicts his sitter displaying her work to the beholder, whose gaze she meets. The likeness she holds may be a love token or a pictorial confession of attachment, in the manner of Honthorst's woman painter in Sacramento. At the same time, the miniature portrait, drawing, and artistic tools complicate the woman's status as simply a sitter or object of the gaze. Lely instead emphasizes her manual practice of painting, something that professional artists like Van Dyck, Rubens, and Lely himself scrupulously avoided in their own self-portraits.[64]

Richard Lovelace ascribed a political significance to Princess Louise Hollandine's artistry as a form of Royalist reparation. Similarly, some Restoration writers framed their praise of accomplished women as part of a larger cultural project of recovering Caroline court values. Tributes to women painters operating in the Van Dyckian mode allowed writers of the late seventeenth century to position themselves as outsiders to their own era, praising women who embodied the putative virtues of the bygone court. This attempted restoration of Charles I's

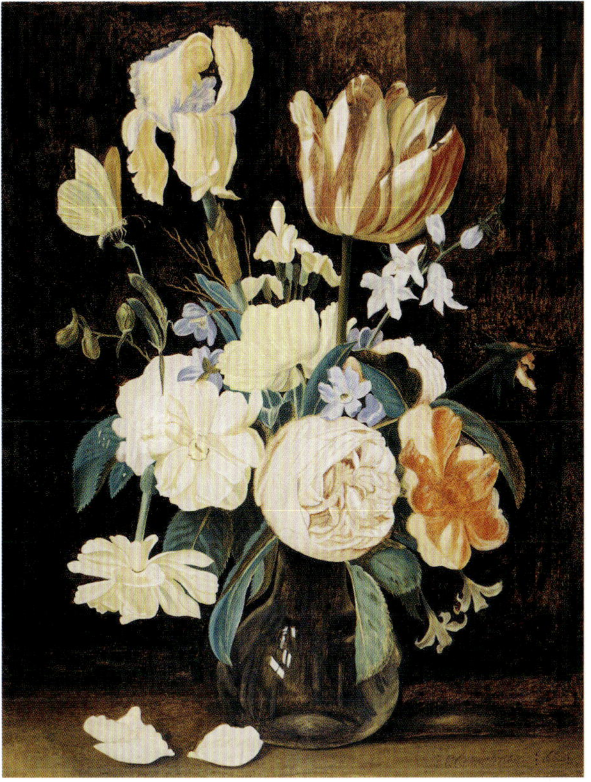

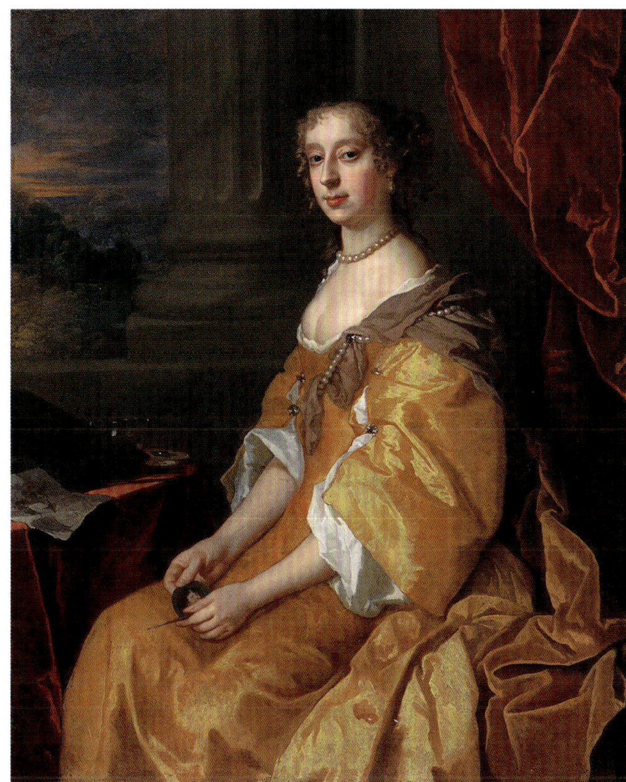

44 Elizabeth, Countess of Carnarvon, *Flowers in a Vase*, 1662, gouache on paper, mounted on panel, 40.65 × 30.5 cm, Royal Collection

45 Peter Lely, *Portrait of a Woman*, ca. 1660, oil on canvas, 122.3 × 98 cm, private collection (courtesy of Philip Mould)

court culture was inextricable from the ongoing engagement of English painters with the king's favorite portraitist and occurred simultaneously with attempts by Charles II and the aristocracy to recover ancestral collections, including many portraits by Van Dyck. For example, when the Duke of Newcastle, whom we have previously encountered praising Van Dyck's conversation, returned from exile after the Restoration to find his estates in ruins, he was relieved to discover that a few paintings "had been saved by the care and industry of his eldest daughter … (which My Lord esteemed very much, the pictures being drawn by Van Dyck)."[65]

This recuperation of Caroline court culture, and of Van Dyck in particular, provides important context for a poem by Anne Killigrew entitled "On My Aunt Mrs. A.K. Drowned under London-bridge, in the Queen's Barge, Anno 1641."[66] Killigrew, who served in the court of Mary of Modena, came from a family with a long tradition of royal service and literary talent.[67] After Killigrew's death from smallpox in 1685 at the age of twenty-five, her father oversaw the publication of her poems, prefaced by elegies from other writers, including a poem by John Dryden that long overshadowed Killigrew's own work.[68]

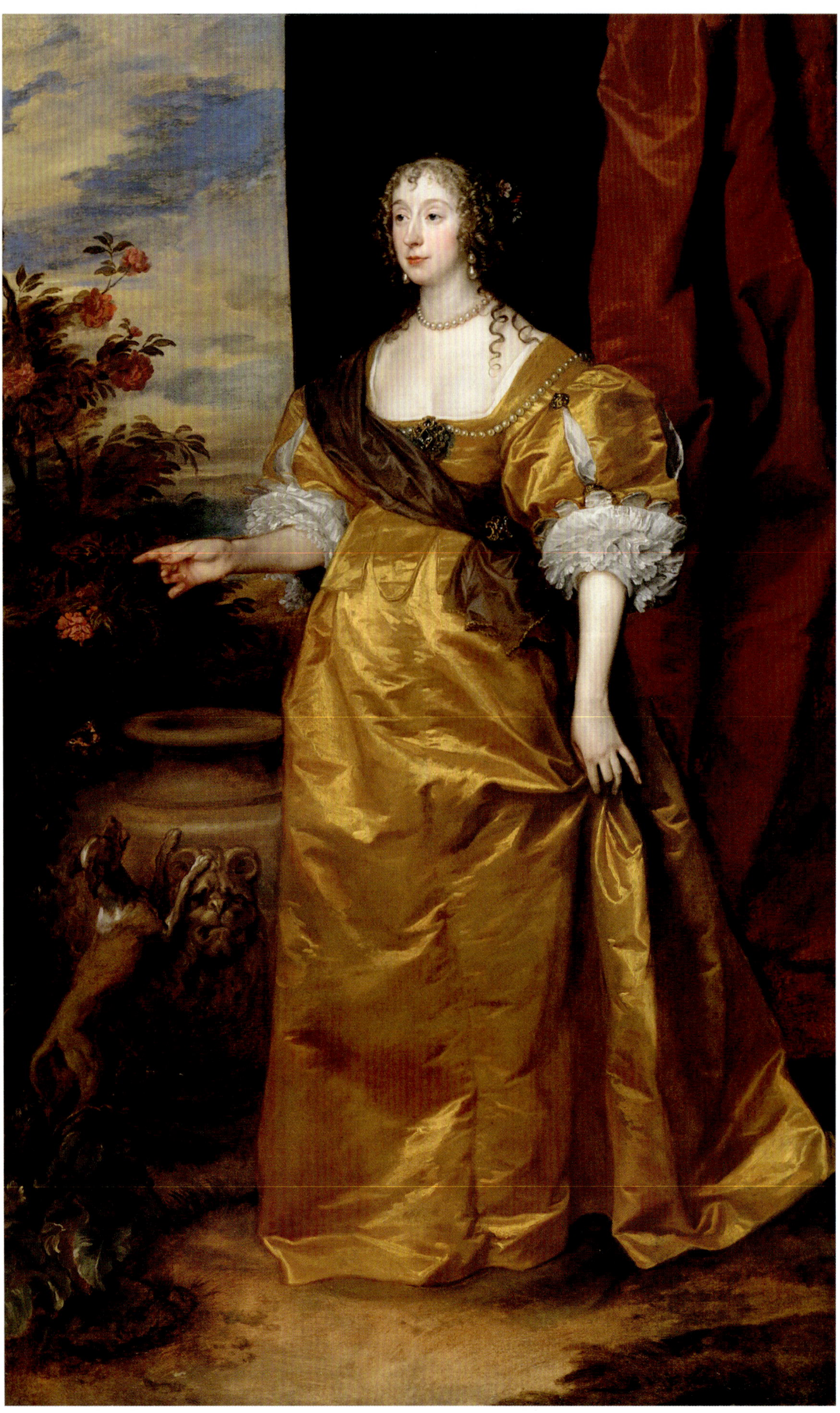

Killigrew's poem commemorates her aunt Anne Kirke, who drowned when the queen's barge capsized in 1641. Kirke was a favorite at the court of Charles I, serving as dresser to Queen Henrietta Maria and a performer in at least one court masque.[69] In implicit contrast to the court mistresses of the Restoration, Killigrew describes her aunt as "The Virtue, which a Virtuous Age did prize," and a paragon of meritorious royal favor. Kirke's worth and court service allowed her to transcend her relatively modest birth, and she was acknowledged even by "those who most upon their Title stood."[70] Killigrew's emphasis on her aunt's place at court builds upon the elegies written in the immediate aftermath of Kirke's drowning, such as Henry Glapthorne's claim that "with her gentle 'haviour and deport, / [She] Did gain the love, not envy of the Court."[71] Killigrew explains her aunt's friendship with Henrietta Maria not only as stemming from her virtue, but also from her dignified appearance: "So Noble was her Air, so Great her Mien, / She seem'd a Friend, not Servant to the Queen." In writing thus, Killigrew may have been informed by Van Dyck's portrait of Anne Kirke, "one of the most carefully devised and sumptuously painted of Van Dyck's later English works" [fig. 46].[72]

In this painting, Mistress Kirke occupies the familiar liminal space of Van Dyck's English portraits, neither exterior nor interior, its background bifurcated between drapery and landscape. Pinching the golden silk of her skirts together

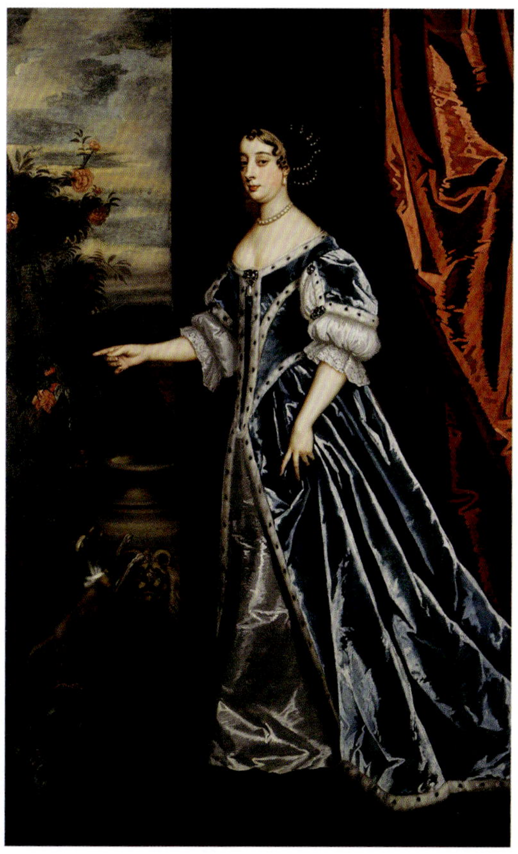

46 Anthony van Dyck, *Anne Kirke*, ca. 1637, oil on canvas, 222.3 × 130.5 cm, San Marino, Huntington

47 Peter Lely and workshop, *Barbara, Countess of Castlemaine*, ca. 1670, oil on canvas, 231 × 137 cm, private collection (courtesy of Sotheby's)

with one hand, she gestures beyond the limits of the frame with the other. The area below Kirke's index finger is the most animated passage of the composition, featuring a small dog who leaps to catch a butterfly. The dog's extended forelegs overlap the grimacing face of a lion on a terracotta urn. Leaping dog, grimacing lion, and fluttering butterfly all combine to reinforce the grand indifference of the sitter.[73]

Van Dyck's portrait of Anne Kirke was one of many paintings by him that Lely collected and drew upon for his renewal of court portraiture during the Restoration.[74] Indeed, Lely's workshop produced a portrait of the royal mistress Barbara Villiers that neatly slots her into Van Dyck's composition [fig. 47].[75] Lely's ability to acquire Anne Kirke's portrait was almost certainly a result of the vicissitudes suffered by the sitter's family during the Civil War.[76] For Anne Killigrew, who allied herself in verse with Charles II's long-suffering queen, Lely's use of her virtuous aunt's portrait as the prototype for the image of an ermine-clad royal mistress must have seemed a travesty.[77]

In her own self-portrait, Killigrew reprised the pictorial building blocks of Van Dyck's painting of her aunt, with its terrace, sculpted urn, and framing drapery [fig. 48]. These were generic elements of female portraiture in the Van Dyckian mode, but Killigrew's saffron-colored skirt and extended index finger may more explicitly link her self-image to the portrait of Anne Kirke. Whereas her aunt's gesture is difficult to read, perhaps directing our eye to the rose bushes, a lost pendant, or nothing at all, Killigrew points emphatically to a scroll of paper held in one hand. The self-portrait commemorates Killigrew's identity as a poet, providing a visual complement to the ekphrastic verse that she wrote about her own paintings.

Caroline writers expressed discomfort with the independence and visibility of court women whose cultural influence extended to their patronage of Van Dyck and their performances in court masques. With the hindsight of the Restoration, however, when professional actresses openly shared the bed of the king, women like Anne Kirke came to represent the virtues of a lost golden age. Her niece's poem even interprets Kirke's drowning as an omen of the societal collapse to come:

> *When angry Heav'n extinguisht her fair Light,*
> *It seem'd to say,* Nought's Precious in my sight;
> As I in Waves this Paragon have drown'd,
> The Nation next, and King I will confound.
> [emphasis in the original]

After Killigrew's death, her elegists further associated the poet with her aunt, portraying her as an avatar of the values of Charles I's court, even as her brief life neatly coincided with the dissolute reign of his son.[78]

In the most important of these elegies, Dryden contrasts Killigrew's own posthumously published verse with the "prostitute and profligate" commercial literary world of the Restoration, and particularly the "steaming Ordures

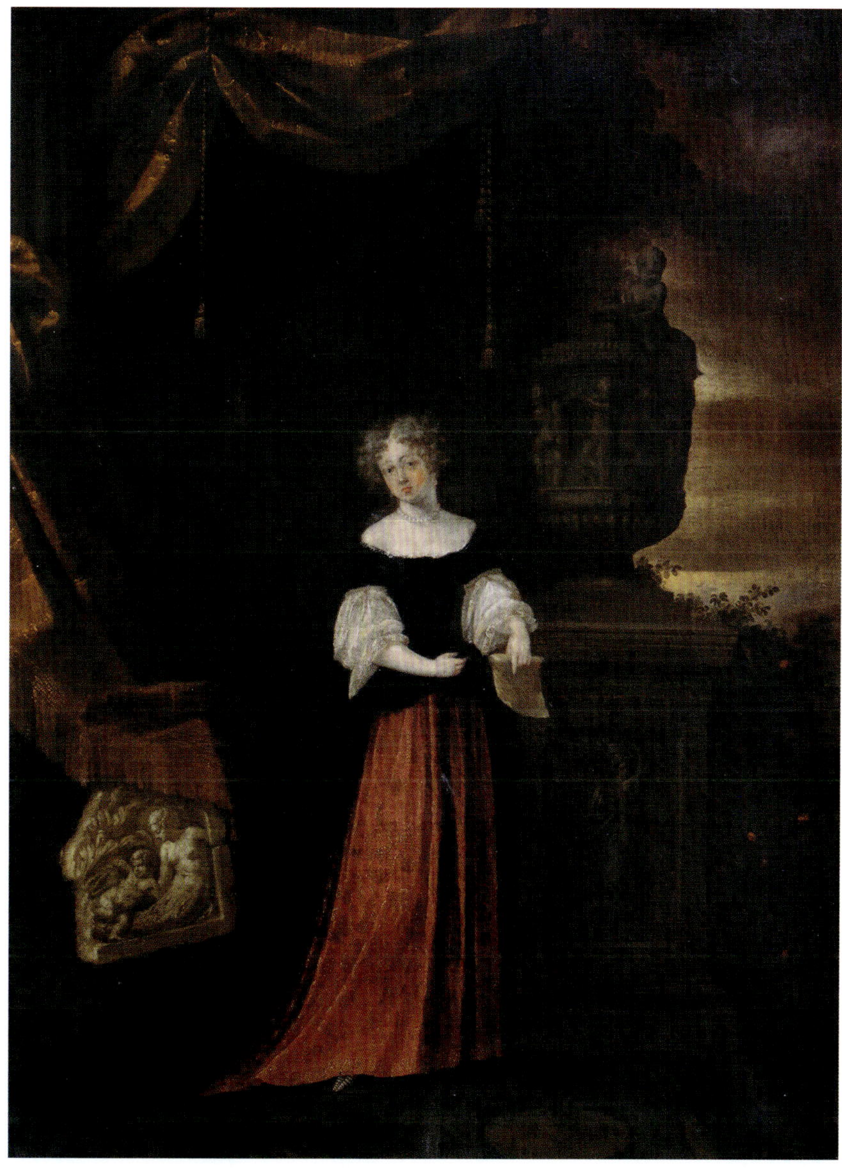

48 Anne Killigrew, *Self-Portrait*, 1685, oil on canvas, 74.3 × 55.9 cm, Berkeley, Berkeley Castle

of the Stage" to which he himself was a major contributor.[79] Seeking to praise a woman writer operating outside of the literary marketplace (and presumably without the classical education that was so critical to his own poetry), Dryden emphasizes Killigrew's inborn talent, declaring: "Art she had none, yet wanted None. / For Nature did that Want supply, / So rich in Treasures of her Own, / She might our boasted Stores defy." Dryden's emphasis on Killigrew's artless excellence has misled many commentators into reading his praise of her poetry and painting as ironic.[80] In fact, Killigrew's non-commercial artistic performances positioned her as a royal favorite and fit companion to the celebrated amateurs of the Stuart dynasty.

In his discussion of Killigrew's paintings, Dryden focuses on her work as the portraitist of both James II and Mary of Modena [fig. 49]. Recalling the terms in which Lovelace praised Lely's double portrait of James and his father, Dryden emphasizes Killigrew's ability to capture both the king's appearance and his character:

> *For not content t'express his Outward Part,*
> *Her hand call'd out the Image of his Heart,*
> *His Warlike Mind, his Soul devoid of Fear,*
> *His High-designing Thoughts, were figur'd there,*
> *As when, by Magic, Ghosts are made appear.*

Meanwhile, in his description of Killigrew's portrait of Mary of Modena, Dryden implies a certain equivalence between artist and royal sitter: "Beauty alone could Beauty take so right." Here the physical beauty of the woman painter supplements that of her paintings.

Dryden's discussion of Killigrew's paintings restages the *paragone* of painting and poetry while recasting feminine accomplishment as martial conquest. Vigorously asserting the subordination of one medium to another, Dryden describes painting as "A plenteous Province, and alluring Prey" for the poet:

> *The Country open lay without Defense:*
> *For Poets frequent Inroads there had made,*
> *And perfectly could represent*
> *The Shape, the Face, with ev'ry Lineament;*
> *And all the large Domains which the* Dumb-sister *sway'd,*
> *All bow'd beneath her Government,*
> *Received in Triumph wheresoe'er she went.*
> *Her Pencil drew, what e'er her Soul design'd,*
> *And oft the happy Draught surpass'd the Image in her Mind.*

Although more invested in a hierarchical relationship between painting and poetry than Lovelace, Dryden shared with the earlier poet a fascination with the figure of the amateur woman artist as an exemplar of inborn talent unsullied by contact with the marketplace.

In her own ekphrastic poetry, Killigrew ventriloquized such figures as John the Baptist, Salome, or "two nymphs of Diana's."[81] All of the poems are in the first person and can only be identified as descriptions of paintings by their titles, which repeat the phrase "Painted by herself." Interestingly, none of the three paintings Killigrew describes in her ekphrastic work is known to survive, raising the question of whether the poems describe real paintings at all. The final tercet of her poem on Diana's nymphs does, however, make a witty allusion to the debate between speaking poetry and mute painting:

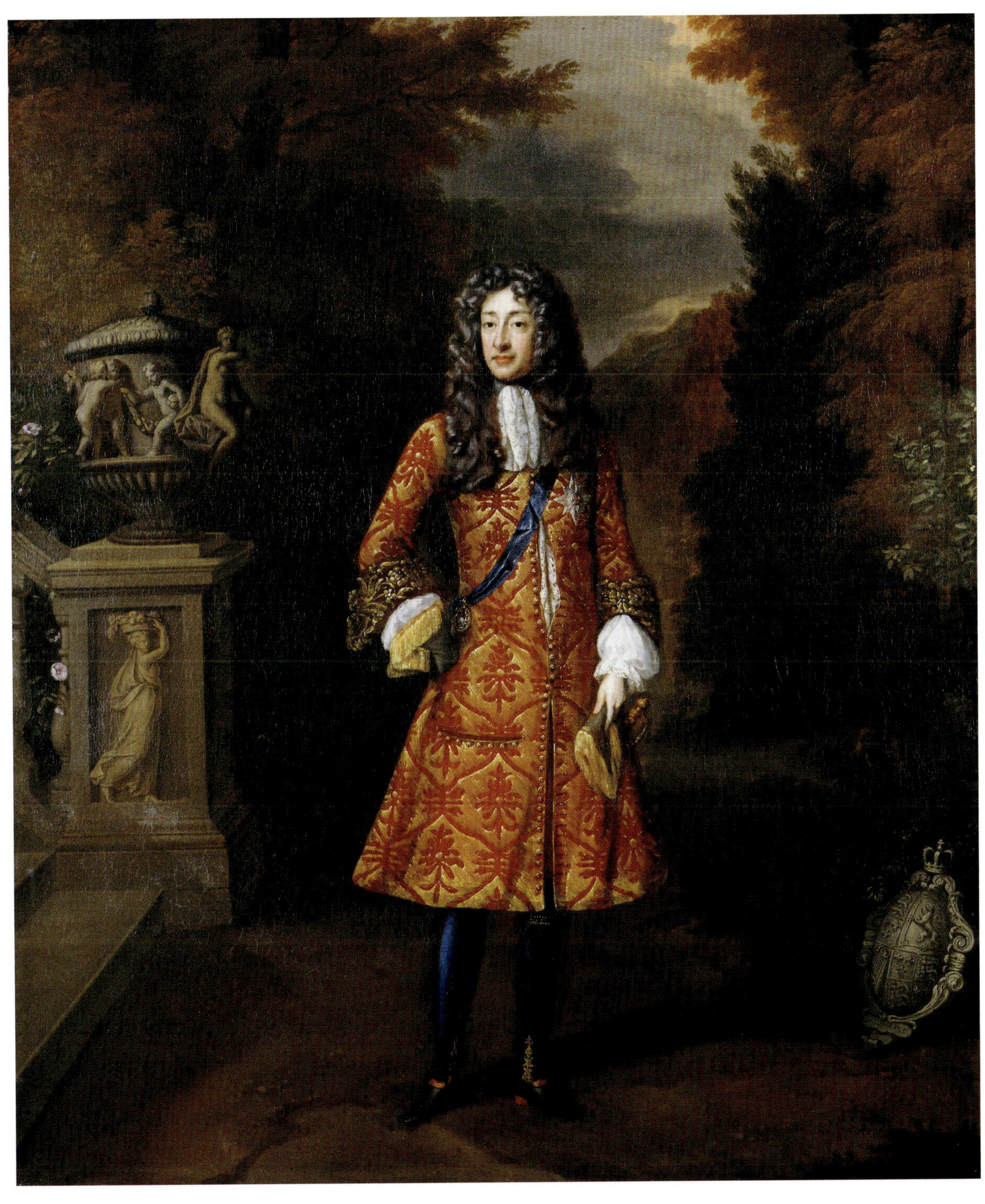

49 Anne Killigrew, *James II*, 1685, oil on canvas, 104.7 × 86.4 cm, Royal Collection

If you ask where such Wights [i.e., the nymphs] *do dwell,*
In what Bless't Clime, that so excel?
The Poets only that can tell.

A similar play on painting's muteness occurs in the poem on Salome's presentation of the head of John the Baptist, where the speaker glories to "present you here; / The Tongue ty'd up, that made all *Jury* [Jewry] quake."[82] In both cases, Killigrew reinforces the silence of painting at the same time that she counteracts it with her own poetic voice.

While Dryden praised Killigrew for existing in a state of purity outside of the literary marketplace, she herself expressed ambivalence about the conditions of authorship imposed by her status as a female courtier. In her poem "Upon the saying that my Verses were made by another," Killigrew reworked Aesop's fable of a jay bird who dresses in the discarded plumes of peacocks.[83] Appearing before real peacocks in this borrowed finery, the imposter is soon exposed and plucked bare. Aesop's jay is a figure of the forger, counterfeiter, or plagiarist, whose deception might also be more charitably described as an act of creative self-fashioning. Killigrew reflected on a false accusation of plagiarism by comparing herself to the jay:

What ought t'have brought me Honour, brought me shame!
Like Aesop's *Painted Jay I seem'd to all,*
Adorn'd in Plumes, I not my own could call:
Rifl'd like her, each one my Feathers tore,
And, as they thought, unto the Owner bore.
My Laurels thus an Others Brow adorn'd,
My Numbers they Admir'd, but Me they scorn'd ...

Intensifying the violence of the jay's exposure with the words "Rifl'd" and "tore," Killigrew casts the accusation as an injustice and a physical violation. The accusation of plagiarism denies the creative capacity of the accused, severing her violently from her work.[84]

Killigrew was particularly susceptible to such accusations because her work circulated in manuscript, "commit[ed]" in the words of her poem, to "some few hands." Accused of plagiarism, the poet experiences disillusionment on the heels of inspired rapture. Brought down to earth, she once again finds herself relegated to the role of admonishing outsider: "I willingly accept *Cassandra*'s Fate, / To speak the Truth, although believ'd too late." Only with her death could Killigrew's poems be brought to press and her name circulated publicly. As we have seen with Lodowick Carlile, even male courtiers made a show of reluctance when they published their works, just as painters might attempt to beg off producing self-portraits for princely benefactors. But for a woman artist and writer like Killigrew, whose cultural power was linked to her avoidance of publicity and commerce, fame presented an impossible double-bind, seemingly permitted only beyond the grave.[85]

Texts like Carlile's and Killigrew's reveal the ambivalence that the open market inspired in courtly performers even during a period when the court retained relative cultural dominance. The marginalization of court culture that followed the "Glorious Revolution" created a new dynamic within English art that would prove ultimately fatal to the central position of the Van Dyckian painter.[86] Celebrated in many histories as the foundational moment for a truly English art, this period also saw the repression of more cosmopolitan identities and entanglements. In the decades after Bainbrigg Buckeridge ranged Joan Carlile alongside Van Dyck, an increasing hostility to women artists, and to male artists coded as feminine, would become a defining feature of the emergent English school.

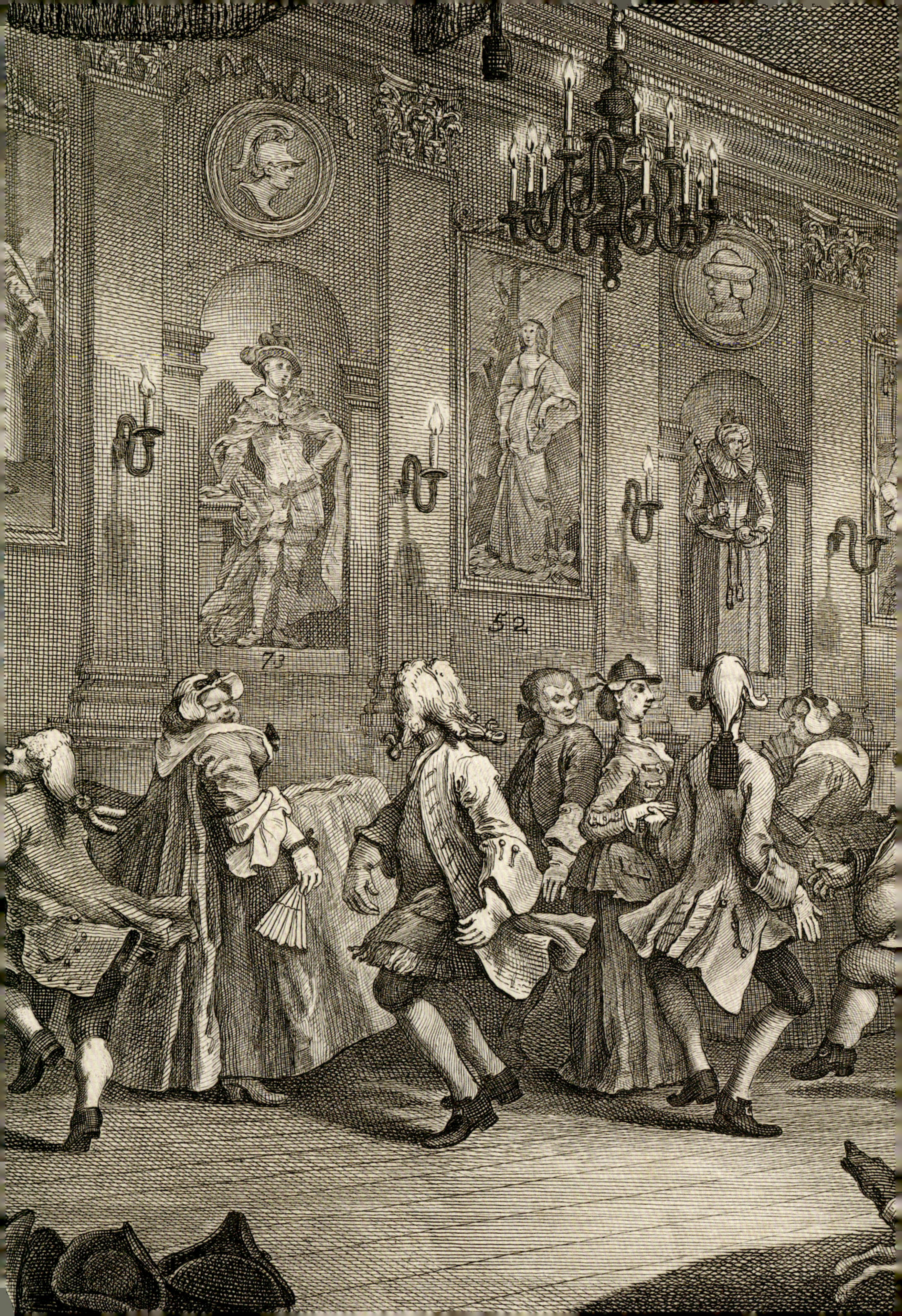
73
52

[CHAPTER FOUR]

Genealogies of Portraiture

IN THE SPRING OF 1726, LADY MARY WORTLEY MONTAGU FOUND HERSELF "in open Wars" with a certain Mrs. Murray. As she told her sister, the Countess of Mar, Lady Mary first endured Mrs. Murray "attack[ing] me in very Billingsgate language at a Masquerade." When the two women next met at an "assembly," the writer asked Mrs. Murray "how I had deserv'd so much abuse at her hands," only to have her antagonist deny the charges. The conflict reached its culmination at Covent Garden on April 20th, during the estate sale of the painter Sir Godfrey Kneller. Lady Mary intended to buy her sister's portrait from among the many unclaimed paintings at the artist's studio, but found to her dismay that Mrs. Murray "not only came to the Auction, but with all possible spite bid up the picture." The wealthy Lady Mary noted with complacency that Mrs. Murray's malice only cost her an extra "ten guineas." In the end, the writer was happy to inform her sister: "The picture is in my possession, and at your service if you please to have it."[1]

Moving from the masquerade ball to the assembly to the salesroom, Mrs. Murray's vendetta traversed the social spaces that structured fashionable life in eighteenth-century London. Within these spaces, elite women put themselves on display – dancing, bidding at auction, or engaging in very visible feuds.[2] Writing several decades later, Horace Walpole marveled that aristocratic parents continued to let their daughters "act plays, and go to painters by themselves," noting that sittings with the painter Katherine Read had facilitated the elopement of Lady Susan Fox-Strangways with an Irish actor.[3] The fact that auctions, like portrait sittings, had become "arenas" for women's competitive consumption and self-display by the early eighteenth century speaks to the importance of art collecting and connoisseurship to elite British identity at this date.[4] But such sales were also one mechanism through which historical portraits became alienated from their original conditions of viewing over the course of the eighteenth century.[5] As will be seen, this process of alienation had notable consequences for the ongoing reception of Van Dyck.

A portrait like the Countess of Mar's put its sitter on view within a domestic (and dynastic) interior, perhaps commemorating successful navigation of the marriage market or recording the costume worn to a masquerade. But because

Detail of William Hogarth, Plate Two from *The Analysis of Beauty*, 1753 [see fig. 58]

portraits also circulated as commodities, they could easily slip from the grasp of their original patrons. Rather than visualizing ancestry, portraits might serve, when openly bought and sold, to broadcast familial distress. Likewise, the relatively new phenomenon of the public auction, a practice imported from the Netherlands, publicized the dismantling of private collections and patrimony.[6] In the case of the Countess of Mar, her husband's support of the Jacobite rebellion and their subsequent shared exile in France meant that she was never able to claim her portrait from Kneller's studio.[7] The countess thus unwittingly exposed her sister to the potential humiliation of losing a family portrait to a social rival.

Artists' posthumous studio sales differed from other auctions. They pulled back the curtain on the mechanics and economics of art production, revealing preparatory works and unsold paintings. Such dispersals had the potential to embarrass those – like the Countess of Mar – who had never paid for their portraits, but also to enlighten others who wished to become artists themselves. In the case of famous painters like Lely or Kneller, the studio auction benefitted from the aura of celebrity, propelling onto the marketplace the contents of a site for encounters between political and cultural elites.

The records of artists' estate sales indicate that the countess's portrait was hardly alone in going unclaimed for years by its sitter (other portraits, of royal or famous sitters, may have been painted on speculation). Kneller's sale lasted three days and contained 340 lots, all of them portraits.[8] These included both originals by Kneller and studio copies, with sitters ranging from George I to an unidentified "Negro Woman."[9] (Long absent from London, the countess was herself mislabeled as "Lord Mar's first Lady," when in fact she was his second.)[10] Stocked with portraits either unclaimed or painted on speculation, studios like Kneller's were major sites for the viewing, as well as the making, of art in early modern London. Visiting the studio of Jacob Huysmans on August 26, 1664, Pepys admired portraits of Queen Catharine of Braganza and the maids of honor.[11] Several decades later, Kneller's studio functioned as shorthand for the display of commercialized female beauty. The *Spectator* declared it "a low and degrading Idea of" women "to consider them meerly as Objects of Sight. This is … to put them upon a Level with their Pictures at Kneller's."[12] Both this analogy and the attendance at studio sales by fashionable women attest to the increasingly semi-public nature of the studio in this period.

Lady Mary Wortley Montagu's erstwhile friend Alexander Pope commemorated the studio of Charles Jervas in a verse epistle that combined the admiration of female portraiture with an elevating association of painting and poetry.[13] Pope described how "Smit with the love of Sister-Arts," painter and poet "met congenial" in the space of the studio. Here, rather than a site of rivalry, the studio became the scene of generative encounters between practitioners of parallel arts. Pope and Jervas worked side by side, both engaged in the project of celebrating and commemorating female beauty. In their complementary tributes to the recently deceased Countess of Bridgewater, the painter "preserv[ed] a Face" and the poet "a Name," a mutual reinforcement of two media that continued the long tradition in English poetry of using the female aristocratic portrait as a stand-in for painting itself [fig. 50].

If the bidding war for the countess's portrait, like the cultural currency of the studio, speaks to the emergent institutions of artistic life in 1720s London, the painting itself reveals the self-referentiality and historical consciousness that had linked ambitious portraitists in England since the mid-seventeenth century [fig. 51]. Kneller depicted his sitter outdoors, dressed in a light pink riding habit.[14] The black hat tucked under her arm provides a curious vacuum at the heart of the image, while the tip of a shoe peeking out from the sitter's skirt along the painting's vertical axis gives a sense of the elegantly posed body beneath her voluminous skirts. Lady Mar (or Lady Frances Pierrepont, as she probably was at the date of the portrait) extends her tasseled walking stick to the left of the portrait, breaking the frame and calling attention to the background, where a young groom tends to her restive horse.

All of the painting's key iconographic elements – woodland setting, black hat, one bare and one gloved hand, walking stick, groom, and horse with raised foreleg – derive from the Van Dyck portrait of Charles I now known as *Le Roi à la Chasse* [fig. 52].[15] In creating this image, Van Dyck had himself drawn upon earlier Jacobean portraits that depicted members of the royal family at the hunt, but his own formulation, with its emphasis on the king's self-mastery and distinction, marked a highly influential turning point in English portraiture. The countess's portrait was separated from its Van Dyckian prototype by the traumas of civil war, regicide, restoration, and revolution, not to mention the differing genders and ranks of the respective sitters. But the persistence of Van Dyck's Caroline iconography into the eighteenth century (and beyond) speaks to its powerful ideological importance as a marker of continuity in the face of societal transformations. Kneller's self-positioning with regard to his most celebrated predecessors in English portraiture was clear to his contemporaries; as Benjamin Victor wrote in a poem on Kneller's death, "He strove *Vandike* and *Lilly* to excel."[16] While Lady Mary's success at auction restored her sister's picture to its status as an inalienable family portrait (it hangs at the Mar family's seat to this day), Kneller's citation of Van Dyck grounded the portrait in the visual culture of enduring aristocracy and artistic prestige.

At first glance, then, the story of Lady Mar's portrait might appear to offer a contrast between the emergence of a modern art world, where auctions accelerated the circulation of artistic commodities, and the persistence of certain retrograde motifs within painting. It is not, after all, Kneller's elegant female portraits that have provided the focal point for discussions of the emergence of the "English school" in the early decades of the eighteenth century.[17] Contrasted with the portraits that the ambitious young William Hogarth would paint in the years following Kneller's death, the countess's portrait looks like an attenuated relic, its rehearsal of Stuart iconography as hopeless as the sitter's dedication to

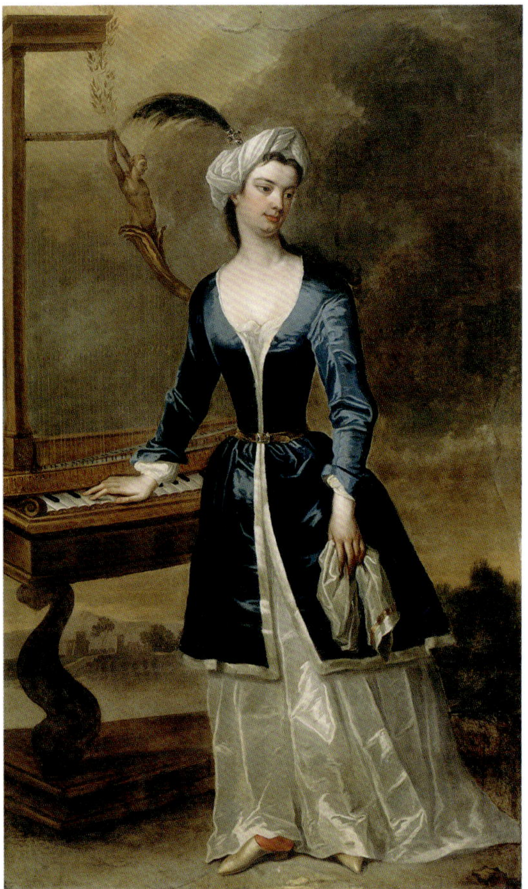

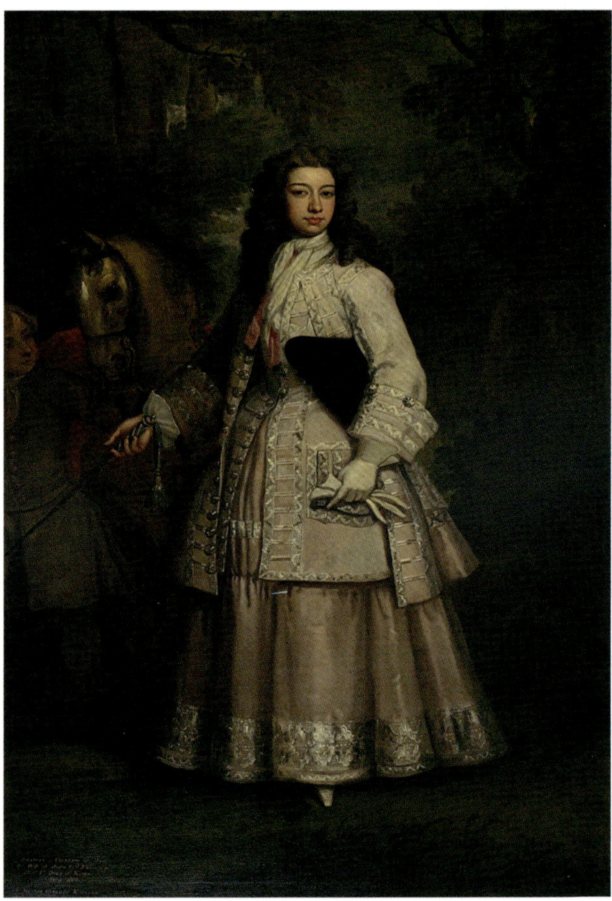

50 Charles Jervas, *Elizabeth, Countess of Bridgewater*, ca. 1710–14, oil on canvas, 215.2 × 125.8 cm, Dublin, National Gallery of Ireland

51 Sir Godfrey Kneller, *Lady Frances Pierrepont, Later Countess of Mar*, ca. 1715, oil on canvas, 228.6 × 152.4 cm, Alloa Tower (National Trust of Scotland)

the Jacobite cause.[18] But Van Dyck's pictorial motifs were by no means extinguished by the emergence of other forms of portraiture in the Georgian period. Rather, over the course of the eighteenth century Van Dyck's legacy appears to split in two. On the one hand, stylistic emulation of the artist endured, and even flourished. On the other, those who embraced the Van Dyckian paradigm of social performance encountered ever more deprecation and scorn within the nascent culture of printed art criticism, itself a response to the phenomenon of the public exhibition. While auctions and exhibitions alienated portraits from their sitters, art criticism increasingly estranged Van Dyck's paintings from the charisma of the artist. Himself an alien, in the sense of foreign-born, Van Dyck was an unsatisfactory founding father for an increasingly self-confident national school. His never-to-be-completed repudiation haunts the art criticism of the eighteenth century.

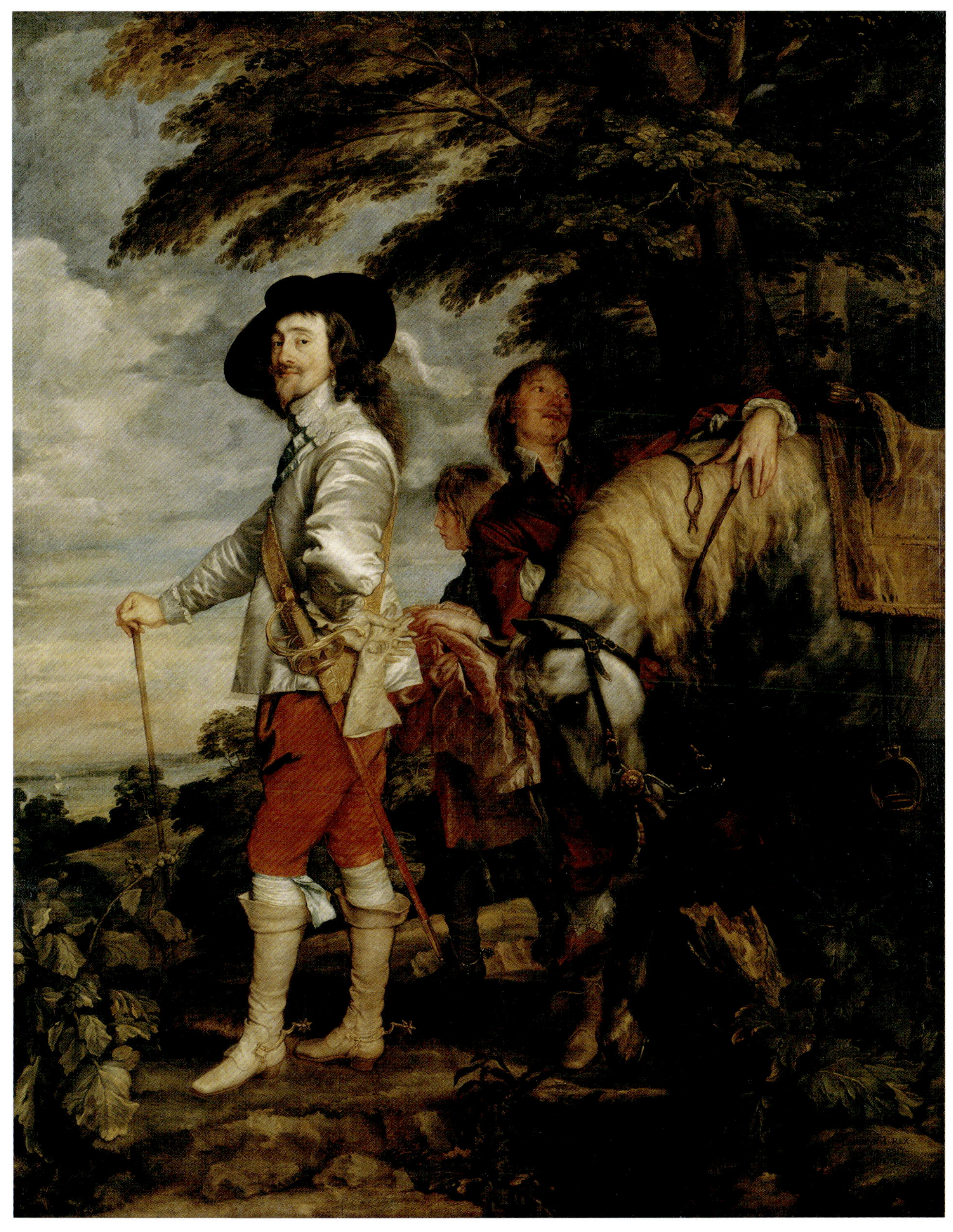

52 Anthony van Dyck, *Charles I at the Hunt* (*"Le Roi à la Chasse"*), ca. 1635, oil on canvas, 266 × 207 cm, Paris, Louvre

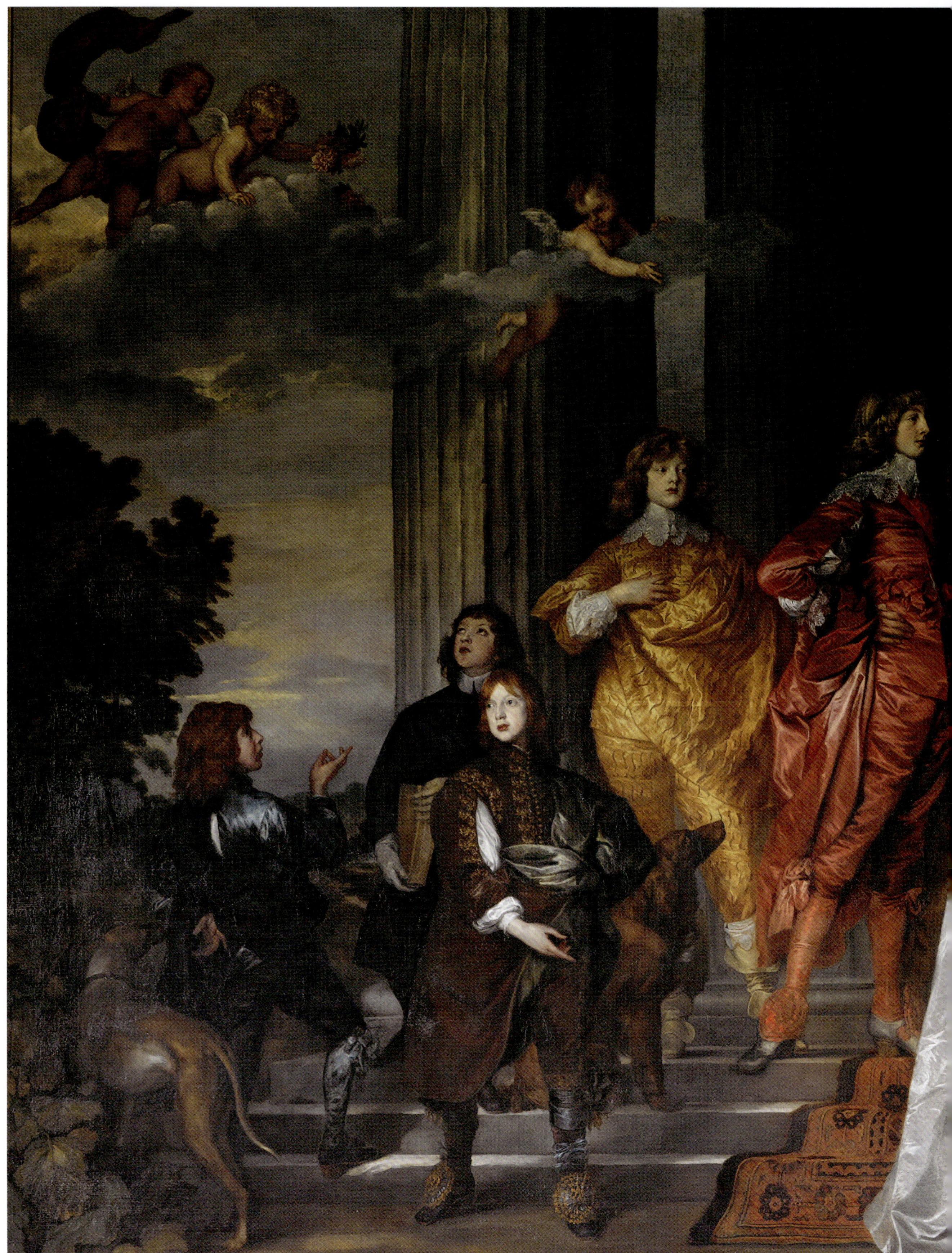

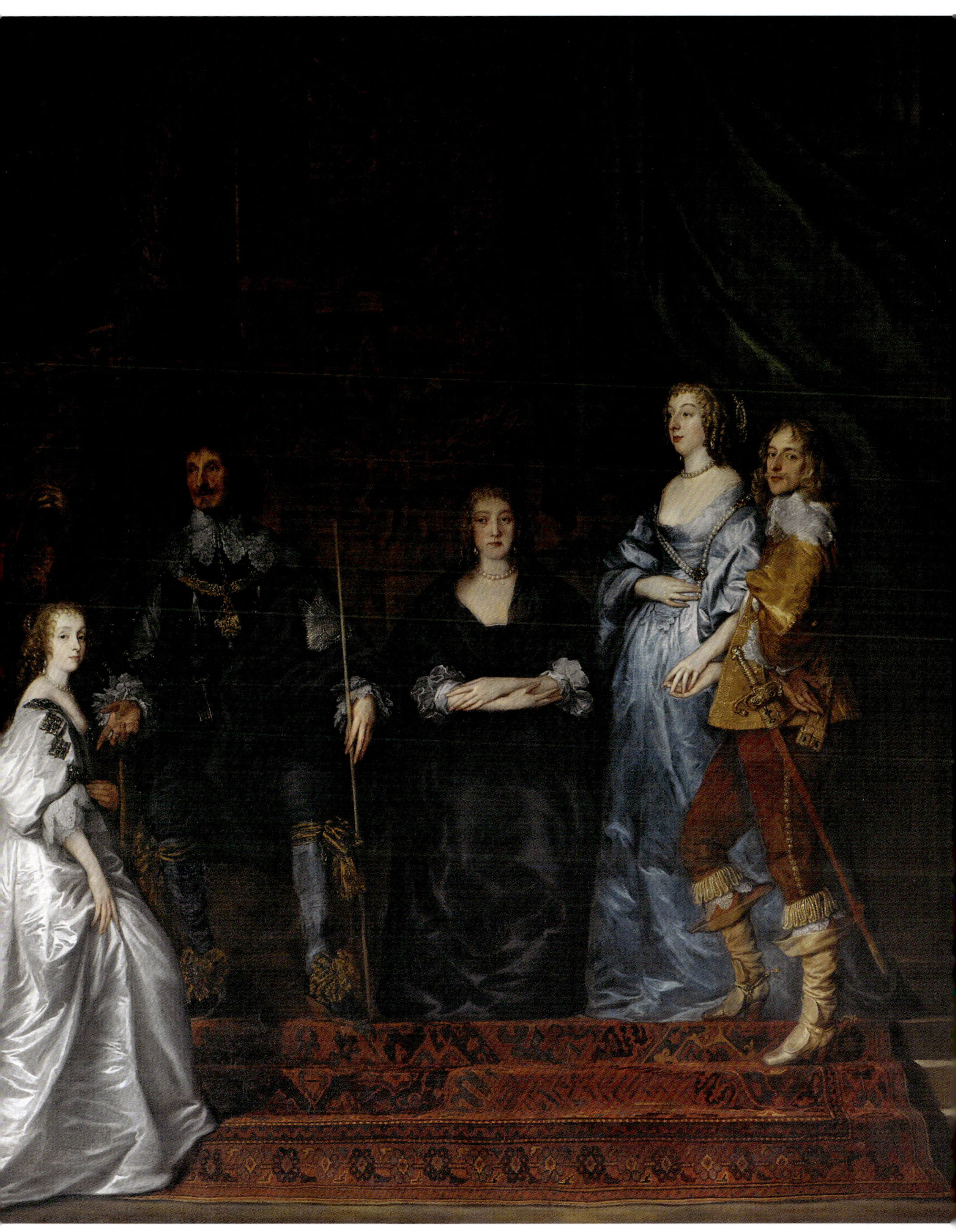

53 Anthony van Dyck, *Philip Herbert, 4th Earl of Pembroke, with His Family*, ca. 1635, oil on canvas, 330 × 510 cm, Salisbury, Wilton House

— "*Fantastic, Apish, Antic*" —

In the series of aesthetic treatises known as the *Second Characters* that he prepared shortly before his death in 1713, the 3rd Earl of Shaftesbury provided an emphatic dismissal of the portraitist's art. According to Shaftesbury, "Face painting being almost the whole of portraiture ... The artist may be and almost ever is ignorant of anatomy, proportions" and other aesthetic precepts. A portraitist "may set up for a painter and [be] great in his way," but Shaftesbury insisted that the genre does not comprise "a liberal art nor [is it] to be so esteemed; as requiring no liberal knowledge, genius, education, converse, manners, moral-science, mathematics, optics, but [is] merely practical and vulgar." Effacing the portrait sittings during which Van Dyckian painters had long displayed their converse and manners, Shaftesbury allied idealist criticism to aristocratic prejudice and declared portraitists to be "not deserving [of the] honour, gentility, [and] knighthood" that leading practitioners had enjoyed in England since Van Dyck's day. Indeed, Shaftesbury named Van Dyck and Lely (both knighted painters) as examples of "genius" that had been "checked and spoilt" by a focus on portraiture.[19]

The terms in which Shaftesbury deprecated portraiture were not original, having long roots in Continental discourse.[20] But Shaftesbury provides a specifically English expression of the hierarchy of genres, grounded in class conflict and a critique of specific paintings by Van Dyck. Indeed, Shaftesbury added a note to his text that provides a scathing account of the artist's more complex, multi-figure compositions [fig. 53]:

> *A portrait painter (as Van Dyck) attempts a family piece, puts figures together in an action, lays a scene, unites, makes a disposition, etc. But this is launching out of his depth. Better a history painter if strongly invited should descend to this work for some great and understanding patron or Prince ... than that the accustomed face-painter should offer to ascend so high as this, in which he will prove an Icarus. For so Van Dyck: fantastic, apish, antic in his action, and wretched and false in his composition.*[21]

Although he does not name Rubens in this passage, Shaftesbury, like so many commentators before and since, may have had him in mind as Van Dyck's foil, a history painter commonly considered to have "descended" to portraiture only at the behest of a "patron or Prince."[22] His discussion also recalls Bellori's description of Maratta's exceptional elevation of portraiture, discussed in Chapter 1, in which high patronage and the inventive disposition of figures ennobled the genre.

The contrast between Shaftesbury's approach to portraiture and that of Jonathan Richardson the Elder from the same decade could scarcely be stronger. Both Shaftesbury and Richardson were interested in the social status of painters and in the question of portraiture's fitness as a vehicle for artistic invention. But Richardson, a working artist, was eager to defend portraiture's narrative and intellectual heft, particularly as practiced by Van Dyck. Modeling his own response to portraiture as both an aesthetic and an affective experience, Richardson provided his readers with one exemplary "Specimen" of the description of portraits in a long passage devoted to Van Dyck's *Frances Bridges, Dowager Countess of Exeter* [fig. 54].[23]

Richardson owned Van Dyck's painting, as well as the artist's preparatory drawing, so that singling out this work advertised his own status as a connoisseur and collector.[24] He began with a formal reading, declaring Van Dyck's composition, built around the "Equilateral Triangle" of the countess's highlighted face and hands, to be "Defective."[25] He then proceeded to the "Admirable Harmony" of other parts of the picture, noting how Van Dyck has "very Artfully broken" the "streight line" of the countess's stomacher "by the Bowes of a Knot of narrow Ribbon."[26] Having "dispatch'd" these formal preliminaries, Richardson was "at liberty to consider" what he termed "the Invention" of the countess's portrait.[27] As he pored over the picture, Richardson felt able to reconstruct the widowed countess's emotional state and relationship to the beholder, deducing from her ungloved hands and other details that Van Dyck's intention had been "that the Lady should be sitting in her Own Room receiving a Visit of Condolance from an Inferiour with great Benignity."[28] Richardson's novelistic description, attuned to the visual encodings of social class, imagines the site of the portrait as the Countess's "Own Room" and projects onto the beholder a specific subordinate relationship to her. But it also recalls the actual encounter between the countess and an inferior that resulted in her portrait: namely, the sitting she granted to Van Dyck.

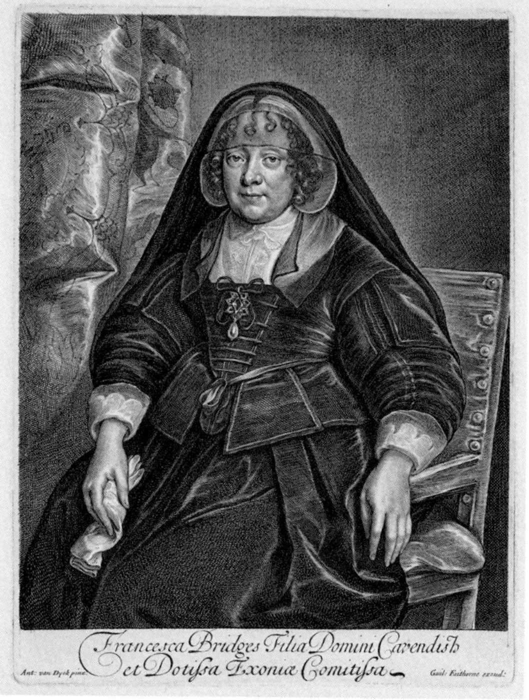

54 William Faithorne, after Anthony van Dyck, *Frances Bridges, Dowager Countess of Exeter*, 1660s, engraving, 28.5 × 21.5 cm, London, British Museum

In asserting the ingenuity of Van Dyck's invention, Richardson attributed to him "not an Insipid Representation of a Face, and Dress," but rather a deeply affecting "Picture of the Mind."[29] With this claim, Richardson took a stance in the debate about portraiture's ability to convey a mind or soul that we have already encountered in, for example, Ben Jonson's response to Van Dyck's portraits of Venetia Digby. Within this debate, Richardson adopted a diametrically opposed position to that of Shaftesbury. Noting that affective response is contingent, operating "More, or Less as my Fancy, Judgment, or other Circumstances happen to be,"[30] the writer made a disarmingly intimate revelation: "There is such a Benignity, such a Decent Sorrow, and Resignation Express'd here, that a Man must be very Insensible that is not the Better for considering it ... But what I confess I am particularly affected with, I who (I thank God) have for many Years been happy as a Husband, is the Circumstance of Widdowhood, Not that it gives Sorrow as remembring the Conjugal Knot must be cut, but I Rejoyce that it Yet subsists."[31]

A great portrait, according to Richardson's reading, prompts beholders not only to position themselves in a social relationship to the depicted, but also engages their emotions with the imagined life of the sitter. This entails an act of empathy, by which the sitter's circumstances are compared to the viewer's own at the time that he or she views the portrait. Himself an English portraitist, Richardson had a particular stake in this elevation of Van Dyck's work; as he noted elsewhere, "When *Van-Dyck* came Hither, he brought *Face-Painting* to Us; ever since which time ... *England* has excell'd all the World in that great Branch of Art."[32] Where Shaftesbury dismissed Van Dyck and his followers as upstart mechanics who flew too close to the sun, Richardson saw Van Dyck as the founding figure of a proud lineage of English portraitists, whose work could and should make intellectual and emotional claims upon the beholder. Nevertheless, he acknowledged that Van Dyck had "brought" his brand of portraiture from elsewhere, that it remained a foreign import.

Van Dyck had also played a key role in Bainbrigg Buckeridge's attempt, discussed in the previous chapter, to formulate an "English school" that could hold its own against Continental traditions. Buckeridge's aims with his essay were explicitly patriotic and entailed a liberal assimilation of foreign-born painters in his attempts to rival the French tradition sketched by Roger de Piles; he declared the English school "more than a match for the *French*; and the *German*, and *Flemish-Schools*, only excel it by the performances of those *Masters* whom we claim as our Own," notably Holbein and Van Dyck.[33] Two factors, according to Buckeridge, distinguished the English tradition: patronage and portraiture. After all, "'twas the Protection and Friendship of the Duke of *Buckingham*, that procur'd [Rubens] the Opportunities he had of distinguishing himself above others of his Contemporaries and Country-Men of the same Profession."[34] Meanwhile, citing the achievements of Isaac Fuller, William Dobson, and Samuel Cooper, Buckeridge asserted that the English "have not only infinitely out-done [the

French] in *Portraits*, but have produc'd more *Masters* in that kind, than all the rest of Europe."[35]

In practical terms, Buckeridge and Richardson's shared vision of an English school defined by excellence in portraiture and the dependence of artists on aristocratic patronage continued to hold sway even as academicism made increasing inroads in England. Shaftesbury's hierarchies were never going to dissuade ambitious young painters from making a living through portraiture, in emulation of the great foreign-born masters Van Dyck, Lely, and Kneller. Nor would erudite art criticism discourage the expanding clientele for commissioned likenesses. But whatever its limited consequences for artistic practice, Shaftesbury's critique fed into a growing unease about the intellectual status of portraiture that reflected the absorption of idealist theories like Bellori's into English artistic discourse and that explains the subtle defensiveness of Richardson's text. At the same time, changing social norms and gender ideals meant that the practices of fashion, flattery, and self-display that had secured the Van Dyckian painter's elevation at court increasingly came to seem alien and effeminate to patriotic defenders of the "English school." The Van Dyckian paradigm continued to exert a powerful hold on artists looking to shape their careers and public personae as expressions of self-ennoblement. But those who did so faced an ever-greater risk of critical opprobrium.

Art writers and artists who opposed the Van Dyckian paradigm needed to find different models for an ambitious career. Heroic history painting remained the most lauded academic ideal, but in eighteenth-century England success also increasingly meant embracing a vision of the artist as proudly commercial, emphatically English, and unimpeachably masculine.[36] No one embodied this threat to the Van Dyckian tradition better than William Hogarth, the artist who more than any other has functioned as the founding father for nationalist narratives of British art.[37] Hogarth's conflicted relationship to Van Dyck provides a leitmotif in both his portraits and his writings, as well as his earliest biography, published by John Nichols in 1785. For example, Nichols tells the following story about the artist's studio at Leicester Fields:

> Hogarth *made one essay in sculpture. He wanted a sign to distinguish his house in* Leicester-fields; *and thinking none more proper than the* Golden Head, *he, out of a mass of cork made up of several thicknesses compacted together, carved a bust of* Vandyck, *which he gilt and placed over his door. It is long since decayed, and was succeeded by a head in plaster, which has also perished; and is supplied by a head of Sir* Isaac Newton. Hogarth *modelled another resemblance of* Vandyck *in clay; which is likewise destroyed.*[38]

Nichols records a sequence of ephemeral works made for purposes of self-promotion. The first of these, a mass of gilded cork, sounds a distinctly Hogarthian note of deceptive surface refinement. Even more striking, however, is Hogarth's choice of Van Dyck as the figurehead for his studio. As has been made clear, Van Dyck provided *the* standard by which ambitious English portraitists measured themselves in the century prior to Hogarth's move to Leicester Fields in 1733. Yet the potential note of satire in Hogarth's display of Van Dyck as a shop sign – apparently interchangeable with a head of Sir Isaac Newton – aligns with the ambivalent attitude toward his predecessor that Hogarth expressed in both his art and his critical writings.

Another of John Nichols's studio anecdotes captures Hogarth's self-positioning as an antitype of Van Dyckian politesse. According to the biographer, early in his career Hogarth was tasked with portraying "a nobleman, who was uncommonly ugly and deformed." Hogarth portrayed him skillfully "but the likeness was rigidly observed, without even the necessary attention to compliment or flattery." The nobleman, "disgusted," refused payment. Hogarth then informed the nobleman that he intended to add "a tail ... and some other little appendages" to the portrait in order to sell it to "the famous wild-beast man" for exhibition as a curiosity. Needless to say, Hogarth's threat resulted in prompt payment of his outstanding fee.[39]

Van Dyck's eighteenth-century biographers also told stories of his impudent quips to high-born patrons. But Nichols's account is important for the link it makes between Hogarth's assertiveness toward his betters and the artist's refusal to practice "compliment or flattery" within portraiture. A defining feature of the Van Dyckian mode, flattery also aligned with idealist aesthetics. But as Hogarth increasingly attained the status of founding father to a native-born English school, the flattering portrait became ever more suspect. The portraitist as a disrespecter of persons surfaced as a new ideal for one segment of patriotic art critics.

For all that his bluff and chauvinistic manner makes him appear the opposite of the smooth and cosmopolitan Van Dyck, Hogarth had a far more complicated relationship with the old master's legacy than his social persona and biography would imply. Not only did he advertise his studio by hanging the golden head of Van Dyck as a shop sign, but he also painted a copy of the earlier artist's portrait of Inigo Jones, an alternative founding father for an English tradition in the visual arts.[40] In *The Analysis of Beauty*, Hogarth described Van Dyck as "one of the best portrait painters in most respects ever known," but lamented his lack of a systematic approach to the depiction of beauty, declaring that "there seems not to be the least grace in his pictures more than what the life chanced to bring before him."[41]

Hogarth's description of Van Dyck as a mere ape of nature, unable to assimilate chance appearances to an aesthetic system, presents a surprising moment of agreement between Hogarth and the connoisseurial class represented by Shaftesbury. Hogarth's critique of Van Dyck also distinguished him from other portraitists, like Richardson, who saw in Van Dyck's life and art the potential for their own elevation. Perhaps responding to Richardson's ekphrasis of the Countess of Exeter's portrait, Hogarth declared another female portrait by the artist, that of Jane, Lady Wharton, to be "thoroughly divested of every elegance" and symptomatic of the painter's inability to improve upon natural imperfection [fig. 55].[42] This portrait, known to Hogarth through a print by Pieter van Gunst, is a typical production of Van Dyck's late English period that places his full-length female sitter in a garden or on a terrace, the background bisected by a blank wall. Hogarth's claim that Van Dyck merely imitated nature coexists uneasily with the portrait's highly polished artifice. Plucking roses from a potted bush, Lady Wharton extends both of her arms in a mannered, cradling gesture. Moreover, the portrait assimilates its sitter to a prototype that Van Dyck had recycled in multiple portraits. Hogarth's insistence on Van Dyck's artlessness, his mere copying of whatever graces the sitter brought to his studio, provides not so much an accurate account of Lady Wharton's portrait as a gesture of rivalrous erasure. Indeed, Hogarth's claim to originality in conforming his figures to the "line of beauty" elides the long history of elegant poses in English portraiture.

At the same time that he criticized Van Dyck in his theoretical writings, Hogarth's autobiographical fragments make clear that he considered the painter to be a yardstick against which to measure his own ambitions.[43] Summoning his youthful frustration with the lack of recognition given to native-born English painters, Hogarth recalled: "about 20 years agoe being perswaded in my mind that I could paint a portrait as well (not to mince the matter) ... [as] vandike my query [to] all the painters then at the [St. Martin's Lane] academy ... was whether a man could get it ackno[w]ledg[ed] in his life[. T]he unanimouss answer was positively no."[44]

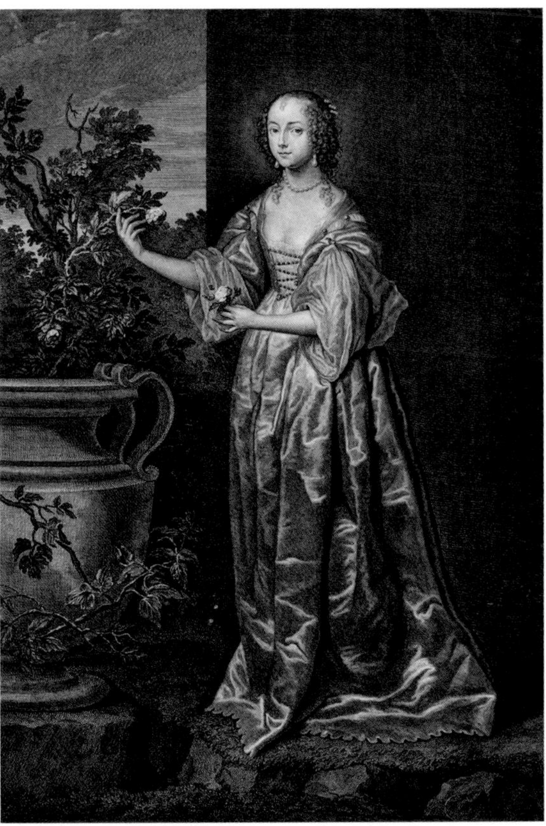

55 Pieter van Gunst, after Van Dyck, *Jane, Lady Wharton*, ca. 1713–15, engraving, 50.5 × 30.5 cm, London, British Museum

In the highly ambitious portraits of the early 1740s, in which Hogarth attempted to vie with Van Dyck and assert the achievements of the contemporary English school, his agonistic relationship to Van Dyck's legacy is everywhere in evidence. Celebrated as an unvarnished icon of the commercial class, Hogarth's *Captain Thomas Coram* is also a refashioning of Charles I in the "Greate Peece," Van Dyck's first royal commission [figs. 56 and 57]. Hogarth extracted the king's pose, identifying him as the father of the nation, for his own image of the benevolent creator of the Foundling Hospital.[45]

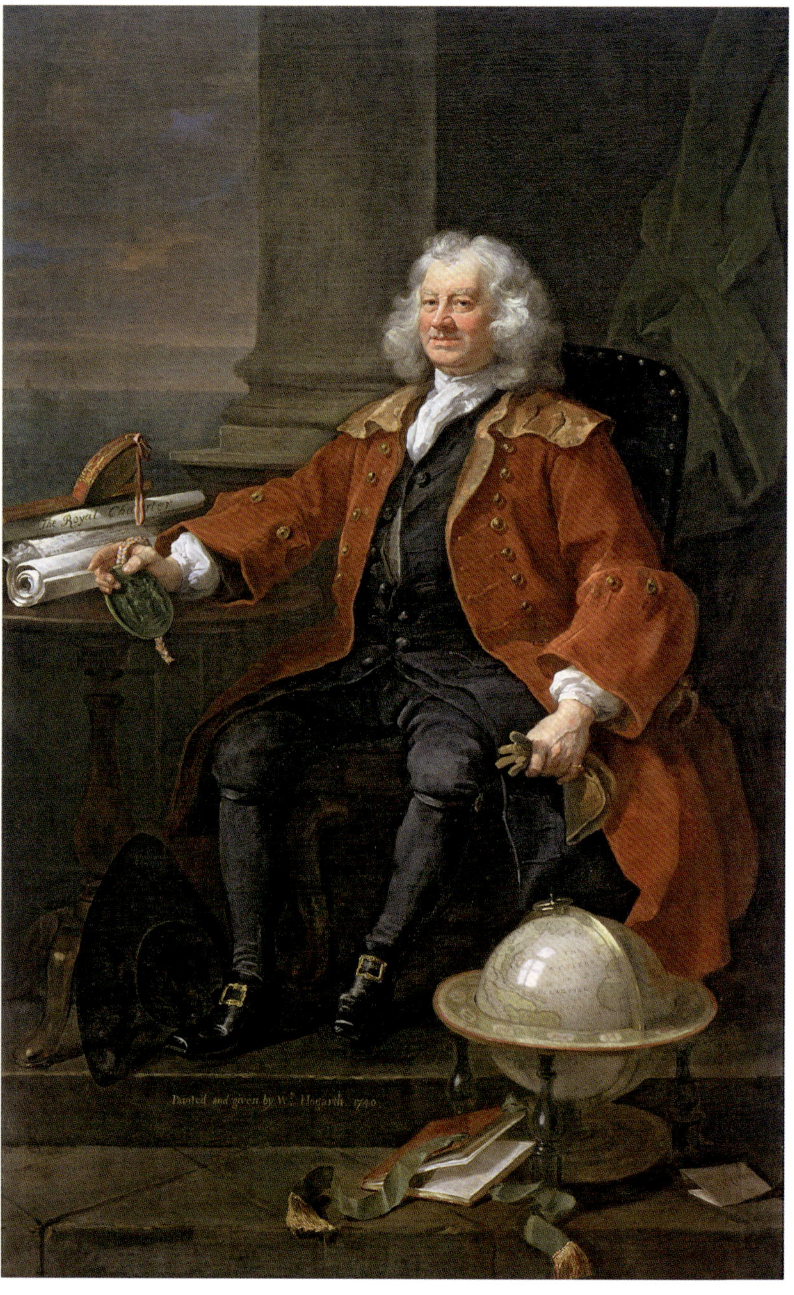

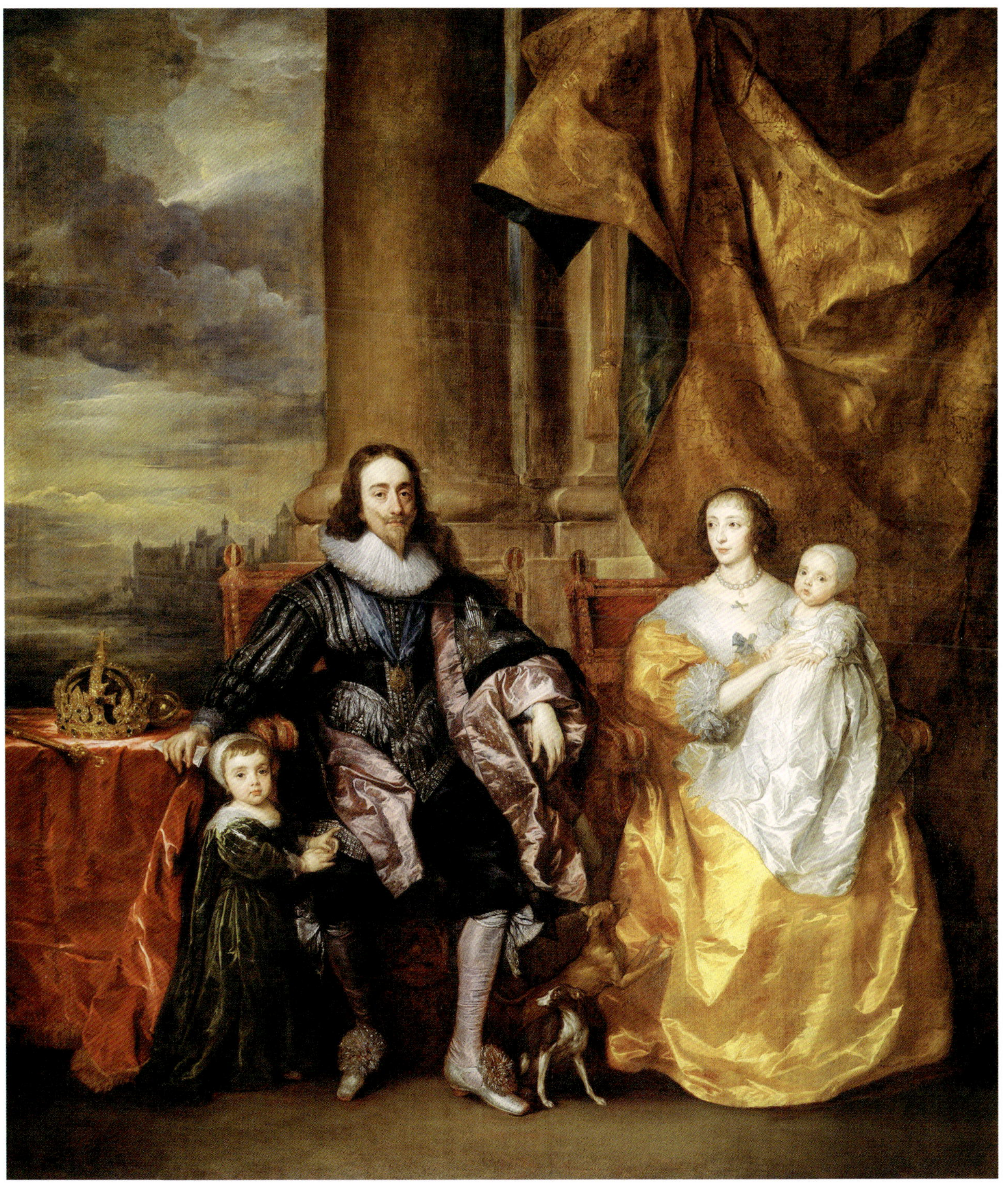

56 William Hogarth, *Captain Thomas Coram*, 1740, oil on canvas, 238.7 × 147.3 cm, London, Foundling Hospital

57 Anthony van Dyck, *Charles I and Henrietta Maria with Their Two Eldest Children, Prince Charles and Princess Mary*, 1632, oil on canvas, 303.8 × 256.5 cm, Royal Collection

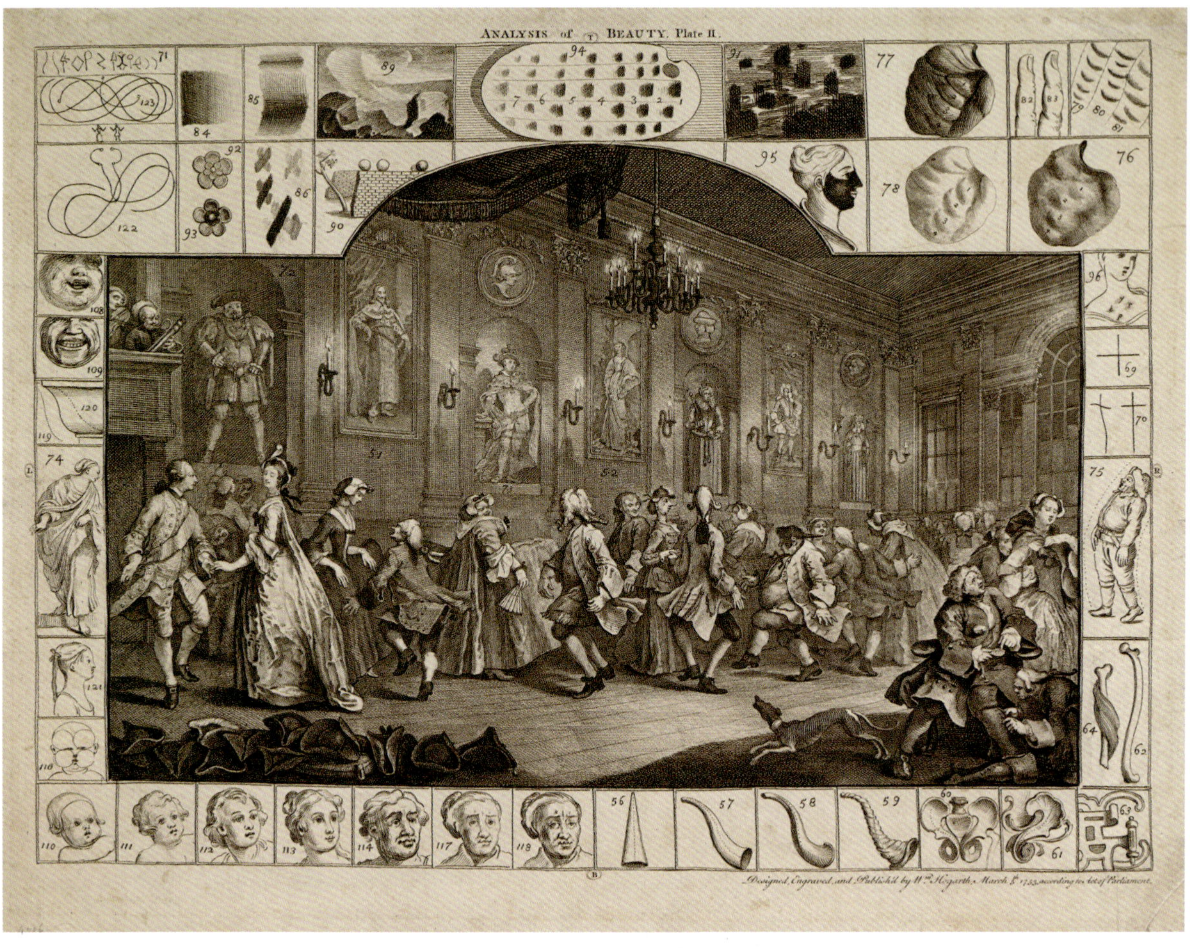

58 William Hogarth, Plate Two from *The Analysis of Beauty*, 1753, engraving, third state, 42.5 × 53.5 cm, New York, Metropolitan Museum of Art

Hogarth provided a further meditation on the history of English royal portraiture within *The Analysis of Beauty*. In the book's second plate, a riotous dance takes place in a ballroom hung with a sequence of portraits ranging from a Holbein-inspired Henry VIII to two Van Dycks, a late seventeenth-century portrait in the manner of Kneller, and a series of sculpted images [fig. 58]. In the text, Hogarth makes clear that these "statues and pictures" are meant to serve as an "illustration" by contrasting with the twirling, stomping bodies on the dance floor. Thus "Henry viii ... makes a perfect X with his legs and arms; and the position of Charles the first ... is composed of less-varied lines than the statue of Edward the sixth."[46] In other words, Hogarth demotes iconic images of royalty by his foreign-born predecessors to mere waystations in an evolutionary narrative. Within this sequence, his own art of unbridled embodiment represents a joyous climax.

Hogarth's most ambitious independent likeness of a female sitter, the portrait of Mary Edwards, sheds further light on his efforts to distinguish himself from Van

Dyck's precedent and to articulate an alternative model for English portraiture [fig. 59].[47] Individual components of the heiress's portrait – the dog and pearls, drapery and sculpture – might all recall earlier images of elite women such as Van Dyck's *Anne Kirke*. But Hogarth's composition, which crops Edwards's skirts just below the knee, brings the viewer face to face with the sitter in an encounter of cozy intimacy totally alien to Van Dyck's portraits. The sitter's gaze is similarly frank and engaging, her wide mouth just curling into a smile. Moreover, Hogarth insisted on the Englishness of his portrait by placing his sitter alongside busts of Queen Elizabeth I and King Alfred, with one of Elizabeth's most famous speeches inscribed on the sheet of paper next to Miss Edwards. Whereas artists from Lely to Kneller had reached back to a Van Dyckian pose or gesture to anchor their portraits in a prestigious lineage, Hogarth emphasized his textual relation to the English past, promoting his portraits as a new beginning for a national art. At the same time, Mary Edwards's scandalous marital career allied Hogarth's work with a raffish social celebrity very different from the idealized aristocratic femininity of Van Dyck's portraits.

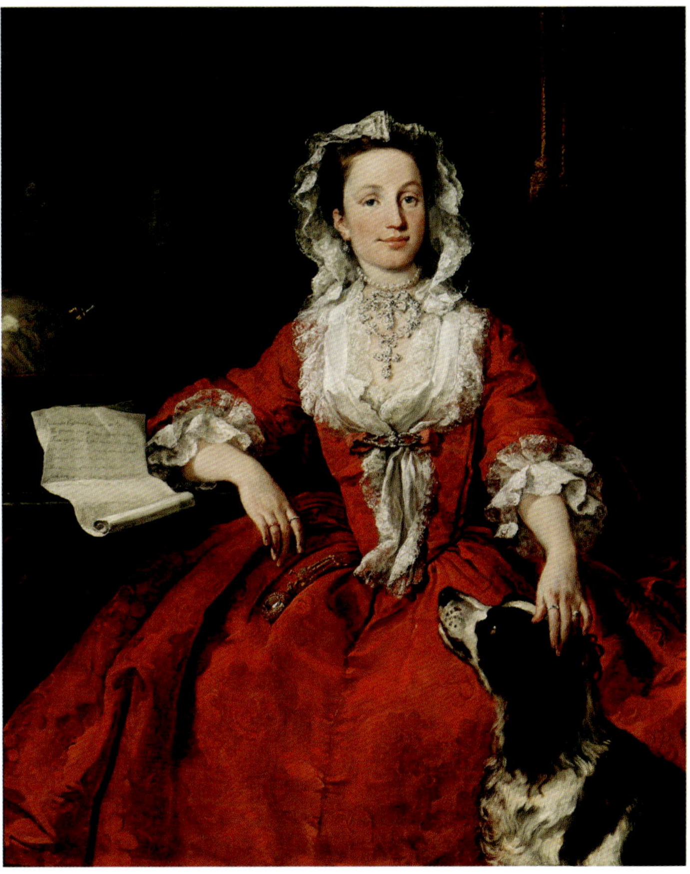

59 William Hogarth, *Mary Edwards*, 1742, oil on canvas, 126.4 × 101.3 cm, New York, Frick Collection

In his most famous self-portrait, Hogarth made explicit his roots in an English tradition that was primarily literary, not visual [fig. 60].[48] Hogarth began the portrait by depicting himself in a wig, as a traditional statement of status and self-confidence. Gradually, however, he replaced this with an informal cap and constructed an elaborately self-referential image, in which a painting-within-a-painting rests on bound leather volumes of Shakespeare, Milton, and Swift. The portrait promotes Hogarth as the dealer in home truths who has blossomed out of a vernacular literary culture and finally shaped a visual language of equal accomplishment.[49] As the previous chapters have shown, this English literary tradition consistently had an ambivalent, if not outright hostile, attitude to the visual arts in general and foreign-born portraitists in particular. Hogarth's foundational status within narratives of English art rests on this Oedipal dismantling of Van Dyckian precedent.

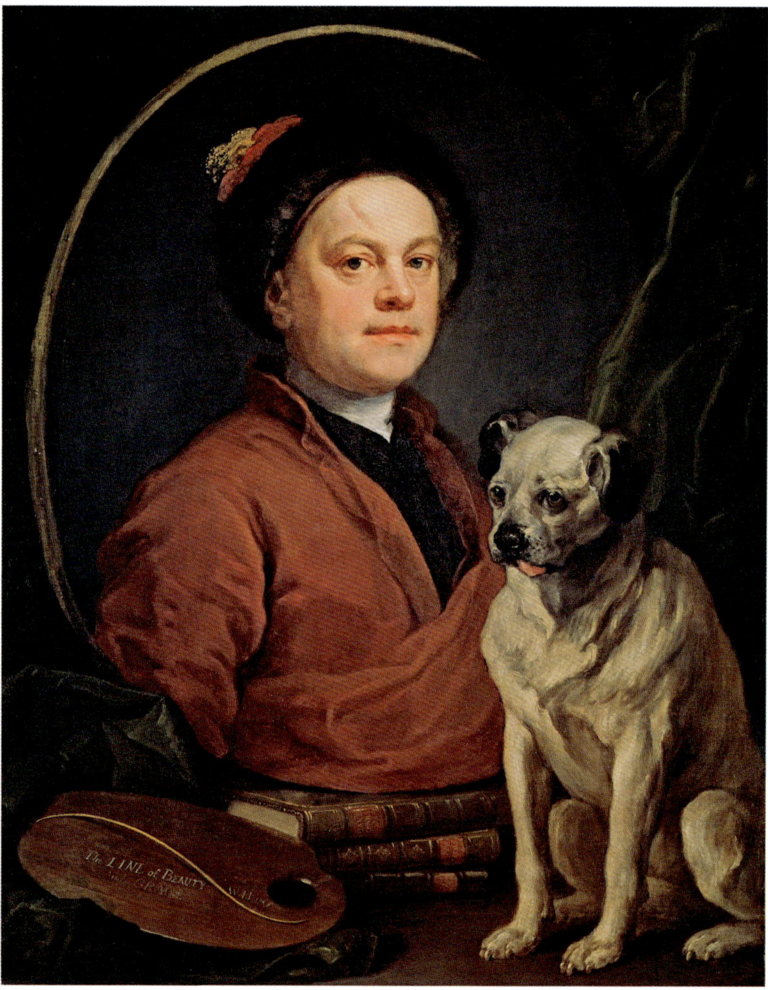

60 William Hogarth, *The Painter and His Pug*, 1745, oil on canvas, 90 × 69.9 cm, London, Tate

— *A Dynastic Art* —

Even as critiques like Shaftesbury's and Hogarth's dented Van Dyck's reputation among cognoscenti, collecting practices and dynastic politics solidified his stature as a particularly English kind of "old master." As noted in the previous chapters, the Civil War launched Van Dyck's portraits onto the open market as circulating commodities. At the same time, the post-Restoration recovery of many portraits by royal and aristocratic collectors reinforced these portraits' status as markers of continuity with an increasingly idealized past. Borne on successive waves of alienation and recovery, they acquired a powerful cultural charge. While Charles II or the Duke of Newcastle reclaimed a Van Dyckian birthright that they had lost in their youth, other, newer elites acquired Van Dyck portraits to manufacture a lineage or express aesthetic discernment. This tension between a dynastic and an aesthetic relationship to Van Dyck quickly came to a head on the art market. In 1678, for example, Sir Ralph Verney spent £30 on a portrait of his father, who had been killed at the Battle of Edgehill, beating out collectors who coveted the painting "for noe other reason, But because it was don by Vandike."[50]

Circulating on the market and in printed reproduction, Van Dyck's portraits came to function as the definitive pictorial record of the Caroline past.[51] Defenders of portraiture might cite this historical function to enhance the genre's prestige. As Richardson wrote, "*Painting* gives us not only the persons, but the Characters of Great Men ... Let a Man read a Character in my Lord *Clarendon*['s history of the Civil War] ... he will find it improv'd, by seeing a Picture of the same Person by *Van Dyck*."[52] Indeed, Clarendon had furnished his London mansion, when Lord Chancellor, with Van Dyck portraits, given to him by those eager, in John Evelyn's words, "to make their Court by such Presents."[53] Families that had been ennobled in the wake of the Restoration or Glorious Revolution had a particular interest in the Van Dyckian mode as a way of papering over obscure origins or conflicted relationships with the Stuart dynasty. In some cases, as with the dukes of Marlborough, this dynastic engagement with Van Dyckian portraiture could extend over the course of two centuries.

In a letter dated June 7, 1734, for example, Sarah, the dowager Duchess of Marlborough, informed her granddaughter that she wished to have Isaac Whood paint portraits of the latter and her husband, the Duke of Bedford. The duke was to appear in his "coronation robes," the duchess in the "white satin clothes and the posture" of "that picture that was done by Vandyke for that charming Countess of Bedford."[54] With these stipulations, the dowager duchess made clear that she wanted portraits that would emphasize the status of her granddaughter and her granddaughter's husband, who came from more venerably aristocratic stock than her own. In the duke's case, coronation robes would broadcast his rank, but the duchess's portrait was to provide a somewhat subtler pedigree by emulating her husband's elegant great-grandmother (and a painting from his family collection).[55]

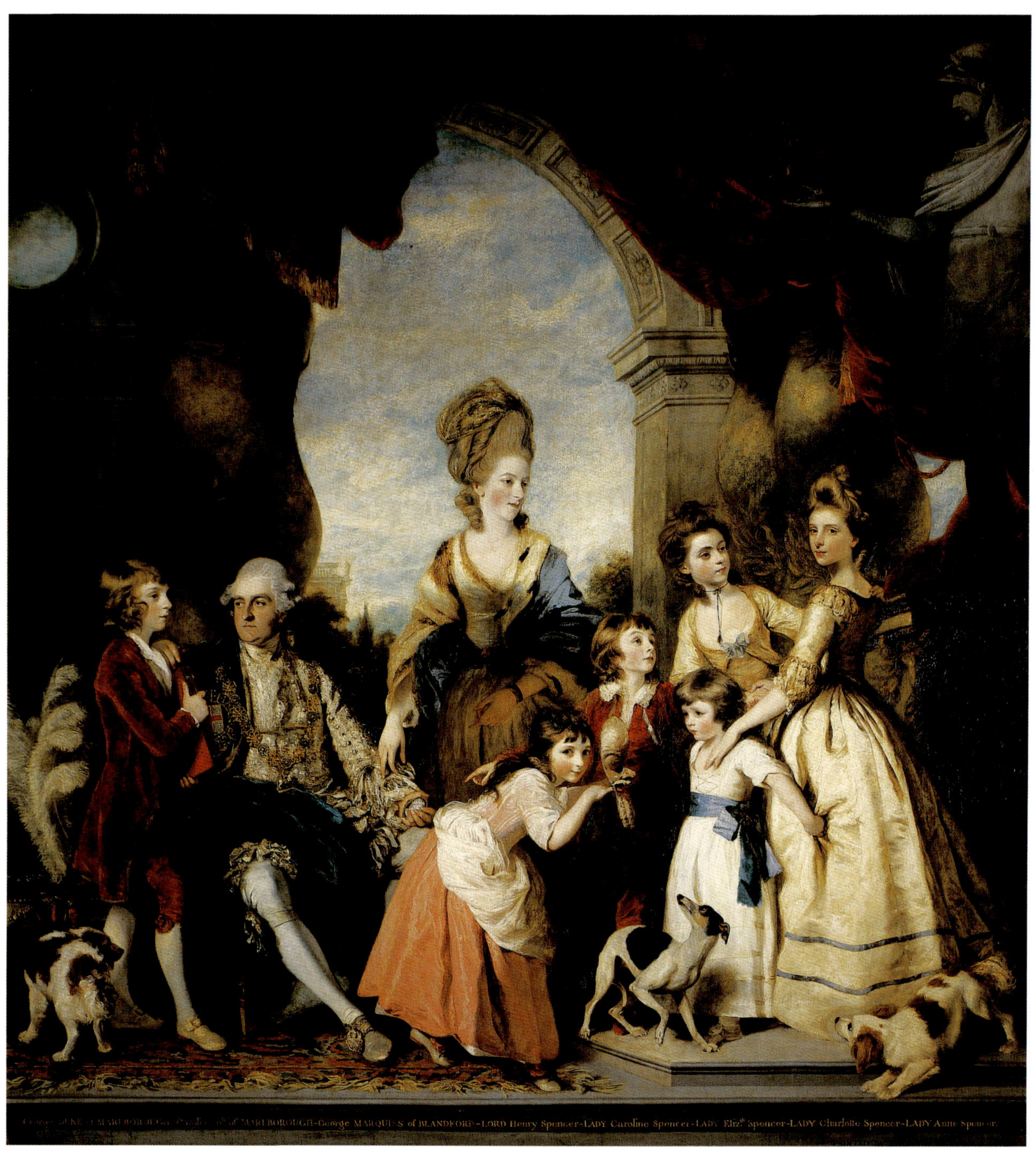

61 Joshua Reynolds, *The 4th Duke of Marlborough and His Family*, ca. 1777–78, oil on canvas, 318 × 289 cm, Woodstock, Blenheim Palace

62 Anthony van Dyck, *Katherine, Duchess of Buckingham, with Her Children*, ca. 1633, oil on canvas, 250 × 196 cm, Antwerp, Rubenshuis

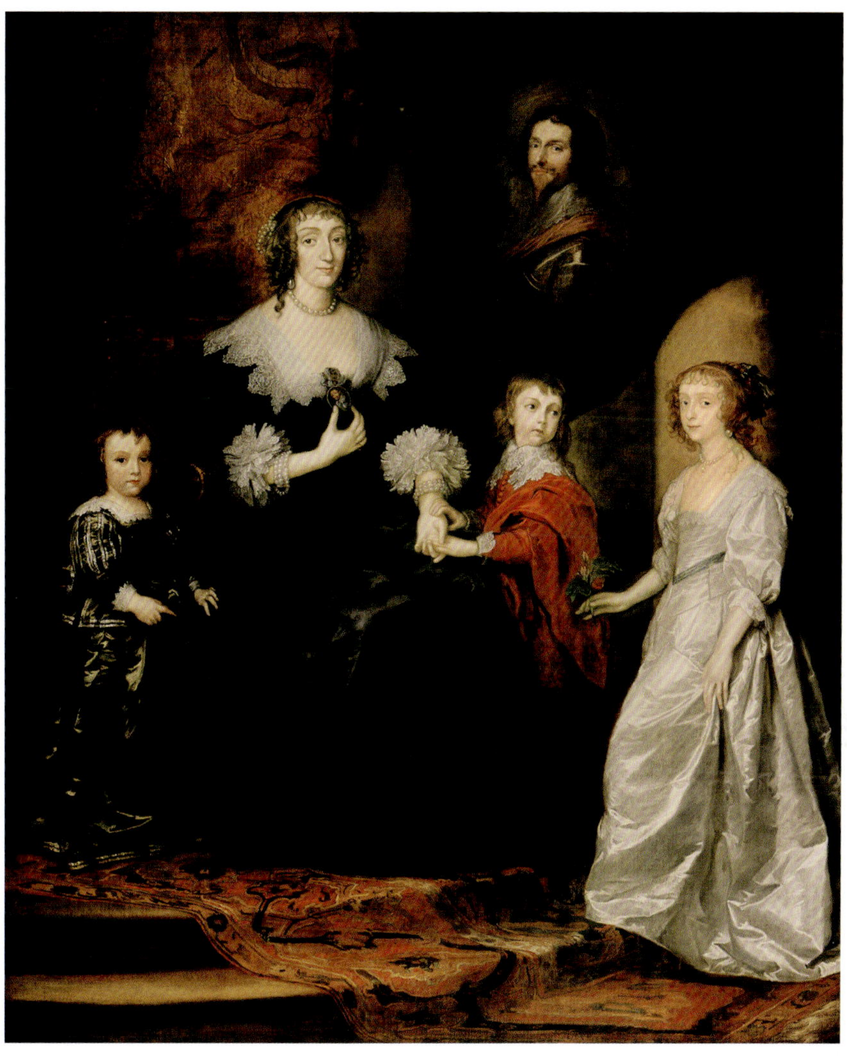

Subsequent generations of the family returned to Van Dyckian precedent, particularly the dynastic group portraits that had so disgusted the Earl of Shaftesbury. In one celebrated example, the fourth duke commissioned a monumental family portrait from Reynolds that responded to Van Dyck's painting of the widowed Duchess of Buckingham and her children, which hung close by at Blenheim [figs. 61 and 62].[56] As revealed in his commonplace book, the young Reynolds had been an avid reader of Richardson, noting to himself the precept, "Van Dyck's model to be follow'd."[57] The mature artist's continued self-positioning as the heir to Van Dyck was lost neither on critics who praised the Marlborough portrait nor on those who condemned it; while the *Public Advertiser* described the Marlborough portrait as "perhaps the best Piece of Portrait Painting, that has been produced since the Days of Vandycke," the *Morning Post* derided Reynolds's "servile imitation of [Van Dyck's] draperies."[58]

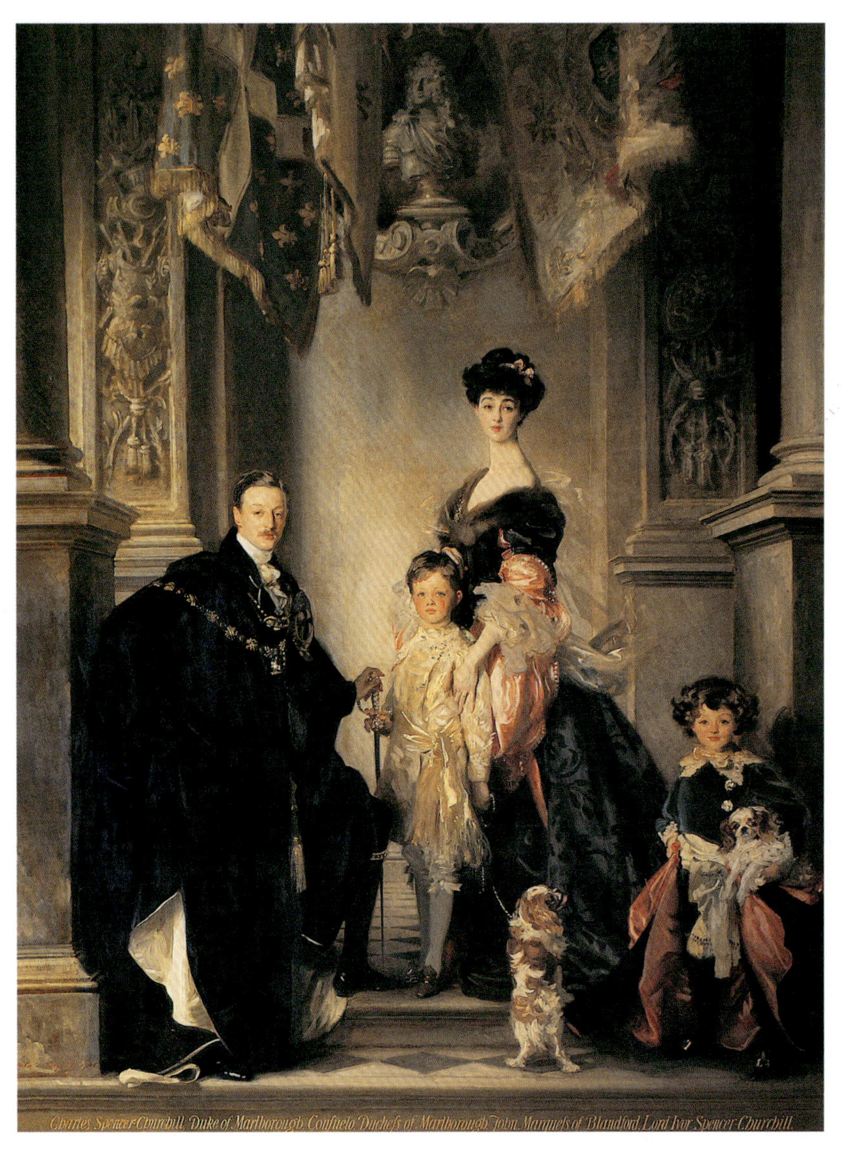
Charles Spencer-Churchill, Duke of Marlborough, Consuelo, Duchess of Marlborough, John, Marquess of Blandford, Lord Ivor Spencer-Churchill

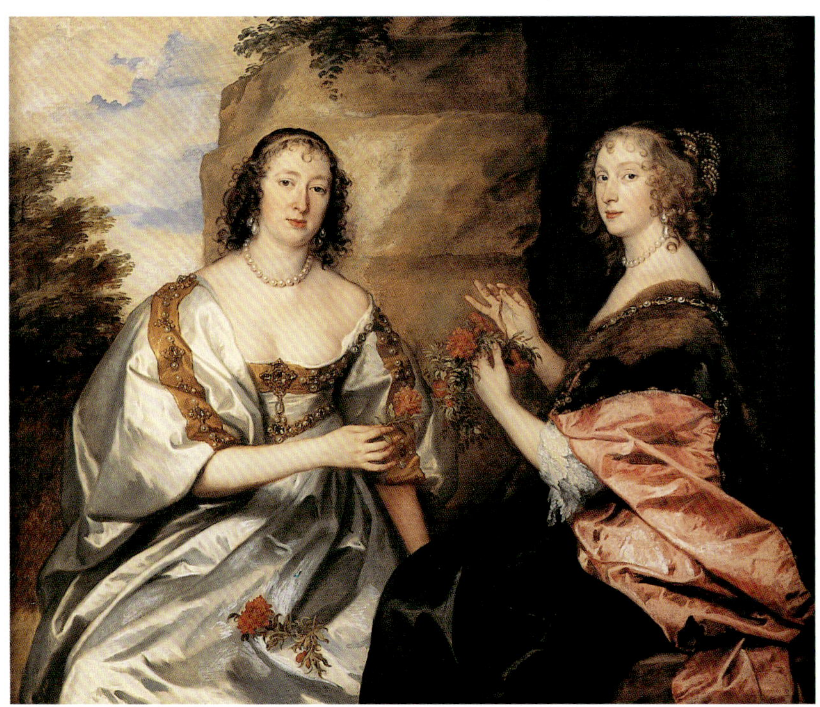

Almost 130 years later, the ninth duke commissioned a pendant to Reynolds's portrait from John Singer Sargent that brought the family's embrace of Van Dyckian dynastic imagery into the twentieth century [fig. 63].[59] In addition to arranging the family members on a tiered set of steps that recalls Van Dyck's Pembroke family portrait, Sargent made a further explicit citation in the form of the duchess's costume. The juxtaposition of fur, black silk, and rose-colored satin derived from a double portrait by Van Dyck hanging in Blenheim's Red Drawing Room [fig. 64].[60] The Marlborough family group may have cemented Sargent's reputation as "the American Van Dyck," but it inevitably further linked Van Dyckian emulation with hopeless political and aesthetic conservatism.[61] Indeed, no institution has been more associated with the collecting, display, and study of Van Dyck's portraits than the British Royal Collection, whether in the eighteenth century or today. The prominence of his portraits within the royal palaces largely stems from their dynastic function, but by the mid-eighteenth century, as genealogical ties to Charles I became more tenuous and cultural memory of the Civil War more distant, an aesthetic rediscovery of Van Dyck becomes apparent in court circles as well.

In his memoirs, for example, Lord Hervey recounts a domestic dispute between George II and Queen Caroline in which two paintings by Van Dyck played a central role:

> *In the absence of the King, the Queen had taken several very bad pictures out of the great drawing-room at Kensington* [Palace], *and put very good ones in their places. The King, affecting, for the sake of contradiction, to dislike this change, or, from his extreme ignorance in painting, really disapproving it, told Lord Hervey … that he would have every new picture taken away, and every old one replaced. Lord Hervey, who had a mind to make his court to the Queen by opposing this order, asked if His Majesty would not give leave for the two Vandykes, at least, on each side of the chimney to remain, instead of those two sign-posts, done by nobody knew who, that had been removed to make way for them. To which the King answered, "My Lord, I have a great respect for your taste in what you understand, but in pictures I beg leave to follow my own. I suppose you assisted the Queen with your fine advice when she was pulling my house to pieces and spoiling all my furniture … As for the Vandykes, I do not care whether they are changed or no."*[62]

Here, aesthetic appreciation of Van Dyck marks Hervey as belonging to the camp of the intelligent and sophisticated queen; the king's indifference to the artist, by contrast, is characteristically boorish and old-fashioned. The actual identities of Van Dyck's sitters are so unimportant as to go unmentioned by Hervey. What matters is Van Dyck's status as a byword for courtly good taste.

63 John Singer Sargent, *The 9th Duke of Marlborough with His Family*, 1905, oil on canvas, 332.7 × 238.8 cm, Woodstock, Blenheim Palace

64 Anthony van Dyck, *Mary, Lady Killigrew, and an Unknown Woman (Mrs. Morton?)*, ca. 1638, oil on canvas, 127 × 145.5 cm, Woodstock, Blenheim Palace

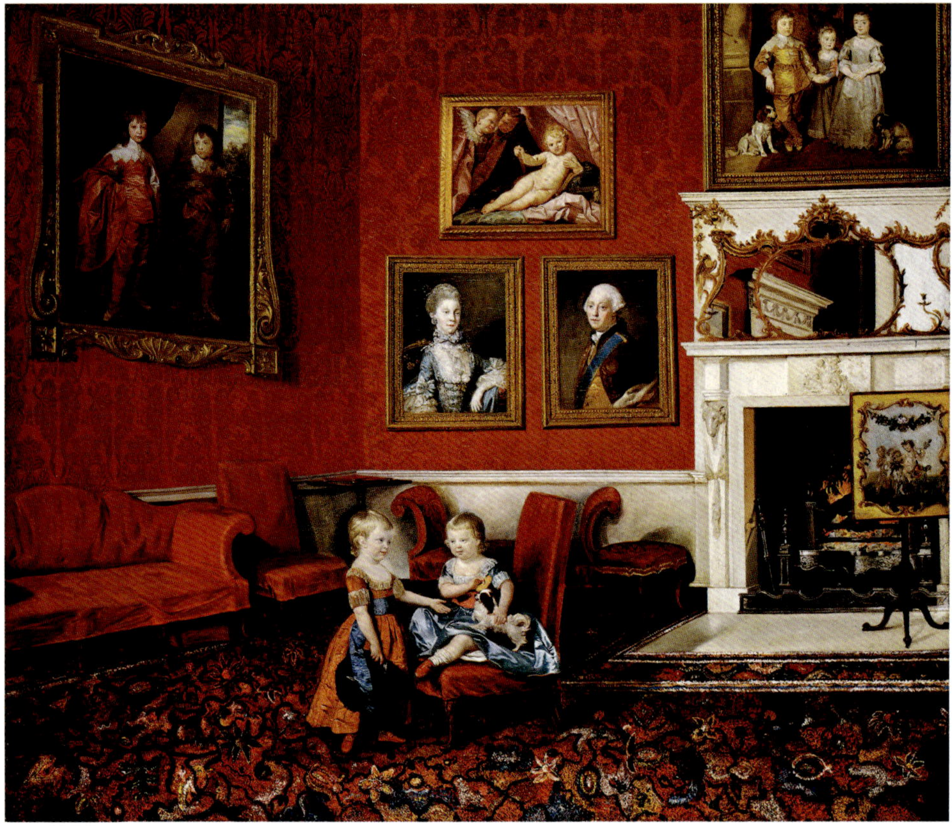

65 Johan Zoffany, *George, Prince of Wales, and Frederick, later Duke of York, at Buckingham House*, 1765, oil on canvas, 111.9 × 127.9 cm, Royal Collection

In their own portraiture and display practices, George III and Queen Charlotte both embraced Van Dyck, acquiring the artist's portraits and posing numerous times in Van Dyck dress.[63] A more complex staging of the artist's legacy occurs in Johan Zoffany's conversation piece depicting the royal couple's two eldest sons in the Queen's Second Drawing Room at Buckingham House [fig. 65]. Here, the two young boys, not yet breeched, appear as small figures within the overwhelming crimson interior, its walls hung with paintings. Of these, three appear to be Zoffany's own invention, flanked by two real portraits of children by Van Dyck [fig. 66].[64] The portrait on the left, depicting George Villiers, 2nd Duke of Buckingham, and his brother, Lord Francis Villiers, both rhymes with and threatens to overshadow the two young princes below. With this metapictorial inclusion, Zoffany staged a history of the English royal portrait that emphasized the modernity of his own approach and, implicitly, the antiquated nature of Van Dyck's. Compared with the tenderness of the young princes' interaction, the Villiers boys look like stiffly miniaturized adults. The genealogy of the English royal portrait that Zoffany proposes presents Van Dyck less as an endlessly renewable prototype than as a collectible artifact of the distant past.[65] In doing so,

Zoffany most likely had Hogarth's ballroom from *The Analysis of Beauty* in mind; as Ronald Paulson has written, "It is the Hogarthian room that lies behind Zoffany's royal conversations."[66]

Even while they provoked aesthetic critique, the display of Van Dyck's portraits at the royal palaces contributed to their continued cultural visibility, prompting, for example, Reynolds to a defense of the artist. In one of his articles for Samuel Johnson's *Idler*, Reynolds recounted a visit to Hampton Court in the company of a "connoisseur ... his mouth full of nothing but the grace of Raffaelle, the purity of Domenichino ... with all the rest of the cant of criticism."[67] As the artist and his pedantic companion "were passing through the rooms," Reynolds pointed out "a whole length of Charles the first, by Vandyke, as a perfect representation of the character as well as the figure of the man." In doing so, Reynolds reprised Richardson's praise for Van Dyck's portraits as both artworks and historical records. Reynolds's companion "agreed [that the portrait] was very fine, but it wanted spirit and contrast, and had not the flowing line, without which a figure could not possibly be graceful."[68] The inclusion of the "flowing line" reads as an intentional dig at Hogarth's attempts at aesthetic systematization through "the line of beauty." In his dismissal of Van Dyck's portraits, Hogarth appears to have struck Reynolds as a homegrown connoisseur whose fatuousness rivaled that of Continental academicians.

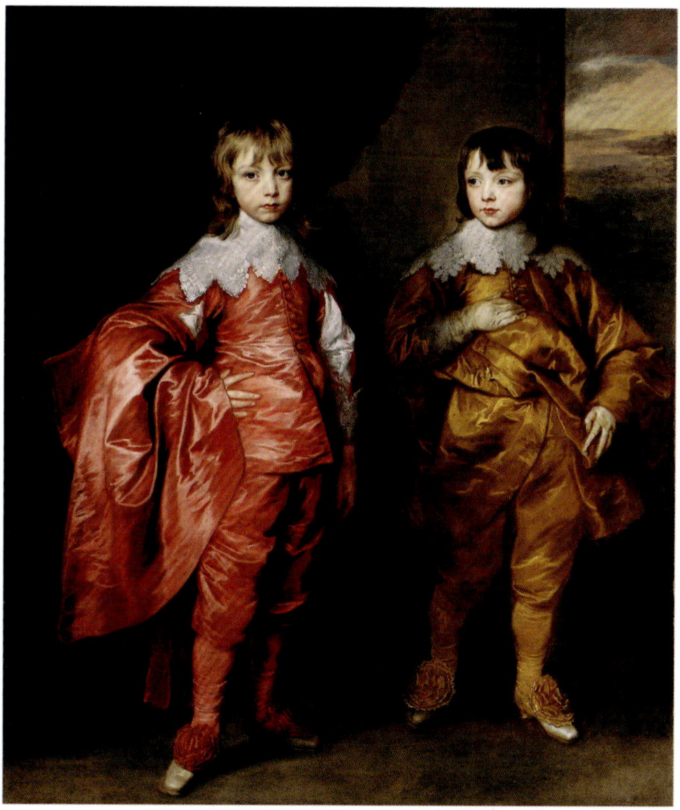

66 Anthony van Dyck, *George Villiers, 2nd Duke of Buckingham, and Lord Francis Villiers*, 1635, oil on canvas, 137.2 × 127.7 cm, Royal Collection

— *Dressing Up* —

As noted above, Zoffany not only placed his royal sitters in interiors hung with Van Dyck portraits, but also depicted them in costumes derived from the artist's paintings. In one portrait of the royal family, dismissed by Horace Walpole as "ridiculous," the two eldest princes appear to have grown into the pose and costumes of Van Dyck's portrait of the Villiers boys, although Zoffany again captures a greater naturalness of childlike comportment [fig. 67].[69] In fact, the use of Van Dyck's paintings as source material for masquerade costumes and fancy-dress portraits remains the best studied aspect of the artist's eighteenth century reception.[70] This is an epiphenomenon of the broader centrality of the masquerade – a public, ticketed event at which classes mingled and identities shifted – in studies of eighteenth-century culture.[71] Artists ranging from the amateur painter Oldfield Bowles to the ambitious young colonial Benjamin West all chose Van Dyck dress to position themselves as heirs to the most glamorous pedigree in English art, while exploiting the contemporary fashion for masked public assemblies.[72] The ubiquity of Van Dyck dress became something of a bugbear for promoters of academic classicism in portraiture. As Reynolds said to the students of the Royal Academy: "The great variety of excellent portraits with which Vandyck has enriched the nation, we are not content to admire for their real excellence, but extend our approbation even to the dress which happened to be the fashion of that age. We all very well remember how common it was a few years ago for portraits to be drawn in this fantastic dress; and this custom is not yet entirely laid aside."[73] Reynolds's criticism, conceding Van Dyck's "real excellence" while opposing wholesale imitation of his work, reprised the unease that Gérard de Lairesse had expressed about the modern manner, with its dependence on mutable fashions that might quickly become ridiculous.

Portraits in Van Dyck fancy dress unsettled commentators not just for transgressing idealist decorum but also through their connection with the social mobility of both painters and patrons. Gainsborough's Van Dyckian portraits, touchstones for the earlier artist's reception in the eighteenth century, conveyed not only his internalization of Continental technique, but also his clientele of "demireps" and new money, who lent themselves to a flamboyantly loose and demonstrative facture.[74] A paradigmatic example is his portrait of the Hon. Frances Duncombe, painted during the sitter's short-lived engagement to Lord Folkestone, heir to the Earl of Radnor [fig. 68].[75] Recently ennobled, the Radnors compensated for their Huguenot and mercantile origins both by collecting Van Dyck's portraits and by commissioning their own in Van Dyck dress. In Gainsborough's portrait, Miss Duncombe occupies an Arcadian landscape,

67 John Zoffany, *George III, Queen Charlotte and Their Six Eldest Children*, 1770, oil on canvas, 104.9 × 127.4 cm, Royal Collection

68 Thomas Gainsborough, *The Honourable Frances Duncombe*, ca. 1777, oil on canvas, 234.3 × 155.3 cm, New York, Frick Collection

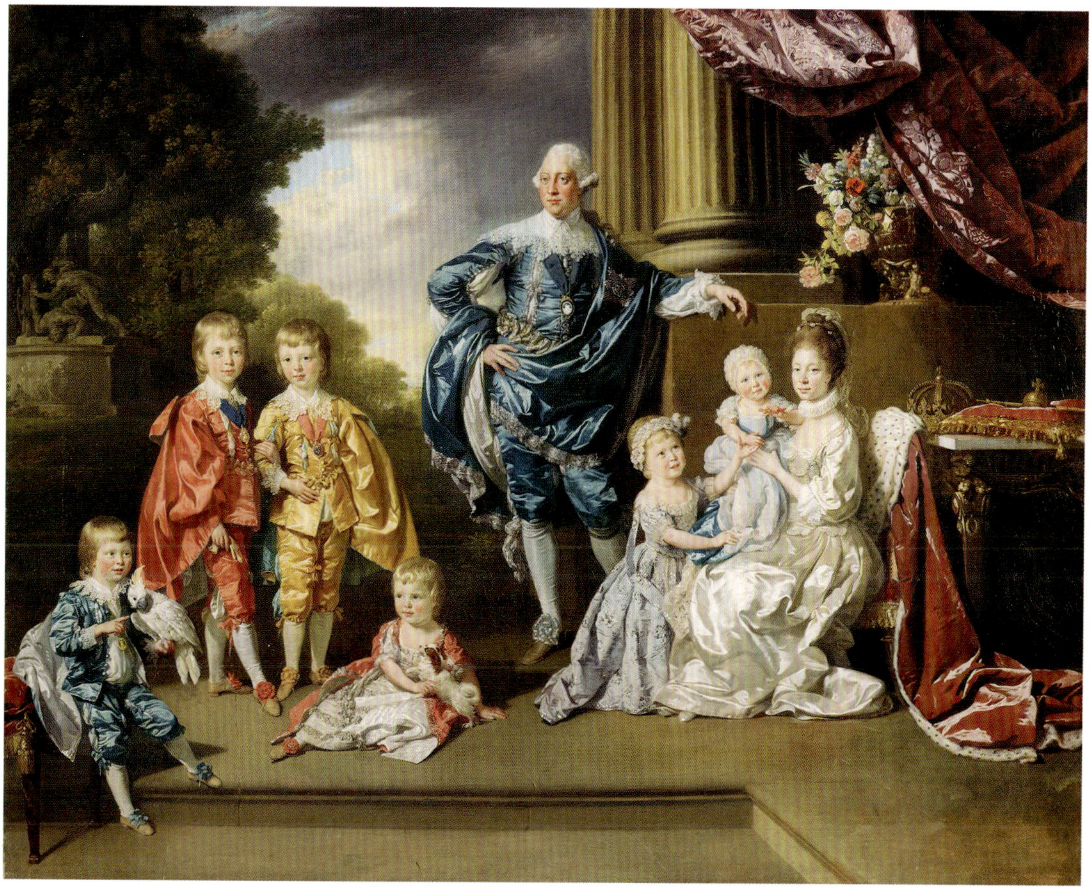

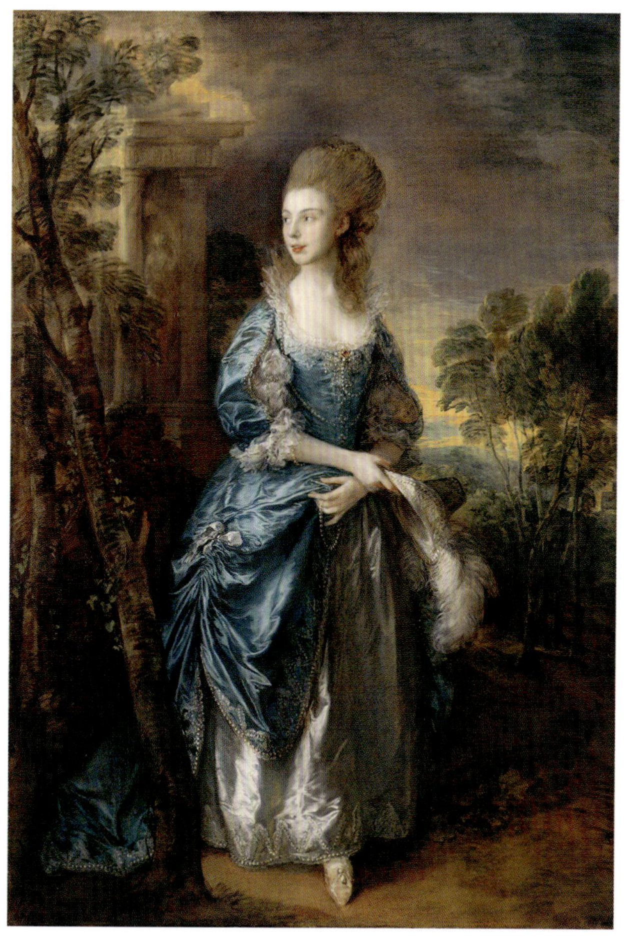

dressed for a masquerade. Her virago sleeves, plumed riding hat, jeweled bodice, and standing lace collar are all standard elements of Van Dyck costume, associating the sitter with fashionable entertainments and her portraitist with the prestigious artistic tradition he had studied in country house collections. Now evacuated of the moral associations bestowed on Van Dyck's portraits by Restoration writers, *The Honourable Frances Duncombe* is an exposition of the Van Dyckian mode as a gorgeously empty style.

Gainsborough's pictorial affiliation with Van Dyck contrasts with the persona he cultivated in his letters. Where Van Dyck's aristocratic friendships were a defining feature of his identity, Gainsborough chastised the composer and amateur painter William Jackson for "dayly throwing your Gift away upon Gentlemen & only studying how you shall become the Gentleman too." Rather than clamoring for his superiors' "Company & notice," Gainsborough claimed to "blow away all the chaff ... know[ing] that they have but one part worth looking at, and that is their Purse."[76] When Jackson took his tirade amiss, Gainsborough clarified in his next letter: "If I meant any thing ... it was this, that many a real Genius is lost in the fictitious Character of the Gentleman."[77] Precisely through his understanding that painters were only enacting a fiction when they posed as gentlemen, Gainsborough broke the Van Dyckian paradigm into two component parts: a stylistic emulation that he embraced and a social performance that he rejected. The Gainsborough of the letters, lamenting or ironizing his economic dependence upon portraits and their sitters, has allowed for a historiographic redemption, incorporating him into a nationalist narrative of British art, granted to no other Van Dyckian painter. At the same time, the fraught social status of Gainsborough's daughters, who trained as artists but never practiced professionally, indicates some of the anxieties behind Gainsborough's seemingly blasé pronouncements.[78] This ambivalence adds nuance to the painter's famous last words: "Van Dyck was right."[79]

Reynolds presents a different case of conflicted Van Dyckian reception. As noted above, emulation of the painter was an important facet of his portraiture, but he also continued the tradition of operating his studio as a cultural attraction. Like Van Dyck, he achieved a knighthood, but much of his social prominence derived from his affiliation with academic rigor and as a founder of institutions that explicitly placed portraiture beneath history painting within a hierarchy of genres. His extensive friendships and cultivation of patrons reflected not a Van Dyckian self-assertion, but rather the affability that Richard Wendorf has situated within a contemporary cultural ideal of "complaisance."[80] Reynolds's social persona has been amply studied elsewhere, but one less obvious aspect of his negotiation of power relations in both academy and studio is particularly relevant here – namely, his relationship to the live model.

If portrait sittings challenged the painter's autonomy and authority, particularly when the sitter was a social superior, then work from the hired model reinforced the artist's stature by confronting him (the male pronoun is used here advisedly) with a subordinate in a state of vulnerability or even abjection.[81] Both Bellori and de Piles noted the presence of professional models in Van Dyck's studio. According to Bellori, "He kept men and women to serve as models for the portraits of lords and ladies when, after achieving the likeness of the face, he would then complete the rest from live models."[82] De Piles similarly records that Van Dyck "had in his studio hired persons of one or the other sex who served him as models," particularly for the hands in his portraits. A key function of the state-sponsored academies that emerged across Europe in the seventeenth and eighteenth centuries was the provision of live models to students, resulting in the emergence of the artist's model as a distinct professional identity. This arrangement contrasted with an earlier fluidity, in which young apprentices were the most frequent models for their masters. But even with the regularization of life drawing in the academy, the presence of the model in the individual studio, drawn from the lower orders and relatively powerless, continued to serve as a powerful foil for the gentleman-painter.

One such model features prominently in an anecdote told by Reynolds's student and biographer, James Northcote. Reading the newspaper one morning in 1769, Reynolds, "to his great astonishment, saw that a prisoner had been tried and condemned to death for a robbery committed on the person of one of his own servants, a negro who had been with him for some time." Northcote adds, "This black man had lived in his service as footman for several years, and has been pourtrayed in several pictures, particularly in one of the Marquis of Granby."[83] Having questioned this servant about the case, Reynolds then dispatched another retainer to visit the condemned man before his execution. There, "he beheld the most wretched spectacle that imagination can conceive – a poor forlorn criminal, without a friend on earth ... reduced almost to a skeleton by famine and by filth, waiting till ... he was to be rendered a terrible example by a violent death." Setting his own example of benevolence, Reynolds "ordered fresh cloathing to be sent to him, and also that the black servant as a penance, as well as an act of charity should carry to him every day a sufficient supply of food from his own table." The artist then interceded on the prisoner's behalf with his friend Edmund Burke, "and by their joint interest they got his sentence changed to transportation; when, after being furnished with all necessaries, he was sent out of the kingdom."[84]

With the convict's transportation, both he and "the black servant" sail out of Northcote's narrative. Their function is to enact an episode that Northcote terms "highly illustrative of [Reynolds's] character."[85] Reprimanding a servant and reprieving a criminal, Reynolds displays kindly paternalism as the head of his household. From a twenty-first-century vantage point, "what strikes us rather more forcefully is Reynolds's determination to humiliate his black servant by forcing the victim of the crime to become the servant of the perpetrator."[86] Within this miniature drama of crime and punishment, the servant's status as the model for "several pictures" is particularly salient. The relationship between artist and model lays the foundation for the grand manner portrait's binaries of dominance and servitude.

Northcote does not record the name of Reynolds's servant, but earlier in his biography he gives some fleeting information about the man's life: that he was born enslaved in the West Indies and came to England with a governor's widow whose daughter, an actress, was Reynolds's friend and sitter.[87] Northcote also names one painting for which the footman served as model, a portrait of the Marquess of Granby standing before a battlefield [fig. 69]. This portrait, along with one of the Count of Schaumburg-Lippe, formed a pair depicting heroes of the Seven Years' War.[88] Both commanders appear with turbaned Black grooms, apparently based on two different models. In the Schaumburg-Lippe portrait, the groom looks up at the count from a position in the background. The Granby portrait adopts a more ambiguous structure, placing the heads of marquess and groom on the same plane, the two men each in three-quarter profile as they look off to either side of the scene. Rather than establishing parity between the two men, their rhymed poses heighten the binaries of race and power that structure Reynolds's composition.[89] Breaking with certain conventions for the depiction of Black pages, Reynolds nevertheless reinforced their function in the naturalization of social hierarchies.

In the Granby portrait, Reynolds combines two separate traditions of Van Dyckian portraiture, strengthening their respective binaries of power and deference by making them overlap. In one of these traditions, as in *Le Roi à la Chasse*, a noble rider appears alongside his groom, the two men posed in such a way that the primary sitter's self-governed autonomy is heightened by the groom's occupation with a restive animal [see fig. 52]. In his portrait of the Marquess of Granby, Reynolds overlaid onto this juxtaposition of rider and groom the racial dichotomies of portraits where the primary sitter appears in the company of a Black servant or page. Because the model for the general's groom was Reynolds's own footman, his presence in the painting implies for insiders like Northcote an equivalence between the mastery of the sitter and that of the artist, positioning both as white subjects who dispose over Black labor.

Northcote's anecdote functions primarily within his text as evidence for Reynolds's character, even if that evidence reads very differently today than it did at the end of the eighteenth century. But in its domestic detail, the story also entails an interesting demystification of grand manner portraiture. Like a studio sale, the anecdote sheds light on the different components that go into the making of a finished portrait. By identifying the servant as the model for the groom in Granby's portrait, Northcote underscores the image's artificiality. If the groom is not a groom, but in fact the artist's own servant and, moreover, a servant remembered for a criminal imbroglio, then what does that say about the heroic pose of the general himself?

Artists' use of their own servants as models was both a longstanding commonplace of artistic practice and a bête noire of art criticism. Seventeenth-century inventories record a head study of "Rubens's washerwoman" or "a laughing *tronie* of Rubens's pigment grinder [painted] by Van Dyck."[90] De Lairesse scorned

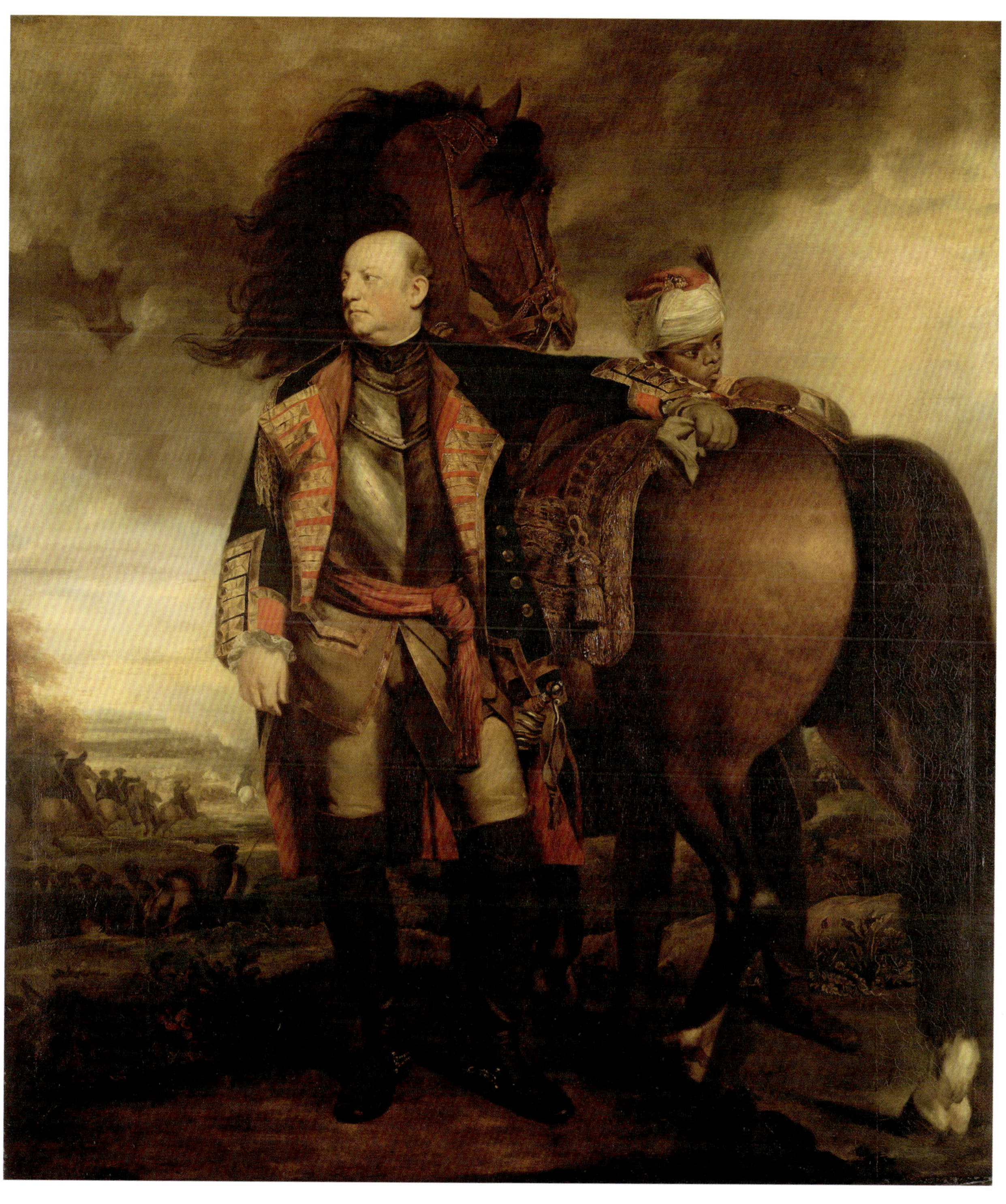

69 Joshua Reynolds, *John Manners, Marquess of Granby (1721–70) and a Groom*, ca. 1766–70, oil on canvas, 245.5 × 207.0 cm, Royal Collection painters who made a "young lady" of their "ill-mannered serving maid," or posed their own son in the "garb of a gentleman."[91] From de Lairesse's perspective, models drawn from the household travestied social decorum. But the presence of models in the household was also a display of wealth embraced by painters in the Van Dyckian mode. Placing his footman in his pictures, Reynolds declared himself an heir to Van Dyck's studio practices as well as to his compositional prototypes. Even as he recruited models from his household, Reynolds played an essential role in the provision of professional models to English art students at the Royal Academy. But as Reynolds's own practice indicates, the professional academic model never replaced the occasional model who was also a servant, beggar, or prostitute. Indeed, the lowliness of the model that is such a constant theme of early modern art writing persisted into the nineteenth century as a correlative for the elevation of gentlemen-painters.

The professional model, like the academy itself, arrived belatedly in England. Early in the seventeenth century, Edward Norgate, with whom Van Dyck lodged in London, jestingly defined the drawing academy as "a *Roome* where in the middle, a hired Long sided Porter or such like is to be set, stand or hang naked sometimes in a posture for two or three howres," presenting drawing from life as a distinctly foreign, even comical practice.[92] Many of the most vivid anecdotes about artists' models in early English art writing have to do with the experiences of foreigners or of English artists abroad. For example, Vertue recalled that the Flemish artist Peter Angellis, sojourning in Rome after his successful career in England, employed a "young man that he made use of for his model to draw after ... it causd much sport and laughter to his companions ... when Angellis us[e]d to dress up this young man ... into womens dresses or habits, he made such aukard – queere figures."[93] Vertue's amusement at the standard Continental practice of having young men model for female figures may reflect the fact that by the time he recorded his anecdote, nude female models had become a staple of private drawing academies in England.[94]

The earliest of these informal academies, predating the Royal Academy by nearly a century, met in the early 1670s under Lely's guidance. In 1656, the Painter-Stainers' Company had rejected a petition to hold life drawing classes in its hall, and this first academy most likely met in Lely's own studio in Covent Garden.[95] The primary evidence for this early academy is an album of drawings by various hands now at Dulwich College. The drawings range from copies after Van Dyck to studies of plaster casts and engravings. There are also a few drawings apparently after live models, both male and female.[96]

A drawing from 1714 by Jonathan Richardson the Elder records the identity of one notable artist's model, the "gladiator" James Figg [fig. 70].[97] Famous for the prizefights held at his amphitheater in Oxford Road, Figg has been identified with figures in Hogarth's *Southwark Fair* and *A Rake's Progress*.[98] In contrast to these genre scenes, Richardson's drawing appears to come from an academic session, probably in the academy in Great Queen Street, where Figg posed bare-chested,

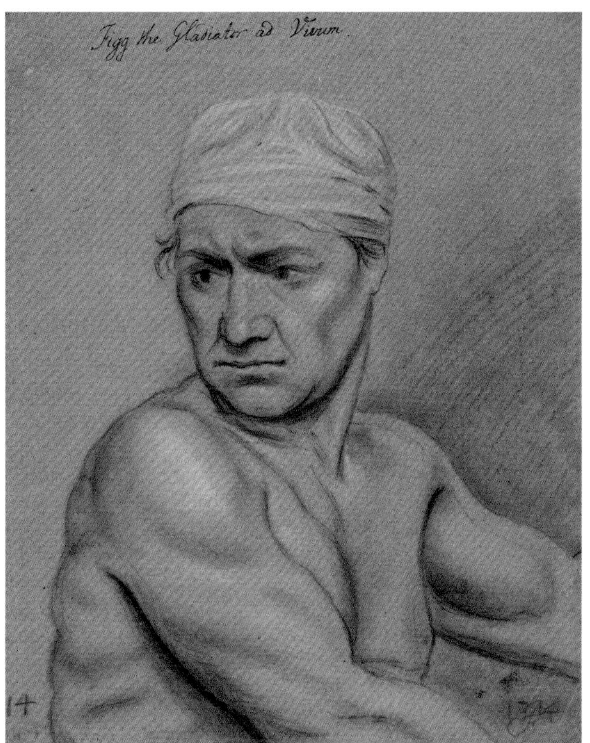

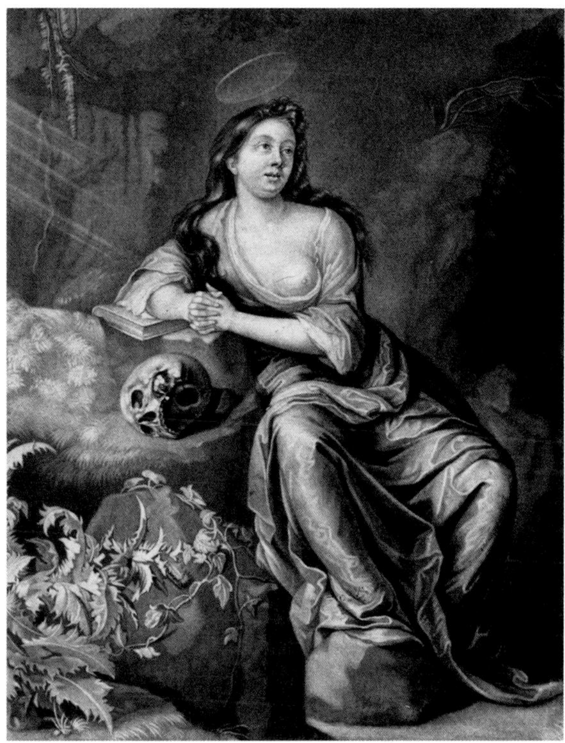

70 Jonathan Richardson, *James Figg*, 1714, black and white chalk on blue paper, 29 × 22.5 cm, Oxford, Ashmolean Museum

71 Jacob Gole, after Gaspar Smits, *Saint Mary Magdalene*, n.d., engraving, 25.5 × 18.2 cm, Amsterdam, Rijksmuseum

a cap on his head. Twisting to look over one shoulder in a pose that recalls Michelangelo's Isaiah from the Sistine Chapel, Figg displays the musculature of a powerful but middle-aged body. Richardson depicted his model in black and white chalk on blue paper, adopting the prestigious medium of the Van Dyck drawings that had already become coveted collectors' items among English artists. While the drawing could be preparatory to a larger composition, the artist's inscription, "Figg the Gladiator ad Vivum," and the particularity of the face lend the drawing an ambiguous status, somewhere between figure study and portrait.

Records of live modeling in England oscillate between a prurient fixation on the female model's sexual availability and an acknowledgment of the precarious social realities operating for models of both sexes. Bainbrigg Buckeridge recounted of Gaspar "Magdalen" Smits that "his Inclination led him most to Drawing of *Magdalens*, from whence he had his Name, and whereof he drew a great number by a certain *English* Gentlewoman, who past for his Wife."[99] This brief anecdote is onomastic, accounting for the origin of Smits's byname at the same time that it reads the artist's life through his art. Buckeridge explains the eroticism of Smits's Magdalens [fig. 71] not through market demand but rather the artist's own "Inclination" and "irregular way of Living," epitomized by an illicit relationship with a woman who passed for, but was not in fact, his wife.

Alternative sources, such as inscriptions on drawings and payment records, indicate that most early English models were servants.[100] Sketchbooks by Mary Beale's son Charles contain some of the most remarkable English drawings of the seventeenth century, documenting a young artist's training as he drew plaster casts, copied details from Van Dyck's portraits, and portrayed the family's servants and tradespeople as they posed or slept [fig. 72].[101] The names inscribed on the backs of some of these drawings – Susan Gill, Su Jaxon, T Porter – record identities otherwise lost to history, while the portraits themselves capture with nearly unique directness the appearance of seventeenth-century working people.[102] Beale's drawings document the artist's household as a socially porous space, frequented not just by Mary Beale's genteel friends and clientele, but also by the men and women who swept the floors or carted off paintings.

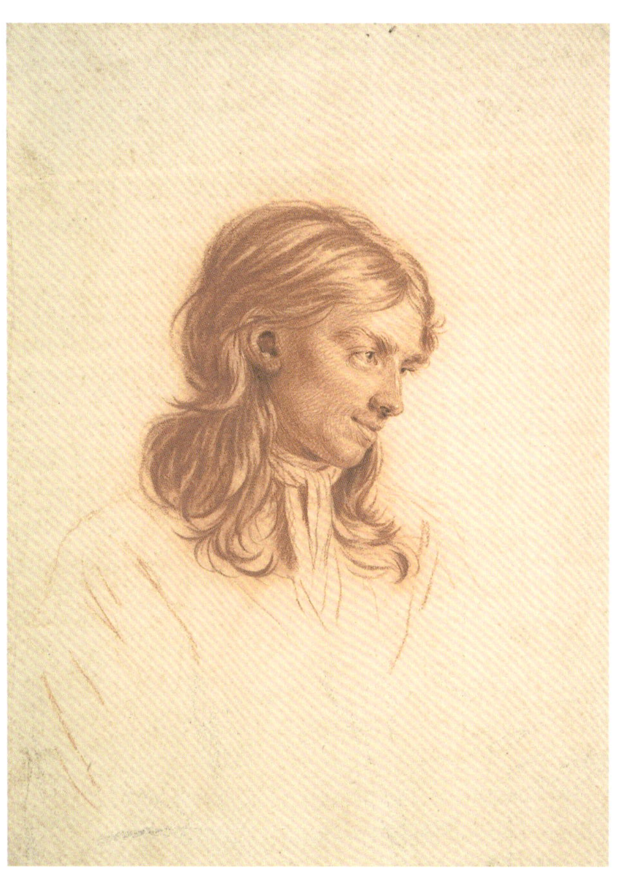

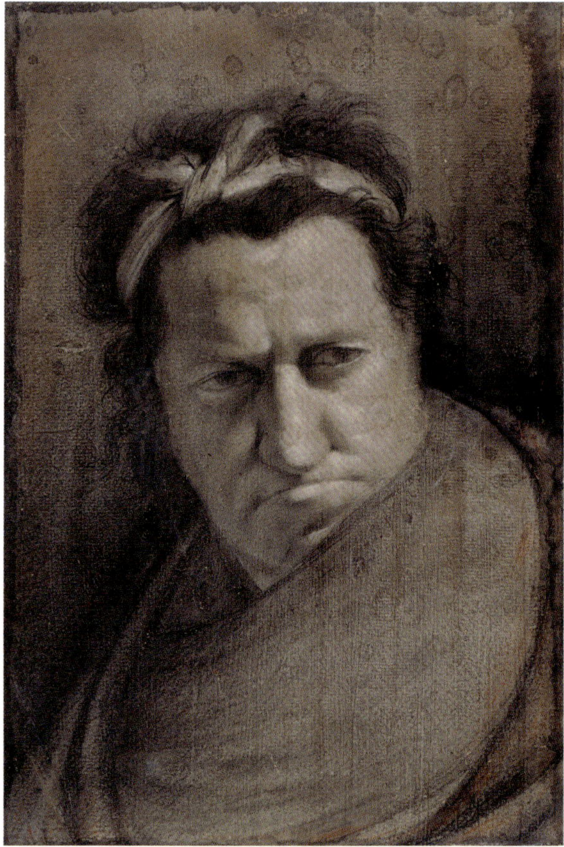

72 Charles Beale, *Carter, the Colorman*, ca. 1680, red chalk heightened with touches of black chalk and graphite, on paper, 26 × 20.3 cm, New York, Metropolitan Museum of Art

73 Thomas Banks, *John Malin*, ca. 1768–69, black and red chalk, heightened with white, on paper, 48.5 × 37 cm, London, Royal Academy

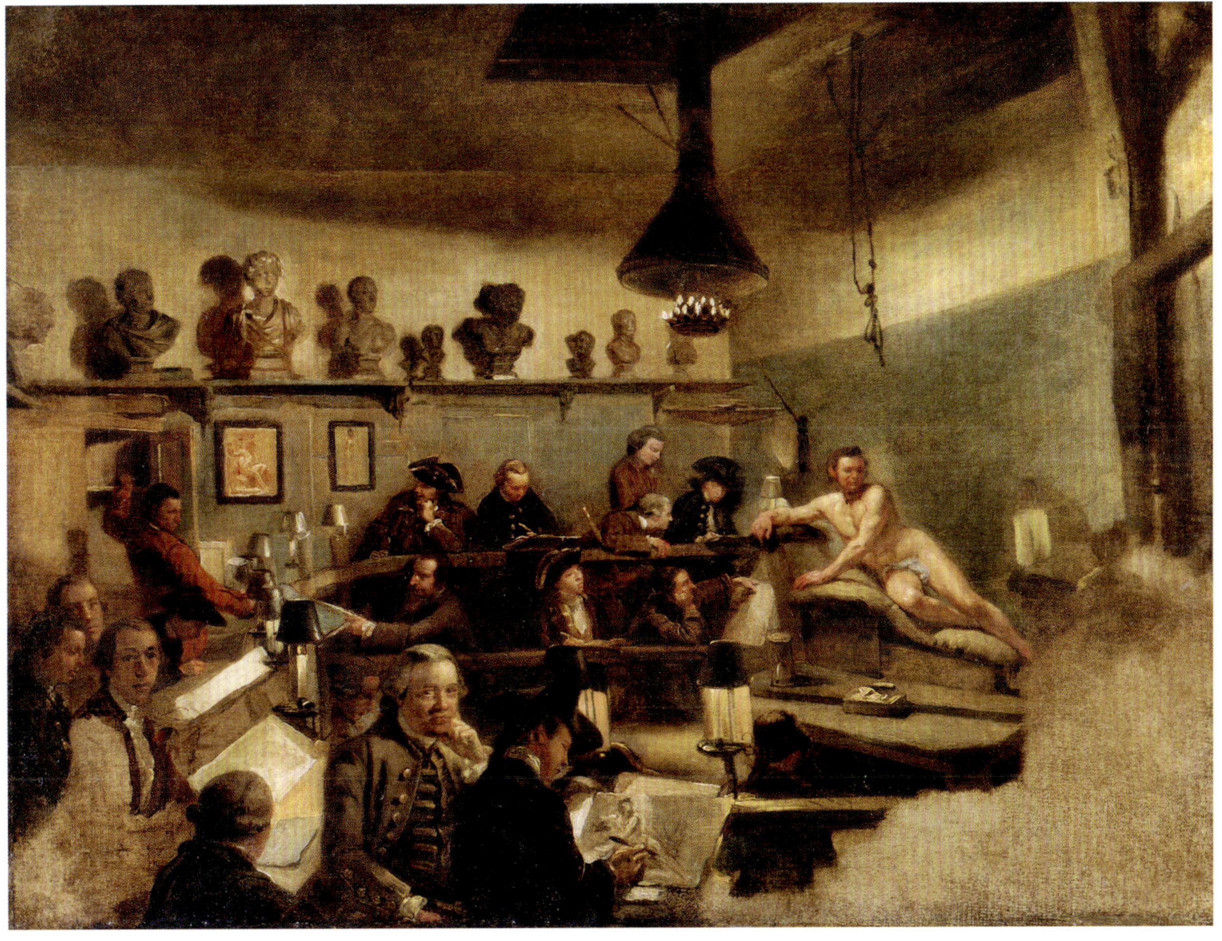

74 Johan Zoffany, *A Life Class at St Martin's Lane Academy*, 1761–62, oil on canvas, 50.5 × 66 cm, London, Royal Academy

Within this context, it is hardly surprising that the first model of the Royal Academy was its porter, John Malin. A drawing by Thomas Banks made shortly before Malin's death in 1769 depicts Malin wrapped in a shawl, with his hair tied back, frowning intensely [fig. 73].[103] This study of an expressive face recalls the Netherlandish tradition of the head study, practiced extensively by both Van Dyck and Rubens. The inscription on the verso, calling the drawing "equal to anything by Leonardo da Vinci," associates it with a prestigious old master tradition at the same time that it identifies the sitter as "the first porter and model at the Royal Academy." Malin also appears in Zoffany's unfinished depiction of a life class at the St. Martin's Lane Academy [fig. 74].[104] The porter stands at the left of the composition, reaching into a cupboard. Marked out from the other figures by his red coat, Malin brackets the composition along with the reclining, barely draped model on the right. The two men appear here as studio laborers, distinct from the artists in their midst. The fact that Malin's identity was recorded attests to his long

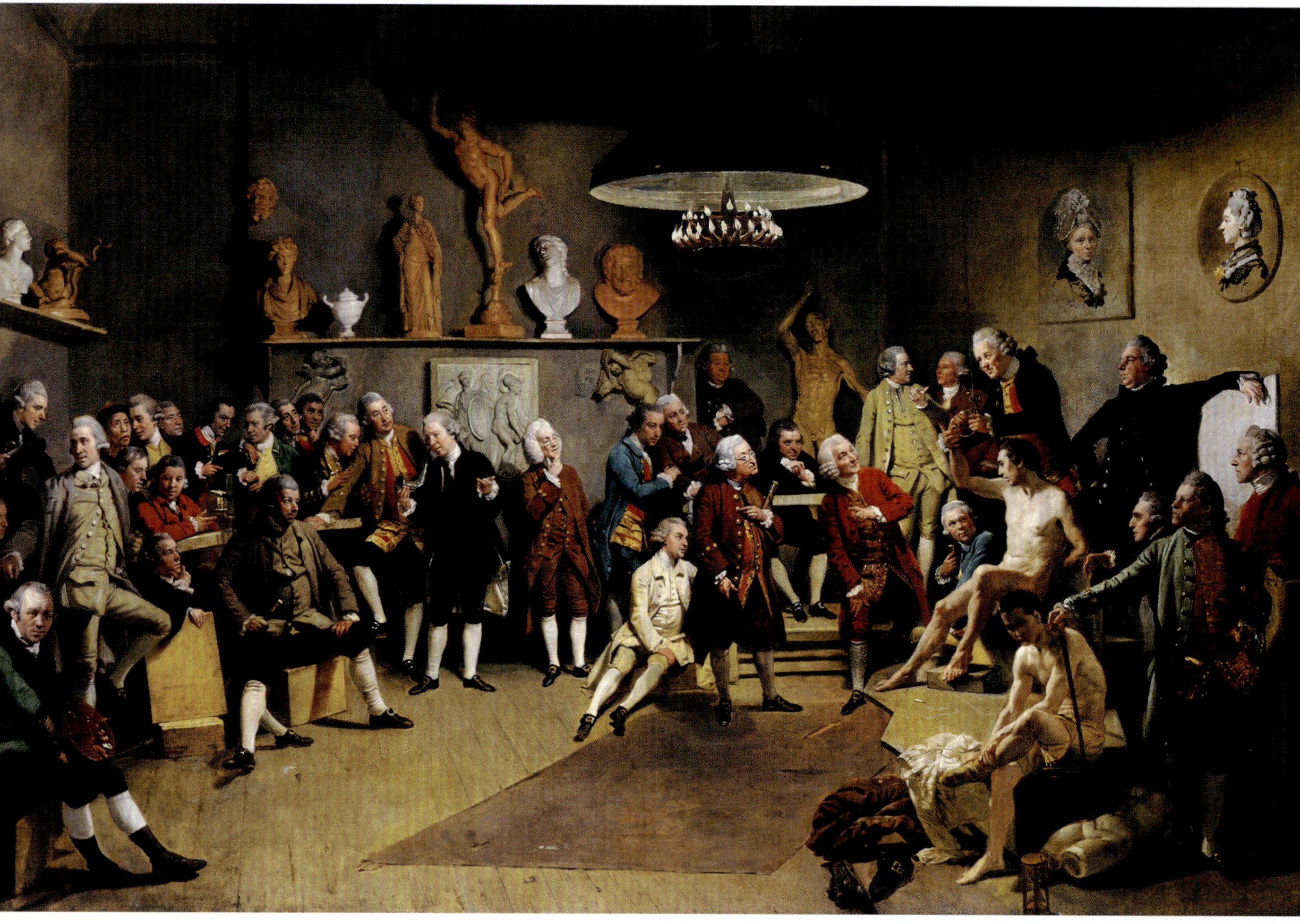

75 Johan Zoffany, *The Academicians of the Royal Academy*, 1771–72, oil on canvas, 101.1 × 147.5 cm, Royal Collection

institutional service and the affection with which the academicians, who paid for his funeral, regarded him.

As befitted their role in the institution's pedagogical mission, models figure prominently in Zoffany's celebrated depiction of the Royal Academy, first exhibited in 1772 [fig. 75].[105] A triumphant image of the institutionalization of English art, it shows the academicians watching as a model is posed, his wrist slipped into a kind of noose by George Michael Moser. Another model occupies the foreground on the right, looking out as he adjusts the wrappings on his foot. In contrast to the aging, powdered academicians, the models are young, beautiful, and nameless – their identities left off the eighteenth-century key to the painting that scholars have relied on ever since.[106] In a characteristic pictorial joke, Zoffany placed his own self-portrait at the far left of the painting, facing the model in the foreground and nearly mirroring his pose. Even as the academy reinforced the divide between artists and models, between the named and nameless, Zoffany harkened back to a recent past of fraught intimacies between these studio actors.

Another figure in Zoffany's painting, striking in his bright green coat at the far right of the canvas, extends his arm as he plants his cane on a plaster torso, so that he casts a shadow on one of the models. This is Richard Cosway, portrayed on the cusp of a career that would make him, along with his wife Maria, a cynosure of cultural and social life in late eighteenth-century London. Famously fashionable, the friends of aristocrats and the Prince of Wales, the Cosways made clear their Van Dyckian affiliation through sustained references to seventeenth-century portraiture in their art. But despite their success, the Cosways' disastrous critical reception, extending from their lifetimes into the present day, reveals just how fraught Van Dyck's legacy became in an artistic culture where the academy and the newspaper had replaced the court in guiding national taste.

[CHAPTER FIVE]

Old Master Poses

RICHARD COSWAY'S BOLD STANCE AT THE VERY EDGE OF ZOFFANY'S DEPICTION of the Royal Academy captures two essential features of his career: the flamboyance of his public persona and his marginalization within institutional narratives of English art [see fig. 75]. But Zoffany's all-male scene was painted a decade before an event that would prove even more determinative for Cosway's life and art: his marriage to the Italian-born artist Maria Hadfield. Together, Richard and Maria Cosway represent a late chapter in the trajectory of Van Dyckian reception that this book has traced so far. Indeed, the Van Dyckian paradigm provides an essential framework for understanding this union of a notoriously effeminate man and a famous female painter, both of whose various social performances threatened to eclipse their actual artistic achievements.

In his biographical sketch of Richard Cosway, John Thomas Smith, whose father, Nathaniel, studied with Cosway as a young man, evokes some of the caustic skepticism that the painter inspired:

> *Richard Cosway when a boy, was noticed by Mr. Shipley, the proprietor of the Drawing-school in the Strand ... who took him to wait upon the students, and carry in the tea and coffee ... The students ... good-temperedly gave Dick, for so he was called, instructions in drawing, and also advised him, finding him to have some talent, to try for a prize in the Society of Arts ...* [After winning several prizes] *he left his master, and became a teacher in Parr's Drawing-school, in the Strand. He was also employed to make drawings of heads for the shops, as well as fancy-miniatures, and free subjects for snuff-boxes for the jewellers, mostly from ladies whom he knew; and from the money he gained, and the gaiety of the company he kept, he rose, from one of the dirtiest boys, to one of the smartest of men.*[1]

Eliding Cosway's respectable origins as the son of a schoolmaster, Smith vividly captures the artist's reputation as a "ridiculously foppish" social climber "with a small three-cornered hat on the top of his powdered toupée, and a mulberry silk coat, profusely embroidered with scarlet strawberries."[2] Smith also emphasizes Cosway's production, not of proper paintings, but rather miniatures and "subjects for snuff-boxes" modeled after "ladies whom he knew." From the beginning of his career, Cosway's name was synonymous with sartorial display, high living, and feminine frivolity.

Detail of Richard Cosway, *Self-Portrait in Masquerade Costume*, ca. 1770 [see fig. 76]

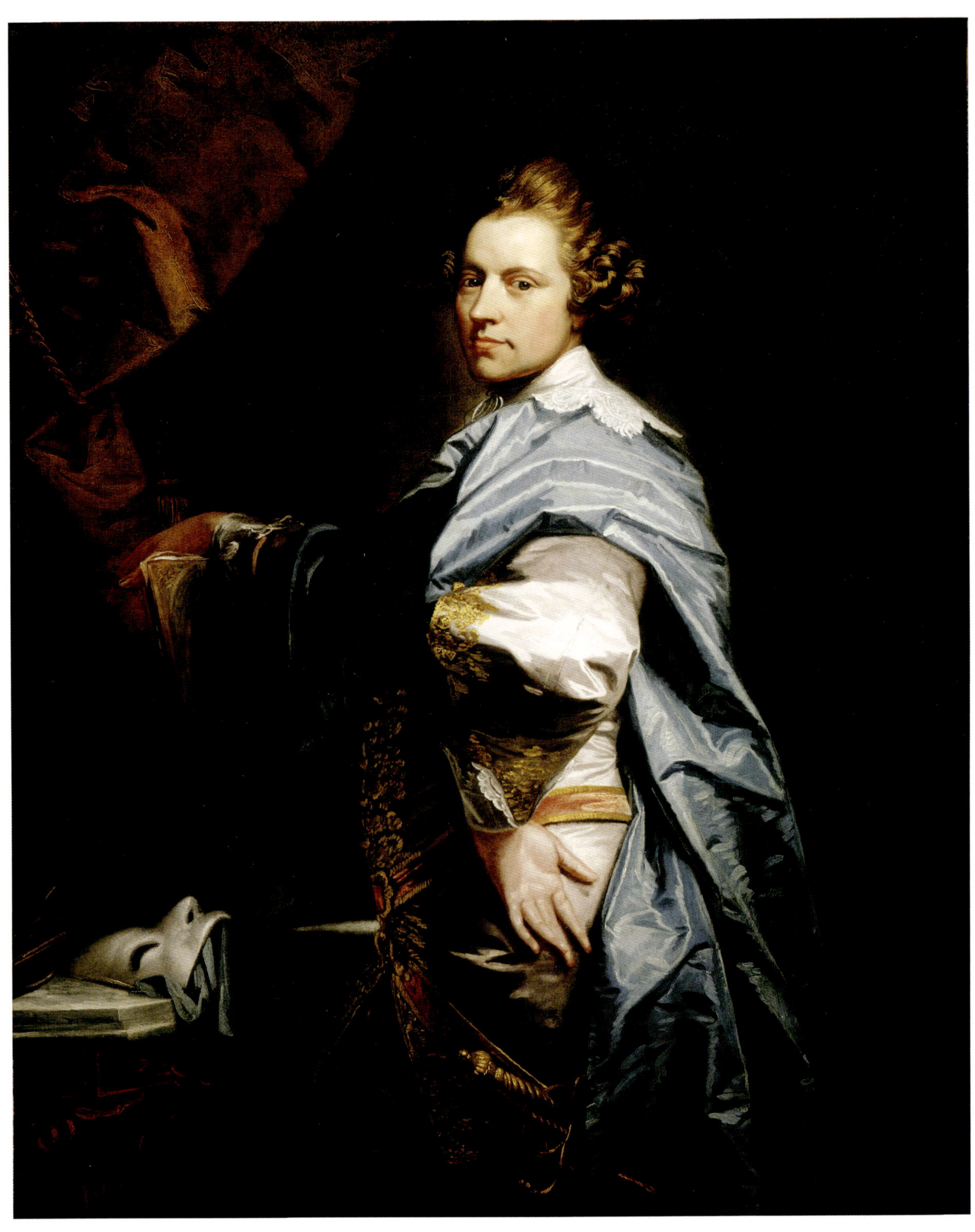

76 Richard Cosway, *Self-Portrait in Masquerade Costume*, ca. 1770, oil on canvas, 129.5 × 101.6 cm, Shrewsbury, Attingham Park (National Trust)

In society portraits, Cosway commemorated real Van Dyck costumes, such as the spectacular attire worn by William Courtenay for his coming-of-age celebrations in 1789.[3] But he also returned to seventeenth-century prototypes throughout his lifelong practice of self-portraiture and in images of his wife and fellow artist, Maria. In the earliest of Cosway's self-portraits, from around 1770, he adopts the twisted pose, slung cape, and provocative glance of Van Dyck's self-portrait with Endymion Porter, extracted from that painting's context of a deferential relationship between patron and protégé [fig. 76].[4] The prominently foreshortened elbow at the composition's dead center calls attention to Cosway's virtuosity and his internalization of baroque motifs, while his elaborate costume both ennobles the sitter and displays his skillful reproduction of luxurious surfaces. Amidst all this, the discarded mask sounds a note of irony, suggesting that Cosway's self-presentation in the Van Dyckian mode may be no more than fancy dress.

Cosway was a leading figure among the young men known as macaroni, whose boldly colored fashions and towering hairstyles represented a striking transgression of social and gender norms in the 1770s.[5] Another self-portrait from early in that decade, a miniature on ivory, captures Cosway's macaroni style with his high toupee wig, black solitaire hair ribbon, and hand tucked inside a brocaded coat trimmed with ermine [fig. 77].[6] Although they derived their fashions from formal court dress, macaroni came from a variety of backgrounds and appeared

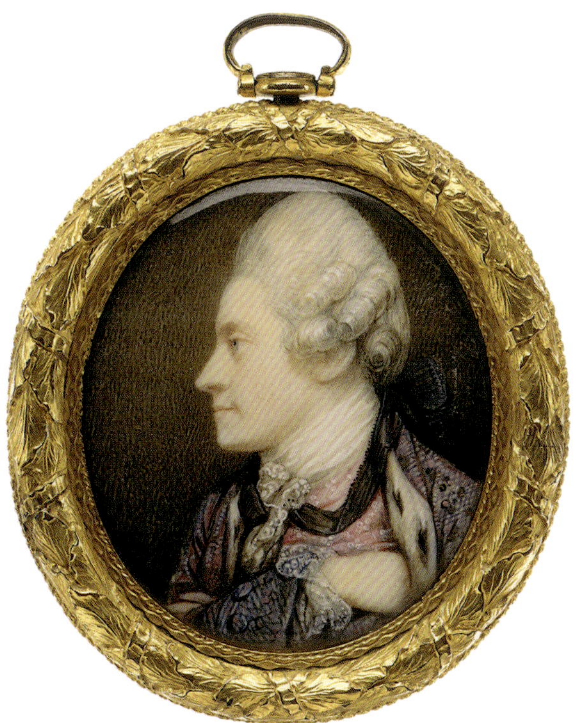

77 Richard Cosway, *Self-Portrait*, ca. 1770–75, watercolor on ivory, 5 × 4.2 cm, New York, Metropolitan Museum of Art

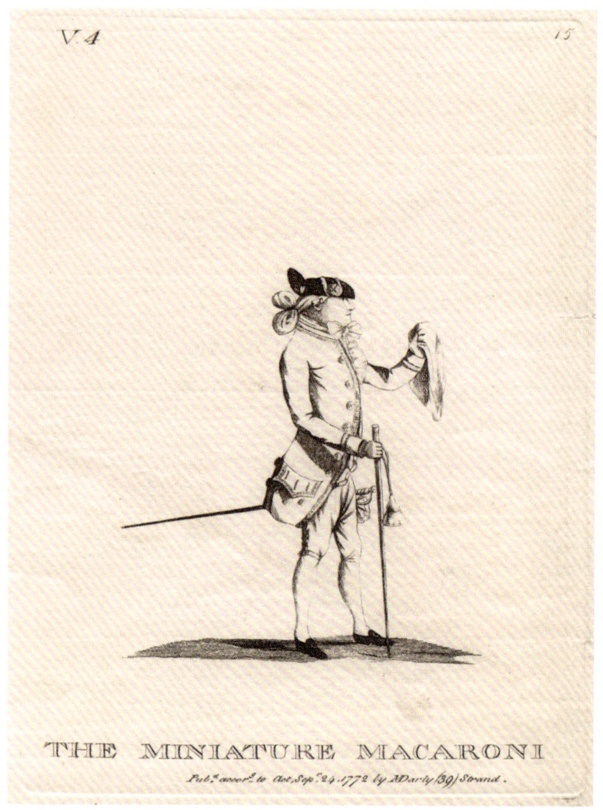

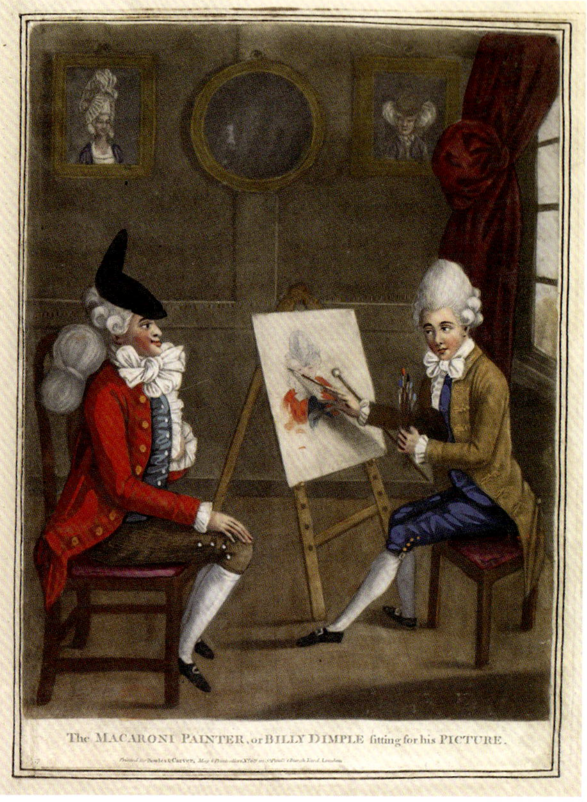

78 Matthew and Mary Darly, *The Miniature Macaroni*, 1772, etching, 17.4 × 12.6 cm, London, National Portrait Gallery

79 Richard Earlom, after Robert Dighton, *The Macaroni Painter, or Billy Dimple Sitting for His Picture*, 1772, hand-colored mezzotint, 35.2 × 25.2 cm, London, British Museum

in contemporary satires as paradigmatic social upstarts. They struck a nerve in a country whose expanding prosperity and consumer culture had stirred fears of growing national "effeminacy."[7]

Described by Smith as "a well-made little man, [though] very much like a monkey in his face," Cosway's bold self-presentation and social aspirations provided ample fodder for the caricaturists whose work exploited the tensions, contradictions, and deceptions of more formal Georgian portraiture.[8] In 1772, Mary and Matthew Darly lampooned both Cosway's stature and his artistic medium by portraying him as "the miniature macaroni," his diminutive body contrasting with a jutting sword and oversized handkerchief [fig. 78]. A second caricature published that same year, based on a drawing by Robert Dighton, labeled Cosway "the Macaroni Painter" and depicted him in his studio at work on the likeness of another effete young man [fig. 79]. Dighton's caricature transforms the studio from a porous space of (sometimes transgressive) heterosexual encounters into a closed circuit of effeminate self-admiration and display.

Zoffany's *Academicians of the Royal Academy* provides its own subtly satiric meditation on the homosocial spaces of art-making. Painted shortly after Cosway's election to the Academy, Zoffany's painting shows the artist standing at the far right, striking an elegant pose with his walking stick and wearing the bold green color favored by the macaroni. Cosway's outstretched hand nearly grazes the cheek of the barely dressed model seated beside him, who has instinctively struck the pose of the Roman *Spinario* as he takes off his shoe. In Zoffany's witty composition, brimming with art historical citations and erotic innuendo, Cosway, "the smartest of men," overlaps with the "dirty boy" he used to be. At the same time, he balances his walking stick on the abdomen of a toppled plaster cast of a female torso. This seemingly careless gesture makes an unsettling association of his coxcomb stance with powerless femininity.[9]

Seventeenth-century costume remained a touchstone for Cosway in the mature self-portraits that developed the macaroni poses of his youth. Richard Cosway's public persona in the latter half of his career depended on his artistic and personal collaboration with his wife, whom he married in 1781. Raised in Florence by British parents, Maria Cosway's career recalls in many aspects the tightrope walked by the women artists already discussed in this book. Apparently intended by her parents to emulate Angelica Kauffman's success, Cosway received an early training in both the visual arts and music. An important autobiographical account of her artistic formation, in a letter written toward the end of her life, provides further details:

> *When four years old I was put into a Convent, under the protection of the Grand Duke and Duchess of Tuscany … I had natural dispositions* [and] *I was immediately put to learn Music and at Six and more at Ten years of age did what I since have thought extraordinary. At eight years I began drawing* [since] *having seen a young Lady draw I took a passion for it … I was taken home and put under the care of an old Celebrated Lady who's* [sic] *portrait is in the* [Uffizi] *Gallery. I had a number of Masters but painting had my preference. This Lady soon found I could go farther than she could instruct me and Mr Zofani being at Florence my father aske'd him to give me some instructions. I went to study in the Gallery & the Palazzo Pitti and copied many of the finest pictures.*[10]

Cosway's account of her education strikes many familiar notes from the lives of other "accomplished" women, with an emphasis on precociousness, a combination of multiple artistic talents, the mentorship of professional artists, and copying from the old masters. Her parents' investment in her career, meanwhile, reflects the extent to which female accomplishment had become a potentially lucrative cultural phenomenon.

Brought to London at the age of nineteen after her father's death, Maria soon met Richard Cosway. In her autobiographical narrative, she reflects with ambivalence on the impact of their marriage upon her artistic development and career: "Mr Cosways wish was that I should occupy myself as hitherto done in the Arts and so I did. The first pictures I exhibited made my reputation. The novelty & my Age Contributed more than the real Merit ... encouraged but never proud I followed entirely the impulse of my imagination[;] had Mr C. permitted me to rank professionally I should have made a better painter but left to myself by degrees instead of improving I lost what I had brought from Italy of my early studies." The knotty syntax conveys some of the conflicting impulses guiding Richard's management of Maria Cosway's career.[11] Aware that her talents attracted notice and patronage, Richard encouraged them to the extent that they could function as domestic accomplishments, but not as professional exertions. From Maria's own vantage point, her seclusion from formal training and the marketplace, even as she continued to paint, draw, and exhibit, had a disastrous effect on her art.

Throughout the early years of their marriage, Richard Cosway repeatedly used Maria's portrait, widely distributed in print, to bolster his claims to a kind of old master status. Intriguingly, however, Rubens supplants Van Dyck in these works as the lodestar of Cosway's self-aggrandizement. A pair of prints by Francesco Bartolozzi and Marino Bova after drawings by Richard depict the artist and Maria in costumes taken directly from Rubens's own marital self-portraiture [figs. 80–82]. Bova's engraving links the two artists even more explicitly by placing Cosway next to a book inscribed "Vita Di Rubens," as though he were studying the life of his paragon. Elsewhere, Cosway posed himself alongside busts of Rubens and Michelangelo; he collected the former's oil sketches and even claimed to use Rubens's pigment box as his own.[12]

By the time he made these explicitly Rubensian self-portraits, Cosway's career had come to revolve almost entirely around the production of miniature portraits as he abandoned the more ambitious conversation pieces he painted in the 1770s. His skill at miniatures earned him an appointment as Principal Painter to the Prince of Wales, a title trumpeted in Latin in the inscription to Bova's engraving. Focused on portraiture and sustained by the patronage of a future British monarch, Cosway was far more of a Van Dyckian than a Rubensian painter. His shift toward explicitly naming Rubens as his model can perhaps be read as an act of compensation for the decreasing ambition of his actual practice, as well as a reflection of Van Dyck's lesser status within an academic discourse that sought to move beyond the distinctive lineage of English portraiture sketched by figures like Buckeridge and Richardson. Cosway's self-depiction as Rubens's epigone immediately inspired withering critique. A pair of etchings by an unknown artist appeared shortly after Bova's and Bartolozzi's, lampooning "Dicky Causway" and "Maria Costive" [figs. 83 and 84].[13] The etching replaces Richard's finery with rags and his life of Rubens with a penny ballad of Dick Whittington, the medieval Lord Mayor of London whose social mobility had become the stuff of legend. For her part, Maria appears to have established her studio in Bedlam, the cruel nickname "Maria Costive" recasting her emulative relationship to the old masters as a grotesque indigestion.

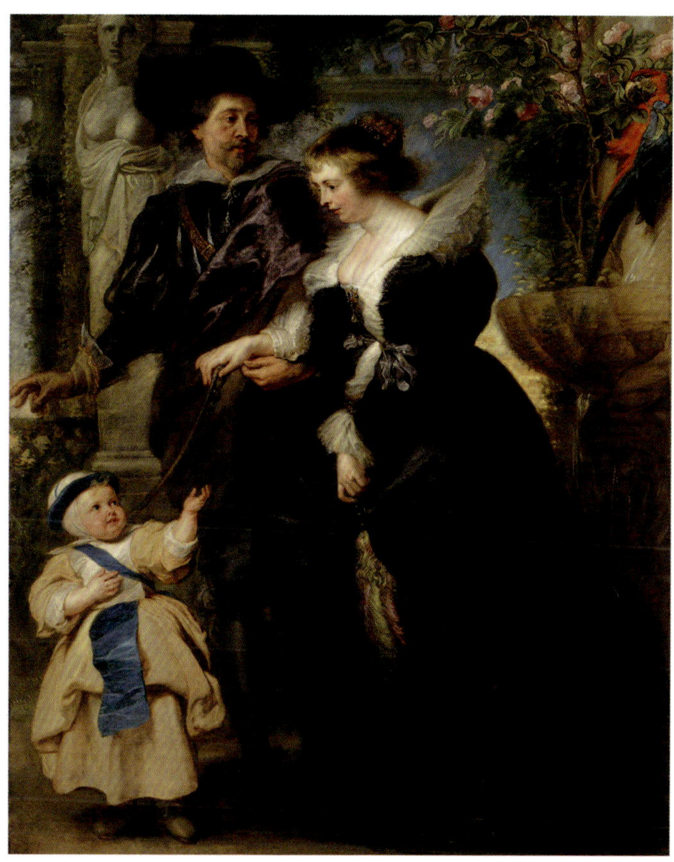

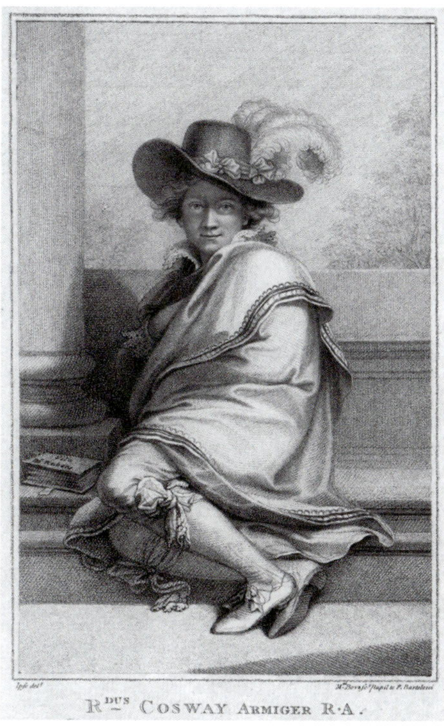

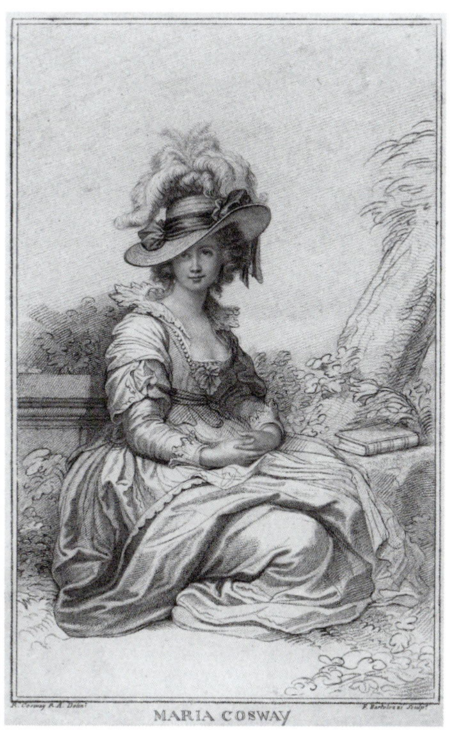

80 Peter Paul Rubens, *The Artist with His Wife Helena and Their Son Frans*, ca. 1635, oil on panel, 203.8 × 158.1 cm, New York, Metropolitan Museum of Art

81 Marino Bova, after Richard Cosway, *Richard Cosway*, 1786, stipple engraving, 27.4 × 16.5 cm, London, National Portrait Gallery

82 Francesco Bartolozzi, after Richard Cosway, *Maria Cosway*, 1785, stipple etching, 23.7 × 15.0 cm, London, British Museum

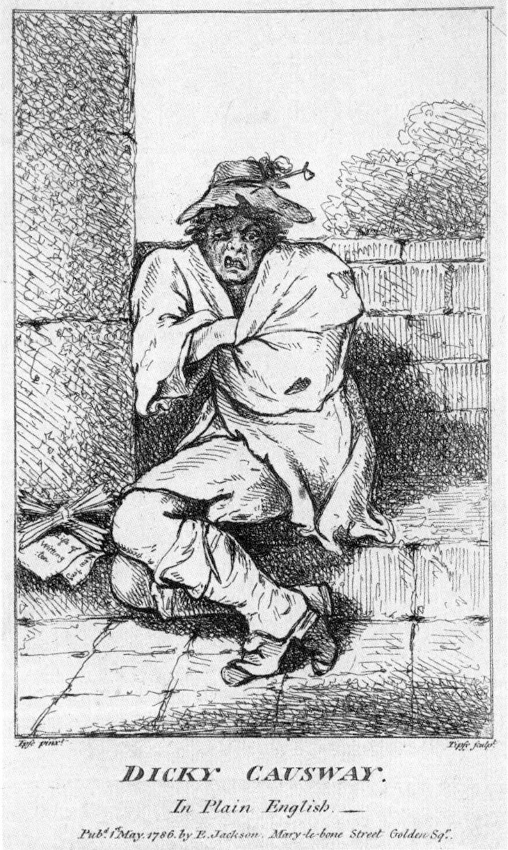

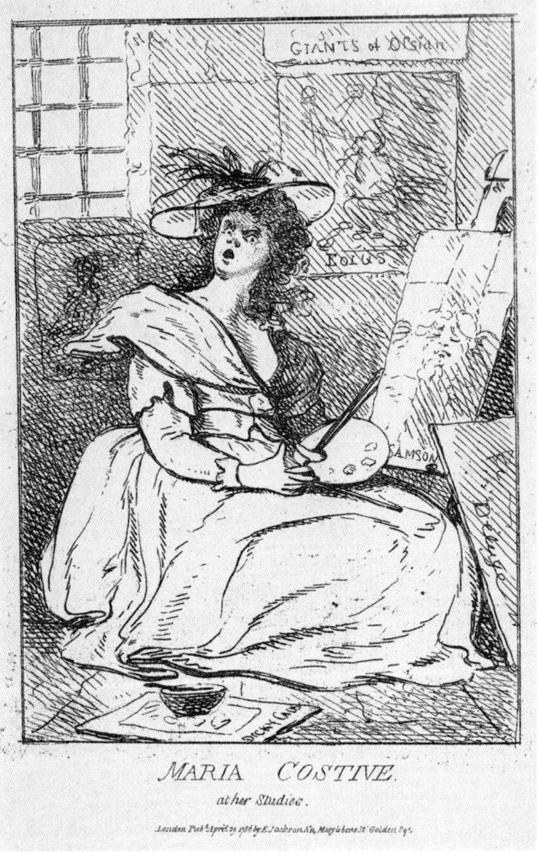

83 Unknown artist, *Dicky Causway in Plain English*, 1786, etching, 24 × 15.1 cm, London, British Museum

84 Unknown artist, *Maria Costive at Her Studies*, 1786, etching, 24 × 15.4 cm, London, British Museum

With his gradual shift toward the mass production of repetitive works, Richard Cosway's career enacted a key feature of the Van Dyckian paradigm. In this later phase of his career, Cosway's ambition manifested itself as much in his social life and art collecting as in his actual work. For her part, navigating the tensions between public display and domestic accomplishment, Maria Cosway became the object of intense public fascination and critical scorn until her eventual departure from England. The Cosways' marriage itself was the subject of much innuendo, with Richard more frequently cast as a cuckold than a lothario. Rather than speculating about the actual sexual lives of the couple, I am interested in the way that erotic gossip structured negative responses to their art, particularly the condemnation of Richard as an effeminate social climber and Maria as a promiscuous woman posing as an artistic genius. That the seeds of this hostility predated Richard's first meeting with Maria becomes clear from a close reading of one of his most ambitious early paintings.

— *"Coxcomical and Ridiculous"* —

In the first week of May 1779, a reviewer for the *St. James's Chronicle* published a brief but damning notice of two paintings by Richard Cosway on display at the newly opened exhibition of the Royal Academy in London: "The Portraits of this Artist are drawn with Precision, and finished with a painful and minute attention to little Circumstances. By these Means, a Bouquet of Flowers, or a Lady's Ruffles, become the principal Object; and his productions acquire a coxcomical and ridiculous air."[14] As decorum dictated, Cosway's portraits were exhibited without identifying their sitters, under the titles "A Lady, Kit-cat" (referring to a half-length format) and "A ditto [that is, another lady] playing on the harp, small whole length."[15] Visitors to the Royal Academy's exhibition enjoyed naming the sitters of portraits while they mingled and gossiped together.[16] For their part, modern scholars have identified Cosway's harpist with Marianne Dorothy Harland, as depicted in a painting now in New York [fig. 85].[17]

At first glance, Cosway's portrait may seem a puzzling target for the reviewer's vehement response in the *St. James's Chronicle*. The painting depicts Miss Harland, the daughter of a vice-admiral, in her dressing room, playing the harp while a lap-dog slumbers at her feet. The sitter occupies a fashionable interior, recognizable as a private feminine space through such features as the dressing table bearing a pincushion, scent bottles, and powder puff. Miss Harland's clothing, a white morning dress and so-called powdering mantle, ties the scene to a specific time of day, before the sitter has presented her public face to the world.[18]

With its lush "Bouquet of Flowers" and the skittering white highlights marking out the sitter's "Ruffles," Miss Harland's portrait is clearly the one that aroused the ire of Cosway's critic. But the epithet "coxcomical and ridiculous" suggests that it was not simply the work but also the painter himself who agitated contemporaries. By the time he exhibited *Marianne Dorothy Harland*, Cosway was thirty-six years old and established in London, having been elected a Royal Academician in 1771. *Marianne Dorothy Harland*, made prior to Cosway's marriage and the beginning of his association with the Prince of Wales, represents his most successful attempt to exhibit ambitious oil paintings at the Royal Academy.

Cosway's painting has a significance beyond the artist's emergence as an ultra-fashionable portraitist and flamboyant cynosure in late eighteenth-century London. It reveals a path not taken in Cosway's own career, while also illuminating debates about gender, luxury, and painting as mediated through female portraiture. In eighteenth-century England, images of women, whether aristocrats, actresses, or courtesans, achieved a new and controversial public status through exhibitions like the Royal Academy's and an ever-expanding market for reproductive prints.[19] English art theorists in the civic humanist tradition founded by Shaftesbury had long associated female beauty with the corrupting effects of luxury and effeminacy, a distraction from art's true purpose of promoting virtue in the ruling class.[20] As the *St. James's Chronicle*'s reviewer attested, Cosway's portrait unsettled contemporary viewers both through an aesthetic defined by the careful

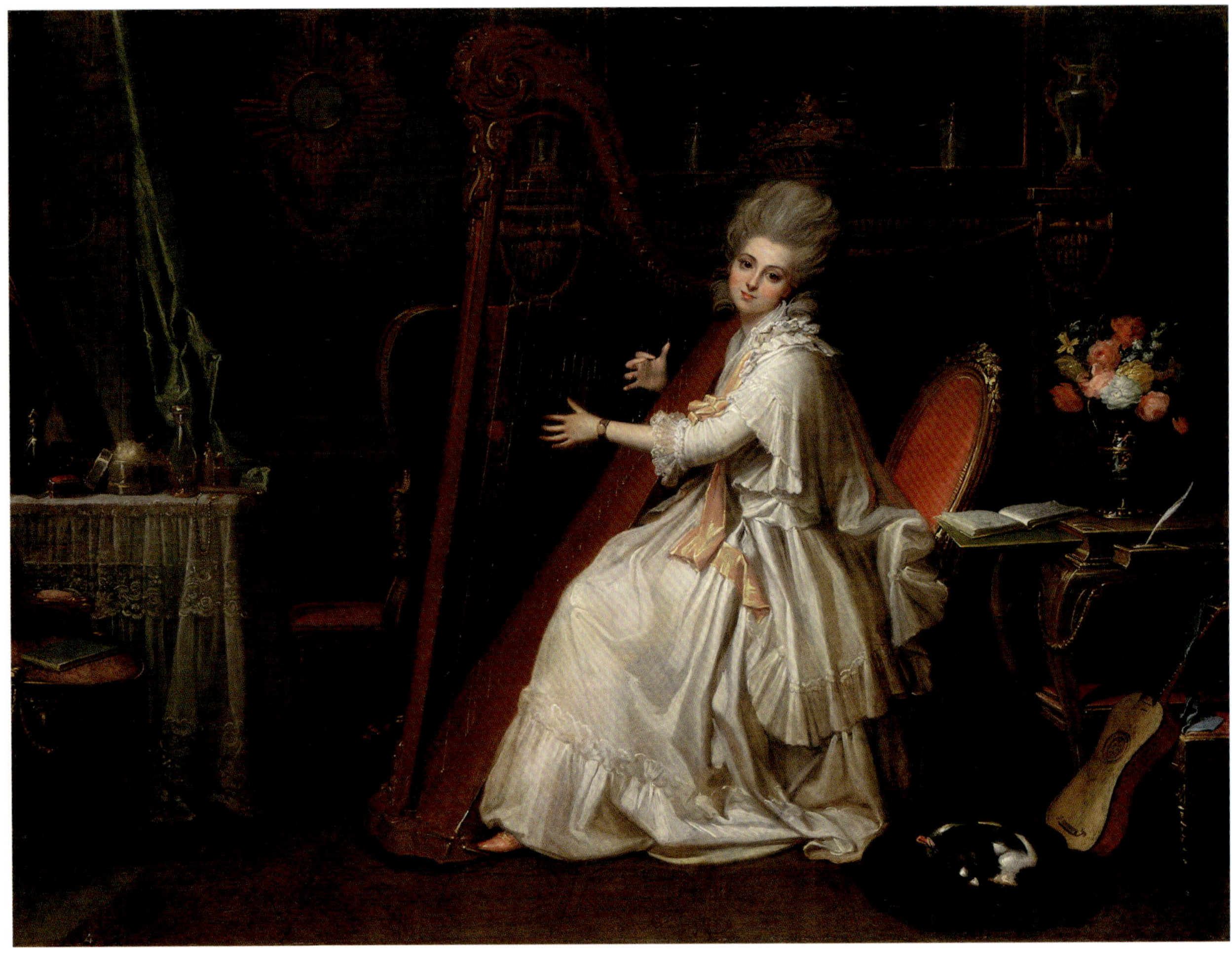

85 Richard Cosway, *Marianne Dorothy Harland*, 1779, oil on canvas, 71.1 × 91.8 cm, New York, Metropolitan Museum of Art

observation of fashionable detail and a male artist who flaunted his identification with feminine luxury.

What did it mean for an artist to announce his ambition with a portrait of a woman? Since the sixteenth century, female portraits had functioned for English writers as stand-ins for painting in general, whether in sonnets or aesthetic treatises. As the previous chapters have shown, Van Dyck's female portraits captured the literary imagination in a way his male portraits never could. Building on this tradition, Gainsborough linked his emulation of Van Dyckian style to his portraits of beautiful women, many of them figures of public controversy. But to an art world increasingly focused on the establishment of institutions and the defense of an English school, portraiture, and particularly female portraiture, could never be an adequate vehicle for national ambition. It was "the art par excellence of selfish interests and particular appearances."[21] The rise of heroic male portraits as exhibition pictures placed further stress upon women's images. Reynolds's series of female portraits of the 1760s, depicting marriageable beauties in mythological guises, proposed one solution to this dilemma, infusing the female likeness with the erudite claims of history painting.[22] Cosway's *Marianne Dorothy Harland*, by contrast, is insistently contemporary and modish in its address to the viewer. Intended for public exhibition and critique at the Royal Academy, it was an unapologetic act of self-identification with the pleasures of feminine consumption and the intimate spaces of the upper-class home.

Today Cosway is remembered, if at all, for miniatures like his self-portrait, painted with minute strokes of a squirrel-hair brush on wafer-thin pieces of ivory. But this was not the medium Cosway chose to exhibit at the Royal Academy, instead submitting oil portraits like *Marianne Dorothy Harland*.[23] For his first exhibition piece, in 1770, he provided a group portrait of three members of the Witts family in classical dress, adopting "the Character of Fortitude introducing Hope as the Companion to Distress" [fig. 86].[24] With its rhetorical gestures and classical costumes, the Witts family group reflected Cosway's initial desire to emulate the heroic portraiture of Reynolds. *Marianne Dorothy Harland*, exhibited nine years later, represents an evolution beyond this first attempt, reconciling Cosway's ambition to paint in oils with his attunement to contemporary fashion and his response to Zoffany's conversation pieces. At the same time, what appears to be a miniature portrait on Miss Harland's bracelet, visible as she raises her hand to the harp, provides a knowing reference to Cosway's other medium.

For over two centuries following the emergence of miniature painting at the Tudor courts, the medium's delicacy and expensive materials gave it a genteel status compared to other branches of painting. By the eighteenth century, however, miniature painting was a decidedly minor art, aptly described by Marcia Pointon as existing "on an axis between portrait painting and the pawnshop, between the Royal Academy and the treasure hoard, between the body and the vitrine."[25] Painted shortly before he cemented his status as one of the greatest of all miniature painters, *Marianne Dorothy Harland* speaks to Cosway's ultimately unsuccessful attempt to make a reputation in the more critically prestigious genre of oil on canvas while retaining the deft and meticulous touch that defined his career.

Viewed up close, *Marianne Dorothy Harland* reveals Cosway's mastery of his oil medium in bravura painterly passages, particularly in the highlights on gilt furniture or the lacey ruffles that so disturbed the *St. James's Chronicle* reviewer [fig. 87]. Nevertheless, the latter's assertion that Cosway's works were "drawn with Precision, and finished with a painful and minute attention" indicates that Cosway was unable to escape his identity as a miniaturist even when working in oils. A more favorable contemporary commentator, the miniaturist Ozias Humphry, said of Cosway, "He inclined more to the neat, the graceful, and the lovely, than toward the serene, the dignified, and the stern, and though his admiration for the antique was great, this was modified by his continuous study of living nature, and from a taste for whatever was soft and delicate."[26] Littleness

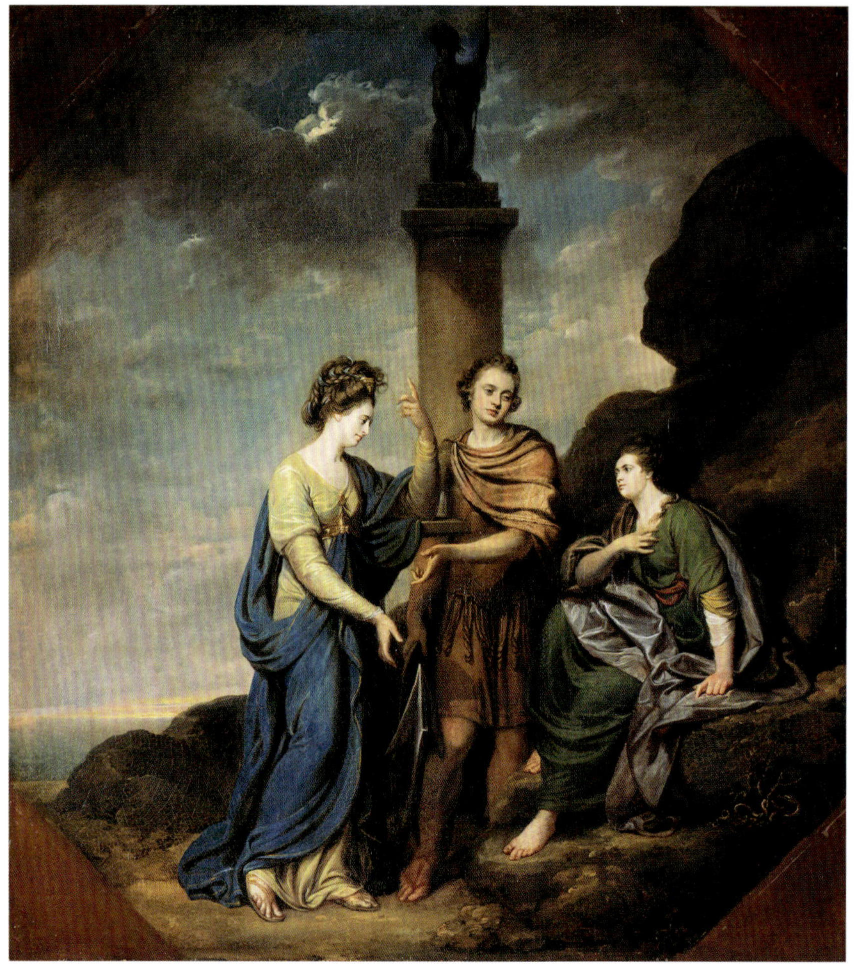

86 Richard Cosway, *The Witts Family*, 1770, oil on canvas, 118 × 104 cm, London, Tate
87 Richard Cosway, *Marianne Dorothy Harland* [detail of fig. 85]

and neatness, qualities of Cosway's art that struck caricaturists as humorously in accord with his body, had long awakened unease on the part of art theorists.[27] For some eighteenth-century critics, a taste for the neat was an obstacle to the heroic (but, in England, perennially beleaguered) genre of history painting. In *An Inquiry into the Real and Imaginary Obstructions to the Acquisition of the Arts in England*, published in 1775, the history painter James Barry decried the fixation of the English on portraiture: "Being attached to little things, we naturally came to admire and to over-rate the little men who succeeded in them."[28] Diminutive Cosway, the "dirty boy" turned "miniature macaroni," embodied for such commentators the effeminate degeneration of English painting.

The gendered dynamics inflecting the reception of Cosway's *Marianne Dorothy Harland* become all the more clear when we consider other paintings on view at the Royal Academy in the spring of 1779. Further down the column from his

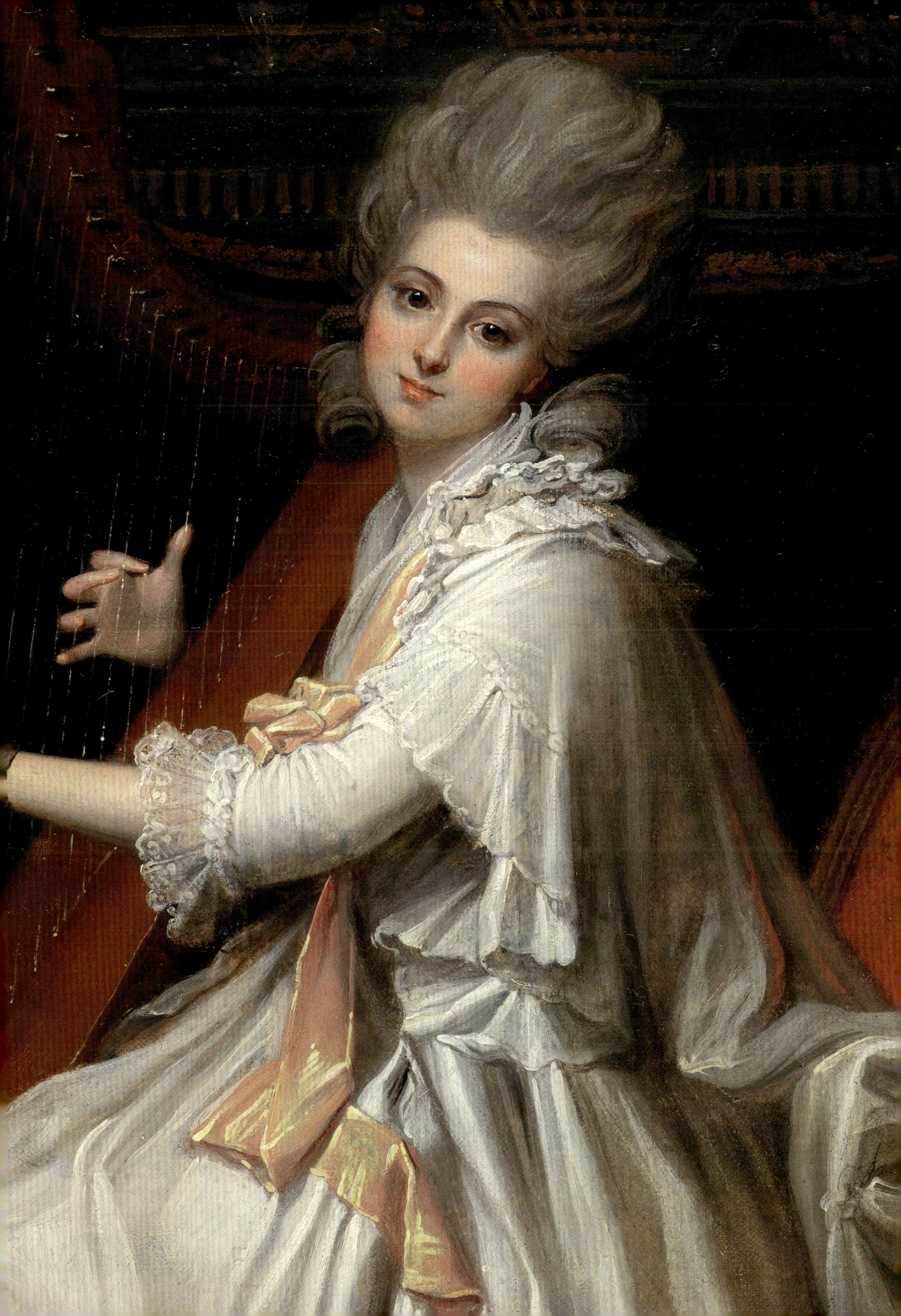

criticism of Cosway, the *St. James's Chronicle* reviewer singled out for praise several works by Angelica Kauffman. While quibbling about a few details of her compositions and titles, the reviewer declared Kauffman's *Magdalen* to be "one of the most beautiful, affecting, and characteristic Figures, we have ever seen," while asserting that "Nothing can exceed the Truth and Delicacy" of a figure entitled *Conjugal Peace* [fig. 88].[29] Kauffman's allegorical portraits, eschewing contemporary fashions in favor of the simplicity of an academic high style, represented the inverse of Cosway's minutely fashionable manner and the "little Circumstances" that absorbed his attention. But as a female painter succeeding in the genres of allegory and history painting, Kauffman was an even more subversive figure than the effete miniaturist.[30] With their works hanging side by side at the most prestigious exhibition venue in London, Cosway and Kauffman both presented conservative critics with an art world whose traditional hierarchies seemed on the brink of toppling.

A poem published in the *Literary Fly* on March 13, 1779, gives further insight into Cosway's standing among contemporary painters at the time he exhibited *Marianne Dorothy Harland*.[31] The poem's preface makes the argument that "There cannot be a more mistaken opinion, than that women in general are attached to trifling objects."[32] Framed as an "Epistle to a Lady, Who Has Retired into the Country," the poem contrasts her sober virtue with contemporary frivolity, pleading with her to return to London and "reign the first and fairest of the fair." Such a return will ensure that "Almighty Fashion shall ... / Deem misplaced ornament the worst abuse; / Keep wealth and whim and novelty in awe, / And fix good sense the standard of her law." With a predictably xenophobic turn, the author declares that the "nymph's" reign will cause "Britain's locusts [to] all be swept away: / French milliners, French dancers; and French plays, / French barbers, French cosmetics, and French stays." Naturally, the poet's muse will inspire painters as well, each contributing his characteristic strengths to her portrayal. Thus, Reynolds brings "his chaste, yet animate design" and Benjamin West a "Grecian figure." For his part, Cosway is distinguished by "Luxuriant fancy." In a poem that dismisses "wealth and whim and novelty," this was at best a back-handed compliment.

The vilification of luxury as a source of corruption and enervation for the national elite had been a recurrent theme of civic humanist discourse throughout the eighteenth century. By the time Cosway exhibited *Marianne Dorothy Harland*, however, some writers, such as Bernard Mandeville or, to a lesser extent, David Hume, had articulated a defense of luxury as a civilizing force and economic spur.[33] At the same time, the culture of sensibility gave rise to a new model of refined masculinity, closely associated with the polish acquired in mixed company.[34] Even the writer for the *Literary Fly* did not outright banish Cosway's "Luxuriant fancy" along with the French barbers and stays, instead placing him on a spectrum of permissible approaches to the depiction of female beauty. Nonetheless, with her hair high and powdered, occupying an interior cluttered

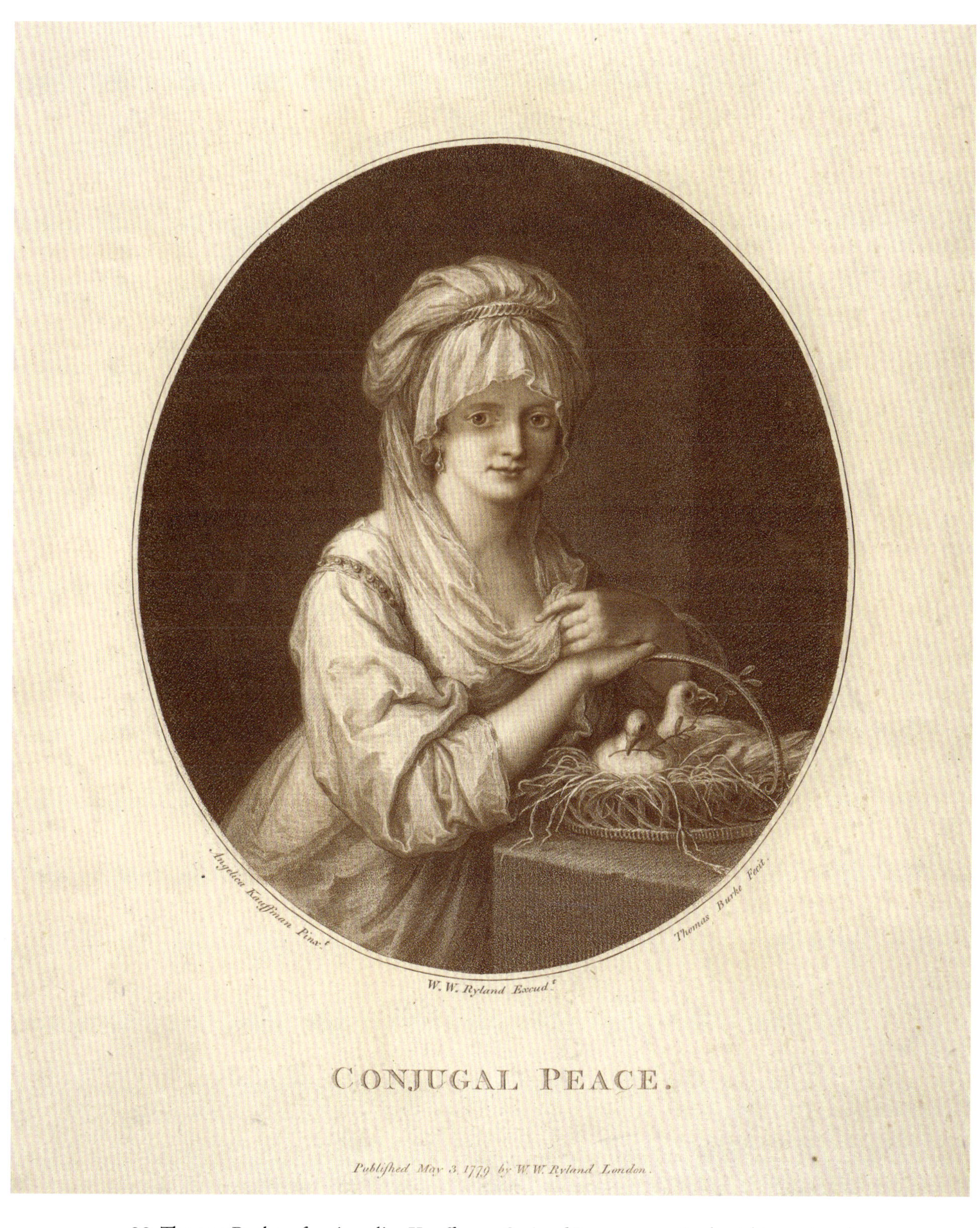

88 Thomas Burke, after Angelica Kauffman, *Conjugal Peace*, 1779, stipple etching printed in red-brown ink, 37 × 31.2 cm, London, British Museum with "trifling objects," *Marianne Dorothy Harland* embodies the fashionable, Francophile, and luxurious femininity targeted by the poem's author. Hostile critics saw in Cosway's paintings the mere painstaking reproduction of fashionable reality. In fact, taking his lead from Zoffany, Cosway populated Miss Harland's dressing room with a range of signifying objects. By examining these objects and considering the identity of his sitter, we can arrive at a closer understanding of the multiple meanings of her portrait.

Marianne Dorothy Harland, born in 1759, was the daughter of Sir Robert Harland, who held the rank of vice-admiral of the red in the spring of 1779 and had been made a baronet in 1771.[35] In the same year that his daughter's portrait hung at the Royal Academy, Sir Robert's name was frequently in the newspapers due to his entanglement in a major naval scandal.[36] On July 27, 1778, Sir Robert had taken part under Admiral Augustus Keppel in the inconclusive Battle of Ushant against the French fleet, commanding the van while Sir Hugh Palliser commanded the rear. After the battle's conclusion, Palliser, responding to rumors that Keppel had accused him of disobedience, successfully demanded the admiral's court-martial in February 1779. Keppel's case became a cause célèbre for the opposition Whigs, with rioters burning Palliser in effigy and gutting his London house following Keppel's acquittal. Sir Robert Harland was the first witness Keppel called to testify on his behalf, after which his testimony was printed in full in the *St. James's Chronicle*.[37] After Keppel's acquittal, Palliser was himself court-martialed in a trial that lasted three weeks, beginning on April 12, 1779. At the end of this rancorous affair, both Keppel's and Palliser's naval careers were ruined, while Harland resigned his command on May 10, 1779 (a week after his daughter's portrait was reviewed in the same newspaper that had printed his testimony). Harland's resignation prompted heated debate in Parliament about the dysfunctional state of the British navy in the midst of the American Revolutionary War.[38]

Sir Robert Harland was almost certainly the patron of Cosway's portrait of his daughter, which was painted four years before her marriage and which remained in the possession of his male descendants until the early twentieth century. Cosway could not have exhibited the portrait at the Royal Academy without Sir Robert's approval. An image of feminine accomplishment in a setting of fashionable luxury, Marianne Dorothy Harland's portrait advertised her father's status as a man who had obtained both a title and a fortune through his naval career: in other words, a man whose social mobility paralleled Cosway's. Viewed in the context of Harland's patronage, the painting can be understood not only as an expression of Cosway's artistic ambition, but also as fulfilling a father's desire to project an image of domestic gentility.

When Cosway's portrait left the possession of Sir Robert's descendants in 1914, it had an apparent pendant, a now untraced portrait also by Cosway depicting Marianne's sister Frances, later Countess Dillon. The two paintings had the same dimensions and remained together until they were sold with other pictures from Wherstead Park. The auction catalogue describes Frances's portrait as "In

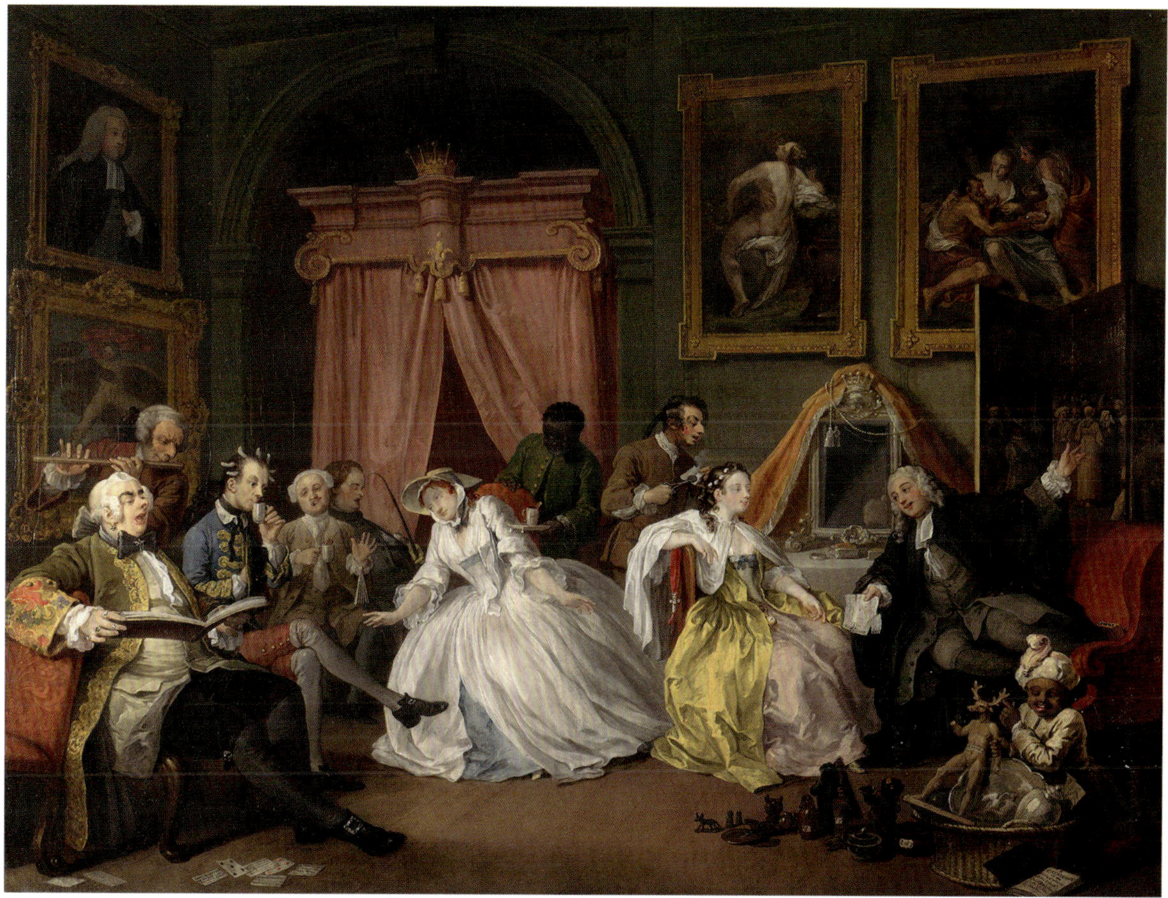

89 William Hogarth, *Marriage-à-la-Mode, 4: The Toilette*, 1743, oil on canvas, 70.5 × 90.8 cm, London, National Gallery

blue dress with white lace trimming; seated in an apartment, holding a letter."[39] Six years later, when the painting was sold again, it was described as "Seated in an apartment before a window, resting her right elbow on a table."[40] Frances Harland's portrait may have been a simultaneous commission with that of Marianne, but it was certainly not the kit-cat composition exhibited that same year at the Royal Academy. From the description, it is clear that both portraits of the vice-admiral's daughters adapted a conversation piece format to depict single sitters. The letter in Frances Harland's portrait may have been a device to link her with the open writing desk and quill pen in the painting of Marianne.

Cosway's depiction of Marianne in her dressing room was itself a significant choice, with clear art historical and social resonances. Cosway exhibited his sitter in attire that she would never have worn in public, in a space of the house accessible only to intimate visitors.[41] Hogarth had parodied the questionably secluded nature of the lady's dressing room in the fourth scene of his *Marriage-à-la-Mode* series from 1743 [fig. 89]. Here, the parvenu countess receives musicians

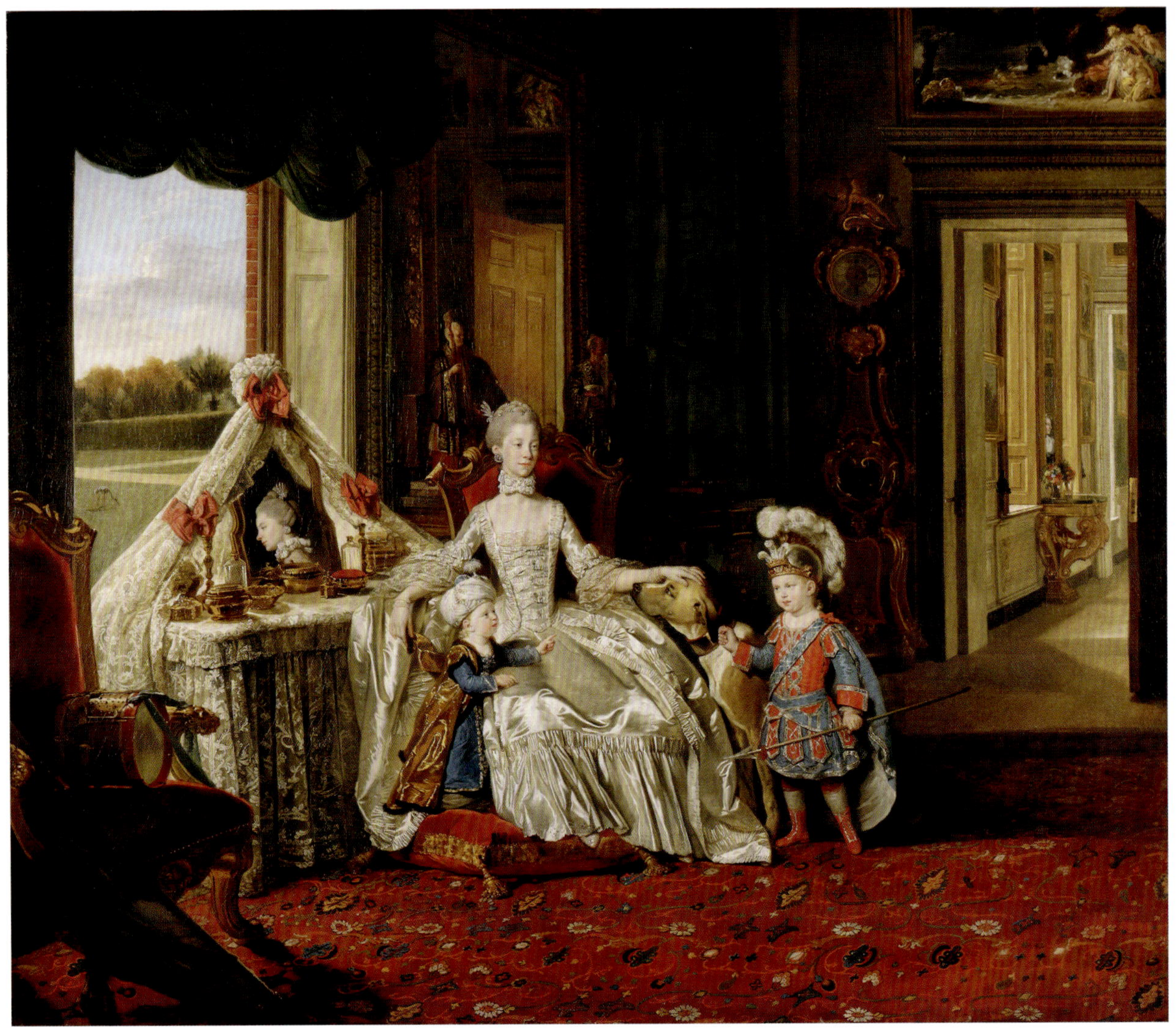

90 Johan Zoffany, *Queen Charlotte with Her Two Eldest Sons*, 1764, oil on canvas, 112.2 × 128.3 cm, Royal Collection

and admirers while having her hair curled. Surrounded by "a microcosm of banal commodities," the countess embodies an amoral form of cosmopolitan consumerism with roots dating back to the Caroline London of Shirley's *Lady of Pleasure*, whose protagonist likewise received her sycophantic callers at home.[42] Indeed, Hogarth's conversation pieces and "modern moral subjects" represent an attempt to fashion a visual satire of the commodity culture that English writers had been critiquing for more than a century. Closer to Cosway's representation of Marianne Dorothy Harland, both in its positive depiction of the dressing room as an intimate space and its embrace of luxury goods, is Zoffany's portrait of Queen Charlotte at her dressing table from 1764 [fig. 90]. Here, the queen appears in her preferred guise of devoted mother, receiving her two eldest sons in the early afternoon, after she has dressed but before she dines with the king.[43]

Zoffany depicts the dressing room as a private space for family intimacy that is also shaped by the queen's exquisite taste. Cosway's portrait pays similar tribute to the Harland family's refinement with its careful attention to such objects as the sunburst clock, mounted celadon vases, or cabriole-legged writing desk.[44] At the same time, the book resting on a chair, the opened desk, and the sleeping dog convey the intimacy of the scene, as though not yet tidied for company. Unlike Hogarth or Zoffany, Cosway does not depict interactions within the dressing room. Instead, Miss Harland, shown by herself, directs her gaze outward, positioning the viewer of the picture as the auditor of her intimate concert.

As a private space of refined consumption, artistic performance, and the entertainment of privileged guests, Miss Harland's dressing room provides a feminine, domestic analogue to the Van Dyckian studio. Indeed, her harp playing locates her in a lineage extending back to the ostensibly amateur "performances" of Joan Carlile, Mary Beale, or Anne Killigrew. As his own wealth grew and his social persona overtook his artistic ambition, Cosway himself increasingly blurred the distinctions between studio, home, exhibition space, and concert venue. His staging of an artistic persona within the context of the luxurious studio-residence was vividly evoked by his biographer Smith, who could "recollect seeing him stand at the fireside, upon one of Madame Pompadour's rugs, leaning against a chimney-piece, dedicated to the Sun, the ornaments of which were sculptured by Banks, giving instructions to a picture-dealer."[45] Smith's memory echoes those of visitors to the homes of Van Dyck and Rubens, where collecting and making similarly mingled, and where the curiosities on display might provide the pretext for a royal visit. In Cosway's case, the lavishly appointed home of his later years surpassed even the luxurious interior he had minutely recreated (or imagined) for *Marianne Dorothy Harland*. In much the same way, his identification with feminine accomplishment, as expressed in Miss Harland's portrait, gave a foretaste of his marital and creative partnership with Maria Cosway.

In a studio an artist paints sitters, and in the eighteenth-century dressing room both men and women were painted with cosmetics. Cosway depicted Marianne Dorothy Harland with powdered hair and a powder puff prominently visible on her dressing table. (The dressing table was itself a highly fashionable and luxurious piece of furniture.)[46] By emphasizing his sitter's use of cosmetics, Cosway may have intended an ironic allusion to contemporary criticisms of portraiture as a kind of "face painting" that encouraged feminine vanity and deception.[47] The fraught nature of powder and the dressing room's status as a liminal space of transformation become clear in a scene from *The Sylph*, a novel published anonymously in 1778 by Cosway's friend and patron, Georgiana, Duchess of Devonshire. Upon her arrival in London, the novel's newly married heroine must undergo the ordeal of powdering and hairdressing at the hands of a macaroni-esque "Monsieur" before her presentation at court:

Monsieur bowed and shrugged, just like an overgrown monkey. In a moment I was overwhelmed with a cloud of powder. "What are you doing? I do not mean to be powdered," I said. "Not powdered!" repeated Sir William; "why you would not be so barbarous as to appear without – it positively is not decent."

"I thought," answered I, "you used to admire the colour of my hair – how often have you praised its glossy hue! and called me your nut-brown maid!"

"Pho! pho!" said he, blushing, perhaps lest he should be suspected of tenderness, as that is very vulgar, "I can bear to see a woman without powder in summer; but now the case is otherwise.[48]

This scene exposes the artifice (and discomfort) behind the curled and powdered appearance that Cosway's portrait seeks to naturalize. Himself a kind of artistic "Monsieur," Cosway did not depict the actual procedures for which a dressing room was intended. Instead, Marianne appears already powdered but not yet formally dressed, displaying her accomplishment as she plays the harp that dominates her dressing room.

Another account of Cosway's studio likewise plays upon the double-edged analogy of painter and hairdresser. The solicitor William Hickey commissioned a portrait of his mistress Charlotte Barry from Cosway before the couple was to depart for India together early in 1782. Upon first receiving Hickey's commission, Cosway "replied that he never had been so deeply engaged in business," but, "as he really wished to oblige me, and saw a peculiar character of countenance in Mrs. Barry of which he was sure he should succeed in making a superior picture, he would for once in his life act a deceitful part by shutting himself up and refusing admittance to anybody under the plea of illness, until he had completed the work." Cosway "requested [Mrs. Barry] would come and sit to him the following morning. I accordingly accompanied her, and was much amused by observing the progress of the picture, soon perceiving that he would make a beautiful thing of it." With his protestations and ultimate granting of exclusivity, Cosway was, of course, reviving a timeworn trope of studio politesse, familiar already from Rubens's concession of a sitting to the Countess of Arundel. Hickey, "observing the progress of the picture," also placed himself within the long lineage of English virtuosi who occupied an ambivalent spectator position within the atelier. At the same time, Cosway, Hickey, and Mrs. Barry together reenacted the triangular structure so characteristic of literary accounts of the portrait sitting.

Hickey notes that for her sittings with Cosway, Mrs. Barry's hair was dressed by Hickey's manservant Freskini "in the most fashionable elegant style, so much so as to draw from Cosway the remark that he never had seen a finer head of hair." But on another occasion,

After Charlotte had sat twice we, one morning upon our return from riding, called at Cosway's in Berkeley Row, not with any idea of her then sitting again, she being in her

> *riding habit, but merely to see the progress he had made during the preceding day. The weather being uncommonly clear and fine for the time of year, we had taken so long a ride as to put her quite in a glow, and she looked remarkably well. Some of her curls having blown loose, she had taken off her hat and was standing before a glass arranging them when Cosway entered the room. He gave a start of surprize, exclaiming, "Good God! what an alteration for the better. I declare on my honour I should not know you for the same woman. Come here, come along with me this moment, just as you are. No more dressed head, powder, or pomatum. I never saw such a change, so now is the time to show you off to advantage." Then presenting his hand he led her into his painting room, rubbed out the elegantly arranged hair* [from her portrait], *and drew her exactly as she then sat before me, making as he predicted one of the most beautiful pictures I ever beheld, the likeness being inimitable. After sitting full three hours, I saw evidently that he was greatly delighted with it himself. With some difficulty I prevailed upon him not to touch it any more, feeling satisfied it could not be improved and might be hurt by attempting at a higher finishing. I would willingly have carried it away at that time, but that he would not hear of, saying he must touch the drapery a little, besides which he was too proud of his performance not to be desirous of showing it to a few persons who were real connoisseurs. A week afterwards I received it from Cosway, and it has ever since been my inseparable companion.*[49]

By now, we can recognize in Hickey's tale many of the classic features of the studio anecdote, built around the encounter between male writer, his demimondaine mistress, and the fashionable painter who portrays her. Within this encounter, Charlotte Barry is notably silent and passive, while Hickey and Cosway enact a mild male rivalry. Hickey fears that the painter will ruin his portrait with "higher finishing," and Cosway refuses to part with it before showing the miniature off to a few "real connoisseurs." Cosway's willingness to shut off his studio to all other clients confers a special status upon Mrs. Barry and, by extension, her lover. Rather than being yet another product of Cosway's large-scale portrait production, this miniature emerges from an intense and exclusive triangle of sitter, painter, and lover. Cosway's fixation on the sitter's coiffure associates him, somewhat demeaningly, with the Italian hairdresser Freskini, at the same time that his preference for a more natural style without "powder, or pomatum" marks his greater discernment (and perhaps native-born English virility).

Like his depiction of Charlotte Barry, Cosway's representation of Marianne Dorothy Harland blended cosmetic artifice with claims to intimacy and naturalness. At the same time, his sitter's central attribute, the harp, emphasizes her status as an accomplished woman and not merely an ornamental beauty. The harp, played by none other than Marie Antoinette, had strong associations with femininity and amateur accomplishment in the late eighteenth century.[50] A year before Cosway's painting was exhibited, Mozart composed his famous flute and harp concerto for two French aristocratic amateurs, the Duc de Guines and his daughter.[51] Alongside its social prestige, the harp required a display of the performer's body that some observers found unsettlingly seductive. Placed between the player's legs, the harp calls attention to shapely arms and fingers, while the pedal requires the visible animation of the foot, as Cosway's portrait makes clear.[52] English novels associated harp playing with flirtation and worse: Mary Crawford, the heroine's glamorous but morally corrupt romantic rival in Jane Austen's *Mansfield Park*, infamously attempts to requisition a cart to transport her harp in the middle of the harvest.[53] The delicate play of Marianne Harland's fingers evokes a lover's caress but also allegorizes the deft touch of the miniaturist, recorded in the highlights carefully placed on each shimmering string.

Miss Harland's painted concert takes place in a part of the home explicitly coded as private, the dressing room. Ann Bermingham has discussed a shift in the late eighteenth century away from feminine display in public spaces such as the assembly room and toward the performance of accomplishment in a domestic setting.[54] Cosway's portrait of Miss Harland located her in precisely such a putatively private place of intimate recreation, but it was destined for exhibition at the Royal Academy. Contrasting her with a professional musician, Gillian Perry has characterized Miss Harland's address of the beholder as "safely flirtatious," arguing that her social status insulated her from "connotations of coquetry."[55] But the exhibition of the portrait to an audience who could identify its sitter by means of gossip (and who might subject the portrait to excoriating reviews in the press) meant that Miss Harland's security as a genteel young lady only went so far. If she visited the exhibition at the Royal Academy, others in attendance might have attempted to compare her portrait with its original, drawing attention that could be compromising for a gentleman's unmarried daughter, particularly a gentleman implicated in a very public naval scandal. A writer for the *Public Advertiser* noted that when Cosway exhibited a portrait of the notorious Duchess of Cumberland in 1781, the presence of the sitter herself on opening day "*confronting* her own portrait" gave rise to animated discussions about Cosway's likeness.[56]

Commissioned by her father and relying on conventional tropes of feminine accomplishment, the portrait tells us very little about Marianne Dorothy Harland herself. The historical record is scarcely more informative, attesting merely to Harland's marriage, in 1783, to William Dalrymple and her death two years later. It is only in her will that a faint and largely formulaic echo of her own voice survives.[57] The will primarily concerns the fate of the £500 in annuities settled upon her by Sir Robert at her marriage, but also records more personal wishes, as when she gave "all my Trinkets Cloathes and wearing apparel" to her sister and executrix Susan Edith Rowley, or expressed the desire "that my Body may be deposited in the vault of my ffathers family ... unless I happen to depart this life in a fforeign country and in that case I desire that my heart may be put into an urn and sent home and deposited in the said vault and that my body may be thrown into the sea." As noted above, Cosway's portrait was unlikely to have ever been in the sitter's own possession, remaining in that of her father, brother, and their descendants until the early twentieth century. It is a painting of a woman by a man, made for another man, that adopts feminine domesticity as the vehicle of male ambitions.

— *"The Grey Mare"* —

Both the individual portrait of Marianne Dorothy Harland and Richard Cosway's entire career demonstrate the fraught nature of a male artist's self-identification with female portraiture. As noted above, Richard Cosway publicly circulated his wife Maria's image and encouraged her to exhibit her own work, while prohibiting her from engaging with the commercial art market. In the context of his *Marianne Dorothy Harland*, the compensatory role for Maria Cosway's career played by semi-private musical performances is particularly striking. Immediately following her lament, in the autobiographical letter cited above, about the decline in her artistic studies as a result of her amateur status, Cosway continues:

> *My exercise in Music made my Evenings very agreeable. Lady Lyttelton and the Hon*[oura]*ble Mrs Damer Countess of Ailesbury, Lady Cecilia Johnston, The Marchioness of Townsend were my most intimate friends ... Lady M. Duncan, Miss Wilks and General Paoli, the Foreign Ministers, the distinguished foreigners Lord Sands, Mr Erskine the most distinguished talents and many such formed the agreeable evening society Until they became great Concerts and these Concerts have been mentioned in a work on Music published in Germany of the first professors. H.R.H the Prince of Wales honor'd constantly.*[58]

Richard Cosway's portrait of Miss Harland imagined a private concert in the most intimate of domestic spaces, but then transgressed that intimacy through the work's exhibition at the Royal Academy. Likewise, the Cosways' musical evenings turned feminine and domestic accomplishment into the spectacle of social arrival. Some of the vitriol the couple inspired can be traced to this insistent blurring of public and private, home and studio, and amateur and professional.

A print by William Birch, after a painted collaboration between William Hodges and Richard Cosway, neatly captures Maria Cosway's status as liminal performer, occupying a threshold between public and private display [fig. 91]. In the print, Maria gazes out of an enormous picture window, sitting in a space the inscription identifies as "MR. COSWAY'S BREAKFAST-ROOM PALL MALL." With a book dangling from one hand and a dog leaping up at her, Maria figures as an embodiment of cultured but resolutely inactive femininity. She adorns her husband's home and, by implication, his studio. Moreover, he permits images of her to circulate as reproductions on the open market. Like the row of potted plants on the windowsill, Maria strains toward the sun and the outer world while remaining irrevocably a product of domestic cultivation.

Of course, Maria's public image was shaped by her own self-portraits as well as by her husband's depictions of her. In responding to these works, contemporary critics enjoyed playing the artistic spouses off against one another.

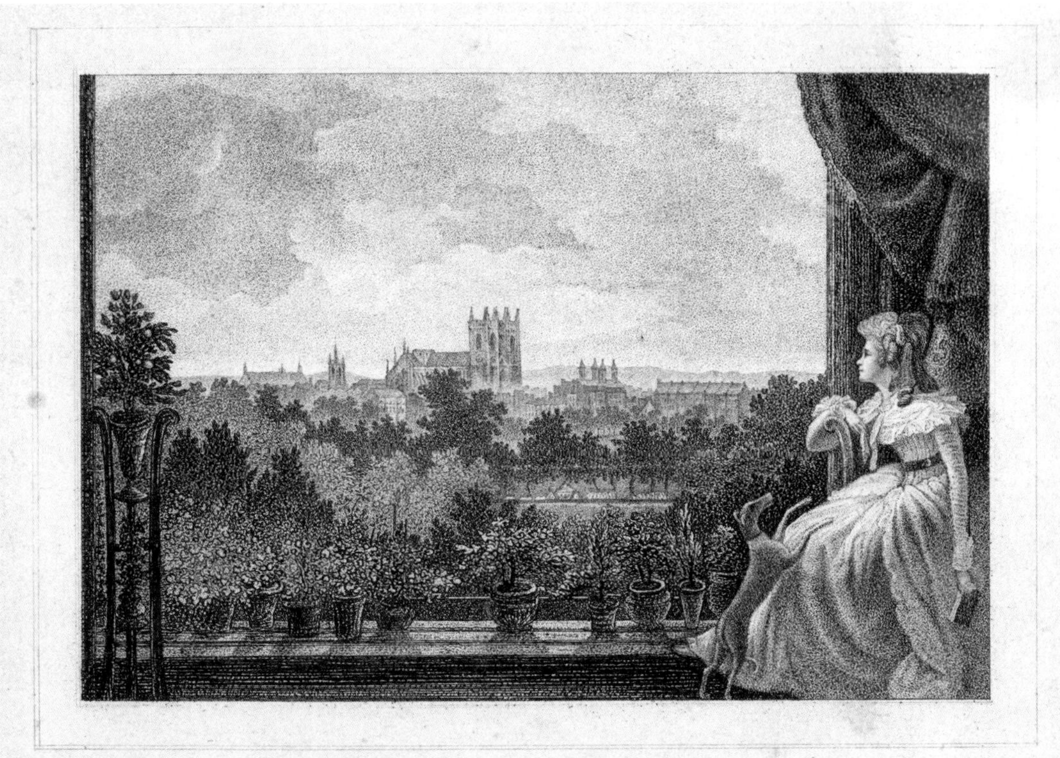

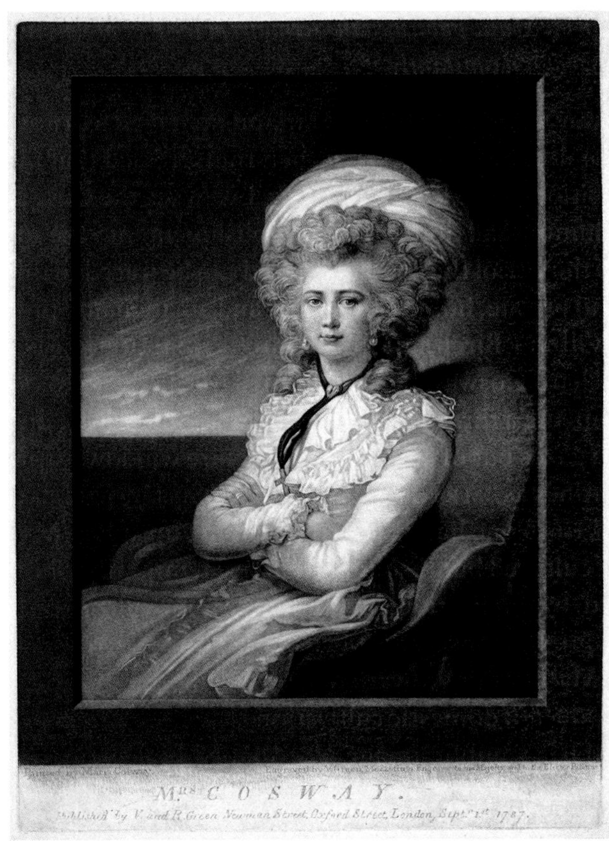

91 William Birch, after Richard Cosway and William Hodges, *A View from Mr. Cosway's Breakfast-Room Pall Mall*, 1789, stipple etching and engraving, 18.3cm × 21.8 cm, London, Victoria and Albert Museum

92 Valentine Green, after Maria Cosway, *Maria Cosway*, 1787, mezzotint, 46.7 × 34 cm, Royal Collection

Summarizing the Royal Academy's exhibition in May 1787, the reviewer for the *St. James's Chronicle* began with a caustic discussion of Richard's submission: "No. 93. *Portraits of a Lady and Child*. – This is said to be Lady Page, formerly the buxom milliner of St. James's-Street. Cosway, as usual, has stiffened her figure. He would be an excellent Painter for the Humane Society."[59] Implying that Richard's sitter resembles a drowned woman (in need of the Humane Society's rescue), the reviewer traffics in exhibition gossip, unmasking a sitter's dubious social origins at the same time as he cuts her portraitist down to size. The next paragraph shifts to Maria's own two submissions, including her self-portrait [fig. 92]:

> *To apply a common Phrase to the Family of the Cosways, "The Grey Mare is the better Horse" – the Productions of Maria are much superiour to those of her Husband ... the Portrait of herself, No. 251, though a Symptom of the Family Vanity, possesses considerable Merit. We congratulate this Lady, on her Departure from the extravagant Stile of Composition she first adopted, with so little success.*[60]

The reviewer repeats a pattern from the same newspaper's earlier discussion of *Marianne Dorothy Harland*, in which a dismissal of Cosway's work precedes a more positive, if condescending, discussion of a woman painter (in the earlier case,

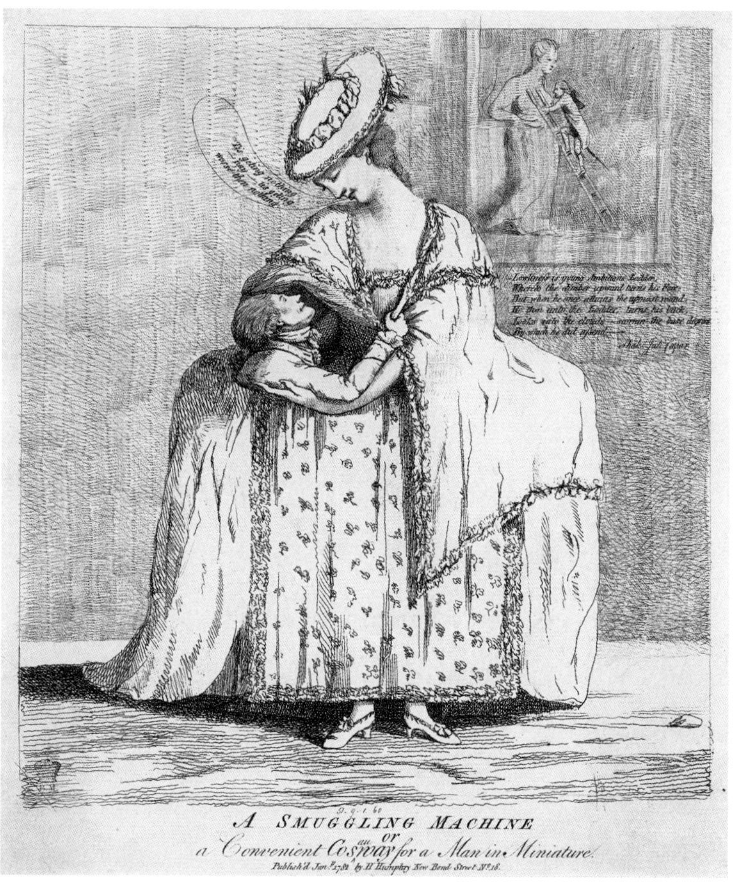

93 Unknown artist, *A Smuggling Machine* ..., 1781, engraving, 27.7 × 23.6 cm, London, British Museum

Angelica Kauffman). Given his antipathy toward Richard, the reviewer's validation of Maria may primarily reflect her usefulness to him as a foil, a wife who outclassed her husband even after Richard forbade her "to rank professionally." Such invidious comparisons had already found an even more pointed expression in a caricature from 1781, in which a tiny and infantilized Richard emerges from Maria's monumental hoop skirt [fig. 93].[61]

More than "a Sympton of ... Vanity," Cosway's 1787 self-portrait is also her own redaction of an iconic seventeenth-century image, Rubens's so-called *Chapeau de Paille* [fig. 94].[62] This painting had already inspired the self-portrait of another celebrated woman artist, Elisabeth Vigée Le Brun [fig. 95]. Here, the painter uncrossed the arms of her Rubensian prototype to display her palette and brushes.[63] Maria Cosway, by contrast, heightened the constriction of the gesture. Whereas the crossed arms in Rubens's painting appear to function largely as a framing device for the sitter's décolletage, Cosway adapted them as a protective

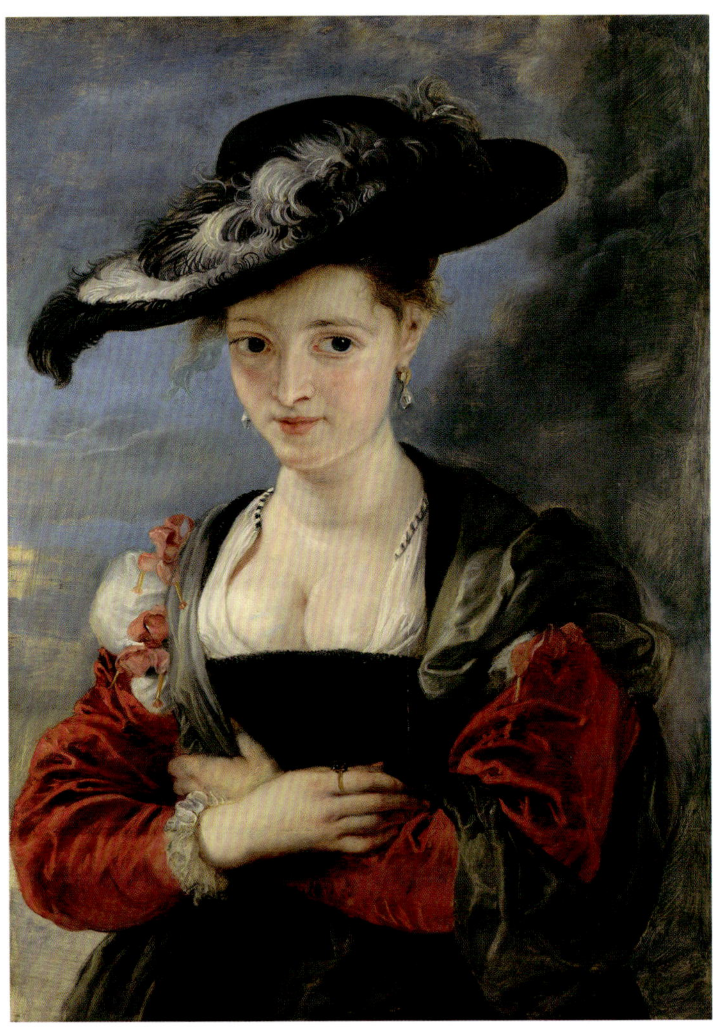

94 Peter Paul Rubens, *Susanna Lunden ("Le Chapeau de Paille")*, ca. 1622–25, oil on panel, 79 × 54.6 cm, London, National Gallery

or defensive pose. Displaying her self-portrait in a public exhibition, but prohibited by her husband from working professionally, she makes a show of idle arms and feminine restraint far more ambivalent than Richard Cosway's depiction of her breakfast room reverie. At the same time, she successfully emulated her husband's idol, Rubens, to the extent that contemporary critics perceived her as a stronger painter than Richard.

Prohibited by her husband from selling her work, Maria Cosway was nevertheless an artist very much in the public eye, both through the printed circulation of her likeness and through her regular contributions to the exhibitions of the Royal Academy. The extensive contemporary critical response to her work reveals both her prominence as well as the changed circumstances of artistic culture in England by the 1780s. A painter operating in the Van Dyckian mode no longer had to contend only with the work of coterie poets or veiled allusions in drama. Instead, Maria Cosway saw her work, persona, and even morality dissected in newsprint.

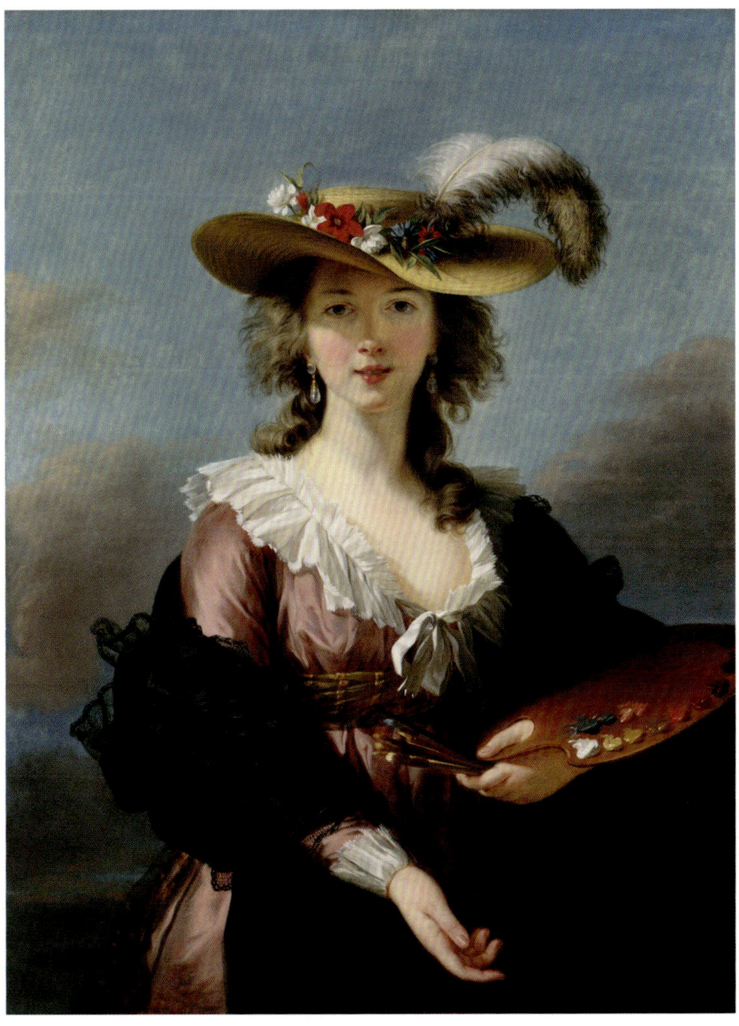

95 Elisabeth Vigée Le Brun, *Self-Portrait in a Straw Hat*, 1782, oil on canvas, 97.8 × 70.5 cm, London, National Gallery

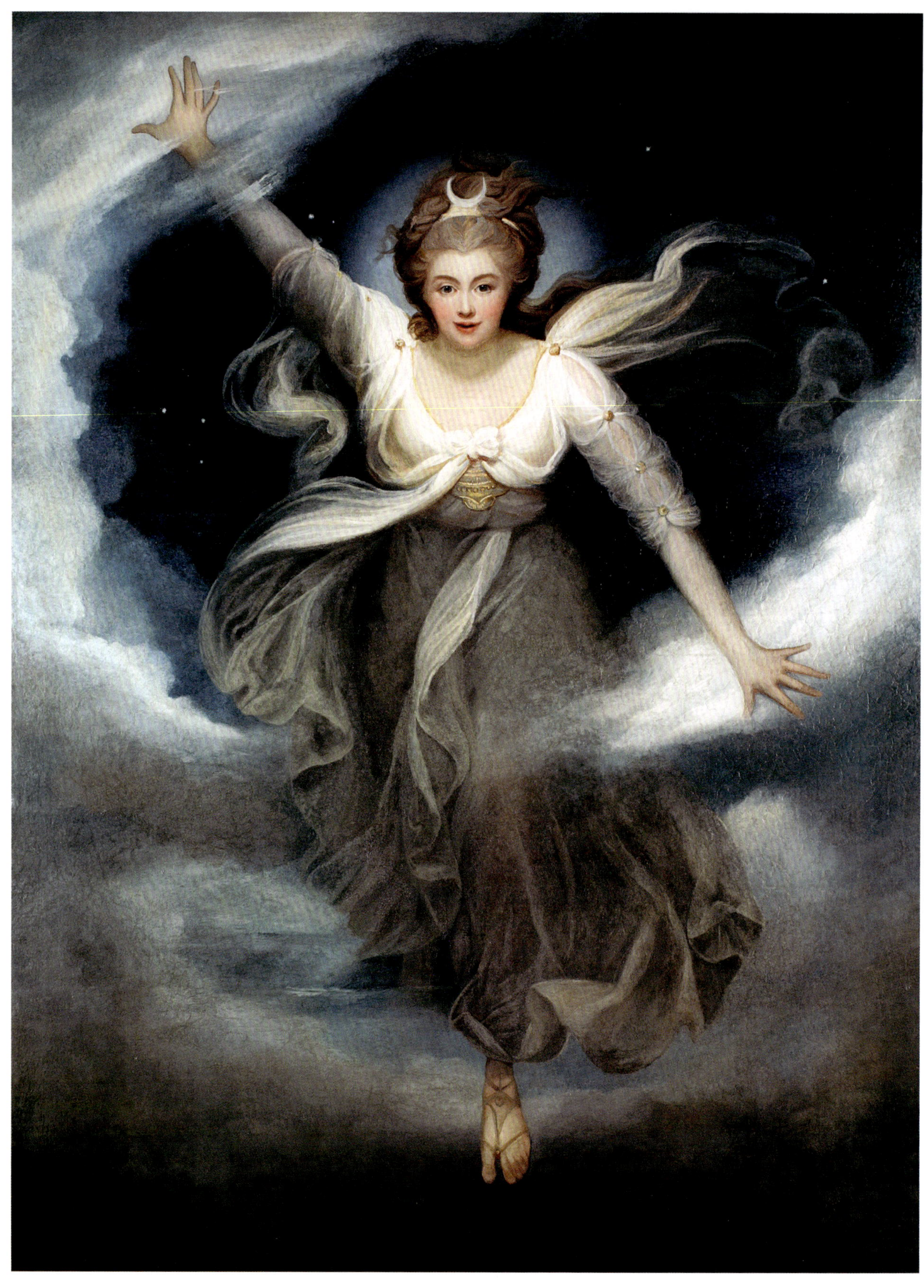

96 Maria Cosway, *Georgiana, Duchess of Devonshire, as Cynthia*, 1782, oil on canvas, 219.7 × 160 cm, Bakewell, Chatsworth

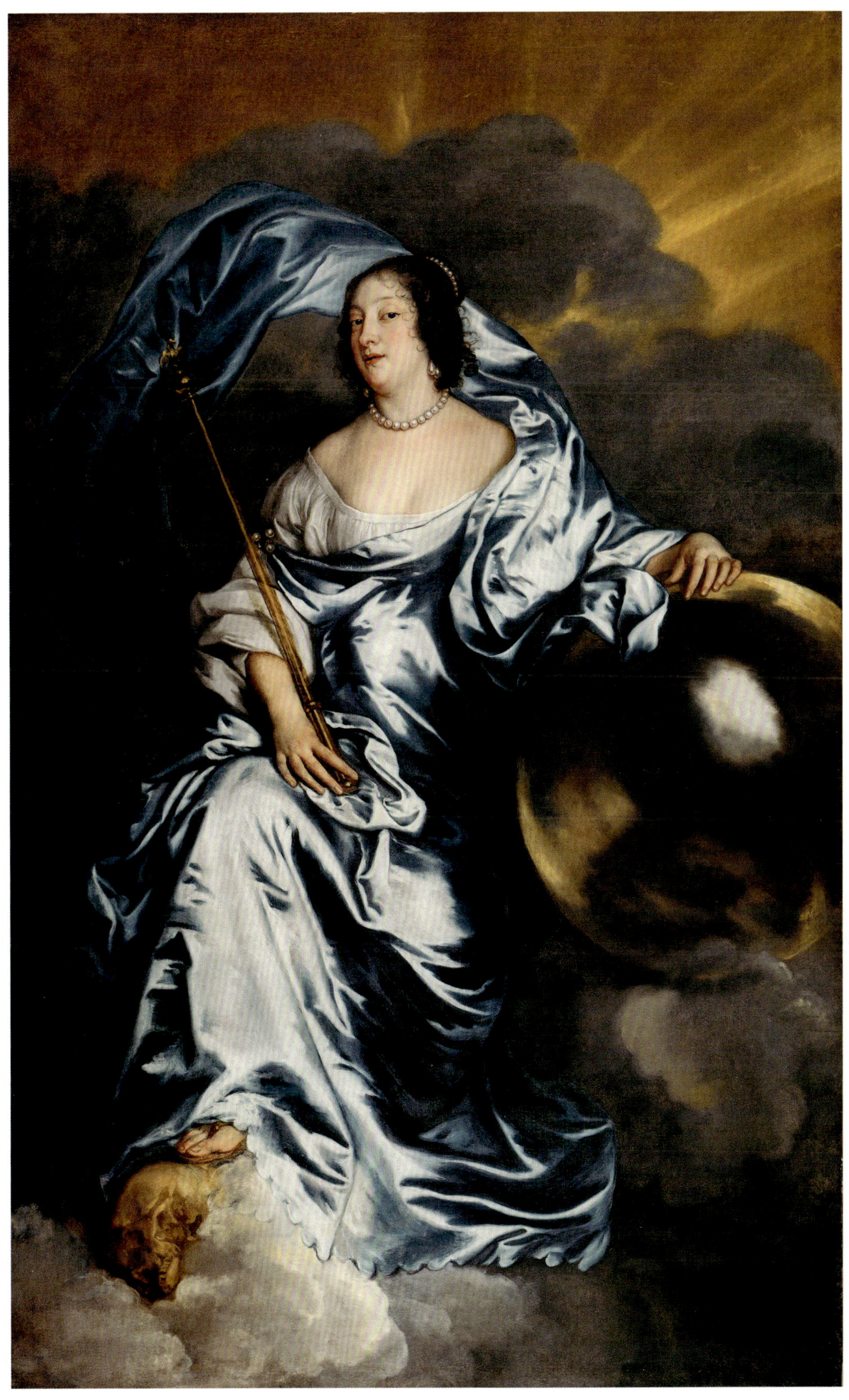

97 Anthony van Dyck, *Rachel de Ruvigny, Countess of Southampton, as Fortune*, ca. 1638, oil on canvas, 219.5 × 132.5 cm, Cambridge, Fitzwilliam Museum

Cosway's portrait of Georgiana, Duchess of Devonshire, one of her most ambitious paintings, prompted a revealing outpouring of both praise and ridicule when it was exhibited in 1782 [fig. 96]. The portrait depicts the duchess in full-length, in the guise of Cynthia, the goddess of the moon, as described in Spenser's *Faerie Queene*. Drawing its motif from English Renaissance literature, Cosway's composition takes its visual cues from the *portraits historiés* of the seventeenth century. The duchess appears in classical drapery, her sandal-clad foot grounding a plumb line that bisects the composition. Parting the clouds, the sitter's arms extend like spokes of a wheel as she appears to stride out of the canvas and into the space of the viewer. The portrait's dynamic forward movement animates the more static configuration of works like Van Dyck's portrait of the Countess of Southampton as the goddess of fortune, while proposing a similar apotheosis of a titled female sitter [fig. 97].

Exhibited under the title "Cynthia," the painting's status as a portrait of a contemporary celebrity was obvious to its first commentators. It divided the critics, with one notably effusive response coming from a contributor to the *Morning Chronicle*, writing under the name "Candid." The critic praised the portrait of "the Duchess of Devonshire in the character of the Moon, illuminating our lower hemisphere," noting both "the elegant compliment every way conveyed by it" from painter to sitter, as well as "the originality and delicacy of the thoughts [which do] this tasteful female painter the highest credit." From there, Candid built to a laudatory crescendo:

> *When I add to this, that from the action we may learn grace, from the chaste style of colouring natural effect, that the portrait has strong likeness, accompanied with character, and that the whole partakes as largely as the subject will admit of the sublime, I think I can hardly be suspected of paying this lady a compliment at the expence of truth, by asserting that she is the first of female painters, and inferior only among the male sex to her husband, and to Sir. J. Reynolds ... But what most pleases me in this lady's compositions, is, that they bespeak a mind adorned with picture learning, and taste to distinguish the great from the little, and all her errors are on the right side. She is often carried into the regions of wild imagination, but never travels the barren road of common nature.*[64]

While Candid notably avoids praising Maria Cosway over her husband, he does laud her art in terms that distinguish it from Richard's characteristic littleness and neatness, declaring that Maria can "distinguish the great from the little" and even endow portraiture with an effect "of the sublime." He implies that she has achieved heroic qualities in portraiture which perennially evaded her husband.

Candid's panegyric swiftly evoked a devastating response, published by "C.D." in *Parker's General Advertiser* on May 21, 1782. Accusing Candid of being a hack in the service of the Cosways, with the intention "to erect the fame of that gemini of artists, whom he so lavishly extols, on the ruins of the reputation of several of the first painters [of] England," C.D. skewered every aspect of Candid's praise

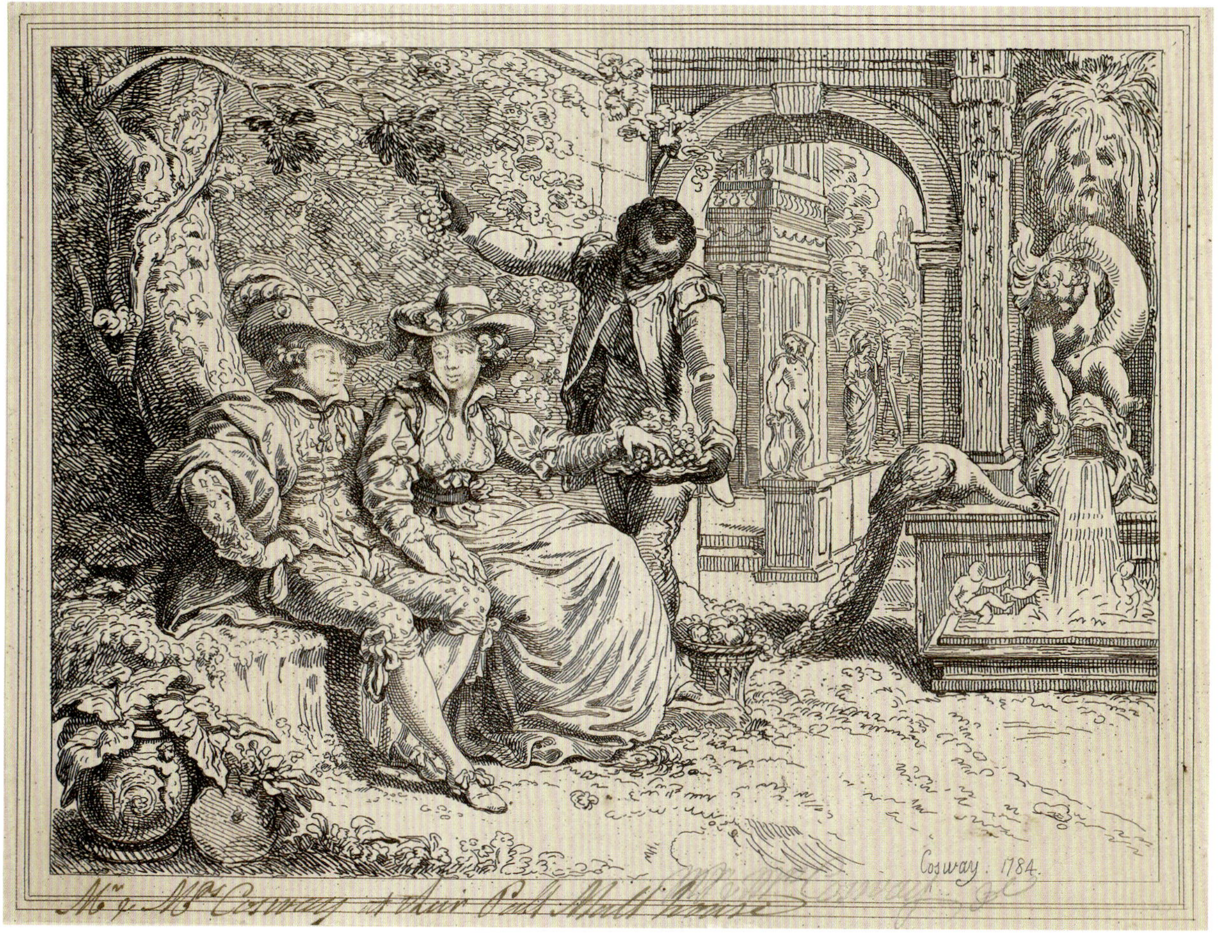

98 Richard Cosway, *A Self-Portrait with Maria Cosway and Ottobah Cugoano*, 1784, etching, 24.5 × 31.5 cm, Royal Collection

for the two painters, such as the notion that Maria's "very *errors* are perfections." He finally arrived at a grudging concession of certain merits to Richard Cosway, very much at the cost of Maria's own achievement: "He is certainly no mean artist. Many of his pictures deserve praise, and even the Cynthia of Mrs. Cosway, I suspect, owes much of its moderate value to conjugal affection."[65] Here, C.D.'s admission of Richard Cosway's talent took the form of a conservative restoration of the natural order, in which the wife's talent is subsumed within, or attributed to, her husband's.

Such critiques appear to have had no effect on Richard Cosway's promotion of his marriage as a key facet of his public persona. In an etching dated 1784, he again adopted a Rubensian prototype to advertise the couple's domestic contentment [fig. 98]. This etching depicts the Cosways in seventeenth-century dress, seated under a grapevine in a garden that represents a pastiche of elements from Rubens's own family portraits [see fig. 80]. Yet this is not a simple depiction of a couple or a family, but rather that of three individuals linked by ambiguous gestures. The Cosways are attended by a Black servant who occupies the center of the composition as he proffers a platter of grapes to Maria. Through his inclusion of this figure within the etching, Cosway again positioned himself within a Van Dyckian lineage, drawing upon one of its most enduring, and disturbing, compositional devices, the Black page who attends a primary white sitter.

J. T. Smith recalled that at "No. 4, Berkeley-street, opposite the Duke of Devonshire's wall, I first saw Mr. Cosway; and at that time he kept a black servant, who published an octavo work upon Slavery."[66] Smith's biographical sketch conveys the artist's upward social trajectory through real estate, charting moves from Portman Square to Berkeley Street and Schomberg House on Pall Mall.[67] Smith juxtaposes Cosway's proximity to a ducal wall with his employment of a "black servant," harnessing both details as signifiers of a fashionable household. At the same time, Cosway's employment of a Black domestic who was also an artist's model places him within a lineage of British artists, Reynolds among them. Smith notes that Cosway's quarters at Schomberg House were previously occupied by Nathaniel Hone, "who kept a famous black woman in it as his model."[68]

Unlike Hone's unnamed model, Cosway's servant can now be identified as Ottobah Cugoano, alias John Stuart, whose letters bore the address "at Mr. Cosway's" and whose abolitionist treatise, *Thoughts and Sentiments on the Evil ... of ... Slavery*, counted Reynolds among its subscribers.[69] Cugoano almost certainly posed for the servant who appears in the etching of 1784 depicting the Cosways in a Rubensian garden. Artists had long recruited servants as models, but making an identifiable servant like Cugoano a prominent figure in this engraving was clearly a specific strategy on Cosway's part, intended to advertise the opulent life he shared with Maria.

Portraying himself and his wife with a Black servant who was also a noted abolitionist writer, Cosway both embraced and ironized this pictorial motif. By the time he made his etching, some Black Londoners had achieved heightened visibility through their embrace of the macaroni style. This was particularly the case with Julius Soubise, a protégé of the Duchess of Queensberry parodied as the "Mungo Macaroni" by the same caricaturists who targeted Cosway [fig. 99].[70] Another well-known Black Londoner, and Soubise's correspondent, was the celebrated man of letters Ignatius Sancho, who once sat for his portrait by Gainsborough [fig. 100].[71] An old note on the back of Gainsborough's canvas records that "This sketch ... was done in one hour and forty minutes, November 29th, 1768." This note, part of the tradition of anecdotes about the swiftness of portrait sittings, suggests that Sancho sat to Gainsborough at the same time as his employer, the

99 Mary and Matthew Darly, *A Mungo Macaroni*, 1772, etching, 17.6 × 12.5 cm, Lewis Walpole Library, Yale University

100 Thomas Gainsborough, *Ignatius Sancho*, 1768, oil on canvas, 73.7 × 62.2 cm, Ottawa, National Gallery of Canada

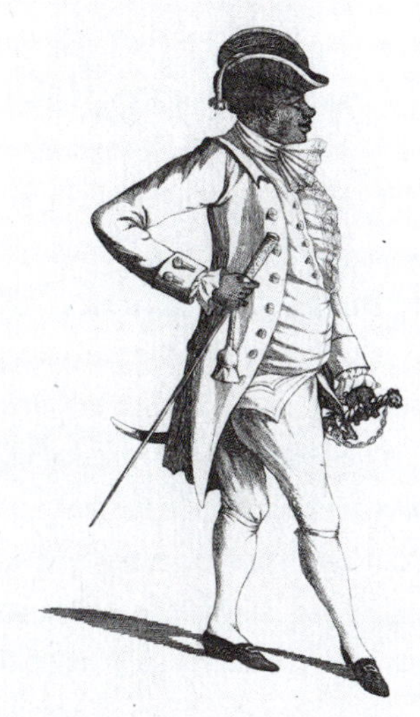

A MUNGO MACARONI.

Publish'd according to Act, by MDarly, 39 Strand, Septr 10. 1772.

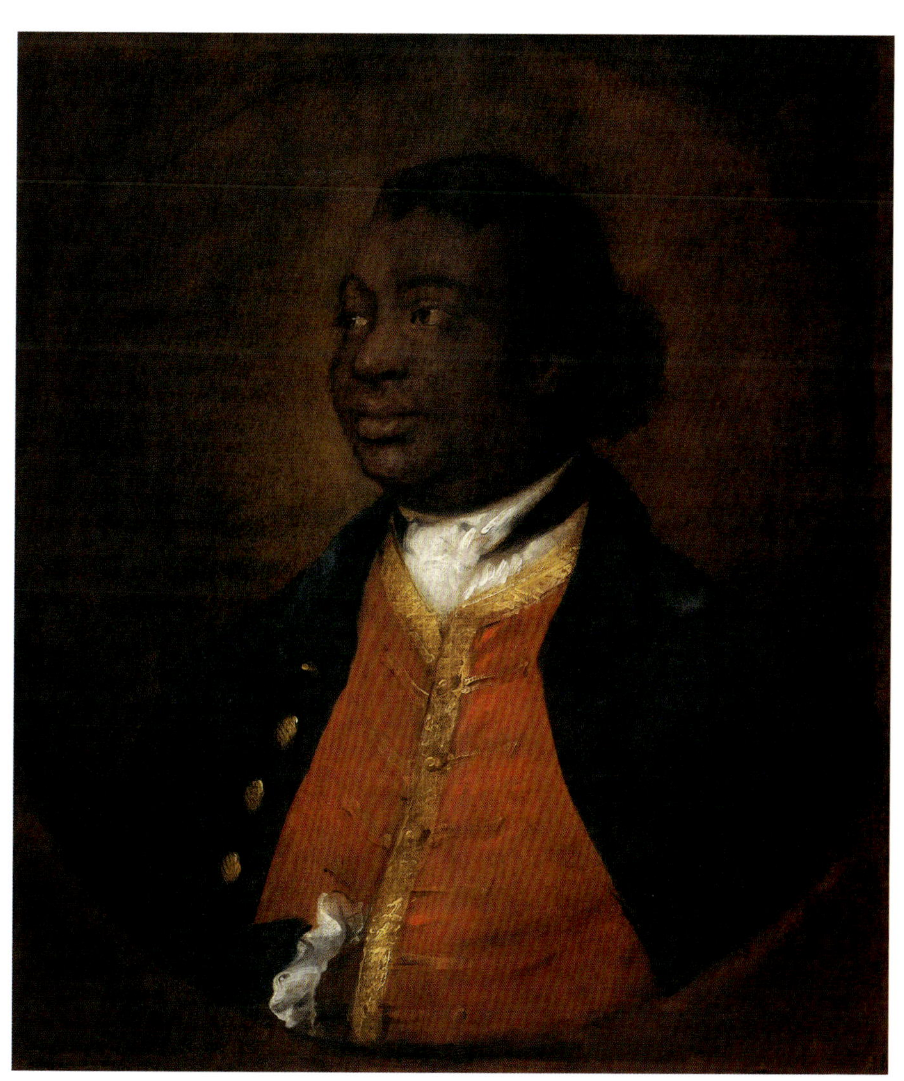

Duchess of Montagu, who was also painted by the artist at Bath in November of that year.[72] While Sancho may have accompanied the duchess to her sitting, Gainsborough's portraits split the Van Dyckian convention of pairing a white aristocrat and a Black attendant into two independent images, providing Sancho with an autonomy denied to most sitters of color.

Unlike Gainsborough, Cosway did not take the step of depicting a Black sitter by himself. In the etched self-portrait with Maria and Cugoano, Cosway instead enlisted his Black model for a pose à trois that had its origins in an emulation of Rubens. Notably, however, Rubens's family portraits never featured such a figure of color. This was a signifier of aristocratic identity that Cosway instead borrowed from Van Dyck and grafted onto Rubens's domestic scenes. At the same time, Cugoano's position within the etching suggests an ambivalent relationship to Van Dyckian tradition on the part of the artist. Whereas most Black attendant figures are diminutive, flanking the central sitter, Cugoano dominates the composition as its focal point, looming over the Cosways even as he stoops to offer grapes to Maria. Not only his skin, but also his clothes and hair, are far more intensely worked with the etcher's needle than his employers', drawing the eye and recording the artist's investment of time in this figure. He holds his scalloped platter below his waist, adding a suggestive note to Maria's gluttonous gesture of gathering a handful of grapes, even as she twines the fingers of her other hand with her husband's.

Just as he objectified Cugoano as an ornament of his household, Cosway instrumentalized him within the etching for a winking meditation on the history of portraiture in the Van Dyckian mode. The degree to which Cugoano's presence in the Cosways' ménage informed the artists' public personae becomes clear from a reading of one of the most violent diatribes directed against them. Under the racist moniker "Pompey," Cugoano features in a vicious satire of the Royal Academy published in 1786 by John Williams, alias Anthony Pasquin.[73] In the farce, Pasquin aims particular venom at Cosway in the guise of the Academician "Tiny Cosmetic":

> *a miniature painter of merit; but where he possesses an ounce of capability, it is sicklied over with a pound of vanity – he looks upon himself as one of the greatest men of the age, and will admit of no competitor but the King of Prussia; he is as mischievous as a monkey, and as illiterate as a Savoyard; and though a contemptible animal in his person, he firmly believes that the first beauties of the nation are sighing for his favours … to remove the approaches of jealousy from every husband in Great-Britain, he married the daughter of a drunken stay-maker at Florence, and has absolutely turned his wife's brain, by calling her the Queen of Taste, and the Empress of Sublimity; he has got her engraved in a wanton attitude for the amusement of every ragged rascal in the metropolis, and nothing warms the channels of his contracted heart so much as to tell him you adore his* MARIA.[74]

Pasquin's vitriol is colored with racial hostility, as when he says of the Academicians: "As for Candour ... they have no more idea of its being a virtue, than a copper-coloured Savage at the Cape, has of cleanliness being salubrious."[75] He likewise mocks Cugoano's presence in the Cosway household by having Tiny Cosmetic recount his and Maria's attempt to conceive an heir "just after Pompey our negro had removed the dinner cloth."[76]

It is ultimately Cosway's inadequate masculinity, as manifested in Maria's sexual freedom, that most offends Pasquin. In a characteristically obscene passage, "Cosmetic" recounts the following episode of studio cuckoldry:

> *the Prince* [of Wales] ... *was drawing in the same study with my dear little angelic* MARIA ... *but the Prince not giving* MARIA *entire satisfaction by his performance, what does* MARIA *do, but lay hold of the prince's* hair pencil, *which he took with infinite good humour; but not being willing to be left in a state of idleness, what do you think his Highness did? ... A monstrous good joke upon my soul; to be even with my poor* MARIA *for snatching his pencil so rudely, damme, what does the Prince, but catches hold of my wife's* brush! *ha, ha, ha! – though it was cover'd with hog's hair, as stiff as the beard of a Jew Rabbi, and as black as my hat.*[77]

This studio farce, with its infantile doubles entendres, drives to a point of extremity the eroticized, triangular relationship between painter, mistress, and patron that this book has shown to be fundamental to English responses to the visual arts since Van Dyck's arrival in London. Pasquin's character assassination of Cosway represents the opposite side of the coin to contemporary defenses of artists as heroic, masculine, and independent. Shocking in its vitriol, Pasquin's text lays bare the motivations for a rejection of Van Dyckian painters that would be given more decorous expression in twentieth-century unease with their narcissism or effeminacy.

The old story of Apelles and Campaspe tantalized male audiences with a fantasy of masculine genius, autonomy, and sexual conquest. It offered a vision of an artist whose talent made a cuckold of a prince and carved out a space for art insulated from the abasement of courtly life. In his own lifetime, Van Dyck appeared to some commentators to pose a similar threat, sequestered with beautiful sitters in his studio, where his effrontery extended to flirtation across class lines. In the centuries since his death, however, Van Dyck has struck most of his critics as too much enamored of the prince and too little in possession of the mistress. The fact that many women artists saw in his career a model for their own ambitions added fuel to Van Dyck's feminine recoding. As English art writers became increasingly invested in a normative masculinity that kept its distance from the court and fashionable life, accusations of effeminacy (for male artists) or promiscuity (for women) became a means of writing undesirable figures out of the national canon. Pasquin's elision of Maria's brush with her pudendum neatly encapsulates the misogyny animating so much anti-Van Dyckian critique and its particularly brutal mobilization against women artists.

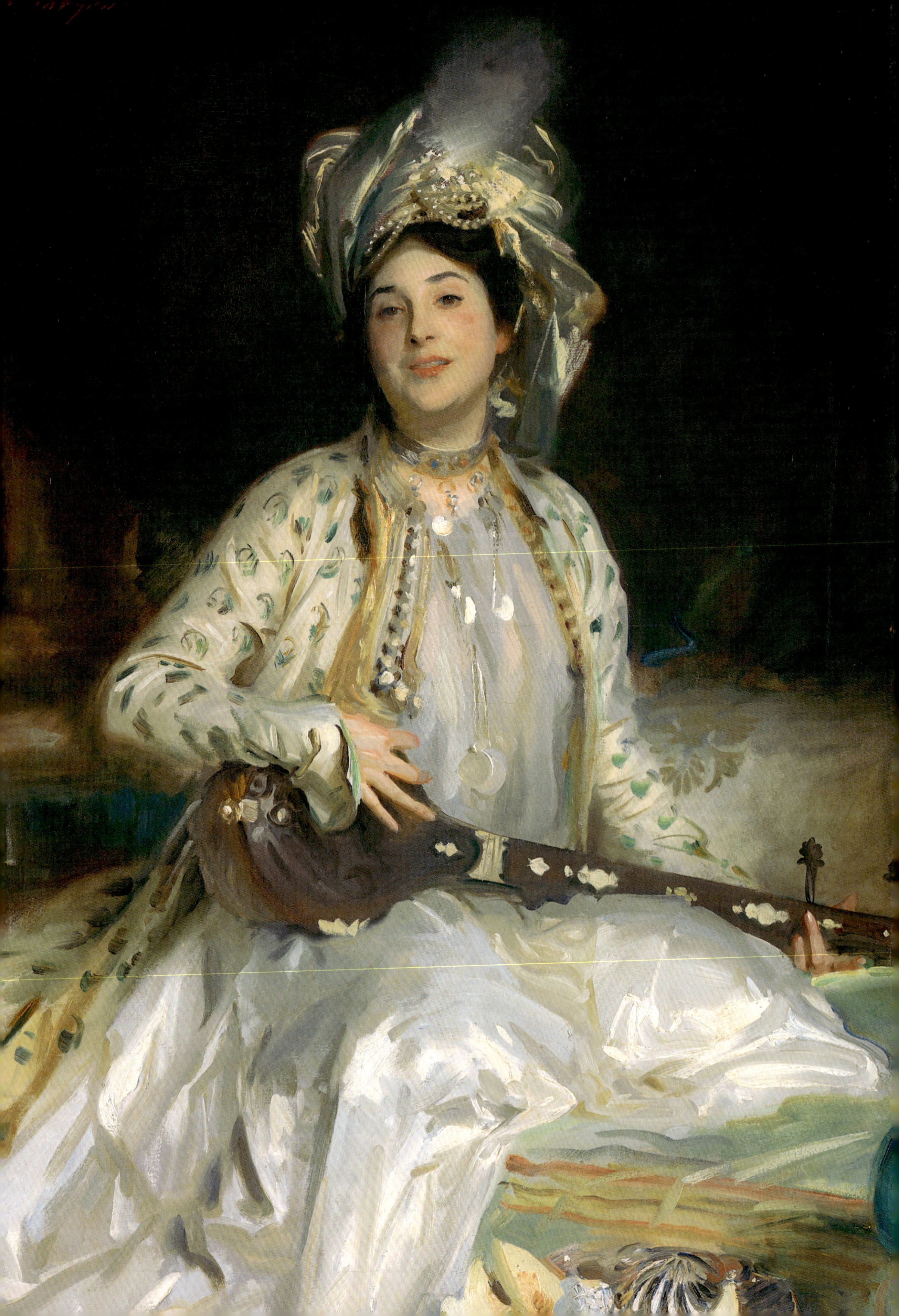

Afterword

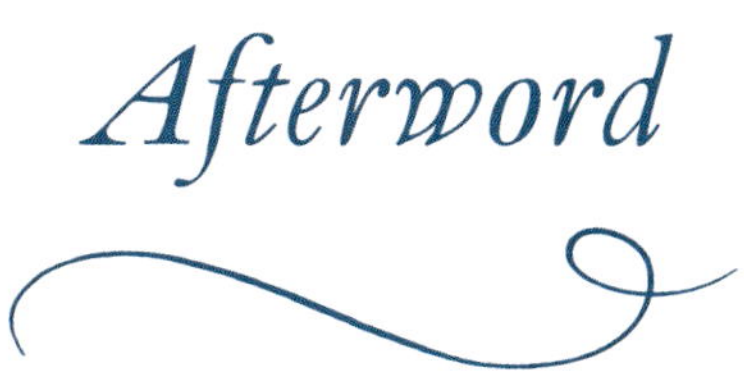

THIS BOOK HAS BEEN MY ATTEMPT TO ANSWER QUESTIONS I FIRST HAD more than fifteen years ago: why do people write (or more often *not* write) about Van Dyck the way that they do? Why does he function so often as a prefatory figurehead in surveys of British portraiture and so rarely as a protagonist in accounts of European baroque painting? Why was I not shown a single one of his works during my academic training, when they were to be encountered, often en masse, in nearly every museum I visited?

As this book has shown, by making his studio the site for the performance of personal charisma, even as the artworks he produced became ever more formulaic, Van Dyck launched a self-aware lineage of English artists. At the same time, his close affiliation with court culture and absolutist politics meant that the Van Dyckian paradigm became increasingly embattled and marginalized in an English art world centered on public exhibitions, civic monuments, and male patriotism. That court culture might provide possibilities for artists – and lives – that the market and academy eventually foreclosed has largely been forgotten within a history of art still wedded to narratives of male independence and political progress. Profound shifts in gender norms at the close of the eighteenth century (a transformation we still live with today) resulted in a consistent misreading of Van Dyck's social persona as irredeemably effeminate. The class-based hostility of some contemporary writers toward his sartorial display or his flirtations with aristocratic women planted a seed that blossomed, perversely and ahistorically, in the homophobia of the twentieth and twenty-first centuries.

I have chosen to end this book at the close of the Georgian era, at a moment when the Van Dyckian poses of Richard and Maria Cosway made them the objects of a critical vitriol that still scalds today. Although this period marks one caesura in the history of Van Dyck's reception, another volume might carry the narrative further, tracing a paradigm of twinned commercial success and historiographic damnation in the careers of figures like Lawrence or Sargent. A nineteenth-century chapter would also need to account for Van Dyck's incorporation into national museum collections, and the attendant phenomenon of the many history paintings that depict the artist in his studio, portraying a king or seducing a model [fig. 101].[1]

Detail of John Singer Sargent, *Almina Wertheimer*, 1905 [see fig. 102]

The persistence of Van Dyckian facture and motifs within portraiture well into the twentieth century is one of the most striking historical continuities of art in England. Just as evergreen, however, is the hostility facing painters who have consciously affiliated themselves with this tradition as a matter not only of style but also of social practice. Opponents of the Van Dyckian paradigm have drawn energy not only from the xenophobia and chauvinism of the late eighteenth century, but also from the imperatives of modernism and its cult of male independence. Writing in response to an exhibition of Sargent's works in 1926, Roger Fry offered a damning critique of the artist that began by quoting enthusiastic remarks overheard in the galleries at Burlington House – remarks that explicitly ranked Sargent among the old masters. Fry explained the initial enthusiasm of English audiences for Sargent's paintings as a result of their ignorance of Impressionism, which the Anglo-American painter rendered only as a "feeble echo," "a vulgarisation," and, most tellingly, "an emasculated version."[2]

Fry defined his standard for good art as "the delight in certain visual relations regarded in and for themselves," a neat encapsulation of an aesthetics grounded in formalism and autonomy.[3] Because Sargent's paintings failed to provide him with this pleasure, Fry asserted, "We must look at these pictures not as works of

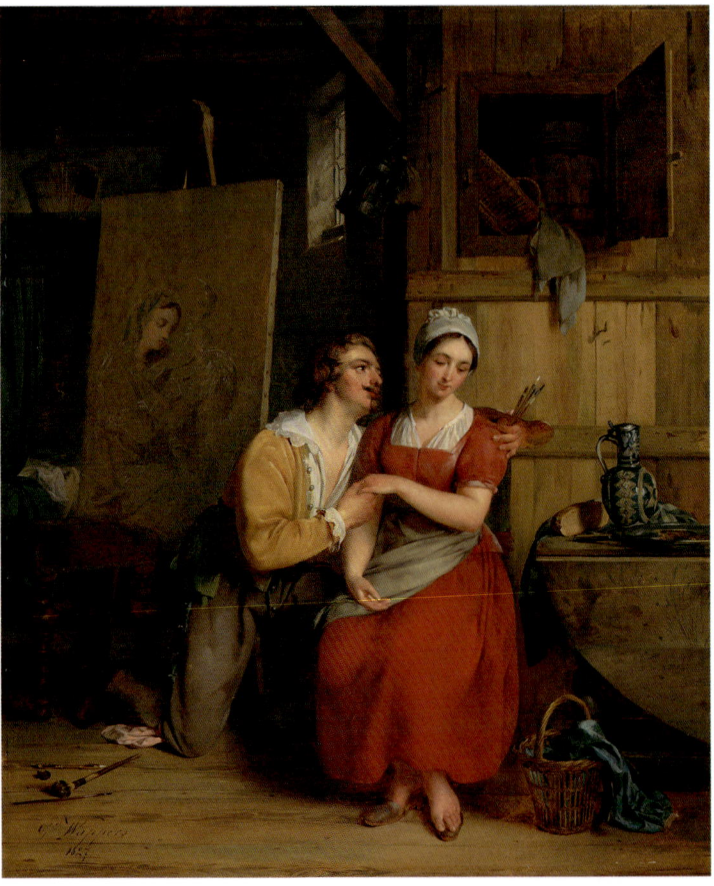

101 Gustave Wappers, *Anthony van Dyck Wooing His Model*, 1827, oil on panel, 58 × 47.5 cm, Amsterdam, Rijksmuseum

art with a value in and of themselves, but as illustrations or reports." According to Fry, Sargent's only "authentic and solid gifts" lay in the sociological acuity of his portraits, the "extreme clearness" with which he captured the "superficial social aspect" of his sitters.[4] From this concession, Fry built to a crescendo in his concluding discussion of Sargent's portraits of the art dealer Asher Wertheimer and his family, viewed by Fry as "art applied to social requirements and social ambitions ... a social transaction quite analogous to the transactions between a man and his lawyer."[5] Fry wrote less than a quarter century before Wilhelm Valentiner's dismissal of Van Dyck as "little more than a man of wealth, pampered by courts and women, having to do only with persons of high rank."[6] Both critics wrote from a modernist vantage point that celebrated male autonomy, as embodied in formal innovation quarantined from the imperatives of patronage.

The rise of the social history of art, with its fascination for the language of contracts and commissions, has made great strides in the recuperation of art as a form of "social transaction" and of artists as cultural actors embedded within a wider societal and economic panorama. Such approaches have, of course, been transformative for the study of British art, particularly of the Georgian period.[7] Yet by some trick of fate or historiography, these developments within art history have left Van Dyck's reputation almost entirely untouched. His portraits – endlessly exhibited, endlessly catalogued, endlessly bought and sold – have remained largely beyond the pale of academic analysis informed by critical theory. By contrast, artists themselves have returned to his work with insight and rigor, formulating redactions of compositions that run like a red silk thread through the history of British art.

In one such painting, Sargent depicted Almina Wertheimer, daughter of the man he served, in Roger Fry's formulation, like the family lawyer [fig. 102].[8] Perched on a cushion, wearing a turban and a Turkish jacket that Sargent kept in his studio, Almina cradles another of the artist's props, the long-necked Indian string instrument known as a *sarod*. Layering colonialist collecting and Orientalist fantasy in his representation of a Jewish woman, Sargent almost appears to taunt the anti-Semites who so often attacked his portraits, buffeting them with an archly overdetermined cosmopolitanism.[9] Sargent's eclecticism extended not only across geography but also to the seventeenth-century portrait that clearly inspired Sargent's own composition, Van Dyck's *Teresa, Lady Shirley* [fig. 103].[10] Van Dyck's painting depicts the Persian-born, Circassian wife of an English adventurer who ended her days as a nun in Rome.[11] Both works, separated by nearly three hundred years, approach identity as a pose that is knowingly struck or a costume that may be put on and then cast aside. Where some critics have attempted to redeem portraiture by claiming for it what Fry called "profound psychological insight into character,"[12] Van Dyck and Sargent masterfully, joyfully imply that true character may have no reality separate from surface appearances.

In mapping Van Dyck's legacy through a cultural history of the portrait sitting, this book has attempted to show an alternative function for portraiture than the capturing of some putative true self. Perhaps the poets were right. How could a painting ever stand in for a person, even in the flickering candlelight of Sir Kenelm Digby's bedside? Van Dyck's achievement was to create a model of portraiture that neither yielded the field to the poets entirely nor anxiously paraded the claims to erudition of a lesser Rubens. Those who sat to Van Dyck never forgot the experience – what he said and how he painted. For centuries, poets lamented portraiture's failure to capture the voice of the beloved. We might also mourn the loss of Van Dyck's "sweetness of conversation" so admired by his friend, the Earl of Newcastle. Such conversation was integral to Van Dyck's art, and it is lost forever. Yet the paintings remain, on museum walls from New York to Melbourne. Face to face with their virtuosity, we still have the chance to be, like Newcastle, "astonished in the right place."

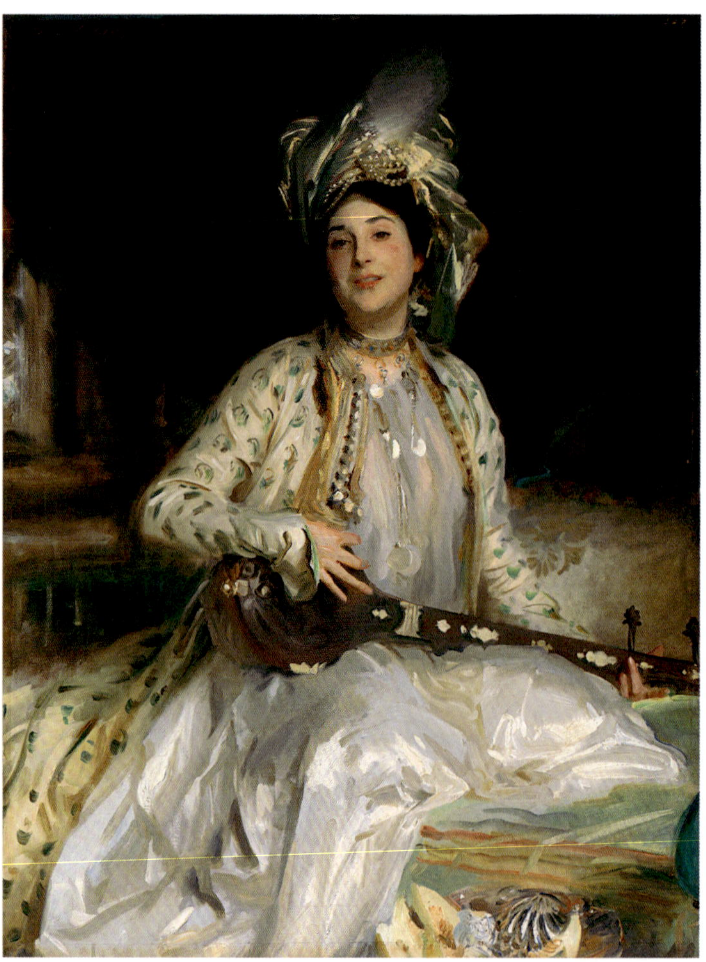

102 John Singer Sargent, *Almina Wertheimer*, 1905, oil on canvas, 134 × 101 cm, London, Tate

103 Anthony van Dyck, *Teresa, Lady Shirley*, 1622, oil on canvas, 200 × 133.4 cm, Petworth, Petworth House (National Trust)

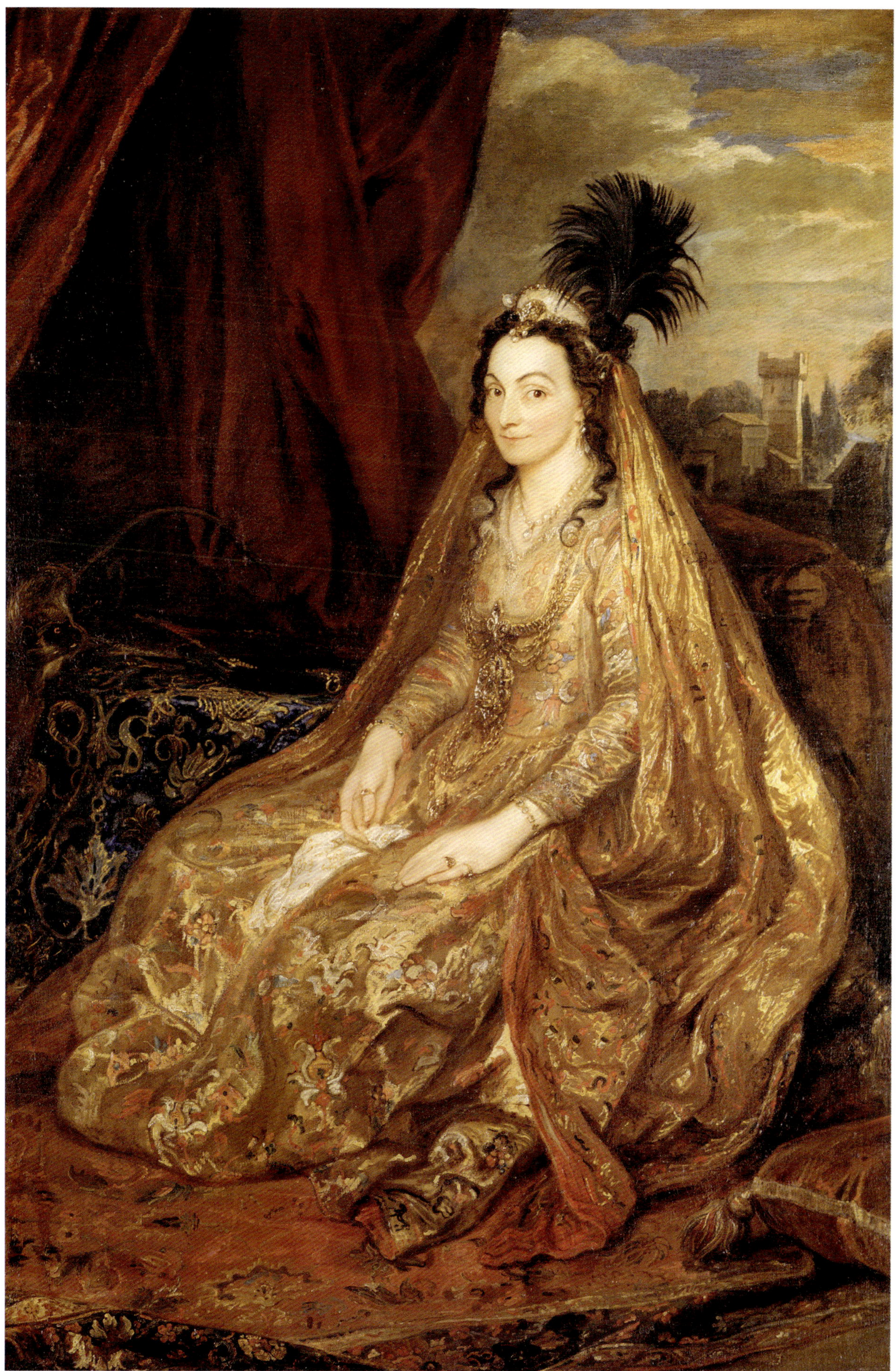

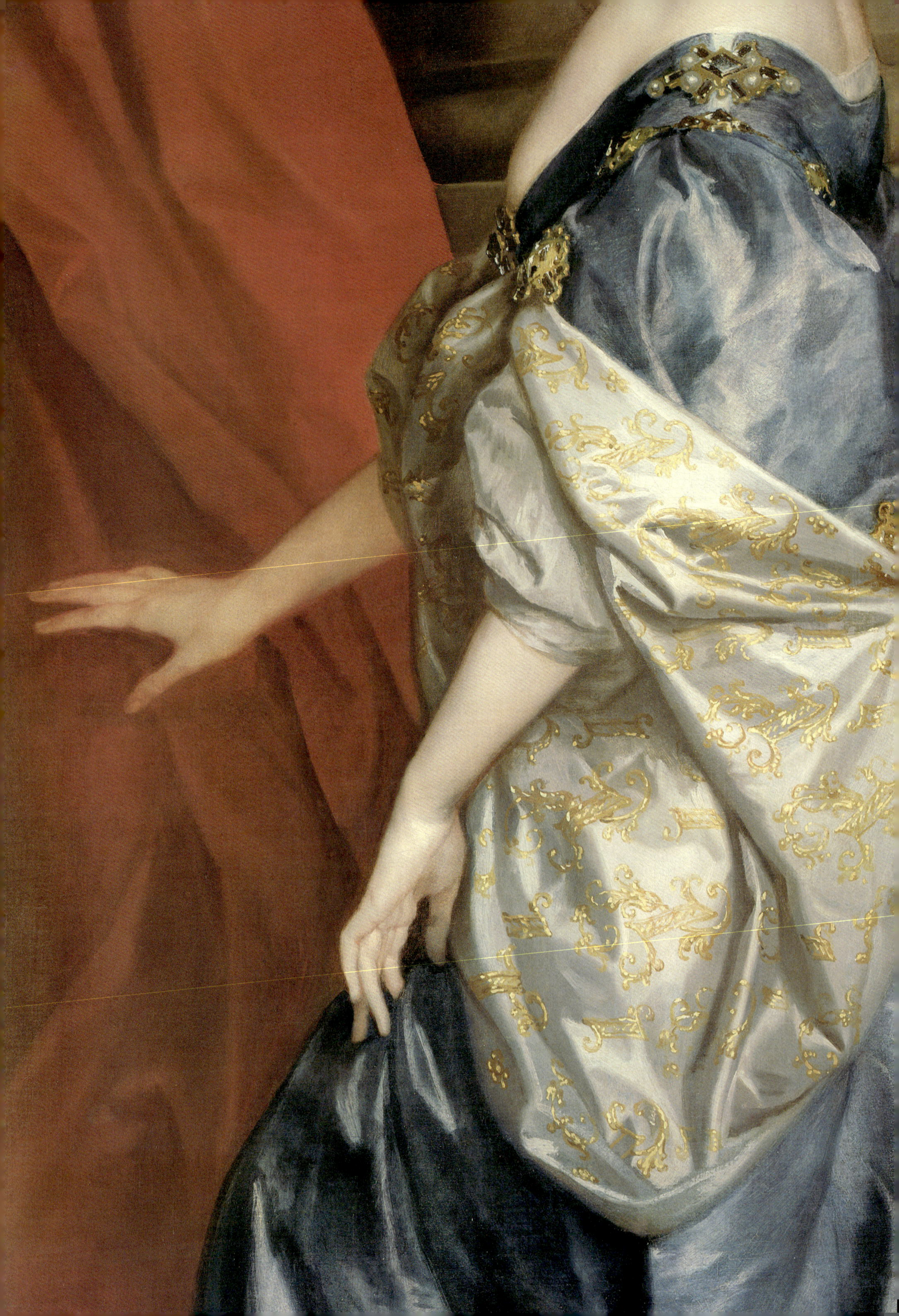

Notes and References

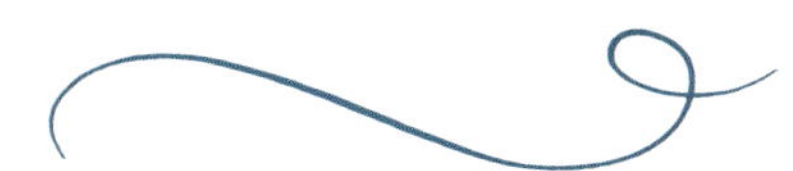

Introduction

1 Horace Walpole, *Anecdotes of Painting in England*, 4 vols. (New York: Arno Press, 1969), vol. 1, p. x.

2 Ibid., p. ix.

3 For example, a recent general history of eighteenth-century British art cites as features of "Van Dyck's legacy" an "ideal of a master painter who mixed on equal terms with even the grandest of his patrons," "a repertoire of poses and compositional types," and the operation of "the workshop as a virtual assembly line"; see David H. Solkin, *Art in Britain 1660–1815*, Pelican History of Art (New Haven and London: Yale University Press, 2015), pp. 3–4.

4 Throughout this book, I have generally used the term "English" as opposed to "British" to reflect the limited geographic terrain covered and the fact that much of the work under discussion predates the Acts of Union in 1707. Moreover, it was under the nomenclature of an "English school" that the writers surveyed here attempted to formulate a national canon.

5 My use of the term "studio" throughout this book to designate Van Dyck's place of work is pragmatic but admittedly anachronistic. The early modern sources simply speak of Van Dyck's house or home, without a separate term for the room in which he painted. Evidence exists, however, that the room in which an artist worked was considered a distinct and special place during the period covered in this book; see, for example, references to Mary Beale's "paynting roome" in her husband's pocket books. For a discussion of this terminology, see Michael Cole and Mary Pardo, "Origins of the Studio," in *Inventions of the Studio: Renaissance to Romanticism*, ed. Michael Cole and Mary Pardo (Chapel Hill: University of North Carolina Press, 2005), pp. 1–35; for Beale's "paynting roome," see Helen Draper, "'Her Painting of Apricots': The Invisibility of Mary Beale (1633–1699)," *Forum for Modern Language Studies* 48, no. 4 (October 2012): 389–405, esp. p. 397.

6 The classic statement of this narrative is Iain Pears, *The Discovery of Painting: The Growth of Interest in the Arts in England, 1680–1768* (New Haven and London: Yale University Press for the Paul Mellon Centre for Studies in British Art, 1988). Pears's account relies on a negative assessment of Charles I's patronage, asserting, "Ultimately it did more harm than good to the cause of painting in England. It set up a model against which all those who followed onto the throne had necessarily to be seen as pale and inadequate imitations. Moreover, the disruption caused by the destruction of the patronage network and the consequent flight of many foreign painters probably set back the development of a solid, home-grown school of English painters by at least a generation" (pp. 134–35). More recent years have witnessed an important reassessment of English art before the Civil War, with an emphasis on émigré artists and outstanding patrons; see, among other works, Karen Hearn, ed., *Dynasties: Painting in Tudor and Jacobean England, 1530–1630* (London: Tate Publishing, 1995); Tarnya Cooper et al., eds., *Painting in Britain, 1500–1630: Production, Influences, and Patronage* (Oxford: Oxford University Press for the British Academy, 2015); Christiane Hille, *Visions of the Courtly*

Detail of Anthony van Dyck, *Lucy Hay, Countess of Carlisle*, 1637 [see fig. 11]

Body: The Patronage of George Villiers, First Duke of Buckingham, and the Triumph of Painting at the Stuart Court (Berlin: Akademie Verlag, 2012); and Elizabeth Goldring, *Robert Dudley, Earl of Leicester and the World of Elizabethan Art: Painting and Patronage at the Court of Elizabeth I* (New Haven and London: Yale University Press for the Paul Mellon Centre for Studies in British Art, 2014).

7 An important exception is Ellis Waterhouse, *Painting in Britain, 1530–1790*, Pelican History of Art (London: Penguin, 1953). The fact that Solkin's successor text in the Pelican History of Art series (see note 3 above) covers the period 1660–1815 instead of Waterhouse's wider span reflects the emergence in the past few decades of sixteenth- and seventeenth-century English art as distinct sub-specialties. For a more recent master narrative extending from the Elizabethan period to the nineteenth century, see Ann Bermingham, *Learning to Draw: Studies in the Cultural History of a Polite and Useful Art* (New Haven and London: Yale University Press for the Paul Mellon Centre for Studies in British Art, 2000). By contrast, the exhibition *British Baroque* at Tate Britain reinforced the trend of viewing the art of the Restoration in isolation from its Caroline precedents; see Tabitha Barber, ed., *British Baroque: Power and Illusion* (London: Tate, 2020).

8 For an important new assessment of Hilliard, see Elizabeth Goldring, *Nicholas Hilliard: Life of an Artist* (New Haven and London: Yale University Press for the Paul Mellon Centre for Studies in British Art, 2019).

9 Arthur F. Kinney and Linda Bradley Salamon, eds., *Nicholas Hilliard's Art of Limning* (Boston, Mass.: Northeastern University Press, 1983), p. 28.

10 Giovanni Pietro Bellori, *The Lives of the Modern Painters, Sculptors and Architects*, ed. Hellmut Wohl, trans. Alice Sedgwick Wohl (New York: Cambridge University Press, 2005), p. 220; original in Bellori, *Le vite de' pittori, scultori e architetti moderni: Parte prima*, ed. Evelina Borea (Turin: Einaudi, 1976), p. 283.

11 English translation taken from Susan J. Barnes, Nora De Poorter, Oliver Millar, and Horst Vey, *Van Dyck: A Complete Catalogue of the Paintings* (New Haven and London: Yale University Press for the Paul Mellon Centre for Studies in British Art, 2004), p. 427, n. 10.

12 Bellori, *The Lives*, p. 218.

13 For an account of Van Dyck's early life grounded in recent archival discoveries, see Katlijne Van der Stighelen, "Van Dyck's First Antwerp Period: Prologue to a Baroque Life Story," in *Van Dyck 1599–1641*, ed. Christopher Brown and Hans Vlieghe (London: Royal Academy of Arts, 1999), pp. 35–48.

14 For an overview of the current state of knowledge about Van Dyck's early career, see Friso Lammertse and Alejandro Vergara, "A Portrait of Van Dyck as a Young Artist," in *The Young Van Dyck*, ed. Friso Lammertse and Alejandro Vergara (Madrid: Museo Nacional del Prado, 2012), pp. 23–74.

15 Quoted in Mary F. S. Hervey, *The Life, Correspondence & Collections of Thomas Howard, Earl of Arundel* (Cambridge: Cambridge University Press, 1921), p. 176, n. 2 (translation slightly modified). The letter is unsigned, but Vercellini's authorship has been generally accepted.

16 See Christopher S. Wood, "Indoor–Outdoor: The Studio around 1500," in *Inventions of the Studio: Renaissance to Romanticism*, ed. Michael Cole and Mary Pardo (Chapel Hill: University of North Carolina Press, 2005), pp. 36–72, esp. p. 38.

17 For the portrait, see Hans Vlieghe, *Corpus Rubenianum Ludwig Burchard, Part XIX (2): Portraits of Identified Sitters Painted in Antwerp* (London: Harvey Miller, 1987), pp. 48–52, cat. no. 72.

18 Upon her return to London from Venice, where Van Dyck accompanied her, the countess brought home both a gondola and a Black maidservant; see Miranda Kaufmann, *Black Tudors: The Untold Story* (London: Oneworld Publications, 2018), pp. 224–25.

19 On Mytens's pendants, see Anastassia Novikova, "Virtuosity and Declensions of Virtue: Thomas Arundel and Aletheia Talbot Seen by Virtue of a Portrait Pair by Daniel Mytens and a Treatise by Franciscus Junius," *Netherlands Yearbook for History of Art / Nederlands Kunsthistorisch Jaarboek (NKJ)* 54 (2003): 308–33.

20 My thinking about the interplay between heraldry and portraiture has been shaped by Hans

Belting with Christiane Kruse, *Die Erfindung des Gemäldes: Das erste Jahrhundert der niederländischen Malerei* (Munich: Hirmer, 1994), esp. pp. 46–47.

21 Joanna Woodall, *Anthonis Mor: Art and Authority* (Zwolle: Waanders, 2007), p. 38.

22 Carlo Cesare Malvasia, *The Life of Guido Reni*, trans. and ed. Catherine Enggass and Robert Enggass (University Park: Pennsylvania State University Press, 1980), pp. 113–14.

23 Bellori, *The Lives*, pp. 215–16; original in Bellori, *Le vite*, p. 272.

24 For an alternative account of Van Dyck's early practice of life study and his response to Rubens, see Adam Eaker, "Van Dyck between Master and Model," *Art Bulletin* 97, no. 2 (June 2015): 173–91.

25 For two previous overviews of different aspects of Van Dyck's reception, see Arthur K. Wheelock, "The Search for 'The Central Orb': Van Dyck and His Historical Reputation," in *Anthony van Dyck*, ed. Arthur K. Wheelock, Julius Samuel Held, and Susan J. Barnes (Washington, D.C.: National Gallery of Art, 1990), pp. 11–16; and Jeffrey M. Muller, "Anthony van Dyck and Flemish National Identity: A Clash of Images between the Two World Wars," in *Van Dyck, 1599–1999: Conjectures and Refutations*, ed. Hans Vlieghe (Turnhout: Brepols, 2001), pp. 305–12.

26 Barnes et al., *Van Dyck*, p. 18.

27 For an overview of Van Dyck's first English sojourn, see Karen Hearn, ed., *Van Dyck & Britain* (London: Tate, 2009), pp. 38–63.

28 The most recent comprehensive discussion of the complicated genesis of Van Dyck's early self-portraits is in Mirjam Neumeister, ed., *Van Dyck: Gemälde von Anthonis van Dyck; Bayerische Staatsgemäldesammlungen, München* (Munich: Alte Pinakothek/Hirmer, 2019), pp. 172–81, cat. no. 6.

29 Bellori, *The Lives*, p. 216.

30 Ibid.

31 My approach to this material aligns with that of Richard Wendorf in his analysis of Joshua Reynolds: "If it is objected that I have puzzled the surviving conversations and anecdotes rather too much, I would reply by arguing that evidence of this kind is meaningful only when it is closely and even playfully analyzed, and – more important still – that the surviving fragmentary evidence from which we attempt to make sense of the mysteries of identity is at least as complicated and challenging to interpretation as any contemporaneous literary form"; Richard Wendorf, *Sir Joshua Reynolds: The Painter in Society* (Cambridge, Mass.: Harvard University Press, 2009), p. 8.

32 For a suggestive account of the way early modern artists might stylize their own behavior with an eye toward artistic biography, see Nicola Suthor, *Bravura: Virtuosität und Mutwilligkeit in der Malerei der Frühen Neuzeit* (Munich: W. Fink, 2010), pp. 13–40.

33 Jonathan Richardson, *An Essay on the Theory of Painting: By Mr. Richardson* (London: printed by W. Bowyer for John Churchill, 1715), p. 18.

34 For an example of this, see the ongoing "Jordaens Van Dyck Panel Paintings Project", http://jordaensvandyck.org (accessed November 29, 2021). A brief but clear-eyed (and still current) assessment of the more recent scholarly literature on Van Dyck appears in Mariët Westermann, "After Iconography and Iconoclasm: Current Research in Netherlandish Art, 1566–1700," *Art Bulletin* 84, no. 2 (June 2002): 351–72; see pp. 354–55.

35 For a forceful statement of this critique, see Joanna Woodall, "Don't Be Seduced," *Art History* 16, no. 4 (December 1993): 657–63.

36 Thomas E. Crow, *Restoration: The Fall of Napoleon in the Course of European Art, 1812–1820*, A. W. Mellon Lectures in the Fine Arts 64 (Princeton: Princeton University Press, 2018), p. 108.

37 There is a parallel between my emphasis on the process of portraiture and Angela Rosenthal's important sociological account of the studios of eighteenth-century women painters, where "the portrait, rather than being considered as an end-product, disconnected from its production, will be seen as a process. Rather than a *reproduction* of a pre-existing self, the portrait is seen as the *production* of sitter and artist, and of the relation between them determined by mobile factors such as class, race, age, and gender"; see Angela Rosenthal, "She's Got the Look! Eighteenth-Century Female Portrait Painters and the Psychology of a Potentially 'Dangerous Employment,'" in *Portraiture: Facing the Subject*, ed. Joanna Woodall (Manchester: Manchester University Press, 1997), pp. 147–66, citation from

p. 148. See also Richard Wendorf's "transactional theory of portraiture," as elaborated through the example of Reynolds; Wendorf, *Sir Joshua Reynolds*, p. 4.

38 W. R. Valentiner, "Van Dyck's Character," *Art Quarterly* 13 (1950): 87–105; for a summary of the traditional views and evidence about the relationship between the two artists, see Julius S. Held, "Van Dyck's Relationship to Rubens," in *Van Dyck 350*, ed. Susan J. Barnes and Arthur K. Wheelock, Studies in the History of Art 46 (Washington, D.C.: National Gallery of Art, 1994), pp. 63–78.

39 See Katlijne Van der Stighelen, "Young Anthony: Archival Discoveries Relating to Van Dyck's Early Career," in *Van Dyck 350*, ed. Susan J. Barnes and Arthur K. Wheelock, Studies in the History of Art 46 (Washington, D.C.: National Gallery of Art, 1994), pp. 17–46; and Katlijne Van der Stighelen, "Van Dyck's Character Revisited: Valentiner versus de zeventiende-eeuwse historiografische traditie," in *Van Dyck 1599–1999: Conjectures and Refutations*, ed. Hans Vlieghe (Turnhout: Brepols, 2001), pp. 229–52.

40 Valentiner, "Van Dyck's Character," pp. 87–88.

41 Ibid., p. 88.

42 Ibid., p. 100.

43 Julius S. Held, "Review of Horst Vey, *Die Zeichnungen Anton van Dycks*," *Art Bulletin* 46, no. 4 (December 1964): 568.

44 Zirka Zaremba Filipczak, *Picturing Art in Antwerp, 1550–1700* (Princeton: Princeton University Press, 1987), p. 108.

45 Christopher White, *Anthony van Dyck & the Art of Portraiture* (London: Modern Art Press, 2021), p. 68.

46 Cited in Fredrika H. Jacobs, *Defining the Renaissance Virtuosa: Women Artists and the Language of Art History and Criticism* (Cambridge: Cambridge University Press, 1997), p. 38.

47 Maike Christadler, *Kreativität und Geschlecht: Giorgio Vasaris "Vite" und Sofonisba Anguissolas Selbst-Bilder* (Berlin: Reimer, 2000), p. 9; see also Jacobs, *Defining the Renaissance Virtuosa*, pp. 27–63.

48 Philip Sohm, "Gendered Style in Italian Art Criticism from Michelangelo to Malvasia," *Renaissance Quarterly* 48, no. 4 (December 1995): 759–808.

49 Ibid., 773–84.

50 For a summary of the literature, see Held, "Van Dyck's Relationship to Rubens."

51 Sperling's German-language account was first published, along with other extracts from his autobiography, in Danish translation in S. Birket Smith, ed., *Dr. Med. Otto Sperlings Selvbiografi (1602–1673), oversat i uddrag efter original-haandskriftet med saerligt hensyn til forfatterens ophold i Danmark og Norge samt fangenskab i Blaataarn* (Copenhagen: Andr. Fred. Høst & Søns Førlag, 1885), pp. 2–3; my translation is based upon the modern German version of the text subsequently published in W. von Seidlitz, "Bericht eines Zeitgenossen über einen Besuch bei Rubens," *Repertorium für Kunstwissenschaft* 10 (1887): 111. For this and other contemporary accounts of visitors to Rubens's house, see also Max Rooses, "De vreemde reizigers Rubens of zijn huis bezoekende," *Rubens-Bulletijn* 5 (1897): 221–29.

52 For an insightful reading of this passage, see Nils Büttner, *Herr P. P. Rubens: Von der Kunst, berühmt zu werden* (Göttingen: Vandenhoeck & Ruprecht, 2006), p. 101.

53 See, among others, Mark Hallett, *Reynolds: Portraiture in Action* (New Haven and London: Yale University Press for the Paul Mellon Centre for Studies in British Art, 2014), pp. 45–47; Marcia Pointon, *Hanging the Head: Portraiture and Social Formation in Eighteenth-Century England* (New Haven and London: Yale University Press for the Paul Mellon Centre for Studies in British Art, 1993), esp. pp. 36–52; and Angela Rosenthal, *Angelica Kauffman: Art and Sensibility* (New Haven and London: Yale University Press for the Paul Mellon Centre for Studies in British Art, 2006), pp. 43–121.

54 For an introduction to the complex relationship between painted and printed portraits during this period, see Peter Moore, "Dialogues in Paint and Print: Mezzotint Portraiture and Intermedial Exchange," in *Court, Country, City: British Art and Architecture, 1660–1735*, ed. Mark Hallett, Nigel Llewellyn, and Martin Myrone (New Haven and London: Yale University Press for the Yale Center for British Art and the Paul Mellon Centre for Studies in British Art, 2016), pp. 433–56.

55 For two oft-cited texts, see Eve Kosofsky Sedgwick, *Between Men: English Literature and Male Homosocial Desire* (New York: Columbia University Press, 1985); and Jonathan Goldberg, *Sodometries: Renaissance Texts, Modern Sexualities* (Stanford: Stanford University Press, 1992).

56 For an exemplary introduction to the state of the field, see the essays collected in Cooper et al., *Painting in Britain, 1500–1630*. A more recent representative publication is Jessica David, Richard Hark, and Edward Town, "'A Real Master Among Hundreds': The Secrets and Techniques of Seventeenth Century Portraiture in Britain," *Materia: Journal of Technical Art History* 1, no. 1 (2021), https://volume-1-issue-1.materia-journal.com/article-jd-rh-et.

57 For one exemplary publication in this regard, see Edward Town, "A Biographical Dictionary of London Painters, 1547–1625," *Walpole Society* 76 (2014): 1–235.

58 Exceptions within the discipline of art history include Marianne Koos, "Wandering Things: Agency and Embodiment in Late Sixteenth-Century English Miniature Portraits," *Art History* 37, no. 5 (2014): 836–59; Hille, *Visions of the Courtly Body*; Matthew C. Hunter, *Wicked Intelligence: Visual Art and the Science of Experiment in Restoration London* (Chicago: University of Chicago Press, 2013); Michael Gaudio, *The Bible and the Printed Image in Early Modern England: Little Gidding and the Pursuit of Scriptural Harmony*, Visual Culture in Early Modernity 52 (Abingdon and New York: Routledge, 2017); and a number of essays contained in Julia Marciari Alexander and Catharine MacLeod, eds., *Politics, Transgression, and Representation at the Court of Charles II*, Studies in British Art 18 (New Haven and London: Yale University Press for the Yale Center for British Art and the Paul Mellon Centre for Studies in British Art, 2007). For examples of literary critics who have engaged with early modern English visual culture, see, among others, Patricia Fumerton, *Cultural Aesthetics: Renaissance Literature and the Practice of Social Ornament* (Chicago: University of Chicago Press, 1991); Juliet Fleming, *Graffiti and the Writing Arts of Early Modern England* (London: Reaktion, 2001); Louis Montrose, *The Subject of Elizabeth: Authority, Gender, and Representation* (Chicago: University of Chicago Press, 2006); Julian Yates, *Error, Misuse, Failure: Object Lessons from the English Renaissance* (Minneapolis: University of Minnesota Press, 2003); and Susan Frye, *Pens and Needles: Women's Textualities in Early Modern England* (Philadelphia: University of Pennsylvania Press, 2011). There is a brief but stimulating discussion of Van Dyck's portraits in Ann Rosalind Jones and Peter Stallybrass, *Renaissance Clothing and the Materials of Memory* (Cambridge: Cambridge University Press, 2000), pp. 44–46.

59 Hille, *Visions of the Courtly Body*, represents an exceptional and important reading of English art through the lens "of the discursive and material practice of homoeroticism" (quotation from p. 102).

60 Sedgwick, *Between Men*, p. 35.

61 Sharon Marcus, "Queer Theory for Everyone: A Review Essay," *Signs* 31, no. 1 (Autumn 2005): 191–218, quote from p. 196.

62 For Pointon's diagrammatic discussion of the various triangular relationships engendered by portrait sittings, see *Hanging the Head*, p. 188; for Rosenthal's description of "the portrait event," see *Angelica Kauffman*, p. 83.

63 See Joel Fineman, "The History of the Anecdote: Fiction and Fiction," in *The New Historicism*, ed. Harold Veeser (London and New York: Routledge, 1989), pp. 49–76.

64 Henry Abelove, *Deep Gossip* (Minneapolis: University of Minnesota Press, 2003), p. xii.

65 Sarah Betzer, "Patch, Walpole, and Queer Complicity," *Art History* 43, no. 5 (November 2020): 1038–64.

66 As Michael Warner writes, "A counterpublic, against the background of the public sphere, enables a horizon of opinion and exchange; its exchanges remain distinct from authority and can have a critical relation to power; its extent is in principle indefinite, because it is not based on a precise demography but mediated by print, theater, diffuse networks of talk, commerce, and the like"; Michael Warner, *Publics and Counterpublics* (New York: Zone Books, 2002), p. 57.

67 Walpole, *Anecdotes*, vol. 1, p. viii.

68 For Walpole's self-fashioning within the *Anecdotes*, see Karen Junod, *"Writing the Lives of Painters": Biography and Artistic Identity in Britain*

1760–1810 (Oxford: Oxford University Press, 2011), pp. 51–79.

69 Ibid., pp. 71–72.

70 Ibid., p. 72, n. 1. Van Mander's anecdote appears in Hessel Miedema, ed., *The Lives of the Illustrious Netherlandish and German Painters, from the First Edition of the Schilder-Boeck (1603–1604): Preceded by the Lineage, Circumstances and Place of Birth, Life and Works of Karel Van Mander, Painter and Poet and Likewise his Death and Burial, from the Second Edition of the Schilder-Boeck (1616–1618)*, 3 vols. (Doornspijk: Davaco, 1994), vol. 1, fol. 221v.

71 For the accuracy of Van Mander's "clearly fictitious" but suggestive account of Holbein's English career, see Susan Foister, *Holbein and England* (New Haven and London: Yale University Press for the Paul Mellon Centre for Studies in British Art, 2004), p. 9.

72 For a recent account of Van Dyck's working method, see Stijn Alsteens, "A Portraitist's Progress," in *Van Dyck: The Anatomy of Portraiture*, ed. Stijn Alsteens and Adam Eaker (New York: Frick Collection in association with Yale University Press, 2016), pp. 1–38.

1 · *The Scene of the Sitting*

1 An earlier version of this chapter appeared as Adam Eaker, "The Scene of the Sitting in Early Modern England," *Art History* 41, no. 4 (September 2018): 650–79.

2 Beale's diary entry survives in a transcription by the engraver and antiquarian George Vertue; see George Vertue, "The Note-books of George Vertue Relating to Artists and Collections in England, vol. IV," *Walpole Society* 24 (1935–36): 168–69. The diary first appeared in print in Walpole's life of Mary Beale (Horace Walpole, *Anecdotes of Painting in England*, 4 vols. [London: J. Dodsley, 1782], vol. 3, pp. 125–26).

3 For the literature on the painting, see Horst Vey's entry in Susan J. Barnes, Nora De Poorter, Oliver Millar, and Horst Vey, *Van Dyck: A Complete Catalogue of the Paintings* (New Haven and London: Yale University Press for the Paul Mellon Centre for Studies in British Art, 2004), p. 321, cat. no. III.92. For the Whitehall inventory, see Oliver Millar, ed., "Abraham van der Doort's Catalogue of the Collections of Charles I," *Walpole Society* 37 (1958–60): 7, no. 34. Lanier's acquisition of the portrait is recorded in Oliver Millar, ed., "The Inventories and Valuations of the King's Goods, 1649–1651," *Walpole Society* 43 (1970–72), p. 70, no. 26. On the Edinburgh drawing, see Horst Vey, *Die Zeichnungen Anton van Dycks*, 2 vols. (Brussels: Verlag Arcade, 1962), vol. 1, pp. 275–76, cat. no. 203. I have previously discussed the drawing, painting, and Lely's anecdote together in Stijn Alsteens and Adam Eaker, eds., *Van Dyck: The Anatomy of Portraiture* (New York: Frick Collection in association with Yale University Press, 2016), pp. 104–106, cat. nos. 20 and 21.

4 Vertue, "The Note-books of George Vertue, vol. IV," 169. For a discussion of the technical information recorded in Charles Beale's notebooks, see Mansfield Kirby Talley, *Portrait Painting in England: Studies in the Technical Literature before 1700* (London: Paul Mellon Centre for Studies in British Art, 1981), pp. 270–305.

5 For more information on Mary Beale, see Tabitha Barber, ed., *Mary Beale (1632/3–1699): Portrait of a Seventeenth-Century Painter, her Family and her Studio* (London: Geffrye Museum Trust, 1999); Helen Draper, "'Her Painting of Apricots': The Invisibility of Mary Beale (1633–1699)," *Forum for Modern Language Studies* 48, no. 4 (October 2012): 389–405; and Helen Draper, "Mary Beale (1633–1699) and her Objects of Affection," in *Writing the Lives of People and Things, AD 500–1700: A Multi-Disciplinary Future for Biography*, ed. Robert F. W. Smith and Gemma L. Watson (London: Routledge, 2016), pp. 115–41.

6 Vertue, "The Note-books of George Vertue, vol. IV," 170.

7 For a persuasive discussion of parallels between portraiture and theater in seventeenth-century Spain, see Laura R. Bass, *The Drama of the Portrait: Theater and Visual Culture in Early Modern Spain* (University Park: Pennsylvania State University Press, 2008).

8 For Bellori's reception of Van Dyck, see Elizabeth Cropper, "'La più bella antichità che sappiate desiderare': History and Style in Giovan Pietro Bellori's 'Lives'", in *Kunst und Kunsttheorie: 1400–1900*, ed. Peter Ganz et al. (Wiesbaden: Otto Harrasowitz, 1991), pp. 145–74, esp. pp. 161–62; for de Piles, see Thomas Puttfarken, *Roger de Piles' Theory of Art* (New Haven and London: Yale

University Press, 1985); for Lely, see Matthew C. Hunter, *Wicked Intelligence: Visual Art and the Science of Experiment in Restoration London* (Chicago: University of Chicago Press, 2013), pp. 98–124, as well as Diana Dethloff, "Lely, Drawing, and the Training of Artists," in *Court, Country, and City: British Art and Architecture, 1660–1735*, ed. Mark Hallett, Nigel Llewellyn, and Martin Myrone, Studies in British Art 24 (London: Yale University Press for the Yale Center for British Art and the Paul Mellon Centre for Studies in British Art, 2016), pp. 291–313.

9 Mary Beal, *A Study of Richard Symonds: His Italian Notebooks and their Relevance to Seventeenth-Century Painting Techniques*, Outstanding Theses from the Courtauld Institute of Art (New York: Garland, 1984), p. 39.

10 For a pertinent discussion of Bernini's method of taking a likeness, see Rudolf Wittkower, *Bernini's Bust of Louis XIV* (Oxford: Oxford University Press, 1951), pp. 6–7.

11 There is a surviving payment from 1635 for "Workes and Repairacions donne and performed ... at the Blackfryers in making a new Cawsey Way and a new paire of Staires for the King's Majesty to land to goe to S[r] Anthoney Vandike's house there to see his paintings"; cited in Lionel Cust, *Anthony van Dyck: An Historical Study of his Life and Works* (London: G. Bell and Sons, 1900), pp. 89–90.

12 As Malcolm Smuts writes, "The residence of a painter a generation removed from a family of Antwerp silk merchants had become one of the centers around which court society revolved. It would be difficult to imagine more forceful testimony to the prestige that artistic skill had attained"; see his *Court Culture and the Origins of a Royalist Tradition in Early Stuart England* (Philadelphia: University of Pennsylvania Press, 1987), p. 188.

13 For Maria's exile, see Toby Osborne, "A Queen Mother in Exile: Marie de Médicis in the Spanish Netherlands and England, 1631–41," in *Monarchy and Exile: The Politics of Legitimacy from Marie de Médicis to Wilhelm II*, ed. Philip Mansel and Torsten Riotte (Houndmills, Basingstoke, and New York: Palgrave Macmillan, 2011), pp. 17–43.

14 Jean Puget de la Serre, *Histoire curieuse de tout ce qui c'est* [sic] *passé à l'entrée de la reyne mère du roi treschrestien dans les villes des Pays Bas* (Antwerp: Imprimerie Plantinienne de Balthasar Moretus, 1632).

15 "La Reyne eut la curiosité de voir toutes les belles & riches peintures qui sont dans la maison de Monsieur Rubens. C'est un homme dont l'industrie, quoy que rare & merveilleuse, est la moindre de ses qualitez: son jugement d'Estat, & son esprit & gouvernement l'eslevent si haut au dessus de la condition qu'il professe, que les oeuvres de sa prudence sont aussi admirables que celles de son pinceau. Sa Majesté receut un extreme contentement à contempler les merveilles animées de ses tableaux ... Mais si faut il que je publie en faveur de la verité, que Monsieur van Dijck à [*sic*] remporté le prix sur tous les plus grands Peintres, qui d'une main toujours trop hardie ont osé tirer la Reyne: car, sans mentir, l'art ne nous sçauroit jamais representer la Majesté en son thrône, que dans le nouveau portraict qu'il en a faict. On tient qu'Apelles desroba les plus beaux traits de divers visages, pour en depeindre un parfaitement beau sous le nom d'Helene: mais ce Peinre plus ingenieux nous fait voir aujourdhuy dans le seul pourtraict de la Reyne toutes les beautez du monde, sans desrober rien à la nature, que l'invention de faire adorer son art. Sa Majesté luy fit l'honneur d'aller chez luy, où elle vid dans la sale le cabinet de Titian: je veux dire, tout les chefs d'oeuvres de ce grand Maistre. Mais j'ose soustenir, sans flatterie, que Monsieur van Dijck partagera bien tost [*sic*] avec luy la gloire de sa renommée: car si cet excellent Peintre a esté l'ornement de son siecle, celuy-cy est la merveille du sien." Ibid., pp. 68–69.

16 For more on Van Dyck's collection, see Jeremy Wood, "Van Dyck's 'Cabinet de Titien': The Contents and Dispersal of his Collection," *Burlington Magazine* 132, no. 1051 (October 1990): 680–96. Van Dyck's self-conscious emulation of Titian is thoroughly discussed in Jeffrey M. Muller, "The Quality of Grace in the Art of Anthony van Dyck," in *Anthony van Dyck*, ed. Susan J. Barnes, Arthur K. Wheelock, and Julius S. Held (Washington, D.C.: National Gallery of Art, 1990), pp. 27–36.

17 "Je remarquois encore la ruse d'un grand nombre de Peintres, qui sous pretexte de voir disner la Reyne, desroboient ingenieusement d'un subtil pinceau tous les traits de son visage." Puget de la Serre, *Histoire curieuse*, p. 65.

18 For the painting, see Horst Vey's entry in Barnes et al., *Van Dyck*, pp. 332–33, cat. no III.105.

19 For the drawing, see Vey, *Die Zeichnungen Anton van Dycks*, pp. 347–48, cat. no. 287.

20 Barnes et al., *Van Dyck*, p. 333.

21 Undated letter from Charles Louis of the Palatine to Elizabeth of Bohemia, transcribed in Nadine Akkerman, ed., *The Correspondence of Elizabeth Stuart, Queen of Bohemia*, 2 vols. (Oxford: Oxford University Press, 2011), vol. 2, pp. 390–91. The correct title of Lodowick Carlile's play, the performance of which gives us an approximate date for the letter, is *Arviragus and Philicia*.

22 As Marguerite Tassi writes, "Because drama was the more popular and economically successful of the two arts, dramatists were in a position to exploit the painter's vulnerable social and artistic status by setting up painting as a foil for their own art"; Marguerite A. Tassi, *The Scandal of Images: Iconoclasm, Eroticism, and Painting in Early Modern English Drama* (Selinsgrove, Penn.: Susquehanna University Press, 2005), p. 25.

23 Act I, Scene 2.78–79; Marilyn J. Thorssen, ed., *A Critical Edition of James Shirley's "The Lady of Pleasure"* (New York: Garland, 1980), p. 100.

24 Act II, Scene 1.22; ibid., p. 135.

25 For a previous account of Van Dyck's early literary reception, see Graham Parry, "Van Dyck and the Caroline Court Poets," in *Van Dyck 350*, ed. Susan J. Barnes and Arthur K. Wheelock, Studies in the History of Art 46 (Washington, D.C.: National Gallery of Art, 1994), pp. 247–62.

26 For introductions to city comedy, see Brian Gibbons, *Jacobean City Comedy*, 2nd edn. (London: Routledge, 1980); Shannon Miller, "Consuming Mothers/Consuming Merchants: The Carnivalesque Economy of Jacobean City Comedy," *Modern Language Studies* 26, no. 2/3 (Spring/Summer 1996): 73–97; and Julie Sanders, *Caroline Drama: The Plays of Massinger, Ford, Shirley and Brome* (Plymouth: Northcote House in association with the British Council, 1999).

27 For women's consumption as a motif in Dutch genre painting, see Elizabeth Alice Honig, "Desire and Domestic Economy," *Art Bulletin* 83, no. 2 (June 2001): 294–315.

28 As Malcolm Smuts writes, "The development of the London season had created a new type: the lady of fashion pining away in the country, amusing herself with books while she dreamed of rejoining the capital's glamorous whirl"; Smuts, *Court Culture*, p. 190.

29 Thomas Clayton and L. A. Beaurline, eds., *The Works of Sir John Suckling*, 2 vols. (Oxford: Clarendon Press, 1971), vol. 1, p. 108.

30 For these portraits, see my entry in Alsteens and Eaker, *Van Dyck: The Anatomy of Portraiture*, pp. 230–32, cat. no. 85.

31 Act I, Scene 1.330–31; Thorssen, *James Shirley's "The Lady of Pleasure,"* p. 119.

32 On this point, see Jean E. Howard, *Theater of a City: The Places of London Comedy, 1598–1642* (Philadelphia: University of Pennsylvania Press, 2011), p. 175.

33 Julie Sanders, "Caroline Salon Culture and Female Agency: The Countess of Carlisle, Henrietta Maria, and Public Theatre," *Theatre Journal* 52, no. 4 (December 2000): 449–64.

34 Oliver Millar, "Strafford and Van Dyck," in *For Veronica Wedgwood These: Studies in Seventeenth-Century History*, ed. Richard Ollard and Pamela Tudor-Craig (London: Collins, 1986), pp. 109–23.

35 Cited ibid., p. 118.

36 For a discussion of the "new woman" controversy, see Thorssen, *James Shirley's "The Lady of Pleasure,"* pp. 51–53.

37 Act I, Scene 1.253–59; ibid., p. 114.

38 Act I, Scene 2.76–90; ibid., pp. 125–26.

39 Giovanni Pietro Bellori, *The Lives of the Modern Painters, Sculptors and Architects*, ed. Hellmut Wohl, trans. Alice Sedgwick Wohl (New York: Cambridge University Press, 2005), p. 218.

40 Howard, *Theater of a City*, p. 184.

41 For Van Dyck's Catholic identity, see Jeremy Wood, "Van Dyck: A Catholic Artist in Protestant England, and the Notes on Painting Compiled by

Francis Russell, 4th Earl of Bedford," in *Van Dyck, 1599–1999: Conjectures and Refutations*, ed. Hans Vlieghe (Turnhout: Brepols, 2001), pp. 167–98. Wood notes that even Van Dyck's Catholic patrons avoided commissioning devotional images from him, and that his religious affiliation did not prevent him from enjoying Puritan patronage.

42 Act II, Scene 1.19–20; Thorssen, *James Shirley's "The Lady of Pleasure,"* p. 135.

43 For an overview of the queen's patronage of Van Dyck, see Gudrun Raatschen, "Merely Ornamental? Van Dyck's Portraits of Henrietta Maria," in *Henrietta Maria: Piety, Politics and Patronage*, ed. Erin Griffey (Aldershot: Ashgate, 2008), pp. 139–63.

44 Erin Griffey, *On Display: Henrietta Maria and the Materials of Magnificence at the Stuart Court* (New Haven and London: Yale University Press for the Paul Mellon Centre for Studies in British Art, 2016), p. 135.

45 Act II, Scene 1.17; Thorssen, *James Shirley's "The Lady of Pleasure,"* p. 135. The fact that the "Belgicke gentleman" paints Aretina at her house should not be taken as evidence of Van Dyck's actual practice, which sources locate at his studio in Blackfriars.

46 For panegyrics dedicated to Lady Carlisle, see Raymond A. Anselment, "The Countess of Carlisle and Caroline Praise: Convention and Reality," *Studies in Philology* 82, no. 2 (Spring 1985): 212–33.

47 Robert Bell, ed., *Poetical Works of Edmund Waller* (London: J. W. Parker, 1854), p. 75.

48 For the actual portrait likely referred to by Waller, see Karen Hearn's entry in Karen Hearn, ed., *Van Dyck & Britain* (London: Tate, 2009), p. 118, cat. no. 53.

49 Jonson, *Eupheme* III.1–12; William B. Hunter, Jr., ed., *The Complete Poetry of Ben Jonson* (Garden City, N.Y.: Anchor, 1963), p. 253.

50 Jonson, *Eupheme* IV.1–2, 7–8.

51 On the distrust of color and "paint" (in the cosmetic sense) within English poems on portraits, see Claire Pace, "'Delineated Lives': Themes and Variations in Seventeenth-Century Poems about Portraits," *Word & Image* 2, no. 1 (January 1986), pp. 1–17, esp. p. 7.

52 On this tradition, see especially Elizabeth Cropper, "On Beautiful Women, Parmigianino, Petrarchismo, and the Vernacular Style," *Art Bulletin* 58, no. 3 (September 1976): 374–94; and Elizabeth Cropper, "The Beauty of Woman: Problems in the Rhetoric of Renaissance Portraiture," in *Rewriting the Renaissance: The Discourses of Sexual Difference in Early Modern Europe*, ed. Margaret W. Ferguson, Maureen Quilligan, and Nancy J. Vickers (Chicago: University of Chicago Press, 1986), pp. 175–90.

53 For an introduction to this genre, see Mary Tom Osborne, *Advice-to-a-Painter Poems, 1633–1856: An Annotated Finding List* (Austin: University of Texas Press, 1949); these poems are also discussed in Judith Dundas, *Pencils Rhetorique: Renaissance Poets and the Art of Painting* (Newark: University of Delaware Press, 1993), pp. 194–205. A close reading of one famous example is provided by Steven N. Zwicker, "Sites of Instruction: Andrew Marvell and the Tropes of Restoration Portraiture," in *Politics, Transgression, and Representation at the Court of Charles II*, ed. Julia Marciari Alexander and Catharine MacLeod, Studies in British Art 18 (New Haven and London: Yale University Press for the Paul Mellon Centre for Studies in British Art, 2007), pp. 123–38.

54 For the background of this episode, see Ann Sumner, ed., *Death, Passion and Politics: Van Dyck's Portraits of Venetia Stanley and George Digby* (London: Dulwich Picture Gallery, 1995).

55 Published in Vittorio Gabrieli, *Sir Kenelm Digby, un inglese italianato nell'età della controriforma* (Rome: Edizioni di Storia e Letteratura, 1957), p. 248.

56 For the literature on the painting, see Oliver Millar's entry in Barnes et al., *Van Dyck*, pp. 506–507, cat. no. IV.97.

57 Cited in Gabrieli, *Sir Kenelm Digby*, p. 248.

58 For an overview of these other memorials, see Clare Gittings, "Venetia's Death and Kenelm's Mourning," in *Death, Passion and Politics: Van Dyck's Portraits of Venetia Stanley and George Digby*, ed. Ann Sumner (London: Dulwich Picture Gallery, 1995), pp. 54–68.

59 For Digby's patronage of Jonson, see Robert C. Evans, "Jonson, Weston, and the Digbys: Patronage Relations in Some Later Poems,"

Renaissance and Reformation / Renaissance et Réforme 28, no. 1 (January 2009): 5–37.

60 Cited in Gabrieli, *Sir Kenelm Digby*, p. 246.

61 Pace, "Delineated Lives," p. 4.

62 For the literature on this painting, see Oliver Millar's entry in Barnes et al., *Van Dyck*, pp. 507–10, cat. nos. IV.98 and IV. 99. Useful discussions of the *paragone* between Jonson and Van Dyck occur in Parry, "Van Dyck and the Caroline Court Poets"; Norman K. Farmer, *Poets and the Visual Arts in Renaissance England* (Austin: University of Texas Press, 1984), pp. 28–30; and Dundas, *Pencils Rhetorique*, pp. 156–63.

63 Neither surviving version of the painting exactly matches the iconography described by Bellori, and both lack the inscription from Juvenal that he cites. My personal inspection of the version at the Palazzo Reale in Milan leads me to suspect it is largely overpainted, which could explain some of the divergences from Bellori's description.

64 Bellori, *The Lives*, p. 219.

65 Ibid., p. 218; original in Bellori, *Le vite de' pittori, scultori e architetti moderni*, ed. Evelina Borea (Turin: Einaudi, 1976), p. 280.

66 Bellori, *The Lives*, p. 219; *Le vite*, p. 280.

67 "Le fameux Jabac ... m'a conté"; Roger de Piles, *Cours de peinture par principes* (Paris: Chez Jacques Estienne, 1708), p. 291.

68 On this point, see Luciano Arcangeli, "Anton van Dyck," in *L'Idea del bello: Viaggio per Roma nel seicento con Giovan Pietro Bellori*, vol. 2 (Rome: Edizioni De Luca, 2000), pp. 305–10.

69 Bellori, *The Lives*, p. 219.

70 Claire Pace and Janis Bell, "The Allegorical Engravings in Bellori's Lives," in *Art History in the Age of Bellori: Scholarship and Cultural Poetics in Seventeenth-Century Rome*, ed. Janis Bell and Thomas Willette (Cambridge: Cambridge University Press, 2002), pp. 191–223, esp. p. 211.

71 Bellori, *The Lives*, p. 411. I am grateful to Diane Bodart for bringing to my attention the significance of Maratta to Bellori's conception of portraiture.

72 Ibid., p. 412.

73 Ibid., p. 411.

74 Ibid., p. 412.

75 Kenelm Digby, *Loose Fantasies*, ed. Vittorio Gabrieli (Rome: Edizioni di Storia e Letteratura, 1968), pp. 64–65.

76 Ibid., p. 121.

77 For the dispute over Venetia's portrait, see Polly Amos and Ann Sumner, "Kenelm Digby and Venetia Stanley: A Great Love Story of the Seventeenth Century," in *Death, Passion and Politics: Van Dyck's Portraits of Venetia Stanley and George Digby*, ed. Ann Sumner (London: Dulwich Picture Gallery, 1995), pp. 26–31, esp. pp. 27–29.

78 *Naturalis Historia* 35.86–87; for visual representations of this anecdote, see Georg-W. Költzsch, *Der Maler und sein Modell: Geschichte und Deutung eines Bildthemas* (Cologne: DuMont, 2000), pp. 87–95. See also the useful material compiled as part of the "Pictor in Fabula" project: http://www.pictorinfabula.com/fiches/14 (accessed December 10, 2021).

79 René Girard, *Deceit, Desire, and the Novel: Self and Other in Literary Structure*, trans. Yvonne Freccero (Baltimore: Johns Hopkins University Press, 1984), pp. 1–52; Eve Kosofsky Sedgwick, *Between Men: English Literature and Male Homosocial Desire* (New York: Columbia University Press, 1985), pp. 21–66; Nancy Vickers, "The Mistress in the Masterpiece," in *The Poetics of Gender*, ed. Nancy K. Miller (New York: Columbia University Press, 1986), pp. 19–41.

80 Christiane Hille, *Visions of the Courtly Body: The Patronage of George Villiers, First Duke of Buckingham, and the Triumph of Painting at the Stuart Court* (Berlin: Akademie Verlag, 2012).

81 For an illuminating discussion of the anxiety provoked by female painters in the eighteenth century, see Angela Rosenthal, "She's Got the Look! Eighteenth-Century Female Portrait Painters and the Psychology of a Potentially 'Dangerous Employment,'" in *Portraiture: Facing the Subject*, ed. Joanna Woodall (Manchester: Manchester University Press, 1997), pp. 147–66.

82 For an extended reading of Lyly's *Campaspe*, see Tassi, *The Scandal of Images*, pp. 66–97.

83 Anat Feinberg-Jütte, "Painters and Counterfeiters: The Painting Artist in Elizabethan and Stuart Drama," *AAA: Arbeiten aus Anglistik und Amerikanistik* 16, no. 1 (January 1991): 3–12.

84 For a useful interpretation of this play and its ambiguous depiction of the painter, see Tassi, *The Scandal of Images*, pp. 114–29.

85 Feinberg-Jütte, "Painters and Counterfeiters," pp. 5 and 11–12. Brome's play also satirizes the courtier playwright Sir John Suckling, whose portrait in theatrical dress Van Dyck painted (Frick Collection, New York); see Matthew Steggle, *Richard Brome: Place and Politics on the Caroline Stage* (Manchester: Manchester University Press, 2004), pp. 158–60.

86 Act III, Scene 1; Richard Brome, *The Dramatic Works of Richard Brome Containing Fifteen Comedies Now First Collected in Three Volumes* (London: John Pearson, 1873), vol. 1, p. 227.

87 For a discussion of the problems of decorum occasioned by Charles I's commission of a suite of paintings depicting the Cupid and Psyche myth, see Elizabeth McGrath, *Jordaens, Psyche and the Abbot: Myth, Decorum and Italian Manners in Seventeenth-Century Antwerp* (Groningen: Stichting Gerson Lezingen, 2009).

88 For the history of these conflicts, see Susan Foister, "Foreigners at Court: Holbein, Van Dyck and the Painter-Stainers Company," in *Art and Patronage in the Caroline Courts: Essays in Honour of Sir Oliver Millar*, ed. David Howarth (Cambridge: Cambridge University Press, 1993), pp. 32–50.

89 Act III, Scene 3; William Gifford and Alexander Dyce, eds., *The Dramatic Works and Poems of James Shirley*, 6 vols. (London: John Murray, 1833), vol. 3, pp. 45–46; the inspiration for this figure is identified as Van Dyck in Smuts, *Court Culture and the Origins of a Royalist Tradition*, p. 188; another discussion of this passage in relation to Van Dyck occurs in Emilie E. S. Gordenker, *Anthony Van Dyck (1599–1641) and the Representation of Dress in Seventeenth-Century Portraiture* (Turnhout: Brepols, 2001), p. 11.

90 Letter from Edward, Viscount Conway, to Thomas, Viscount Wentworth, Lord Deputy of Ireland, January 22, 1636 (Old Style); published in Sir George Radcliffe, ed., *The Earl of Strafforde's Letters and Dispatches, with an Essay towards his Life*, 2 vols. (London: William Bowyer, 1739), vol. 2, p. 48.

91 See, for example, the comments by Valentiner and Filipczak discussed in the introduction.

92 For the painting, see Oliver Millar's entry in Barnes et al., *Van Dyck*, pp. 433–34, cat. no. IV.7, as well as my entry in Alsteens and Eaker, *Van Dyck: The Anatomy of Portraiture*, pp. 247–49, cat. no. 94.

93 William Sanderson, *Graphice: The Use of the Pen and Pensil. Or, The Most Excellent Art of Painting* (London: Robert Crofts, 1658), p. 37.

94 Ibid., p. 36.

95 Ibid.

96 Ibid., p. 37.

97 Ibid. For a more extended version of this argument, see Adam Eaker, "Rubens and the Gallery of Beauties," in *Tributes to David Freedberg: Image and Insight*, ed. Claudia Swan (London: Harvey Miller Publishers, 2019), pp. 61–74.

98 "On the Death of Sir Anthony Vandyck," in Thomas Spratt, ed., *The Poetical Works of Abraham Cowley*, 4 vols. (Edinburgh: Apollo Press, 1784), vol. 1, pp. 218–19.

99 Prado archives, Sign. Sg PRA.Gen. 55 v. 7, p. 57, cat. no. 11888 (694). For more on the portrait, see my entry in Alsteens and Eaker, *Van Dyck*, pp. 247–49, cat. no. 94.

100 For one highly speculative account, see Susan James's entry in the *Oxford Dictionary of National Biography* (https://doi.org/10.1093/ref:odnb/72128, accessed December 10, 2021).

101 Hilary Maddicott, "'Qualis vita, finis ita': The Life and Death of Margaret Lemon, Mistress of Van Dyck," *Burlington Magazine* 160, no. 1379 (February 2018): 92–100.

102 Cited ibid., p. 98.

103 Bellori, *The Lives*, p. 216.

104 For this painting, see Oliver Millar's entry in Barnes et al., *Van Dyck*, p. 552, cat. no. IV.157.

105 For this anecdote, often attributed to Wenceslaus Hollar without substantiation, see Maddicott, "Qualis vita, finis ita," p. 94, n. 12.

106 As transcribed in Vertue, "The Note-books of George Vertue Relating to Artists and Collections in England, vol. 1," *Walpole Society* 18 (1929–30): 114.

107 Maddicott, "Qualis vita, finis ita," pp. 98–99.

108 For a discussion of Killigrew's ties to Van Dyck, see Malcolm Rogers, "'Golden Houses for Shadows': Some Portraits of Thomas Killigrew and His Family," in *Art and Patronage in the Caroline Courts: Essays in Honour of Sir Oliver Millar*, ed. David Howarth (Cambridge: Cambridge University Press, 1993), pp. 220–42.

109 Act II, Scene 3; Thomas Killigrew, *Thomaso, or, the Wanderer: A Comedy, the Scene Madrid* (London: Henry Herringman, 1663), p. 333.

110 On this aspect of Behn's play, see Ashley Brookner Bender, "Moving Miniatures and Circulating Bodies in Aphra Behn's 'The Rover,'" *Restoration: Studies in English Literary Culture, 1660–1700* 31, no. 1 (Spring 2007): 27–46.

111 For the painting, see *Old Master and British Paintings Evening Sale*, London, Sotheby's, July 6, 2011, lot 42.

112 Vertue, "The Note-books of George Vertue, vol. 1," 97.

113 For the painting and its provenance, see Oliver Millar's entry in Barnes et al., *Van Dyck*, pp. 430–31, cat. no. IV.3. Charles II's repossession of his father's collection is discussed in Andrew Barclay, "Recovering Charles I's Art Collection: Some Implications of the 1660 Act of Indemnity and Oblivion," *Historical Research* 88, no. 242 (November 2015): 629–49.

2 · *Impudent Painters*

1 English translation taken from Gérard de Lairesse, *A Treatise on the Art of Painting, in all its Branches: Accompanied by Seventy Engraved Plates, and Exemplified by Remarks on the Paintings of the Best Masters*, ed. William Marshall Craig (London: Edward Orme, 1817), p. 116.

2 Ibid., p. 108.

3 For stimulating discussions of the evolving perception of fashion in early modern Europe, see Alexander Nagel, "Fashion and the Now-Time of Renaissance Art," *Res: Anthropology and Aesthetics*, no. 46 (Autumn 2004): 33–52; and Ann Rosalind Jones and Peter Stallybrass, *Renaissance Clothing and the Materials of Memory* (Cambridge: Cambridge University Press, 2000).

4 De Lairesse, *A Treatise on the Art of Painting*, p. 116.

5 Ibid., pp. 115–16.

6 Ibid., p. 121.

7 For Van Mander's presentation of Bruegel as "a curious ethnographer," see Joseph Leo Koerner, *Bosch and Bruegel: From Enemy Painting to Everyday Life*, A. W. Mellon Lectures in the Fine Arts 57 (Princeton: Princeton University Press, 2016), p. 14.

8 Manuscript letter of William Cavendish, Earl of Newcastle, to Anthony van Dyck, transcribed in Richard William Goulding, *Catalogue of the Pictures Belonging to His Grace the Duke of Portland, K.G. …* (Cambridge: Cambridge University Press, 1936), p. 485.

9 As Jodi Cranston has argued for the early sixteenth-century humanist origins of this genre, such pictures "of two friends depicted for an absent third … implicate the viewer through visual structures of inclusiveness and engagement"; Jodi Cranston, *The Poetics of Portraiture in the Italian Renaissance* (Cambridge: Cambridge University Press, 2000), p. 66; for a discussion of Van Dyck's double portraits of women, see Jennifer L. Hallam, "All the Queen's Women: Female Double Portraits at the Caroline Court," in *Women and Portraits in Early Modern Europe: Gender, Agency, Identity*, ed. Andrea Pearson (Aldershot: Ashgate, 2007), pp. 137–60.

10 For the portrait, see Oliver Millar's entry in Susan J. Barnes et al., *Van Dyck: A Complete Catalogue of the Paintings* (New Haven and London: Yale University Press for the Paul Mellon Centre for Studies in British Art, 2004), pp. 433–34, cat. no. IV.7. Scholars have assumed the portrait belonged to Porter himself, but it is first recorded in the Duarte collection in Antwerp following Porter's death. For a recent reading of the portrait within the context of early modern notions of friendship, see Larissa Weiler, "'For an Assured Freende is the Medicine of Life': Van Dyck and the English Virtuoso," *Netherlands Yearbook for History of Art / Nederlands Kunsthistorisch Jaarboek* 70 (2020): 214–39.

11 For other instances of Van Dyck's manipulation of heraldic convention in double portraits, see Zirka Filipczak, "Van Dyck's Men and Women in Humoral Perspective," *Jaarboek Koninklijk Museum voor Schone Kunsten, Antwerpen* (1999): 63–66.

12 I am grateful to Allison Stielau for aptly suggesting "insinuation" as a description of Van Dyck's self-placement in the painting.

13 For the etymology of the term "conversation piece" as originally applied to Dutch genre paintings, see Kate Retford, *The Conversation Piece: Making Modern Art in Eighteenth-Century Britain* (New Haven and London: Yale University Press for the Paul Mellon Centre for Studies in British Art, 2017), p. 13.

14 For the painting, see Oliver Millar's entry in Barnes et al., *Van Dyck*, pp. 542–43, cat. no. IV.146.

15 For a recent overview of Van Dyck's depictions of Black figures, see Bernadette Haute, "Anthony van Dyck and the Trope of the Black Attendant," *Acta Academica* 48, no. 2 (2016): 18–47.

16 For discussions of the Black attendant figure within early modern English portraiture, see Susan Dwyer Amussen, *Caribbean Exchanges: Slavery and the Transformation of English Society, 1640–1700* (Chapel Hill: University of North Carolina Press, 2007), pp. 191–217; David Bindman, "Subjectivity and Slavery in Portraiture: From Courtly to Commercial Societies," in *Slave Portraiture in the Atlantic World*, ed. Angela Rosenthal and Agnes Lugo-Ortiz (Cambridge: Cambridge University Press, 2013), pp. 71–88. For the role of slavery in defining the "refined" white subject, see Simon Gikandi, *Slavery and the Culture of Taste* (Princeton: Princeton University Press, 2011); and Catherine Molineux, *Faces of Perfect Ebony: Encountering Atlantic Slavery in Imperial Britain*, Harvard Historical Studies 175 (Cambridge, Mass.: Harvard University Press, 2012).

17 Kim F. Hall, *Things of Darkness: Economies of Race and Gender in Early Modern England* (Ithaca: Cornell University Press, 1995), p. 212.

18 For the portrait, see Hans Vlieghe's entry in Barnes et al., *Van Dyck*, pp. 329–30, cat. no. III.102.

19 For the Whitehall inventory, see ibid.

20 For the painting, see Susan Barnes's entry ibid., pp. 186–88, cat. no. II.43.

21 For the painting, see Oliver Millar's entry ibid., pp. 496–97, cat. no. IV.86.

22 For a wide-ranging discussion of this theme, see Beth Fowkes Tobin, *Picturing Imperial Power: Colonial Subjects in Eighteenth-Century British Painting* (Durham, N.C.: Duke University Press, 1999).

23 'een voorbeelt aan andere groote Meesters, die zich dikmaals laaten behandelen als Laqueyen by vergulde Ezels'; Jacob Campo Weyerman, *De levens-beschryvingen der Nederlandsche konst-schilders en konst-schilderessen*, 4 vols. (The Hague: E. Boucquet, H. Scheurleer, F. Boucquet, and J. de Jongh, 1729), vol. 1, p. 305. The anecdote is given in full, in loose translation, in W. R. Valentiner, "Van Dyck's Character," *Art Quarterly* 13 (1950): 94–97. For another eighteenth-century anecdote about Van Dyck's conflict with a patron, see Gaetane Maës, "Van Dyck's Anger in Kortrijk and his Decision to Paint 'Only for People and Not for Donkeys'", in *Facts & Feelings: Retracing Emotions of Artists, 1600–1800*, ed. Hannelore Magnus and Katlijne Van der Stighelen (Turnhout: Brepols, 2015), pp. 187–200.

24 'een extraordinaire belooning', 'een Konstenaar die een open Tafel voor zyn Vrienden, en een open beurs houd voor zyn Maitressen, gelyk als ik doe, is nu en dan niet onbekent met den bodem van zyn Geldkist'; Weyerman, *De levens-beschryvingen*, p. 312.

25 Cited in Wayne E. Franits, *Godefridus Schalcken: A Dutch Painter in Late Seventeenth-Century London* (Amsterdam: Amsterdam University Press, 2018), p. 74. In fact, Schalcken's painting does not show the king holding the candle, but Weyerman may have conflated it with one of the artist's own self-portraits.

26 Ibid.

27 Horace Walpole, *Anecdotes of Painting in England*, 4 vols. (New York: Arno Press, 1969), vol. 3, pp. 244–45.

28 The passages from Walpole and Weyerman are discussed together in Franits, *Godefridus Schalcken*, pp. 74–75.

29 For this painting, see ibid., pp. 64–67.

30 Ibid., pp. 85–86.

31 English translation in Jeremy Wood, ed., *Lives of Rubens* (London: Pallas Athene, 2005), p. 78.

32 For an English translation of this passage from Palomino's life of Velázquez, see Robert

Enggass and Jonathan Brown, eds., *Italy and Spain, 1600–1750: Sources and Documents* (Englewood Cliffs, N.J.: Prentice-Hall, 1970), p. 188.

33 H. Rackham, trans., *Pliny: Natural History*, 10 vols., Loeb Classical Library (Cambridge, Mass.: Harvard University Press, 1949–62), vol. IX, p. 325.

34 For this painting, and other depictions of the subject by Van Haecht, see Gary Schwartz, "Love in the Kunstkamer: Additions to the Work of Guillam van Haecht (1593–1637)," *Tableau* 18 (Summer 1996): 43–52.

35 See also the interesting discussion of this anecdote and its representation in Christopher S. Wood, "Indoor–Outdoor: The Studio around 1500," in *Inventions of the Studio: Renaissance to Romanticism*, ed. Michael Cole and Mary Pardo (Chapel Hill: University of North Carolina Press, 2005), pp. 36–72 (anecdote discussed p. 38).

36 Richard Perrinchief, *The Royal Martyr, or, The History of the Life and Death of King Charles I* (London: printed by J.M. for R. Royston, 1676), pp. 253–54.

37 For another discussion of this passage, see R. Malcolm Smuts, *Court Culture and the Origins of a Royalist Tradition in Early Stuart England* (Philadelphia: University of Pennsylvania Press, 1987), p. 153.

38 Act I, Scene 2; Marilyn J. Thorssen, ed., *A Critical Edition of James Shirley's "The Lady of Pleasure"* (New York: Garland, 1980), p. 119. In the context of Shirley's play, it is not the artist but rather Lady Bornwell's disreputable admirers who provide the "discourse" during her sitting.

39 Arthur F. Kinney and Linda Bradley Salamon, eds., *Nicholas Hilliard's Art of Limning* (Boston, Mass.: Northeastern University Press, 1983), p. 22.

40 Jeffrey M. Muller and Jim Murrell, eds., *Edward Norgate: Miniatura, or, The Art of Limning* (New Haven and London: Yale University Press, 1997), p. 80.

41 Esmond Samuel de Beer, ed., *The Diary of John Evelyn*, 6 vols. (Oxford: Clarendon Press, 1955), vol. 3, pp. 309–10.

42 Andrew Clark, ed., *"Brief Lives": Chiefly of Contemporaries, set down by John Aubrey, between the Years 1669 & 1696*, 2 vols. (Oxford: Clarendon Press, 1898), vol. 1, p. 340.

43 For this portrait and its indications of Van Dyck's working method, see my entry in Stijn Alsteens and Adam Eaker, eds., *Van Dyck: The Anatomy of Portraiture* (New York: Frick Collection in association with Yale University Press, 2016), pp. 240–41, cat. no. 90.

44 My thinking about Van Dyck's performance of his virtuosity in the context of the sitting is indebted to the discussion of portrait sittings in Nicola Suthor, *Bravura: Virtuosität und Mutwilligkeit in der Malerei der Frühen Neuzeit* (Munich: W. Fink, 2010), pp. 131–36. See also the discussion of Lely's practice in Matthew C. Hunter, *Wicked Intelligence: Visual Art and the Science of Experiment in Restoration London* (Chicago: University of Chicago Press, 2013), p. 123.

45 For a relevant discussion of the intersection between amateur artistic practices and courtliness in Stuart England, see Ann Bermingham, *Learning to Draw: Studies in the Cultural History of a Polite and Useful Art* (New Haven and London: Yale University Press for the Paul Mellon Centre for Studies in British Art, 2000), pp. 33–73.

46 For an English translation and discussion of this passage, originally recorded in Dutch, see Mansfield Kirby Talley, *Portrait Painting in England: Studies in the Technical Literature before 1700* (London: Paul Mellon Centre for Studies in British Art, 1981), pp. 150–56.

47 Linda Bauer and George Bauer, "Van Dyck's Club," *Zeitschrift für Kunstgeschichte* 71, no. 2 (2008): 259–71; see also Weiler, "For an Assured Freende."

48 For de Mayerne's manuscript, see Ernst Berger, *Beiträge zur Entwicklungsgeschichte der Maltechnik*, 5 vols. (Munich: G. D. W. Callwey, 1901), vol. 3, pp. 92–410; J. A. van de Graaf, *Het De Mayerne Manuscript als bron voor de schildertechniek van de barok* (Mijdrecht: Drukkerij Verweij, 1958); Talley, *Portrait Painting in England*, pp. 72–149; Donald C. Fels, ed., *Lost Secrets of Flemish Painting: Including the First Complete English Translation of the De Mayerne Manuscript, B.M. Sloane 2052* (Hillsville, Va.: Alchemist, 2001); and Jenny Boulboullé, "Drawn up by a Learned Physician from the Mouths of

Artisans: The Mayerne Manuscript Revisited," *Netherlands Yearbook for History of Art / Nederlands Kunsthistorisch Jaarboek* 68 (2019): 204–49.

49 English translation in Talley, *Portrait Painting in England*, p. 98; for the original, see Van de Graaf, *Het De Mayerne Manuscript*, p. 206.

50 For Van Dyck and Anguissola, see the following chapter.

51 "peintre tresexcellent"; Van de Graaf, *Het De Mayerne Manuscript*, p. 177.

52 Talley, *Portrait Painting in England*, pp. 113–14.

53 Ibid., pp. 116–17.

54 For a conservator's approach to these records of Van Dyck's conversations, see Carol Christensen, Michael Palmer, and Michael Swicklik, "Van Dyck's Painting Technique, His Writings, and Three Paintings in the National Gallery of Art," in *Anthony van Dyck*, ed. Arthur K. Wheelock, Susan J. Barnes, and Julius S. Held (Washington, D.C.: National Gallery of Art, 1990), pp. 45–52.

55 The spectacular nature of portrait sittings at Charles II's court can be connected to the larger phenomenon of "public intimacy" during his reign; for this, see Joseph Roach, "Celebrity Erotics: Pepys, Performance, and Painted Ladies," in *Politics, Transgression, and Representation at the Court of Charles II*, ed. Julia Marciari Alexander and Catharine MacLeod, Studies in British Art 18 (New Haven and London: Yale University Press for the Paul Mellon Centre for Studies in British Art, 2007), pp. 233–50.

56 Transcribed in George Vertue, "The Note-books of George Vertue Relating to Artists and Collections in England, vol. 1," *Walpole Society* 18 (1929–30): 28.

57 Robert Latham and William Matthews, eds., *The Diary of Samuel Pepys*, 11 vols. (Berkeley: University of California Press, 1970–83), vol. 5, p. 209.

58 Critics of the court were also eager to exploit this irony in their parodies of court portraiture; see Steven N. Zwicker, "Sites of Instruction: Andrew Marvell and the Tropes of Restoration Portraiture," in *Politics, Transgression, and Representation at the Court of Charles II*, ed. Julia Marciari Alexander and Catharine MacLeod, Studies in British Art 18 (New Haven and London: Yale University Press for the Paul Mellon Centre for Studies in British Art, 2007), pp. 123–38.

59 Frances Harris, *Transformations of Love: The Friendship of John Evelyn and Margaret Godolphin* (Oxford: Oxford University Press, 2002), p. 183.

60 Diary entry for August 26, 1664; Latham and Matthews, *Diary of Samuel Pepys*, vol. 5, p. 254.

61 Anna Maria Crinò, "The Relations between Samuel Cooper and the Court of Cosmo [*sic*] III," *Burlington Magazine* 99, no. 646 (January 1957): 16–21; for the visit to Rembrandt's studio, see G. J. Hoogewerff, ed., *De twee reizen van Cosimo de' Medici, Prins van Toscane door de Nederlanden (1667–1669): Journalen en documenten*, Werken uitgegeven door het Historisch Genootschap 3, vol. 41 (Amsterdam: Johannes Müller, 1919), p. 67.

62 Letter transcribed in David Bierens de Haan et al., eds., *Oeuvres complètes de Christiaan Huygens*, 22 vols. (The Hague: Martinus Nijhoff, 1888–1950), vol. 4 (1891), p. 361.

63 Ibid., pp. 362–3; Huygens's use of the English phrase, "there was a Lady sitting," indicates that he is perhaps quoting a studio assistant or servant.

64 Ibid., pp. 370–73.

65 "Was smergens met de langhe Browne tot m^rs Remy, een Brabantsche vrouw; haer man had een schilder geweest in tijdt van van Dijck, daer sij veel van wist te vertellen, en hoe hij m^rs Limmon langh in huys gehadt en onderhouden hadde"; Constantijn Huygens, Jr., *Journaal van Constantijn Huygens, den zoon, 21 october 1688 tot 2 september 1696* (Utrecht: Keminck & Zoon, 1876), p. 240. This passage is discussed in the context of Huygens's activity as a collector in Rudolf Dekker, *Family, Culture and Society in the Diary of Constantijn Huygens Jr, Secretary to Stadholder-King William of Orange* (Leiden: Brill, 2013), p. 79.

66 For the drawing's provenance, see my entry in Alsteens and Eaker, eds., *Van Dyck: The Anatomy of Portraiture*, p. 106, cat. no. 21.

67 For these drawings, see An Van Camp's entries in ibid., pp. 211–14, cat. nos. 75 and 76.

68 For Lanier's collection, see Jeremy Wood, "Nicholas Lanier (1588–1666) and the Origins of Drawings Collecting in Stuart England," in *Collecting Prints and Drawings in Europe, c.1500–1750*, ed. Christopher Baker, Caroline Elam and Genevieve Warwick (Aldershot: Ashgate, 2003), pp. 85–122; for Lely's collection, see Diana Dethloff, "Sir Peter Lely's Collection of Prints and Drawings," ibid., pp. 123–39.

69 For Beale's self-portrait, originally intended as a pendant to a painting of her husband, Charles, see Tabitha Barber, ed., *Mary Beale (1632/3–1699): Portrait of a Seventeenth-Century Painter, Her Family and Her Studio* (London: Geffrye Museum Trust, 1999), p. 62, cat. no. 4.

70 Helen Draper writes of Beale's self-portrait, "In this painted statement of intent, in an act of quiet subversion, the absence and presence of her family has become entirely symbolic, while her visual persona is that of the artist, alone in a 'paynting roome' of her own. Far from questioning the viability of motherhood and creativity co-existing in a woman's world, the portrait offers a conclusive example of just such a possibility"; Helen Draper, "'Her Painting of Apricots': The Invisibility of Mary Beale (1633–1699)," *Forum for Modern Language Studies* 48, no. 4 (October 2012): 389–405, quoted p. 399.

71 Georg-W. Költzsch, *Der Maler und sein Modell: Geschichte und Deutung eines Bildthemas* (Cologne: DuMont, 2000), pp. 235–36.

72 Tiarna Doherty, "Painting Connoisseurship: Liefhebbers in the Studio," *Netherlands Yearbook for History of Art / Nederlands Kunsthistorisch Jaarboek* 69, no. 1 (2020): 146–73.

73 For the painting, lost since World War II, see Katja Kleinert, *Atelierdarstellungen in der niederländischen Genremalerei des 17. Jahrhunderts: Realistisches Abbild oder glaubwürdiger Schein?* (Petersberg: Michael Imhof, 2006), p. 266, cat. no. 43.

74 For Jabach, see Blaise Ducos and Olivia Savatier Sjöholm, eds., *Un Allemand à la cour de Louis XIV: De Dürer à Van Dyck, la collection nordique d'Everhard Jabach* (Paris: Musée du Louvre/Le Passage, 2013); an overview of his portraits is given in Horst Vey, "Die Bildnisse Everhard Jabachs," *Wallraf-Richartz-Jahrbuch* 29 (1967): 157–86.

75 Stephan Wolohojian, Melinda Watt, and Michael Gallagher, "A Grand Tableau: Charles Le Brun's Portrait of the Jabach Family," *Metropolitan Museum of Art Bulletin* 75, no. 1 (Summer 2017): 5–48.

76 Sir Joshua Reynolds, *A Journey to Flanders and Holland*, ed. Harry Mount (Cambridge: Cambridge University Press, 1996), pp. 139–40.

77 Vey, "Die Bildnisse Everhard Jabachs," p. 171.

78 The foundational account in this regard is Victor Stoichita, *The Self-Aware Image: An Insight into Early Modern Meta-Painting*, trans. Anne-Marie Glasheen (Cambridge: Cambridge University Press, 1997).

79 Svetlana Alpers, *Rembrandt's Enterprise: The Studio and the Market* (Chicago: University of Chicago Press, 1988).

80 Ibid., pp. 17–18.

81 There is a significant literature on the Dutch reception of Van Dyck, focused primarily on stylistic emulation and the recycling of specific poses; see, for example, Stephanie S. Dickey, "Van Dyck in Holland: The Iconography and Its Impact on Rembrandt and Jan Lievens," in *Van Dyck 1599–1999: Conjectures and Refutations*, ed. Hans Vlieghe (Turnhout: Brepols, 2001), pp. 289–304; and Walter Liedtke, "Van Dyck's 'Influence' in the Dutch Republic," in *Aemulatio: Imitation, Emulation and Invention in Netherlandish Art from 1500 to 1800; Essays in Honor of Eric Jan Sluijter*, ed. Anton W. A. Boschloo et al. (Zwolle: Waanders Publishers, 2011), pp. 304–17.

82 This correspondence appears in Frances Parthenope Verney, *Memoirs of the Verney Family during the Seventeenth Century*, 4 vols. (London and New York: Longmans, Green, and Co., 1892), vol. 1, pp. 257–59. The portrait itself is untraced.

83 Ibid., p. 259.

84 Bendor Grosvenor, "Van Dyck as Andy Warhol," *Art History News*, January 13, 2016, https://www.arthistorynews.com (accessed February 19, 2021).

85 Jonathan Jones, "Rembrandt and Slavery: Did the Great Painter Have Links to this Abhorrent Trade?", *Guardian*, February 9, 2021, https://www.theguardian.com (accessed February 19, 2021).

3 · *Artists and Gentlewomen*

1 Bainbrigg Buckeridge, "An Essay towards an English School of Painters," in Roger de Piles, *The Art of Painting: And the Lives of Painters* ... (London: J. Nutt, 1706), pp. 398–480. For a discussion of Buckeridge's text, see Richard Johns, "Framing Robert Aggas: The Painter-Stainers' Company and the 'English School of Painters,'" *Art History* 31, no. 3 (July 2008): 322–41.

2 Buckeridge, "An Essay," p. 409.

3 Ibid., pp. 410–11.

4 For parallels between Cooper's and Van Dyck's model of the social studio, see Richard Wendorf, *The Elements of Life: Biography and Portrait-Painting in Stuart and Georgian England* (Oxford: Clarendon Press, 1990), p. 125.

5 Buckeridge, "An Essay," p. 411.

6 Ibid., p. 403.

7 Helen Draper has made an important argument along these lines about Mary Beale: "It was through a gradual process of carefully chosen collaborations that the Beales and their circle managed to create a personal persona for Mary that enabled her to become a professional painter. She built upon the virtuous reputation she had gained as a domestic amateur and later relied on this sociable studio model to lend her professional practice the required air of respectability ... Mary capitalized on the courtly culture of gift exchange that was commonplace within her wider circle. Inscribed portraits and texts were given as gestures of affection, but also as payment in kind for favours and loans. The Beales used the established pattern of giving and exchanging likenesses for love to make the selling of portraits acceptable as an extension of the currency of friendship"; Helen Draper, "'Her Painting of Apricots': The Invisibility of Mary Beale (1633–1699)," *Forum for Modern Language Studies* 48, no. 4 (October 2012): 389–405, quote on pp. 392–93.

8 See the previous chapter.

9 Gérard de Lairesse, *A Treatise on the Art of Painting, in all its Branches: Accompanied by Seventy Engraved Plates, and Exemplified by Remarks on the Paintings of the Best Masters*, ed. William Marshall Craig (London: Edward Orme, 1817), p. 114.

10 For the identification of Van Mieris's sitter with his wife, see Claus Kemmer, "In Search of Classical Form: Gerard de Lairesse's 'Groot Schilderboek' and Seventeenth-Century Dutch Genre Painting," *Simiolus: Netherlands Quarterly for the History of Art* 26, no. 1/2 (1998): 87–115, esp. pp. 97–99.

11 "[H]is mother occupied herself with embroidery, and she painted with her needle, fashioning landscapes and figures in stitchery. Given this circumstance, Anthony began on his own to draw at a tender age, and his mother, who was by now no longer adequate to teach him, recognized that nature meant to make him noteworthy in art"; Giovanni Pietro Bellori, *The Lives of the Modern Painters, Sculptors and Architects*, ed. Hellmut Wohl, trans. Alice Sedgwick Wohl (New York: Cambridge University Press, 2005), p. 215.

12 "Een Schou-cleet wonder fraey"; Cornelis de Bie, *Het gulden cabinet van de edel vry schilderconst* (Antwerp: Jan Meyssens, Juliaen van Montfort, 1662), p. 78. For Van Dyck's painting, see Susan Barnes's entry in Susan J. Barnes et al., *Van Dyck: A Complete Catalogue of the Paintings* (New Haven and London: Yale University Press for the Paul Mellon Centre for Studies in British Art, 2004), p. 151, cat. no. II.1.

13 Katlijne Van der Stighelen, "Cornelia Pruystinck en Lynken Cuypers: Over de grootmoederlijke erfenis van Anton van Dyck," *Jaarboek Koninklijk Museum voor Schone Kunsten, Antwerpen* (1995): 243–87.

14 "L'età di essa 96 havendo la memoria et il serverllo prontissimo, cortesissima, et sebene perla vecciaia la mancava la vista, hebbe con tutto cio gusto de mettere gli quadri avanti ad essa et congran stenta mettendo il naso sopra il quadro, venne a discernere qualche poca et piglio gran piacere ancora in quell modo, facende il ritratto de essa, mi diede diversi advertimenti non pigliar il lume troppo alto, accio che le ombre nelle ruge della vecciaia non diventassero troppo grande, et molti altri buoni discorsi come ancora conto parte della vita di essa per la quale se conobbe che era pittora de natura et miraculosa et la pena magiore che hebbe era per mancamento di vista non poter piu dipingere; la mano era ancora ferma senza tremula nessuna"; *Italian Sketchbook*, fol. 110; text transcribed and translated in Barnes et al., *Van Dyck*, pp. 2–3 (translation modified).

15 For the Knole portrait, see Susan Barnes's entry in Barnes et al., *Van Dyck*, p. 171, cat. no. II.27; Xavier F. Salomon, *Van Dyck in Sicily, 1624–1625: Painting and the Plague* (London: Dulwich Picture Gallery, 2012), pp. 72–75, cat. nos. 5 and 6; and Alejandro Vergara's entry in Leticia Ruiz Gómez, ed., *A Tale of Two Women Painters: Sofonisba Anguissola and Lavinia Fontana* (Madrid: Museo Nacional del Prado, 2019), pp. 134–37, cat. nos. 22 and 23.

16 For a useful biographical overview, see Maria Kusche, "Sofonisba Anguissola: Her Life and Work," in *Sofonisba Anguissola: A Renaissance Woman*, ed. Sylvia Ferino-Pagden and Maria Kusche (Washington, D.C.: National Museum of Women in the Arts, 1995), pp. 26–105.

17 Michael W. Cole, *Sofonisba's Lesson: A Renaissance Artist and Her Work* (Princeton: Princeton University Press, 2019), p. 14.

18 For a detailed examination of Anguissola's position within the royal household, see Pamela Holmes Baldwin, "Sofonisba Anguissola in Spain: Portraiture as Art and Social Practice at a Renaissance Court," PhD dissertation, Bryn Mawr College, 1995, pp. 24–63.

19 Kusche, "Sofonisba Anguissola: Her Life and Work," p. 60.

20 "La cui prefata Maestà quando le dava una veste fregiata riccamente d'oro di gran valor, e quando una colana con gioie e vezzi di perle, et altre cose reali di maniera, che si trovava riccamente vestita et ornata"; de Ribera's life of Anguissola is reprinted in Paolo Buffa, ed., *Sofonisba Anguissola e le sue sorelle* (Cremona: Centro Culturale, 1994), pp. 409–11; see also Kusche, "Sofonisba Anguissola: Her Life and Work," p. 67. For a more general discussion of Anguissola's self-portraits, see Baldwin, "Sofonisba Anguissola in Spain," pp. 64–122; and Maike Christadler, *Kreativität und Geschlecht: Giorgio Vasaris "Vite" und Sofonisba Anguissolas Selbst-Bilder* (Berlin: Reimer, 2000), pp. 97–231.

21 Buckeridge, "An Essay," p. 406. Buckridge mistakenly calls the painter "Anne Carlisle."

22 Carlile's biography and oeuvre were first reconstructed in Margaret Toynbee and Gyles Isham, "Joan Carlile (1606?–1679) – An Identification," *Burlington Magazine* 96, no. 618 (September 1954): 273–77. For more recent accounts, see Jane Eade, "Rediscovering the 'Worthy Artiste Mrs Carlile,'" *National Trust Historic Houses & Collections Annual* (2018): 19–24; and Bendor Grosvenor, *"Bright Souls": The Forgotten Story of Britain's First Female Artists* (London: Lyon & Turnbull, 2019), pp. 7–15. An important overview of other women artists whose work is largely lost or unidentified appears in Helen Draper, "Mary Beale and Art's Lost Laborers: Women Painter Stainers," *Early Modern Women* 10, no. 1 (Fall 2015): 141–51.

23 For Susanna Horenbout, see Lorne Campbell and Susan Foister, "Gerard, Lucas and Susanna Horenbout," *Burlington Magazine* 128, no. 1003 (October 1986): 719–27; for Esther Inglis, see Georgianna Ziegler, "'More than Feminine Boldness': The Gift Books of Esther Inglis," in *Women, Writing, and the Reproduction of Culture in Tudor and Stuart Britain*, ed. Mary E. Burke et al. (Syracuse: Syracuse University Press, 2000), pp. 19–37. For a critique of the historiographic emphasis on distinguishing "professional" from "amateur" women painters, see Rosemary O'Day, "Family Galleries: Women and Art in the Seventeenth and Eighteenth Centuries," *Huntington Library Quarterly* 71, no. 2 (2008): 323–49.

24 Eade, "Rediscovering the 'Worthy Artiste Mrs Carlile,'" p. 22.

25 For Joan Carlile's will, see Charles H. Gray, *Lodowick Carliell: His Life, a Discussion of His Plays, and "The Deserving Favourite", a Tragi-Comedy Reprinted from the Original Edition of 1629* (Chicago: University of Chicago Press, 1905), p. 177.

26 Lodowick's last name is often spelled Carliell or Carlell. The primary scholarly discussion of his plays characterizes them as follows: "Carliell's principal characters belong to one class of society, the court; they always act through exalted motives of unselfish love, friendship, or duty; their life is narrow, their sentiments idealistic and impracticable. These plays are court plays; plays written under the patronage of the sovereign, first produced before royalty, and limited to the exploitation of a theory of life that can find place only at court, the theory of *noblesse oblige*"; see ibid., p. 47.

27 Nadine Akkerman, ed., *The Correspondence of Elizabeth Stuart, Queen of Bohemia*, vol. 2 (Oxford: Oxford University Press, 2011), pp. 390–91.

28 Gray, *Lodowick Carliell*, p. 72.

29 Ibid., p. 73.

30 For the broader context of royal artistry, see the essays collected in Annette Caroline Cremer et al., eds., *Fürst und Fürstin als Künstler: Herrschaftliches Künstlertum zwischen Habitus, Norm und Neigung*, Schriften zur Residenzkultur 11 (Berlin: Lukas Verlag, 2018).

31 Buckeridge, "An Essay," p. 472.

32 For an introduction to the literature of this period, see Lois Potter, *Secret Rites and Secret Writing: Royalist Literature, 1641–1660* (Cambridge: Cambridge University Press, 1989).

33 C. H. Wilkinson, *The Poems of Richard Lovelace*, 2nd edn. (Oxford: Clarendon Press, 1953), pp. 27–29. On the dating of the poem and Lovelace's visit to The Hague, see Susan Clarke, "Richard Lovelace: Royalist Poetry in Context, 1639–1649," PhD dissertation, Australian National University, 2010, pp. 61–62.

34 For Louise Hollandine, see Alheidis von Rohr, "'Peint par Madame l'Abesse': Louise Hollandine Prinzessin von der Pfalz (1622–1709)," *Niederdeutsche Beiträge zur Kunstgeschichte* 28 (1989): 143–60; Jorunn Labordus, "Gerard van Honthorst en zijn prinsessen," in *Vrouwen en kunst in de Republiek: Een overzicht*, ed. Els Kloek, Catherine Peters Sengers, and Esther Tobé, Utrechtse Historische Cahiers 19 (Hilversum: Verloren, 1998), pp. 79–88; and Anna Cecilia Koldeweij, "Koninklijke verbeelders verbeeld? Twee recent ontdekte tekeningen van Gerard van Honthorst in perspectief," in *De Verbeelder verbeeld(t): Boekillustratie en beeldende kunst*, ed. Anna Cecilia Koldeweij and Jos Koldeweij (Nijmegen: Vantilt, 2017), pp. 68–76.

35 James Loxley, "Poetry, Portraiture and Praise: Suckling and Van Dyck, Lovelace and Lely," *Seventeenth Century* 32, no. 4 (October 2017): 351–69.

36 "To my Worthy Friend Mr. Peter Lilly: on that excellent Picture of his Majesty, and the Duke of Yorke, drawne by him at Hampton-Court"; Wilkinson, *The Poems of Richard Lovelace*, pp. 57–58. For interpretations of the poem, see Raymond A. Anselment, "'Clouded Majesty': Richard Lovelace, Sir Peter Lely, and the Royalist Spirit," *Studies in Philology* 86, no. 3 (July 1989): 367–87; and Frances Harris, "An Ambivalent Image: Lely's Double-Portrait of Charles I and the Duke of York," *Burlington Magazine* 149, no. 1248 (March 2007): 180–82. Lely's portrait itself revises a Van Dyckian precedent, one of his double portraits of Charles I and Henrietta Maria, supplanting a peacetime image of marital felicity with one of a father's martial legacy to his son.

37 As Matthew Hunter notes, "At least according to Lovelace's reckoning, Lely had achieved the acme of his art by transfiguring his medium so completely as to paint through the eyes of the Stuart kings – elevating himself by seeing *as* his ennobled sitters"; Matthew Hunter, *Wicked Intelligence: Visual Art and the Science of Experiment in Restoration London* (Chicago: University of Chicago Press, 2013) p. 110.

38 For introductions to the masque and its ideological significance, see, among other works, Stephen Orgel, *The Illusion of Power: Political Theater in the English Renaissance* (Berkeley: University of California Press, 1975); and Graham Parry, *The Golden Age Restor'd: The Culture of the Stuart Court, 1603–42* (Manchester: Manchester University Press, 1981), pp. 40–63. For important discussions of the masques of Louise Hollandine's aunt, Henrietta Maria, see Karen Britland, *Drama at the Courts of Queen Henrietta Maria* (Cambridge: Cambridge University Press, 2006); and Erica Veevers, *Images of Love and Religion: Queen Henrietta Maria and Court Entertainments* (Cambridge: Cambridge University Press, 1989).

39 Clare McManus, *Women on the Renaissance Stage: Anna of Denmark and Female Masquing in the Stuart Court (1590–1619)* (Manchester: Manchester University Press, 2002).

40 C. E. McGee, "Cupid's Banishment: A Masque Presented to Her Majesty by Young Gentlewomen of the Ladies Hall, Deptford, May 4, 1617," *Renaissance Drama* 19 (1988): 226–64.

41 Nadine Akkerman, "Cupido en de eerste koningin in Den Haag," *De Zeventiende Eeuw* 25, no. 2 (2009): 73–96.

42 On Elizabeth Stuart's court in exile, see Nadine Akkerman, *Courtly Rivals in the Hague: Elizabeth Stuart and Amalia von Solms* (Venlo: Van Spijk/Rekafa Publishers, 2014); on her self-conception as a heroine of romance, see Barbara Kiefer Lewalski, *Writing Women in Jacobean England* (Cambridge, Mass.: Harvard University Press, 1993), pp. 45–66; and Michele L. Frederick, "Affectionate Sister, Most Faithful Friend: Elizabeth Stuart and Gerrit van Honthorst's *Seladon and Astraea*," *Netherlands Yearbook for History of Art / Nederlands Kunsthistorisch Jaarboek* 70 (2020): 160–91.

43 My reading of Lovelace's poem as grounded in his Royalist politics departs from Lindsay Ann Reid's recent extended interpretation of the poem. Reid argues that Lovelace's poem positions Louise Hollandine as an "Arachne" (a figure never actually named in his text). In this reading, the princess's revisions of mythological narrative "launch a proto-feminist assault on the brutal power dynamics and excoriable sexual politics of classical tradition." Such a reading neglects the context of Royalist politics that inspired Lovelace's poem and the established tradition of Stuart women presenting themselves as pacifying, anti-erotic forces. Attractive as Reid's feminist reading might be to a modern sensibility, the gulf between Louise Hollandine's paintings and the elaborate mythological scenes described in the poem indicates that Lovelace was more interested in promoting a specific idea of female royal agency than in close analysis or even description of real paintings. See Lindsay Ann Reid, "Louise Hollandine and the Art of Arachnean Critique," in *Women Artists and Patrons in the Netherlands, 1500–1700*, ed. Elizabeth Sutton (Amsterdam: Amsterdam University Press, 2019), pp. 113–42.

44 Mary D. Garrard, "Artemisia Gentileschi's Self-Portrait as the Allegory of Painting," *Art Bulletin* 62, no. 1 (March 1980): 97–112.

45 Marten Jan Bok and Jos De Meyere, "Schilderes aan haar ezel: Nieuwe gegevens over het schilderij van Gerard van Honthorst," *Maandblad Oud-Utrecht* 58 (1985): 298–303.

46 For the painting, see Sabine Craft-Giepmans and Annette de Vries, eds., *Portret in portret in de Nederlandse kunst 1550–2012* (Bussum: Uitgeverij Thoth, 2012), p. 126.

47 For a useful introduction to the ekphrastic tradition in early modern English literature, see Claire Preston, "Ekphrasis: Painting in Words," in *Renaissance Rhetorical Figures*, ed. Sylvia Adamson and Gavin Alexander (Cambridge: Cambridge University Press, 2007), pp. 115–30; see also Claire Preston, "The Gallery, the Eye, and the Rhetoric of Observation in Some Seventeenth-Century Descriptions," *Seventeenth Century* 32, no. 4 (October 2017): 371–92.

48 "Peinture," in Wilkinson, *The Poems of Richard Lovelace*, pp. 182–3.

49 Ibid., p. 180.

50 For Flatman, see Graham Reynolds, "A Miniature Self-Portrait by Thomas Flatman, Limner and Poet," *Burlington Magazine* 89, no. 528 (March 1947): 63–67.

51 Thomas Flatman, *Poems and Songs by Thomas Flatman* (London: printed by S. and B.G. for Benjamin Took, 1674), pp. 12–22.

52 For the artist as Pygmalion, see Victor Stoichita, *The Pygmalion Effect: From Ovid to Hitchcock*, trans. Alison Anderson (Chicago: University of Chicago Press, 2008).

53 Parry, *The Golden Age Restor'd*, pp. 189–90.

54 Marika Keblusek, "Entertainment in Exile: Theatrical Performances at the Courts of Margaret Cavendish, Mary Stuart and Elizabeth of Bohemia," in *The Triumphs of the Defeated: Early Modern Festivals and Messages of Legitimacy*, ed. Peter Davidson and Jill Bepler (Wiesbaden: Harrossowitz, 2007), pp. 173–90.

55 Oliver Millar, ed., "Abraham van der Doort's Catalogue of the Collections of Charles I," *Walpole Society* 37 (1958–60): 120–21. For an informative reading of Stuart inventories and practices of display, see Erin Griffey, "Van Dyck Paintings in Stuart Royal Inventories, 1639–1688," *Journal of the History of Collections* 30, no. 1 (March 2018): 49–63.

56 Oliver Millar, ed., "The Inventories and Valuations of the King's Goods, 1649–1651," *Walpole Society* 43 (1970–72), p. 247, nos. 369 and 376.

57 For Lely's double portrait, see Katharine Baetjer, *British Paintings in the Metropolitan Museum of Art, 1575–1875* (New York: Metropolitan Museum of Art, 2009), pp. 17–20, cat. no. 7. My thinking about Van Dyck's female double portraits relies on Jennifer L. Hallam, "All the Queen's Women: Female Double Portraits at the Caroline Court," in *Women and Portraits in Early Modern Europe: Gender, Agency, Identity*, ed. Andrea Pearson (Aldershot: Ashgate, 2007), pp. 137–60.

58 For Mary Capel's early life, see Molly McClain, *Beaufort: The Duke and His Duchess, 1657–1715* (New Haven and London: Yale University Press, 2001), pp. 1–10. Note, however, that in her discussion of the Lely double portrait (p. 5), McClain swaps the identities of the sisters.

59 The lack of botanical precision in Lely's painting makes the plant difficult to identify; for an alternative reading based on an identification as laurel, see Julia Marciari Alexander's entry in Malcolm Warner and Robyn Asleson, eds., *Great British Paintings from American Collections: Holbein to Hockney* (New Haven and London: Yale University Press, 2001), pp. 55–57, cat. no. 4.

60 Oliver Millar, *The Tudor, Stuart and Early Georgian Pictures in the Collection of Her Majesty the Queen*, 2 vols. (London: Phaidon Press, 1963), vol. 1, p. 138, cat. no. 318.

61 O'Day, "Family Galleries," p. 332. For the Duchess of Beaufort's contributions to botany, see, among other works, Julie Davies, "Botanizing at Badminton House: The Botanical Pursuits of Mary Somerset, First Duchess of Beaufort," in *Domesticity in the Making of Modern Science*, ed. Donald L. Opitz, Staffan Bergwik, and Brigitte van Tiggelen (Basingstoke: Palgrave Macmillan, 2016), pp. 19–39; and Mark Laird, *A Natural History of English Gardening, 1650–1800* (New Haven and London: Yale University Press, 2015), pp. 62–123.

62 For one well-documented example, see Carol Gibson-Wood, "Susanna and Her Elders: John Evelyn's Artistic Daughter," in *John Evelyn and His Milieu*, ed. Frances Harris and Michael Hunter (London: British Library, 2003), pp. 233–54.

63 Sold at Sotheby's, London, November 25, 2004, lot 22. I am grateful to Diana Dethloff for discussing with me this portrait and its traditional, but untenable, identification as Anne Killigrew.

64 Lely's self-portrait, now in the National Portrait Gallery, London (NPG 3897), makes an interesting contrast to his images of women painters. Here the artist presents himself as a connoisseur, not practitioner, of art.

65 Ernest Rhys, ed., *Margaret, Duchess of Newcastle: Life of the Duke, Memoirs of Her Own Life & Certain Sociable Letters* (London: J. M. Dent, 1915), p. 92. Newcastle, encountered in the previous chapter as an earl, was elevated to his dukedom following the Restoration.

66 Margaret J. M. Ezell, ed., *Anne Killigrew: "My Rare Wit Killing Sin"; Poems of a Restoration Courtier* (Toronto: Iter/Centre for Reformation and Renaissance Studies, 2013), pp. 90–91.

67 As discussed in the first chapter, her uncle Thomas posed for portraits by Van Dyck and wrote the play *Thomaso*, in which Van Dyck is said to have painted the portrait of a courtesan.

68 Anne Killigrew, *Poems by Mrs Anne Killigrew* (London: Samuel Lowndes, 1686); for a modern edition, see Ezell, *Anne Killigrew*.

69 Ezell, *Anne Killigrew*, p. 22.

70 Note, however, Carol Barash's argument that, in Killigrew's poem, "service to the royal family is ambiguously situated between the spiritual equality of friendship, which undermines the class differences between court ladies and their mistresses, and royal allegory, in which the servants' individual lives cease to matter at all"; Carol Barash, *English Women's Poetry, 1649–1714: Politics, Community, and Linguistic Authority* (Oxford: Clarendon Press, 1996), p. 162.

71 "On the Noble, and Much to be Lamented Mrs. Anne Kirk ..." (25–26); Glapthorne's elegy is reprinted along with a selection of others for Anne Kirke in Ezell, *Anne Killigrew*, pp. 123–29.

72 Oliver Millar in Barnes et al., *Van Dyck*, p. 545, cat. no. IV.150.

73 Of course, the portrait's attributes may also have symbolic weight; Millar notes, "The rose, the butterfly and the dog probably allude respectively to the power of love, to immortality and the transitoriness of mortal life, and to fidelity"; ibid.

74 After Lely's death in 1680, the painting was acquired by the Earl of Kent; ibid. For Lely's collecting, see Diana Dethloff, "Sir Peter Lely's Collection of Prints and Drawings," in *Collecting Prints and Drawings in Europe, c. 1500–1750*, ed. Christopher Baker, Caroline Elam and Genevieve Warwick (Aldershot: Ashgate, 2003), pp. 123–39.

75 Sold at Sotheby's, London, May 3, 2017, lot 248; Van Dyck himself had recycled this successful formula in a portrait of Lady de la Warr (Museum of Fine Arts, Boston [30.445]); see Oliver Millar's entry in Barnes et al., *Van Dyck*, pp. 495–96, IV.85.

76 For the biography of Kirke's widower, George Kirke, who suffered sequestration and loss of office during the Commonwealth, see Philip Lewin's entry in the *Oxford Dictionary of National Biography*, https://doi.org/10.1093/ref:odnb/15662 (accessed December 20, 2021).

77 For Killigrew's alignment with the queen, see her poem "On the Birthday of Queen Catherine," in Ezell, *Anne Killigrew*, pp. 72–73.

78 Jennifer Brady, "John Dryden and Anne Killigrew: Postmortems on the Restoration," in *Emergent Nation: Early Modern British Literature in Transition, 1660–1714*, ed. Elizabeth Sauer, Early Modern Literature in Transition 3 (Cambridge: Cambridge University Press, 2019), pp. 357–72.

79 "To the Pious Memory of the Accomplisht Young Lady Mrs. Anne Killigrew ...", reprinted in Ezell, *Anne Killigrew*, pp. 97–104. Jennifer Brady argues convincingly that Dryden's "illusions of his separation from – and superiority to – the court were challenged, punctured, and exposed by the poems of an earnest and devout young woman poet and painter whose life had been tragically cut short by smallpox"; Brady, "John Dryden and Anne Killigrew," p. 359.

80 Ann Messenger summarizes this interpretation and provides an important corrective to it in "A Problem of Praise: John Dryden and Anne Killigrew," in Ann Messenger, *His and Hers: Essays in Restoration and Eighteenth-Century Literature* (Lexington: University Press of Kentucky, 1986), pp. 14–40.

81 "St John Baptist Painted by herself in the Wilderness, with Angels appearing to him, and with a Lamb by him," "Herodias's Daughter presenting to her Mother St. John's Head in a Charger, also Painted by herself," "On a Picture Painted by herself, representing two Nymphs of Diana's, one in a posture to Hunt, the other Bathing"; these poems are reprinted in Ezell, *Anne Killigrew*, pp. 59–61. For a discussion of Killigrew's ekphrastic poems, see Laura Tallon, "'To Vindicate Her Beauty's Cause': The Sister Arts and Women Poets, 1680–1800," PhD dissertation, Boston University, 2016, pp. 28–37.

82 As Tallon notes, this passage layers the traditional rivalry of the sister arts with the radical assertion of a woman's silencing of male speech; "'To Vindicate Her Beauty's Cause'," pp. 29–30.

83 Ezell, *Anne Killigrew*, pp. 70–72.

84 For a reading of this passage in the context of literary coterie politics, see Margaret J. M. Ezell, "Late Seventeenth-Century Women Poets and the Anxiety of Attribution," in *Early Modern Women and the Poem*, ed. Susan Wiseman (Manchester: Manchester University Press, 2014), pp. 147–61, esp. pp. 154–56.

85 For a discussion of Killigrew's posthumous publication, see Margaret J. M. Ezell, "Posthumous Publication of Women's Manuscripts and the History of Authorship," in *Women's Writing and the Circulation of Ideas: Manuscript Publication in England, 1550–1800*, ed. George L. Justice and Nathan Tinker (Cambridge: Cambridge University Press, 2002), pp. 121–36.

86 For one account of this transformation of English culture, see R. O. Bucholz, *The Augustan Court: Queen Anne and the Decline of Court Culture* (Stanford: Stanford University Press, 1993).

4 · *Genealogies of Portraiture*

1 Letter of April 22, 1726, from Lady Mary Wortley Montagu to Frances, Countess of Mar; published in Robert Halsband, ed., *The Complete Letters of Lady Mary Wortley Montagu*, 3 vols. (Oxford: Clarendon Press, 1965–7), vol. 2, pp. 63–65. For the context of this episode, see Isobel Grundy, *Lady Mary Wortley Montagu* (Oxford: Oxford University Press, 1999), pp. 253–54.

2 For a broad discussion of eighteenth-century women's practices of self-display, see Marcia R. Pointon, *Strategies for Showing: Women, Possession, and Representation in English Visual Culture*,

1665–1800 (Oxford and New York: Oxford University Press, 1997).

3 Letter of April 12, 1764, from Horace Walpole to Francis Seymour Conway, 1st Earl of Hertford; published in W. S. Lewis, ed., *The Yale Edition of Horace Walpole's Correspondence*, 48 vols. (New Haven: Yale University Press, 1937–83), vol. 38, p. 367. I am grateful to the anonymous reviewer for the Paul Mellon Centre for Studies in British Art who pointed out the relevance of this episode to my argument.

4 Brian Cowan, "Arenas of Connoisseurship: Auctioning Art in Later Stuart England," in *Art Markets in Europe, 1400–1800*, ed. Michael North and David Ormrod (Aldershot: Ashgate, 1998), pp. 153–66. On the art market more generally, see Carol Gibson-Wood, "Picture Consumption in London at the End of the Seventeenth Century," *Art Bulletin* 84, no. 3 (September 2002): 491–500, as well as Richard Stephens, "The Palace of Westminster and the London Market for Pictures," in *Court, Country, City: British Art and Architecture, 1660–1735*, ed. Mark Hallett, Nigel Llewellyn, and Martin Myrone (New Haven and London: Yale University Press for the Yale Center for British Art and the Paul Mellon Centre for Studies in British Art, 2016), pp. 29–50.

5 My thinking about the movement of portraits between alienable and inalienable statuses is influenced by the work of Renata Ago; see Renata Ago, *Gusto for Things: A History of Objects in Seventeenth-Century Rome*, trans. Bradford Bouley, Corey Tazzara, and Paula Findlen (Chicago: University of Chicago Press, 2013), esp. pp. 5–6.

6 As Cynthia Wall writes, "the nature of auctions is competitive redistribution, necessarily predicated at the very least on a life change; at most, on disaster or death." Cynthia Wall, "The English Auction: Narratives of Dismantlings," *Eighteenth-Century Studies* 31, no. 1 (Fall 1997): 1–25, quoted p. 10.

7 For Lord Mar's political travails and exile, see Edward Gregg, "The Jacobite Career of John, Earl of Mar," in *Ideology and Conspiracy: Aspects of Jacobitism, 1689–1759*, ed. Eveline Cruickshanks (Edinburgh: J. Donald, 1982), pp. 179–200.

8 "A Catalogue of all the Remaining Works of the Late Sir Godfrey Kneller" (1726); transcribed in "The Art World in Britain 1660 to 1735," http://artworld.york.ac.uk (accessed 12 February 2020).

9 Ibid., lot 164.

10 Ibid., lot 43.

11 Robert Latham and William Matthews, eds., *The Diary of Samuel Pepys*, 11 vols. (Berkeley: University of California Press, 1970–83), vol. 5 (1664), p. 254. For Pepys's voyeuristic viewing of court portraits, see Joseph Roach, "Celebrity Erotics: Pepys, Performance, and Painted Ladies," in *Politics, Transgression, and Representation at the Court of Charles II*, ed. Julia Marciari Alexander and Catharine MacLeod, Studies in British Art 18 (New Haven and London: Yale University Press for the Paul Mellon Centre for Studies in British Art, 2007), pp. 233–50.

12 Cited in Alison Conway, *Private Interests: Women, Portraiture, and the Visual Culture of the English Novel, 1709–1791* (Toronto: University of Toronto Press, 2001), p. 8.

13 The poem was published in 1716 as a preface to Jervas's edition of Dryden's translation of a treatise on painting by Dufresnoy; for a modern edition of the text, see John Butt, ed., *The Poems of Alexander Pope* (London: Routledge, 1966), pp. 249–51.

14 For the portrait, see J. Douglas Stewart, *Sir Godfrey Kneller and the English Baroque Portrait*, Oxford Studies in the History of Art and Architecture (Oxford: Clarendon Press, 1983), p. 116, cat. no. 459. For another female portrait by Kneller with a similar configuration of motifs, see his *Henrietta, Lady Huntingtower*, now at Ham House in Surrey (ibid., p. 111, cat. no. 379).

15 For the literature on the painting, see Oliver Millar's entry in Susan J. Barnes et al., *Van Dyck: A Complete Catalogue of the Paintings* (New Haven and London: Yale University Press for the Paul Mellon Centre for Studies in British Art, 2004), pp. 466–68, cat. no. IV.50. The portrait is undocumented between the record of Van Dyck's payment and its appearance in a French aristocratic collection in 1736; however, Kneller could have known it through one of several surviving copies.

16 Cited in Jacqueline Riding, "'A Session of Painters': Legacy, Succession, and the Prospects for British Portraiture after Kneller," in *Court,*

Country, City: British Art and Architecture, 1660–1735, ed. Mark Hallett, Nigel Llewellyn, and Martin Myrone, Studies in British Art 24 (New Haven and London: Yale University Press for the Yale Center for British Art and the Paul Mellon Centre for Studies in British Art, 2016), pp. 353–79, quotation p. 365.

17 The recent exhibition *British Baroque* did, however, make a compelling case for Kneller's significance; see Tabitha Barber, ed., *British Baroque: Power and Illusion* (London: Tate, 2020).

18 For an account of the "tensions and opportunities" opened up for other portraitists by Kneller's death, see Riding, "A Session of Painters."

19 Anthony Ashley Cooper, Earl of Shaftesbury, *Second Characters, or, The Language of Forms*, ed. Benjamin Rand (Cambridge: Cambridge University Press, 1914), pp. 134–35.

20 On Van Dyck's ambivalent reception by Continental art theorists, who admired his social ascent while lamenting his neglect of history painting, see Edouard Pommier, *Théories du portrait: De la Renaissance aux Lumières* (Paris: Gallimard, 1998), pp. 146–49, and pp. 239–42.

21 Shaftesbury, *Second Characters*, p. 134, n. 2.

22 For another discussion of this passage, see David H. Solkin, *Painting for Money: The Visual Arts and the Public Sphere in Eighteenth-Century England* (New Haven and London: Yale University Press for the Paul Mellon Centre for Studies in British Art, 1993), pp. 9–10.

23 Jonathan Richardson, *Two Discourses: I. An Essay on the Whole Art of Criticism, as It Relates to Painting ... II. An Argument in Behalf of the Science of a Connoisseur; Wherein Is Shewn the Dignity, Certainty, Pleasure, and Advantage of It* (London: W. Churchill, 1719), p. 57. For another discussion of this passage, see Carol Gibson-Wood, *Jonathan Richardson: Art Theorist of the English Enlightenment* (New Haven and London: Yale University Press for the Paul Mellon Centre for Studies in British Art, 2000), pp. 188–91.

24 For the portrait, which survives in damaged and disputed variants, see the entry by Oliver Millar in Barnes et al., *Van Dyck*, p. 633, cat. no. A14. Van Dyck's preparatory drawing is now in the British Museum (Gg,1.423); see Susan Sloman's entry in Karen Hearn, ed., *Van Dyck & Britain* (London: Tate, 2009), p. 210, cat. no. 113. I am grateful to Silvia Davoli for sharing with me her unpublished research, which establishes the provenance of the version owned by Richardson, now at Burghley House.

25 Richardson, *Two Discourses*, p. 58.

26 Ibid.

27 Ibid., p. 62.

28 Ibid., pp. 62–63.

29 Ibid., p. 63.

30 Ibid., p. 66.

31 Ibid., p. 68.

32 Jonathan Richardson, *An Essay on the Theory of Painting: By Mr. Richardson*, 2nd edn. (London: A. Bettesworth, 1725), p. 39.

33 Bainbrigg Buckeridge, "The Dedication," in Roger de Piles, *The Art of Painting: And the Lives of the Painters; Containing, a Compleat Treatise of Painting, Designing, and the Use of Prints: ... Done from the French of Monsieur de Piles. To Which Is Added, an Essay towards an English-School, ...* (London: J. Nutt, 1706), n.p.

34 Ibid.

35 Ibid.

36 As Martin Myrone has noted, Hogarth's aesthetic theory "aligns correct aesthetic judgement with normative sexual appetites"; see Martin Myrone, *Bodybuilding: Reforming Masculinities in British Art 1750–1810* (New Haven and London: Yale University Press for the Paul Mellon Centre for Studies in British Art, 2005), p. 8

37 For a recent attempt to counterbalance nationalist narratives of Hogarth's art by placing him in a pan-European context, see Martin Myrone and Alice Insley, *Hogarth and Europe* (London: Tate, 2022).

38 John Nichols, *Biographical Anecdotes of William Hogarth: With a Catalogue of his Works Chronologically Arranged; and Occasional Remarks*, 3rd edn. (London: John Nichols, 1785), p. 102. I am grateful to Meredith Gamer for suggesting this reference to me.

39 Ibid., pp. 15–16.

40 Elizabeth Einberg, *William Hogarth: A Complete Catalogue of the Paintings* (New Haven and London: Yale University Press for the Paul Mellon Centre for Studies in British Art, 2016), pp. 342–44, cat. no. 229.

41 William Hogarth, *The Analysis of Beauty: With the Rejected Passages from the Manuscript Drafts and Autobiographical Notes*, ed. Joseph Burke (Oxford: Clarendon Press, 1955), p. 9.

42 Ibid., p. 9.

43 For a discussion of Hogarth's ambivalent relationship to portraiture, see Richard Wendorf, *The Elements of Life: Biography and Portrait-Painting in Stuart and Georgian England* (Oxford: Clarendon Press, 1990), pp. 170–88.

44 Hogarth, *The Analysis of Beauty*, p. 225.

45 For Coram's portrait, see Einberg, *William Hogarth*, pp. 209–11, cat. no. 128.

46 Hogarth, *The Analysis of Beauty*, p. 148.

47 For the portrait, see Einberg, *William Hogarth*, pp. 244–46, cat. no. 162; and Nadia Tscherny, "An Un-Married Woman: Mary Edwards, William Hogarth, and a Case of Eighteenth-Century British Patronage," in *The Other Hogarth: Aesthetics of Difference*, ed. Bernadette Fort and Angela Rosenthal (Princeton: Princeton University Press, 2001), 212–23.

48 For the self-portrait, see Einberg, *William Hogarth*, pp. 283–84, cat. no. 194.

49 For an argument that a relationship to English literature was constitutive for the English school of painting, see Ronald Paulson, *Book and Painting: Shakespeare, Milton, and the Bible; Literary Texts and the Emergence of English Painting*, The Hodges Lectures (Knoxville: University of Tennessee Press, 1982).

50 Cited in Michael Jaffé, "*The Standard Bearer*: Van Dyck's Portrait of Sir Edmund Verney," in *Art and Patronage in the Caroline Courts: Essays in Honour of Sir Oliver Millar*, ed. David Howarth (Cambridge: Cambridge University Press, 1993), pp. 90–106, quotation p. 98.

51 For a recent account of the afterlife of the Civil War in the pictorial imagination, with references to Van Dyck's art throughout, see Stephen Bann, *Scenes and Traces of the English Civil War* (London: Reaktion Books, 2020).

52 Richardson, *An Essay on the Theory of Painting*, pp. 12–13.

53 For Clarendon and Van Dyck, see Adam Eaker, "A Taste for Van Dyck," in *Van Dyck: The Anatomy of Portraiture*, ed. Stijn Alsteens and Adam Eaker (New York: Frick Collection in association with Yale University Press, 2016), pp. 39–51, especially pp. 39–40.

54 For the letter, see Gladys Scott Thomson, *Letters of a Grandmother, 1732–1735: Being the Correspondence of Sarah, Duchess of Marlborough, with her Granddaughter Diana, Duchess of Bedford* (London: Jonathan Cape, 1943), pp. 117–18. The Van Dyck portrait in question, to this day in the collection of the Duke of Bedford at Woburn Abbey, depicts Anne, Lady Russell, later Countess of Bedford; see Oliver Millar's entry in Barnes et al., *Van Dyck*, p. 443, cat. no. IV.21.

55 The commission appears never to have been carried out. For a discussion of the duchess's proposal, see Deborah Cherry and Jennifer Harris, "Eighteenth-Century Portraiture and the Seventeenth-Century Past: Gainsborough and Van Dyck," *Art History* 5, no. 3 (September 1982): 287–309, esp. p. 292; Kate Retford, *The Art of Domestic Life: Family Portraiture in Eighteenth-Century England* (New Haven and London: Yale University Press for the Paul Mellon Centre for Studies in British Art, 2006), pp. 159–60; Susan Sloman's entry in Hearn, *Van Dyck & Britain*, p. 212, cat. no. 115; and Eaker, "A Taste for Van Dyck," p. 43. For the duchess's patronage and collecting more generally, see Marcia Pointon, "Material Manoeuvres: Sarah Churchill, Duchess of Marlborough and the Power of Artefacts," *Art History* 32, no. 3 (June 2009): 485–515.

56 For an extended reading of the painting, including its Van Dyckian citations, see Mark Hallett, *Reynolds: Portraiture in Action* (New Haven and London: Yale University Press for the Paul Mellon Centre for Studies in British Art, 2014), pp. 311–39. For Van Dyck's Buckingham family portrait, see Oliver Millar's entry in Barnes et al., *Van Dyck*, pp. 449–50, cat. no. IV.31.

57 Hallett, *Reynolds*, p. 36.

58 Both citations ibid., pp. 312 and 321.

59 For the painting, see Richard Ormond and Elaine Kilmurray, *John Singer Sargent: Complete Paintings*, 9 vols. (New Haven and London: Yale

University Press for the Paul Mellon Centre for Studies in British Art, 1998–2014), vol. 3, pp. 144–47, cat. no. 486.

60 Ibid., p. 144; for the Van Dyck double portrait, traditionally identified as depicting Lady Killigrew and Mrs. Morton, see Oliver Millar's entry in Barnes, et al., *Van Dyck*, p. 545, cat. no. IV.149.

61 For Sargent as Van Dyck's heir, see Adam Eaker, "The American Van Dyck," in *America and the Art of Flanders: Collecting Paintings by Rubens, Van Dyck, and their Circles*, ed. Esmée Quodbach, The Frick Collection Studies in the History of Art Collecting in America 5 (University Park: Pennsylvania State University Press, 2020), pp. 48–57.

62 John, Lord Hervey, *Some Materials towards Memoirs of the Reign of King George II*, ed. Romney Sedgwick, 3 vols. (London: Eyre & Spottiswoode, 1931), vol. 2, pp. 488–89; the episode is situated within the context of Hervey's relationship to the king and queen in Robert Halsband, *Lord Hervey: Eighteenth-Century Courtier* (Oxford: Oxford University Press, 1974), pp. 187–88.

63 On this subject see Wolf Burchard and Kathryn Jones, "The German Princesses as British Patrons," in *Enlightened Princesses: Caroline, Augusta, Charlotte, and the Shaping of the Modern World*, ed. Joanna Marschner (New Haven and London: Yale University Press for the Yale Center for British Art and Historic Royal Palaces, 2017), pp. 109–32, esp. p. 125.

64 For the paintings represented within Zoffany's portrait, see Kate Retford, *The Conversation Piece: Making Modern Art in Eighteenth-Century Britain* (New Haven and London: Yale University Press for the Paul Mellon Centre for Studies in British Art, 2017), p. 205. For a discussion of their dynastic resonance, see Ronald Paulson, *Emblem and Expression: Meaning in English Art of the Eighteenth Century* (Cambridge, Mass.: Harvard University Press, 1975), p. 141.

65 See, however, Simon Schama's argument that Zoffany's inclusion of the Van Dyck portraits expressed a "sentimental revivalism" that also commemorated the restoration of the pictures to the Royal Collection; Simon Schama, "The Domestication of Majesty: Royal Family Portraiture, 1500–1850," *Journal of Interdisciplinary History* 17, no. 1 (Summer 1986): 155–83, esp. 171.

66 Paulson, *Emblem and Expression*, p. 141.

67 Anonymous [Joshua Reynolds], "No. LXXVI. Saturday, September 22," in *The Idler: In Two Volumes* (London: J. Newbery, 1761), vol. 2, pp. 227–28.

68 Ibid., p. 228. On this passage, see Hallett, *Reynolds*, p. 131.

69 For the portrait and Walpole's criticism, see Clarissa Campbell Orr's entry in Martin Postle, ed., *Johan Zoffany RA: Society Observed* (New Haven and London: Yale University Press for the Yale Center for British Art and the Royal Academy of Arts, 2011), pp. 205–6, cat. no. 34.

70 See, for example, the extensive discussion in Aileen Ribeiro, *The Dress Worn at Masquerades in England, 1730 to 1790, and Its Relation to Fancy Dress in Portraiture*, Outstanding Theses from the Courtauld Institute of Art (New York: Garland, 1984), pp. 144–204; as well as Cherry and Harris, "Eighteenth-Century Portraiture and the Seventeenth-Century Past."

71 The classic study is Terry Castle, *Masquerade and Civilization: The Carnivalesque in Eighteenth-Century English Culture and Fiction* (Stanford: Stanford University Press, 1986).

72 For Bowles's self-portrait, see Susan Sloman's entry in Hearn, *Van Dyck & Britain*, p. 229, cat. no. 129; for West, see Susan Rather, *The American School: Artists and Status in the Late Colonial and Early National Era* (New Haven and London: Yale University Press, 2016), pp. 94–98.

73 Cited in Ribeiro, *The Dress Worn at Masquerades*, p. 140.

74 For Gainsborough's relationship to Van Dyck in general, see Cherry and Harris, "Eighteenth-Century Portraiture and the Seventeenth-Century Past"; for his association with Van Dyck's technique, see David A. Brenneman, "Thomas Gainsborough and the 'Thin Brilliant Style of Pencilling of Vandyke,'" *Huntington Library Quarterly* 66, no. 1/2 (2003): 81–95. For the public perception of his clientele, see Benedict Leca, "'A Favourite among the Demireps': Thomas Gainsborough and the Modern Woman," in *Thomas Gainsborough and the Modern*

Woman, ed. Benedict Leca (London: Giles Ltd for the Cincinnati Museum of Art, 2010), pp. 43–105.

75 This discussion of Duncombe's portrait is derived from Eaker, "A Taste for Van Dyck," p. 40; see also Hugh Belsey, *Thomas Gainsborough: The Portraits, Fancy Pictures and Copies after Old Masters*, 2 vols. (New Haven and London: Yale University Press for the Paul Mellon Centre for Studies in British Art, 2019), vol. 1, pp. 93–95, cat. no. 94.

76 John T. Hayes, ed., *The Letters of Thomas Gainsborough* (New Haven and London: Yale University Press for the Paul Mellon Centre for Studies in British Art, 2001), p. 42.

77 Ibid., p. 43.

78 For Gainsborough's daughters, see Ann Bermingham, "Daughters and Sisters: Gainsborough's Portraits of Mary and Margaret," in *Gainsborough's Family Album*, ed. David H. Solkin (London: National Portrait Gallery, 2018), pp. 42–59.

79 For Gainsborough's last words, see David H. Solkin, "Private and Public Relations: Gainsborough's Family Album," in *Gainsborough's Family Album*, ed. David H. Solkin (London: National Portrait Gallery, 2018), pp. 16–39, esp. pp. 38–39.

80 Richard Wendorf, *Sir Joshua Reynolds: The Painter in Society* (Cambridge, Mass.: Harvard University Press, 2009), pp. 12–59.

81 For an extended version of this argument, see Adam Eaker, "Van Dyck between Master and Model," *Art Bulletin* 97, no. 2 (June 2015): 173–91.

82 Giovanni Pietro Bellori, *The Lives of the Modern Painters, Sculptors and Architects*, ed. Hellmut Wohl, trans. Alice Sedgwick Wohl (New York: Cambridge University Press, 2005), p. 218.

83 James Northcote, *The Life of Sir Joshua Reynolds ...: Comprising Original Anecdotes of Many Distinguished Persons, his Contemporaries; and a Brief Analysis of his Discourses*, 2nd edn., 2 vols. (London: Henry Colburn, 1819), vol. 1, p. 204.

84 Ibid., p. 206.

85 Ibid., p. 204.

86 Michael Bundock, *The Fortunes of Francis Barber: The True Story of the Jamaican Slave Who Became Samuel Johnson's Heir* (New Haven and London: Yale University Press, 2015), p. 104.

87 Northcote, *Sir Joshua Reynolds*, vol. 1, pp. 185–86.

88 For a discussion of this portrait, see Hallet, *Reynolds*, pp. 177–82.

89 David Bindman, "Subjectivity and Slavery in Portraiture: From Courtly to Commercial Societies," in *Slave Portraiture in the Atlantic World*, ed. Angela Rosenthal and Agnes Lugo-Ortiz (Cambridge: Cambridge University Press, 2013), pp. 71–88, esp. p. 80.

90 For this, see Eaker, "Van Dyck between Master and Model," esp. p. 182.

91 Cited in Seymour Slive, *Rembrandt and his Critics, 1630–1730*, Utrechtse bijdragen tot de kunstgeschiedenis 2 (The Hague: M. Nijhoff, 1953), p. 162.

92 Jeffrey M. Muller and Jim Murrell, eds., *Edward Norgate: Miniatura, or, The Art of Limning* (New Haven and London: Yale University Press, 1997), p. 108.

93 Cited in Ilaria Bignamini, "The Artist's Model: From Lely to Hogarth," in *The Artist's Model: Its Role in British Art from Lely to Etty*, ed. Ilaria Bignamini and Martin Postle (Nottingham: University Art Gallery, 1991), pp. 8–15, quotation p. 11.

94 Ibid., p. 14.

95 Diana Dethloff, "Lely, Drawing, and the Training of Artists," in *Court, Country, and City: British Art and Architecture, 1660–1735*, ed. Mark Hallett, Nigel Llewellyn, and Martin Myrone, Studies in British Art 24 (New Haven and London: Yale University Press for the Yale Center for British Art and the Paul Mellon Centre for Studies in British Art, 2016), pp. 291–313.

96 My account of the Dulwich album is based on Dethloff, ibid., pp. 299–304.

97 For the drawing, see Ilaria Bignamini's entry in Bignamini and Postle, *The Artist's Model*, pp. 80–81, cat. no. 69. For doubts about the drawing's attribution, see Gibson-Wood, *Jonathan Richardson*, p. 237, n. 66.

98 See Tony Gee's entry on Figg in the *Oxford Dictionary of National Biography*, https://doi.org/10.1093/ref:odnb/9417 (accessed January 14, 2022).

99 Bainbrigg Buckeridge, "An Essay towards an English School of Painters," in Roger de Piles, *The Art of Painting: And the Lives of Painters …* (London: J. Nutt, 1706), p. 462.

100 For a number of examples, including Hogarth's famous group portrait of his servants, see Anne French, "Servants as Artists' Models," in *Below Stairs: 400 Years of Servants' Portraits*, ed. Giles Waterfield and Anne French (London: National Portrait Gallery, 2003), pp. 105–19.

101 For Beale's sketchbooks, see Tabitha Barber, "The Drawings of Charles Beale Junior," in Tabitha Barber, ed., *Mary Beale (1632/3–1699): Portrait of a Seventeenth-Century Painter, Her Family and Her Studio* (London: Geffrye Museum Trust, 1999), p. 70; French, "Servants as Artists' Models," pp. 105–8.

102 At the same time, as Diane Wolfthal notes, "However refreshing Beale's intimate and informal drawings are to modern viewers, they bear clear markers of these sitters' working-class status. Beale lived in a world permeated by an ideology that was invested in seeing the prevalent class hierarchy as natural and ordained, and his drawings, however appealing, are not free of that ideology"; Diane Wolfthal, "Household Help: Early Modern Portraits of Female Servants," *Early Modern Women* 8 (Fall 2013): 5–52, quoted 32–33.

103 For the drawing, see Martin Postle's entry in Bignamini and Postle, *The Artist's Model*, p. 81, cat. no. 70.

104 For the painting, see Martin Postle's entry in Postle, *Johan Zoffany RA*, pp. 214–15, cat. no. 41.

105 See ibid., pp. 218–21, cat. no. 44.

106 Notably, the entry on the painting from Zoffany's most recent monographic exhibition refers to "thirty-six individuals" depicted. As the key in the catalogue makes clear, this count includes the female academicians. Angelica Kauffman and Mary Moser, represented by their portraits, but not the models; see ibid., p. 218.

5 · *Old Master Poses*

1 John Thomas Smith, *Nollekens and his Times: A Life of that Celebrated Sculptor and Memoirs of Several Contemporary Artists, from the Time of Roubiliac, Hogarth and Reynolds to That of Fuseli, Flaxman and Blake* (London: Colburn, 1829), pp. 401–2.

2 Ibid., p. 402. For Cosway's biography, see Stephen Lloyd's entry in the *Oxford Dictionary of National Biography*, https://doi.org/10.1093/ref:odnb/6383 (accessed January 20, 2022), as well as Gerald Barnett, *Richard and Maria Cosway: A Biography* (Tiverton: Westcountry Books in association with Lutterworth Press, 1995).

3 Aileen Ribeiro, "Portraying the Fashion, Romancing the Past: Dress and the Cosways," in *Richard & Maria Cosway: Regency Artists of Taste and Fashion*, ed. Stephen Lloyd (Edinburgh: Scottish National Portrait Gallery, 1995), pp. 101–5, esp. p. 103.

4 For the portrait, see Stephen Lloyd, ed., *Richard & Maria Cosway: Regency Artists of Taste and Fashion* (Edinburgh: Scottish National Portrait Gallery, 1995), p. 113, cat. no. 4.

5 For the macaroni, see Miles Ogborn, "Locating the Macaroni: Luxury, Sexuality and Vision in Vauxhall Gardens," *Textual Practice* 11, no. 3 (December 1997): 445–61; and Peter McNeil, *Pretty Gentlemen: Macaroni Men and the Eighteenth-Century Fashion World* (New Haven and London: Yale University Press, 2018). McNeil discusses Cosway's emblematic status among the macaroni on pp. 105–14.

6 For the self-portrait, see Graham Reynolds, with Katharine Baetjer, *European Miniatures in the Metropolitan Museum of Art* (New York: H. N. Abrams for the Metropolitan Museum of Art, 1996), pp. 131–32, cat. no. 130; and McNeil, *Pretty Gentlemen*, pp. 107–8.

7 Philip Carter, "An 'Effeminate' or 'Efficient' Nation? Masculinity and Eighteenth-Century Social Documentary," *Textual Practice* 11, no. 3 (December 1997): 429–43.

8 Smith, *Nollekens and his Times*, p. 407; for a discussion of Cosway and caricature, see McNeil, *Pretty Gentlemen*, pp. 109–13.

9 Angela Rosenthal argues that "the violence of [Cosway's] gesture against female form can be read on a psychic level as a sign of male anxiety, and particularly anxiety concerning woman's mastering and desiring gaze"; Angela Rosenthal, "She's Got the Look! Eighteenth-Century

Female Portrait Painters and the Psychology of a Potentially 'Dangerous Employment,'" in *Portraiture: Facing the Subject*, ed. Joanna Woodall (Manchester: Manchester University Press, 1997), pp. 147–66, quoted p. 150. I would argue that it simultaneously reflects the anxiety of male artists about Cosway's own perceived effeminacy.

10 Cosway's autobiographical account is transcribed in full in Barnett, *Richard and Maria Cosway*, pp. 260–61.

11 As Ann Bermingham has written, "as the story of an accomplished woman, Cosway's life testifies to the ambiguities, instabilities, and contradictions that the role inevitably produced for women"; Ann Bermingham, "Elegant Females and Gentlemen Connoisseurs: The Commerce in Culture and Self-Image in Eighteenth-Century England," in *The Consumption of Culture, 1600–1800: Image, Object, Text*, ed. Ann Bermingham and John Brewer (London and New York: Routledge, 1995), pp. 489–513, quotation from p. 501. For recent discussions of individual facets of Maria Cosway's art, see Luisa Calè, "Maria Cosway's Hours: Cosmopolitan and Classical Visual Culture in Thomas Macklin's Poets Gallery," in *Romanticism and Illustration*, ed. Ian Haywood, Mary L. Shannon, and Susan Matthews (Cambridge: Cambridge University Press, 2019), pp. 221–42; Diane Boucher, "Maria Cosway (1760–1838): A Commentator on Modern Life," *British Art Journal* 18, no. 3 (Winter 2017–18): 78–86; and Diane Boucher, "Maria Cosway's 'A Persian Going to Adore the Sun,'" *Burlington Magazine* 162, no. 1405 (April 2020): 300–305.

12 For the oil sketches, see Lloyd, *Richard & Maria Cosway*, p. 130, cat. nos. 190, 191; for the pigment box, ibid., p. 132, cat. no. 215.

13 For these caricatures, see ibid., pp. 120–21, cat. nos. 84, 86.

14 "Exhibition," *St. James's Chronicle or the British Evening Post*, May 1–4, 1779, p. 4. The review is unsigned.

15 *The Exhibition of the Royal Academy, M.DCC. LXXIX, The Eleventh* (London: T. Cadell, 1779), p. 7.

16 On this phenomenon, see Marcia Pointon, "Portrait! Portrait!! Portrait!!!," in *Art on the Line: The Royal Academy Exhibitions at Somerset House, 1780–1836*, ed. David H. Solkin (New Haven and London: Yale University Press for the Paul Mellon Centre for Studies in British Art and the Courtauld Institute Gallery, 2001), pp. 93–110.

17 For the painting's provenance, exhibition history, and a summary of the literature, see Katharine Baetjer, *British Paintings in the Metropolitan Museum of Art, 1575–1875* (New York: Metropolitan Museum of Art, 2009), pp. 145–46, cat. no. 65. Stephen Lloyd first identified the Met's picture with Cosway's Royal Academy submission in *Richard & Maria Cosway*, p. 33 and p. 113, cat. no. 7.

18 Ribeiro, "Portraying the Fashion," p. 101.

19 For one introduction to this complex subject, see Alison Conway, *Private Interests: Women, Portraiture, and the Visual Culture of the English Novel, 1709–1791* (Toronto: University of Toronto Press, 2001).

20 John Barrell, "The Dangerous Goddess: Masculinity, Prestige and the Aesthetic in Early Eighteenth-Century Britain," in *The Birth of Pandora and the Division of Knowledge* (London: Palgrave Macmillan, 1992), pp. 63–87.

21 David H. Solkin, *Painting for Money: The Visual Arts and the Public Sphere in Eighteenth-Century England* (New Haven and London: Yale University Press for the Paul Mellon Centre for Studies in British Art, 1993), p. 214.

22 Mark Hallett, *Reynolds: Portraiture in Action* (New Haven and London: Yale University Press for the Paul Mellon Centre for Studies in British Art, 2014), pp. 193–217.

23 The Royal Academy did exhibit miniatures, but in their own separate section of the exhibition.

24 See Lloyd, *Richard & Maria Cosway*, p. 113, cat. no. 2.

25 Marcia Pointon, "'Surrounded with Brilliants': Miniature Portraits in Eighteenth-Century England," *Art Bulletin* 83, no. 1 (March 2001): 48–71, quoted p. 57.

26 Cited in George Charles Williamson, *Richard Cosway, R.A.* (London: G. Bell and Sons, 1905), p. 100.

27 For this earlier history, see Christopher S. Wood, "'Curious Pictures' and the Art of Description," *Word & Image* 11, no. 4 (October–December 1995): 332–52.

28 James Barry, *The Works of James Barry, Esq., Historical Painter ...*, 2 vols. (London, T. Cadell and W. Davies, 1809), vol. 2, p. 246. For a discussion of this passage, see Shearer West, "Patronage and Power: The Role of the Portrait in Eighteenth-Century England," in *Culture, Politics, and Society in Britain, 1660–1800*, ed. Jeremy Black and Jeremy Gregory (Manchester: Manchester University Press, 1991), pp. 131–53, esp. p. 143.

29 "Exhibition," p. 4.

30 For wide-ranging accounts of Kauffman's career and reception, see Angela Rosenthal, *Angelica Kauffman: Art and Sensibility* (New Haven and London: Yale University Press for the Paul Mellon Centre for Studies in British Art, 2006), as well as the recent exhibition catalogue: Bettina Baumgärtel, ed., *Angelica Kauffman* (London, Düsseldorf, and Munich: Royal Academy of Arts, Kunstpalast, and Hirmer, 2020).

31 Anonymous, "Epistle to a Lady, Who Has Retired into the Country," *Literary Fly*, March 13, 1779, pp. 49–54.

32 Ibid., p. 49.

33 M. M. Goldsmith, "Liberty, Luxury and the Pursuit of Happiness," in *The Languages of Political Theory in Early-Modern Europe*, ed. Anthony Pagden (Cambridge: Cambridge University Press, 1990), pp. 225–51; and Solkin, *Painting for Money*, pp. 78–84. For a useful overview of the historiography of eighteenth-century luxury, see Vincent Quinn and Mary Peace, "Luxurious Sexualities," *Textual Practice* 11, no. 3 (December 1997): 405–16.

34 Carter, "An 'Effeminate' or 'Efficient' Nation?"; and Susan Staves, "A Few Kind Words for the Fop," *Studies in English Literature, 1500–1900* 22, no. 3 (Summer 1982): 413–28.

35 For Sir Robert Harland, see the entry by J. K. Laughton, revised by Randolph Cock, in the *Oxford Dictionary of National Biography*, https://doi.org/10.1093/ref:odnb/12333 (accessed January 20, 2022).

36 For an account of the Battle of Ushant and its aftermath, see N. A. M. Rodger, *The Command of the Ocean: A Naval History of Britain, 1649–1815* (London: Allen Lane, 2004), pp. 336–38.

37 "Proceedings of the Court Martial in the Tryal of Admiral Keppel," *St. James's Chronicle or the British Evening Post*, January 30–February 2, 1779, p. 4.

38 As reported, among others, in "House of Lords: Some Account of Yesterday's Business," *Morning Chronicle*, May 14, 1779.

39 *Catalogue of Important Pictures by Old Masters and Works of the Early English School the Property of Arthur M. Grenfell, Esq.: Also Important Pictures Forming the Dashwood Heirlooms Removed from Wherstead Park, Ipswich and Fine Portraits of the Early British School the Property of Sir Frederick Arundell de La Pole, Bart., W. Lindsay Alexander, Esq. and Others* (London: Christie, Manson, and Woods, June 26, 1914), p. 36, lot 93.

40 *Catalogue of the Important Collection of Pictures by Old Masters and Works of the Early English School, also Water Colour Drawings of George Harland-Peck, Esq., Deceased; late of 9 Belgrave Square, S.W., which (by order of Mrs. Harland-Peck, the Executrix) will be sold by Auction by Messrs. Christie, Manson & Woods* (London: Christie, Manson, and Woods, June 25, 1920), p. 9, lot 54.

41 As Hannah Greig notes, "To be invited into a dressing room and be present whilst a woman was at her 'toilette' served as an indication of a privileged connection"; Hannah Greig, *The Beau Monde: Fashionable Society in Georgian London* (Oxford: Oxford University Press, 2013), p. 298, n. 19.

42 Bernadette Fort and Angela Rosenthal, "The Analysis of Difference," in *The Other Hogarth: Aesthetics of Difference*, ed. Bernardette Fort and Angela Rosenthal (Princeton: Princeton University Press, 2001), pp. 3–15, quoted p. 3.

43 For this painting, see Clarissa Campbell Orr's entry in Martin Postle, ed., *Johan Zoffany RA: Society Observed* (New Haven and London: Yale University Press for the Yale Center for British Art and the Royal Academy of Arts, 2011), p. 204, cat. no. 33.

44 I am grateful to Iris Moon and Wolf Burchard for discussing these objects with me.

45 Smith, *Nollekens and his Times*, pp. 407–8.

46 Jane Adlin and Lori Zabar, "Vanities: Art of the Dressing Table," *Metropolitan Museum of Art Bulletin* LXXI, no. 2 (Fall 2013): 1–48, esp. pp. 6–10. There is a discussion of French portraits depicting sitters at their toilettes in

Donald Posner, "The 'Duchesse de Velours' and her Daughter: A Masterpiece by Nattier and its Historical Context," *Metropolitan Museum Journal* 31 (1996): 131–41.

47 For the association between portraiture and cosmetics, see Caroline Palmer, "Brazen Cheek: Face-Painters in Late Eighteenth-Century England," *Oxford Art Journal* 31, no. 2 (2008): 197–213.

48 Anonymous [Georgiana, Duchess of Devonshire], *The Sylph* (London: T. Lowndes, 1778), pp. 64–65.

49 Alfred Spencer, ed., *Memoirs of William Hickey*, 4 vols. (New York: Alfred A. Knopf, 1913), vol. 2, pp. 362–63.

50 Robert Adelson and Jacqueline Letzter, "'For a Woman When She Is Young and Beautiful': The Harp in Eighteenth-Century France," in *History/ Herstory: Alternative Musikgeschichten*, ed. Annette Kreutziger-Herr and Katrin Losleben (Cologne: Böhlau, 2009), pp. 314–35.

51 See David Hennebelle, "Le Rendez-vous manqué entre Mozart et l'aristocratie parisienne (1778)," *Annales Historiques de la Révolution Française*, no. 379 (January–March 2015): 35–45.

52 Adelson and Letzter, "For a Woman," pp. 320–21.

53 For discussions of Mary Crawford's harp, see Juliette Wells, "A Harpist Arrives at Mansfield Park: Music and the Moral Ambiguity of Mary Crawford," *Persuasions* 28 (2006): 101–14; Jeffrey A. Nigro, "'Favourable to Tenderness and Sentiment': The Many Meanings of Mary Crawford's Harp," *Persuasions On-Line* 35, no. 1 (Winter 2014), www.jasna.org/persuasions/on-line/vol35no1/nigro.html; and Linda Zionkowski and Miriam Hart, "'Is She Musical?': Players and Nonplayers in Austen's Fiction," in *Art and Artifact in Austen*, ed. Anna Battigelli (Newark: University of Delaware Press, 2020), pp. 206–23, esp. pp. 214–16.

54 Bermingham, "Elegant Females and Gentlemen Connoisseurs."

55 Gillian Perry, *Spectacular Flirtations: Viewing the Actress in British Art and Theatre, 1768–1820* (New Haven and London: Yale University Press for the Paul Mellon Centre for Studies in British Art, 2007), p. 166.

56 "Exhibition, 1781," *Public Advertiser*, May 2, 1781, p. 2.

57 "Will of Marianne Dorothy Dalrymple late Marianne Dorothy Harland, Wife," PROB 11/1136/293, The National Archives, Kew. For an interesting discussion of eighteenth-century women's wills, see Marcia R. Pointon, *Strategies for Showing: Women, Possession, and Representation in English Visual Culture, 1665–1800* (Oxford and New York: Oxford University Press, 1997), pp. 37–49.

58 Barnett, *Richard and Maria Cosway*, p. 261.

59 "EXHIBITION of PAINTINGS, SCULPTURES, &c., at the Royal-Academy, Somerset-Place, for the year 1787," *St. James's Chronicle or the British Evening Post*, May 10, 1787, p. 4.

60 Ibid.

61 For a discussion of the caricature, see Rosenthal, *Angelica Kauffman*, p. 225; and Cindy McCreery, *The Satirical Gaze: Prints of Women in Late Eighteenth-Century England* (Oxford: Clarendon Press, 2004), pp. 121–22.

62 For the self-portrait, now untraced, see Lloyd, *Richard & Maria Cosway*, p. 134, cat. no. 231. For Richard Cosway's own drawn copy of Rubens's portrait, see Ribeiro, "Portraying the Fashion," p. 104.

63 On this self-portrait, see Mary D. Sheriff, *The Exceptional Woman: Elisabeth Vigée-Lebrun and the Cultural Politics of Art* (Chicago: University of Chicago Press, 1996), pp. 197–203.

64 "To the Printer of the Morning Chronicle," *Morning Chronicle*, May 9, 1782, p. 2.

65 "To the Editor of the General Advertiser," *Parker's General Advertiser, and Morning Intelligencer*, May 21, 1782, p. 2.

66 Smith, *Nollekens and his Times*, p. 402.

67 For the Cosways' urban geography, see Roy Porter, "The Cosways' London," in *Richard & Maria Cosway: Regency Artists of Taste and Fashion*, ed. Stephen Lloyd (Edinburgh: Scottish National Portrait Gallery, 1995), pp. 97–100.

68 Smith, *Nollekens and his Times*, p. 404.

69 Ottobah Cugoano, *Thoughts and Sentiments on the Evil and Wicked Traffic of the Slavery and Commerce of the Human Species ...* (London: sold by T. Becket, Pall-Mall, and others, 1787). For a

modern edition with a selection of Cugoano's letters, see Ottobah Cugoano, *Thoughts and Sentiments on the Evil of Slavery and Other Writings*, ed. Vincent Carretta, Penguin Classics (New York: Penguin Books, 1999). For a biography of Cugoano, see Martin Hoyles, *Cugoano Against Slavery* (Hertford: Hansib Publications, 2015).

70 For Julius Soubise, see Monica L. Miller, *Slaves to Fashion: Black Dandyism and the Styling of Black Diasporic Identity* (Durham, N.C.: Duke University Press, 2009), pp. 57–72; and McNeil, *Pretty Gentlemen*, pp. 118–20.

71 For Sancho, see Reyahn King, ed., *Ignatius Sancho: An African Man of Letters* (London: National Portrait Gallery, 1997).

72 As noted by Reyahn King in "Ignatius Sancho and Portraits of the Black Élite," ibid., pp. 15–44 (see p. 28).

73 Anthony Pasquin [pseud. John Williams], *The Royal Academicians, a Farce* (London: Denew and Grant, 1786).

74 Ibid., p. 20.

75 Ibid., p. iii.

76 Ibid., p. 39.

77 Ibid., p. 23.

Afterword

1 For history paintings of the studio, and Van Dyck's nineteenth-century reception more generally, see Pascal Cornet, ed., *Après & d'après Van Dyck: La Récupération romantique au XIXe siècle* (Antwerp: Hessenhuis, 1999).

2 Roger Fry, "J. S. Sargent as Seen at the Royal Academy Exhibition of His Works, 1926, and in the National Gallery," in *Transformations: Critical and Speculative Essays on Art* (London: Chatto and Windus, 1926), pp. 125–35, quotation from pp. 125–26.

3 Ibid., p. 126.

4 Ibid., p. 130.

5 Ibid., p. 131.

6 W. R. Valentiner, "Van Dyck's Character," *Art Quarterly* 13 (1950): 87–105.

7 Classic texts include David Solkin, *Painting for Money: The Visual Arts and the Public Sphere in Eighteenth-Century England* (New Haven and London: Yale University Press for the Paul Mellon Centre for Studies in British Art, 1993); and Marcia Pointon, *Hanging the Head: Portraiture and Social Formation in Eighteenth-Century England* (New Haven and London: Yale University Press for the Paul Mellon Centre for Studies in British Art, 1993).

8 For the portrait, see Richard Ormond and Elaine Kilmurray, *John Singer Sargent: Complete Paintings*, 9 vols. (New Haven and London: Yale University Press for the Paul Mellon Centre for Studies in British Art, 1998–2014), vol. 3, pp. 202–4, cat. no. 549.

9 The Wertheimer portraits have been a central locus for discussions of Sargent's depictions of Jewish sitters; see Kathleen Adler, "John Singer Sargent's Portraits of the Wertheimer Family," in *The Jew in the Text: Modernity and the Construction of Identity*, ed. Linda Nochlin and Tamar Garb (London: Thames & Hudson, 1995), pp. 83–96; and Norman L. Kleeblatt, ed., *John Singer Sargent: Portraits of the Wertheimer Family* (New York: Jewish Museum, 1999).

10 For this portrait, see Susan Barnes's entry in Susan J. Barnes et al., *Van Dyck: A Complete Catalogue of the Paintings* (New Haven and London: Yale University Press for the Paul Mellon Centre for Studies in British Art, 2004), pp. 203–5, cat. no. II.63.

11 For Lady Shirley (or Sherley)'s biography, see Carmen Nocentelli, "Teresa Sampsonia Sherley: Amazon, Traveler, and Consort," in *Travel and Travail: Early Modern Women, English Drama, and the Wider World*, ed. Patricia Akhimie and Bernadette Diane Andrea, Early Modern Cultural Studies (Lincoln: University of Nebraska Press, 2019), pp. 81–101.

12 Fry, "J. S. Sargent," p. 128.

Bibliography

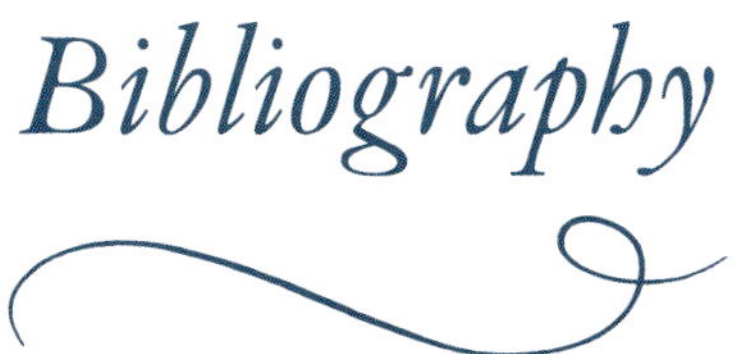

Abelove, Henry. *Deep Gossip*. Minneapolis: University of Minnesota Press, 2003.

Adelson, Robert, and Jacqueline Letzter. "'For a Woman When She Is Young and Beautiful': The Harp in Eighteenth-Century France." In *History/Herstory: Alternative Musikgeschichten*, edited by Annette Kreutziger-Herr and Katrin Losleben, 314–35. Cologne: Böhlau, 2009.

Adler, Kathleen. "John Singer Sargent's Portraits of the Wertheimer Family." In *The Jew in the Text: Modernity and the Construction of Identity*, edited by Linda Nochlin and Tamar Garb, 83–96. London: Thames & Hudson, 1995.

Adlin, Jane, and Lori Zabar. "Vanities: Art of the Dressing Table." *Metropolitan Museum of Art Bulletin* LXXI, no. 2 (Fall 2013): 1–48.

Ago, Renata. *Gusto for Things: A History of Objects in Seventeenth-Century Rome*. Translated by Bradford Bouley, Corey Tazzara, and Paula Findlen. Chicago: University of Chicago Press, 2013.

Akkerman, Nadine, ed. *The Correspondence of Elizabeth Stuart, Queen of Bohemia*. 2 vols. Oxford: Oxford University Press, 2011.

—. *Courtly Rivals in the Hague: Elizabeth Stuart and Amalia von Solms*. Venlo: Van Spijk/Rekafa Publishers, 2014.

—. "Cupido en de eerste koningin in Den Haag." *De Zeventiende Eeuw* 25, no. 2 (2009): 73–96.

Alexander, Julia Marciari, and Catharine MacLeod, eds. *Politics, Transgression, and Representation at the Court of Charles II*. Studies in British Art 18. New Haven and London: Yale University Press for the Yale Center for British Art and the Paul Mellon Centre for Studies in British Art, 2007.

Alpers, Svetlana. *Rembrandt's Enterprise: The Studio and the Market*. Chicago: University of Chicago Press, 1988.

Alsteens, Stijn. "A Portraitist's Progress." In *Van Dyck: The Anatomy of Portraiture*, edited by Stijn Alsteens and Adam Eaker, 1–38. New York: Frick Collection in association with Yale University Press, 2016.

—, and Adam Eaker, eds. *Van Dyck: The Anatomy of Portraiture*. New York: Frick Collection in association with Yale University Press, 2016.

Amos, Polly, and Ann Sumner. "Kenelm Digby and Venetia Stanley: A Great Love Story of the Seventeenth Century." In *Death, Passion and Politics: Van Dyck's Portraits of Venetia Stanley and George Digby*, edited by Ann Sumner, 26–31. London: Dulwich Picture Gallery, 1995.

Amussen, Susan Dwyer. *Caribbean Exchanges: Slavery and the Transformation of English Society, 1640–1700*. Chapel Hill: University of North Carolina Press, 2007.

Anonymous. "Epistle to a Lady, Who Has Retired into the Country." *Literary Fly*, March 13, 1779.

Anonymous [Joshua Reynolds]. "No. LXXVI. Saturday, September 22." In *The Idler: In Two Volumes*. London: J. Newbery, 1761.

Anonymous [Georgiana, Duchess of Devonshire]. *The Sylph*. London: T. Lowndes, 1778.

Anselment, Raymond A. "'Clouded Majesty': Richard Lovelace, Sir Peter Lely, and the Royalist Spirit." *Studies in Philology* 86, no. 3 (July 1989): 367–87.

—. "The Countess of Carlisle and Caroline Praise: Convention and Reality." *Studies in Philology* 82, no. 2 (Spring 1985): 212–33.

ARCANGELI, Luciano. "Anton van Dyck." In *L'Idea del bello: Viaggio per Roma nel seicento con Giovan Pietro Bellori*, vol. 2, 305–10. Rome: Edizioni De Luca, 2000.

BAETJER, Katharine. *British Paintings in the Metropolitan Museum of Art, 1575–1875*. New York: Metropolitan Museum of Art, 2009.

BALDWIN, Pamela Holmes. "Sofonisba Anguissola in Spain: Portraiture as Art and Social Practice at a Renaissance Court." PhD dissertation, Bryn Mawr College, 1995.

BANN, Stephen. *Scenes and Traces of the English Civil War*. London: Reaktion Books, 2020.

BARASH, Carol. *English Women's Poetry, 1649–1714: Politics, Community, and Linguistic Authority*. Oxford: Clarendon Press, 1996.

BARBER, Tabitha, ed. *British Baroque: Power and Illusion*. London: Tate, 2020.

—, ed. *Mary Beale (1632/3–1699): Portrait of a Seventeenth-Century Painter, Her Family and Her Studio: A Catalogue to Coincide with the Exhibition at the Geffrye Museum, 21 September 1999 to 30 January 2000*. London: Geffrye Museum Trust, 1999.

BARCLAY, Andrew. "Recovering Charles I's Art Collection: Some Implications of the 1660 Act of Indemnity and Oblivion." *Historical Research* 88, no. 242 (November 2015): 629–49.

BARNES, Susan J., Nora De Poorter, Oliver Millar, and Horst Vey. *Van Dyck: A Complete Catalogue of the Paintings*. New Haven and London: Yale University Press for the Paul Mellon Centre for Studies in British Art, 2004.

BARNETT, Gerald. *Richard and Maria Cosway: A Biography*. Tiverton: Westcountry Books in association with Lutterworth Press, 1995.

BARRELL, John. "The Dangerous Goddess: Masculinity, Prestige and the Aesthetic in Early Eighteenth-Century Britain." In *The Birth of Pandora and the Division of Knowledge*, 63–87. London: Palgrave Macmillan, 1992.

BARRY, James. *The Works of James Barry, Esq., Historical Painter ...* 2 vols. London: T. Cadell and W. Davies, 1809.

BASS, Laura R. *The Drama of the Portrait: Theater and Visual Culture in Early Modern Spain*. University Park: Pennsylvania State University Press, 2008.

BAUER, Linda, and George Bauer. "Van Dyck's Club." *Zeitschrift für Kunstgeschichte* 71, no. 2 (2008): 259–71.

BAUMGÄRTEL, Bettina, ed. *Angelica Kauffman*. London, Düsseldorf, and Munich: Royal Academy of Arts, Kunstpalast, and Hirmer, 2020.

BEAL, Mary. *A Study of Richard Symonds: His Italian Notebooks and Their Relevance to Seventeenth-Century Painting Techniques*. Outstanding Theses from the Courtauld Institute of Art. New York: Garland, 1984.

BEER, Esmond Samuel de, ed. *The Diary of John Evelyn*. 6 vols. Oxford: Clarendon Press, 1955.

BELL, Robert, ed. *Poetical Works of Edmund Waller*. London: J. W. Parker, 1854.

BELLORI, Giovanni Pietro. *The Lives of the Modern Painters, Sculptors and Architects*. Edited by Hellmut Wohl. Translated by Alice Sedgwick Wohl. New York: Cambridge University Press, 2005.

—. *Le vite de' pittori, scultori et architetti moderni: Parte prima*. Edited by Evelina Borea. Turin: Einaudi, 1976.

BELSEY, Hugh. *Thomas Gainsborough: The Portraits, Fancy Pictures and Copies after Old Masters*. 2 vols. New Haven and London: Yale University Press for the Paul Mellon Centre for Studies in British Art, 2019.

BELTING, Hans, with Christiane Kruse. *Die Erfindung des Gemäldes: Das erste Jahrhundert der niederländischen Malerei*. Munich: Hirmer, 1994.

BENDER, Ashley Brookner. "Moving Miniatures and Circulating Bodies in Aphra Behn's 'The Rover.'" *Restoration: Studies in English Literary Culture, 1660–1700* 31, no. 1 (Spring 2007): 27–46.

BERGER, Ernst. *Beiträge zur Entwicklungsgeschichte der Maltechnik*. 5 vols. Munich: G. D. W. Callwey, 1901.

BERMINGHAM, Ann. "Daughters and Sisters: Gainsborough's Portraits of Mary and Margaret." In *Gainsborough's Family Album*, edited by David H. Solkin, 42–59. London: National Portrait Gallery, 2018.

—. "Elegant Females and Gentlemen Connoisseurs: The Commerce in Culture and Self-Image in Eighteenth-Century England." In *The Consumption of Culture, 1600–1800: Image, Object, Text*, edited by Ann Bermingham and

John Brewer, 489–513. London and New York: Routledge, 1995.

—. *Learning to Draw: Studies in the Cultural History of a Polite and Useful Art*. New Haven and London: Yale University Press for the Paul Mellon Centre for Studies in British Art, 2000.

Betzer, Sarah. "Patch, Walpole, and Queer Complicity." *Art History* 43, no. 5 (November 2020): 1038–64.

Bie, Cornelis de. *Het gulden cabinet van de edel vry schilderconst*. Antwerp: Jan Meyssens, Juliaen van Montfort, 1662.

Bierens de Haan, David, et al., eds. *Oeuvres complètes de Christiaan Huygens*, 22 vols. The Hague: Martinus Nijhoff, 1888–1950.

Bignamini, Ilaria. "The Artist's Model: From Lely to Hogarth." In *The Artist's Model: Its Role in British Art from Lely to Etty*, edited by Ilaria Bignamini and Martin Postle, 8–15. Nottingham: University Art Gallery, 1991.

—, and Martin Postle, eds. *The Artist's Model: Its Role in British Art from Lely to Etty*. Nottingham: University Art Gallery, 1991.

Bindman, David. "Subjectivity and Slavery in Portraiture: From Courtly to Commercial Societies." In *Slave Portraiture in the Atlantic World*, edited by Angela Rosenthal and Agnes Lugo-Ortiz, 71–88. Cambridge: Cambridge University Press, 2013.

Bok, Marten Jan, and Jos De Meyere. "Schilderes aan haar ezel: Nieuwe gegevens over het schilderij van Gerard van Honthorst." *Maandblad Oud-Utrecht* 58 (1985): 298–303.

Boucher, Diane. "Maria Cosway (1760–1838): A Commentator on Modern Life." *British Art Journal* 18, no. 3 (Winter 2017–18): 78–86.

—. "Maria Cosway's 'A Persian Going to Adore the Sun.'" *Burlington Magazine* 162, no. 1405 (April 2020): 300–305.

Boulboullé, Jenny. "Drawn up by a Learned Physician from the Mouths of Artisans: The Mayerne Manuscript Revisited." *Netherlands Yearbook for History of Art / Nederlands Kunsthistorisch Jaarboek* 68 (2019): 204–49.

Brady, Jennifer. "John Dryden and Anne Killigrew: Postmortems on the Restoration." In *Emergent Nation: Early Modern British Literature in Transition, 1660–1714*, edited by Elizabeth Sauer, 357–72. Early Modern Literature in Transition 3. Cambridge: Cambridge University Press, 2019.

Brenneman, David A. "Thomas Gainsborough and the 'Thin Brilliant Style of Pencilling of Vandyke.'" *Huntington Library Quarterly* 66, no. 1/2 (2003): 81–95.

Britland, Karen. *Drama at the Courts of Queen Henrietta Maria*. Cambridge: Cambridge University Press, 2006.

Brome, Richard. *The Dramatic Works of Richard Brome Containing Fifteen Comedies Now First Collected in Three Volumes*. London: John Pearson, 1873.

Bucholz, R. O. *The Augustan Court: Queen Anne and the Decline of Court Culture*. Stanford: Stanford University Press, 1993.

Buckeridge, Bainbrigg. "An Essay towards an English School of Painters." In Roger de Piles, *The Art of Painting: And the Lives of Painters ...*, 398–480. London: J. Nutt, 1706.

Buffa, Paolo, ed. *Sofonisba Anguissola e le sue sorelle*. Cremona: Centro Culturale, 1994.

Bundock, Michael. *The Fortunes of Francis Barber: The True Story of the Jamaican Slave Who Became Samuel Johnson's Heir*. New Haven and London: Yale University Press, 2015.

Burchard, Wolf, and Kathryn Jones. "The German Princesses as British Patrons." In *Enlightened Princesses: Caroline, Augusta, Charlotte, and the Shaping of the Modern World*, edited by Joanna Marschner, 109–32. New Haven and London: Yale University Press for the Yale Center for British Art and Historic Royal Palaces, 2017.

Butt, John, ed. *The Poems of Alexander Pope*. London: Routledge, 1966.

Büttner, Nils. *Herr P. P. Rubens: Von der Kunst, berühmt zu werden*. Göttingen: Vandenhoeck & Ruprecht, 2006.

Calè, Luisa. "Maria Cosway's Hours: Cosmopolitan and Classical Visual Culture in Thomas Macklin's Poets Gallery." In *Romanticism and Illustration*, edited by Ian Haywood, Mary L. Shannon, and Susan Matthews, 221–42. Cambridge: Cambridge University Press, 2019.

CAMPBELL, Lorne, and Susan Foister. "Gerard, Lucas and Susanna Horenbout." *Burlington Magazine* 128, no. 1003 (October 1986): 719–27.

CARTER, Philip. "An 'Effeminate' or 'Efficient' Nation? Masculinity and Eighteenth-century Social Documentary." *Textual Practice* 11, no. 3 (December 1997): 429–43.

CASTLE, Terry. *Masquerade and Civilization: The Carnivalesque in Eighteenth-Century English Culture and Fiction*. Stanford: Stanford University Press, 1986.

CHERRY, Deborah, and Jennifer Harris. "Eighteenth-Century Portraiture and the Seventeenth-Century Past: Gainsborough and Van Dyck." *Art History* 5, no. 3 (September 1982): 287–309.

CHRISTADLER, Maike. *Kreativität und Geschlecht: Giorgio Vasaris "Vite" und Sofonisba Anguissolas Selbst-Bilder*. Berlin: Reimer, 2000.

CHRISTENSEN, Carol, Michael Palmer, and Michael Swicklik. "Van Dyck's Painting Technique, his Writings, and Three Paintings in the National Gallery of Art." In *Anthony van Dyck*, edited by Arthur K. Wheelock, Susan J. Barnes, and Julius S. Held, 45–52. Washington, D.C.: National Gallery of Art, 1990.

CLARK, Andrew, ed. *"Brief Lives": Chiefly of Contemporaries, set down by John Aubrey, between the Years 1669 & 1696*. 2 vols. Oxford: Clarendon Press, 1898.

CLARKE, Susan. "Richard Lovelace: Royalist Poetry in Context, 1639–1649." PhD dissertation, Australian National University, 2010.

CLAYTON, Thomas, and L. A. Beaurline, eds. *The Works of Sir John Suckling*, 2 vols. Oxford: Clarendon Press, 1971.

COLE, Michael W. *Sofonisba's Lesson: A Renaissance Artist and Her Work*. Princeton: Princeton University Press, 2019.

—, and Mary Pardo. "Origins of the Studio." In *Inventions of the Studio: Renaissance to Romanticism*, edited by Michael Cole and Mary Pardo, 1–35. Chapel Hill: University of North Carolina Press, 2005.

CONWAY, Alison. *Private Interests: Women, Portraiture, and the Visual Culture of the English Novel, 1709–1791*. Toronto: University of Toronto Press, 2001.

COOPER, Tarnya, Aviva Burnstock, Maurice Howard, and Edward Town, eds. *Painting in Britain, 1500–1630: Production, Influences, and Patronage*. Oxford: Oxford University Press for the British Academy, 2015.

CORNET, Pascal, ed. *Après & d'après Van Dyck: La Récupération romantique au XIXe siècle*. Antwerp: Hessenhuis, 1999.

COWAN, Brian. "Arenas of Connoisseurship: Auctioning Art in Later Stuart England." In *Art Markets in Europe, 1400–1800*, edited by Michael North and David Ormrod, 153–66. Aldershot: Ashgate, 1998.

CRAFT-GIEPMANS, Sabine, and Annette de Vries, eds. *Portret in portret in de Nederlandse kunst 1550–2012*. Bussum: Uitgeverij Thoth, 2012.

CRANSTON, Jodi. *The Poetics of Portraiture in the Italian Renaissance*. Cambridge: Cambridge University Press, 2000.

CREMER, Annette Caroline, Matthias Müller, and Klaus Pietschmann, eds. *Fürst und Fürstin als Künstler: Herrschaftliches Künstlertum zwischen Habitus, Norm und Neigung*. Schriften zur Residenzkultur 11. Berlin: Lukas Verlag, 2018.

CRINÒ, Anna Maria. "The Relations between Samuel Cooper and the Court of Cosmo III." *Burlington Magazine* 99, no. 646 (January 1957): 16–21.

CROPPER, Elizabeth. "The Beauty of Woman: Problems in the Rhetoric of Renaissance Portraiture." In *Rewriting the Renaissance: The Discourses of Sexual Difference in Early Modern Europe*, edited by Margaret W. Ferguson, Maureen Quilligan, and Nancy J. Vickers, 175–90. Chicago: University of Chicago Press, 1986.

—. "'La più bella antichità che sappiate desiderare': History and Style in Giovan Pietro Bellori's 'Lives.'" In *Kunst und Kunsttheorie: 1400–1900*, edited by Peter Ganz, Martin Gosebruch, Nikolaus Meier, and Martin Warnke, 145–74. Wiesbaden: Otto Harrasowitz, 1991.

—. "On Beautiful Women, Parmigianino, Petrarchismo, and the Vernacular Style." *Art Bulletin* 58, no. 3 (September 1976): 374–94.

CROW, Thomas E. *Restoration: The Fall of Napoleon in the Course of European Art, 1812–1820*. A. W. Mellon Lectures in the Fine Arts 64. Princeton: Princeton University Press, 2018.

CUGOANO, Ottobah. *Thoughts and Sentiments on the Evil of Slavery and Other Writings*. Edited by Vincent Carretta. Penguin Classics. New York: Penguin Books, 1999.

—. *Thoughts and Sentiments on the Evil and Wicked Traffic of the Slavery and Commerce of the Human Species* ... London: sold by T. Becket, Pall-Mall, and others, 1787.

CUST, Lionel. *Anthony van Dyck: An Historical Study of his Life and Works*. London: G. Bell and Sons, 1900.

DAVID, Jessica, Richard Hark, and Edward Town. "'A Real Master Among Hundreds': The Secrets and Techniques of Seventeenth Century Portraiture in Britain." *Materia: Journal of Technical Art History* 1, no. 1 (2021). https://volume-1-issue-1.materiajournal.com/article-jd-rh-et.

DAVIES, Julie. "Botanizing at Badminton House: The Botanical Pursuits of Mary Somerset, First Duchess of Beaufort." In *Domesticity in the Making of Modern Science*, edited by Donald L. Opitz, Staffan Bergwik, and Brigitte van Tiggelen, 19–39. Basingstoke: Palgrave Macmillan, 2016.

DEKKER, Rudolf. *Family, Culture and Society in the Diary of Constantijn Huygens Jr, Secretary to Stadholder-King William of Orange*. Leiden: Brill, 2013.

DETHLOFF, Diana. "Lely, Drawing, and the Training of Artists." In *Court, Country, and City: British Art and Architecture, 1660–1735*, edited by Mark Hallett, Nigel Llewellyn, and Martin Myrone, 291–313. Studies in British Art 24. London: Yale University Press for the Yale Center for British Art and the Paul Mellon Centre for Studies in British Art, 2016.

—. "Sir Peter Lely's Collection of Prints and Drawings." In *Collecting Prints and Drawings in Europe, c. 1500–1750*, edited by Christopher Baker, Caroline Elam and Genevieve Warwick, 123–39. Aldershot: Ashgate, 2003.

DICKEY, Stephanie S. "Van Dyck in Holland: The Iconography and Its Impact on Rembrandt and Jan Lievens." In *Van Dyck 1599–1999: Conjectures and Refutations*, edited by Hans Vlieghe, 289–304. Turnhout: Brepols, 2001.

DIGBY, Kenelm. *Loose Fantasies*. Edited by Vittorio Gabrieli. Rome: Edizioni di Storia e Letteratura, 1968.

DOHERTY, Tiarna. "Painting Connoisseurship: Liefhebbers in the Studio." *Netherlands Yearbook for History of Art / Nederlands Kunsthistorisch Jaarboek* 69, no. 1 (2020): 146–73.

DRAPER, Helen. "'Her Painting of Apricots': The Invisibility of Mary Beale (1633–1699)." *Forum for Modern Language Studies* 48, no. 4 (October 2012): 389–405.

——. "Mary Beale and Art's Lost Laborers: Women Painter Stainers." *Early Modern Women* 10, no. 1 (Fall 2015): 141–51.

—. "Mary Beale (1633–1699) and Her Objects of Affection." In *Writing the Lives of People and Things, AD 500–1700: A Multi-Disciplinary Future for Biography*, edited by Robert F. W. Smith and Gemma L. Watson, 115–41. London: Routledge, 2016.

DUCOS, Blaise, and Olivia Savatier Sjöholm, eds. *Un Allemand à la cour de Louis XIV: De Dürer à Van Dyck, la collection nordique d'Everhard Jabach*. Paris: Musée du Louvre/Le Passage, 2013.

DUNDAS, Judith. *Pencils Rhetorique: Renaissance Poets and the Art of Painting*. Newark: University of Delaware Press, 1993.

EADE, Jane. "Rediscovering the 'Worthy Artiste Mrs Carlile.'" *National Trust Historic Houses & Collections Annual* (2018): 19–24.

EAKER, Adam. "The American Van Dyck." In *America and the Art of Flanders: Collecting Paintings by Rubens, Van Dyck, and their Circles*, edited by Esmée Quodbach, 48–57. The Frick Collection Studies in the History of Art Collecting in America 5. University Park: Pennsylvania State University Press, 2020.

—. "Rubens and the Gallery of Beauties." In *Tributes to David Freedberg: Image and Insight*, edited by Claudia Swan, 61–74. London: Harvey Miller Publishers, 2019.

—. "The Scene of the Sitting in Early Modern England." *Art History* 41, no. 4 (September 2018): 650–79.

—. "A Taste for Van Dyck." In *Van Dyck: The Anatomy of Portraiture*, edited by Stijn Alsteens and Adam Eaker, 39–51. New York: Frick Collection in association with Yale University Press, 2016.

—. "Van Dyck between Master and Model." *Art Bulletin* 97, no. 2 (June 2015): 173–91.

EINBERG, Elizabeth. *William Hogarth: A Complete Catalogue of the Paintings*. New Haven and London: Yale University Press for the Paul Mellon Centre for Studies in British Art, 2016.

ENGGASS, Robert, and Jonathan Brown, eds. *Italy and Spain, 1600–1750: Sources and Documents*. Englewood Cliffs, N.J.: Prentice-Hall, 1970.

EVANS, Robert C. "Jonson, Weston, and the Digbys: Patronage Relations in Some Later Poems." *Renaissance and Reformation / Renaissance et Réforme* 28, no. 1 (January 2009): 5–37.

EZELL, Margaret J. M., ed. *Anne Killigrew: "My Rare Wit Killing Sin"; Poems of a Restoration Courtier*. Toronto: Iter/Centre for Reformation and Renaissance Studies, 2013.

—. "Late Seventeenth-Century Women Poets and the Anxiety of Attribution." In *Early Modern Women and the Poem*, edited by Susan Wiseman, 147–61. Manchester: Manchester University Press, 2014.

—. "Posthumous Publication of Women's Manuscripts and the History of Authorship." In *Women's Writing and the Circulation of Ideas: Manuscript Publication in England, 1550–1800*, edited by George L. Justice and Nathan Tinker, 121–36. Cambridge: Cambridge University Press, 2002.

FARMER, Norman K. *Poets and the Visual Arts in Renaissance England*. Austin: University of Texas Press, 1984.

FEINBERG-JÜTTE, Anat. "Painters and Counterfeiters: The Painting Artist in Elizabethan and Stuart Drama." *AAA: Arbeiten aus Anglistik und Amerikanistik* 16, no. 1 (January 1991): 3–12.

FELS, Donald C., ed. *Lost Secrets of Flemish Painting: Including the First Complete English Translation of the De Mayerne Manuscript, B.M. Sloane 2052*. Hillsville, Va.: Alchemist, 2001.

FILIPCZAK, Zirka Zaremba. *Picturing Art in Antwerp, 1550–1700*. Princeton: Princeton University Press, 1987.

—. "Van Dyck's Men and Women in Humoral Perspective." *Jaarboek Koninklijk Museum voor Schone Kunsten, Antwerpen* (1999): 51–70.

FINEMAN, Joel. "The History of the Anecdote: Fiction and Fiction." In *The New Historicism*, edited by Harold Veeser. London and New York: Routledge, 1989.

FLATMAN, Thomas. *Poems and Songs by Thomas Flatman*. London: printed by S. and B.G. for Benjamin Took, 1674.

FLEMING, Juliet. *Graffiti and the Writing Arts of Early Modern England*. London: Reaktion, 2001.

FOISTER, Susan. "Foreigners at Court: Holbein, Van Dyck and the Painter-Stainers Company." In *Art and Patronage in the Caroline Courts: Essays in Honour of Sir Oliver Millar*, edited by David Howarth, 32–50. Cambridge: Cambridge University Press, 1993.

—. *Holbein and England*. New Haven and London: Yale University Press for the Paul Mellon Centre for Studies in British Art, 2004.

FORT, Bernardette, and Angela Rosenthal. "The Analysis of Difference." In *The Other Hogarth: Aesthetics of Difference*, edited by Bernardette Fort and Angela Rosenthal, 3–15. Princeton: Princeton University Press, 2001.

FRANITS, Wayne E. *Godefridus Schalcken: A Dutch Painter in Late Seventeenth-Century London*. Amsterdam: Amsterdam University Press, 2018.

FREDERICK, Michele L. "Affectionate Sister, Most Faithful Friend: Elizabeth Stuart and Gerrit van Honthorst's *Seladon and Astraea*." *Netherlands Yearbook for History of Art / Nederlands Kunsthistorisch Jaarboek* 70 (2020): 160–91.

FRENCH, Anne. "Servants as Artists' Models." In *Below Stairs: 400 Years of Servants' Portraits*, edited by Giles Waterfield and Anne French, 105–19. London: National Portrait Gallery, 2003.

FRY, Roger. "J. S. Sargent as Seen at the Royal Academy Exhibition of his Works, 1926, and in the National Gallery." In *Transformations: Critical and Speculative Essays on Art*, 125–35. London: Chatto and Windus, 1926.

FRYE, Susan. *Pens and Needles: Women's Textualities in Early Modern England*. Philadelphia: University of Pennsylvania Press, 2011.

FUMERTON, Patricia. *Cultural Aesthetics: Renaissance Literature and the Practice of Social Ornament*. Chicago: University of Chicago Press, 1991.

Gabrieli, Vittorio. *Sir Kenelm Digby, un inglese italianato nell'età della controriforma*. Rome: Edizioni di Storia e Letteratura, 1957.

Garrard, Mary D. "Artemisia Gentileschi's Self-Portrait as the Allegory of Painting." *Art Bulletin* 62, no. 1 (March 1980): 97–112.

Gaudio, Michael. *The Bible and the Printed Image in Early Modern England: Little Gidding and the Pursuit of Scriptural Harmony*. Visual Culture in Early Modernity 52. Abingdon and New York: Routledge, 2017.

Gibbons, Brian. *Jacobean City Comedy*. 2nd edn. London: Routledge, 1980.

Gibson-Wood, Carol. *Jonathan Richardson: Art Theorist of the English Enlightenment*. New Haven and London: Yale University Press for the Paul Mellon Centre for Studies in British Art, 2000.

—. "Picture Consumption in London at the End of the Seventeenth Century." *Art Bulletin* 84, no. 3 (September 2002): 491–500.

—. "Susanna and Her Elders: John Evelyn's Artistic Daughter." In *John Evelyn and His Milieu*, edited by Frances Harris and Michael Hunter, 233–54. London: British Library, 2003.

Gifford, William, and Alexander Dyce, eds. *The Dramatic Works and Poems of James Shirley*. 6 vols. London: John Murray, 1833.

Gikandi, Simon. *Slavery and the Culture of Taste*. Princeton: Princeton University Press, 2011.

Girard, René. *Deceit, Desire, and the Novel: Self and Other in Literary Structure*. Translated by Yvonne Freccero. Baltimore: Johns Hopkins University Press, 1984.

Gittings, Clare. "Venetia's Death and Kenelm's Mourning." In *Death, Passion and Politics: Van Dyck's Portraits of Venetia Stanley and George Digby*, edited by Ann Sumner, 54–68. London: Dulwich Picture Gallery, 1995.

Goldberg, Jonathan. *Sodometries: Renaissance Texts, Modern Sexualities*. Stanford: Stanford University Press, 1992.

Goldring, Elizabeth. *Nicholas Hilliard: Life of an Artist*. New Haven and London: Yale University Press for the Paul Mellon Centre for Studies in British Art, 2019.

—. *Robert Dudley, Earl of Leicester and the World of Elizabethan Art: Painting and Patronage at the Court of Elizabeth I*. New Haven and London: Yale University Press for the Paul Mellon Centre for Studies in British Art, 2014.

Goldsmith, M. M. "Liberty, Luxury and the Pursuit of Happiness." In *The Languages of Political Theory in Early-Modern Europe*, edited by Anthony Pagden, 225–51. Cambridge: Cambridge University Press, 1990.

Gordenker, Emilie E. S. *Anthony Van Dyck (1599–1641) and the Representation of Dress in Seventeenth-Century Portraiture*. Turnhout: Brepols, 2001.

Goulding, Richard William. *Catalogue of the Pictures Belonging to His Grace the Duke of Portland, K.G., at Welbeck Abbey, 17 Hill Street, London, and Langwell House*. Cambridge: Cambridge University Press, 1936.

Graaf, J. A. van de. *Het De Mayerne Manuscript als bron voor de schildertechniek van de barok*. Mijdrecht: Drukkerij Verweij, 1958.

Gray, Charles H. *Lodowick Carliell: His Life, a Discussion of His Plays, and "The Deserving Favourite", a Tragi-Comedy Reprinted from the Original Edition of 1629*. Chicago: University of Chicago Press, 1905.

Gregg, Edward. "The Jacobite Career of John, Earl of Mar." In *Ideology and Conspiracy: Aspects of Jacobitism, 1689–1759*, edited by Eveline Cruickshanks, 179–200. Edinburgh: J. Donald, 1982.

Greig, Hannah. *The Beau Monde: Fashionable Society in Georgian London*. Oxford: Oxford University Press, 2013.

Griffey, Erin. *On Display: Henrietta Maria and the Materials of Magnificence at the Stuart Court*. New Haven and London: Yale University Press for the Paul Mellon Centre for Studies in British Art, 2016.

—. "Van Dyck Paintings in Stuart Royal Inventories, 1639–1688." *Journal of the History of Collections* 30, no. 1 (March 2018): 49–63.

Grosvenor, Bendor. *"Bright Souls": The Forgotten Story of Britain's First Female Artists*. London: Lyon & Turnbull, 2019.

—. "Van Dyck as Andy Warhol." *Art History News*, January 13, 2016, https://www.arthistorynews.com (accessed February 19, 2021).

GRUNDY, Isobel. *Lady Mary Wortley Montagu*. Oxford: Oxford University Press, 1999.

HALL, Kim F. *Things of Darkness: Economies of Race and Gender in Early Modern England*. Ithaca: Cornell University Press, 1995.

HALLAM, Jennifer L. "All the Queen's Women: Female Double Portraits at the Caroline Court." In *Women and Portraits in Early Modern Europe: Gender, Agency, Identity*, edited by Andrea Pearson, 137–60. Aldershot: Ashgate, 2007.

HALLETT, Mark. *Reynolds: Portraiture in Action*. New Haven and London: Yale University Press for the Paul Mellon Centre for Studies in British Art, 2014.

HALSBAND, Robert, ed. *The Complete Letters of Lady Mary Wortley Montagu*. 3 vols. Oxford: Clarendon Press, 1965–7.

—. *Lord Hervey: Eighteenth-Century Courtier*. Oxford: Oxford University Press, 1974.

HARRIS, Frances. "An Ambivalent Image: Lely's Double-Portrait of Charles I and the Duke of York." *Burlington Magazine* 149, no. 1248 (March 2007): 180–82.

—. *Transformations of Love: The Friendship of John Evelyn and Margaret Godolphin*. Oxford: Oxford University Press, 2002.

HAUTE, Bernadette. "Anthony van Dyck and the Trope of the Black Attendant." *Acta Academica* 48, no. 2 (2016): 18–47.

HAYES, John T., ed. *The Letters of Thomas Gainsborough*. New Haven and London: Yale University Press for the Paul Mellon Centre for Studies in British Art, 2001.

HEARN, Karen, ed. *Dynasties: Painting in Tudor and Jacobean England, 1530–1630*. London: Tate Publishing, 1995.

—. *Van Dyck & Britain*. London: Tate, 2009.

HELD, Julius S. "Review of Horst Vey, *Die Zeichnungen Anton van Dycks*." *Art Bulletin* 46, no. 4 (December 1964): 565–68.

—. "Van Dyck's Relationship to Rubens." In *Van Dyck 350*, edited by Susan J. Barnes and Arthur K. Wheelock, 63–78. Studies in the History of Art 46. Washington, D.C.: National Gallery of Art, 1994.

HENNEBELLE, David. "Le Rendez-vous manqué entre Mozart et l'aristocratie parisienne (1778)." *Annales Historiques de la Révolution Française*, no. 379 (January–March 2015): 35–45.

HERVEY, John, Lord. *Some Materials towards Memoirs of the Reign of King George II*. Edited by Romney Sedgwick. 3 vols. London: Eyre & Spottiswoode, 1931.

HERVEY, Mary F. S. *The Life, Correspondence & Collections of Thomas Howard, Earl of Arundel*. Cambridge: Cambridge University Press, 1921.

HILLE, Christiane. *Visions of the Courtly Body: The Patronage of George Villiers, First Duke of Buckingham, and the Triumph of Painting at the Stuart Court*. Berlin: Akademie Verlag, 2012.

HOGARTH, William. *The Analysis of Beauty: With the Rejected Passages from the Manuscript Drafts and Autobiographical Notes*. Edited by Joseph Burke. Oxford: Clarendon Press, 1955.

HONIG, Elizabeth Alice. "Desire and Domestic Economy." *Art Bulletin* 83, no. 2 (June 2001): 294–315.

HOOGEWERFF, G. J., ed. *De twee reizen van Cosimo de' Medici, Prins van Toscane door de Nederlanden (1667–1669): Journalen en documenten*. Werken uitgegeven door het Historisch Genootschap 3, vol. 41. Amsterdam: Johannes Müller, 1919.

HOWARD, Jean E. *Theater of a City: The Places of London Comedy, 1598–1642*. Philadelphia: University of Pennsylvania Press, 2011.

HOYLES, Martin. *Cugoano against Slavery*. Hertford: Hansib Publications, 2015.

HUNTER, Matthew C. *Wicked Intelligence: Visual Art and the Science of Experiment in Restoration London*. Chicago: University of Chicago Press, 2013.

HUNTER, William B., Jr., ed. *The Complete Poetry of Ben Jonson*. Garden City, N.Y.: Anchor, 1963.

HUYGENS, Constantijn, Jr. *Journaal van Constantijn Huygens, den zoon, 21 october 1688 tot 2 september 1696*. Utrecht: Keminck & Zoon, 1876.

JACOBS, Fredrika H. *Defining the Renaissance Virtuosa: Women Artists and the Language of Art History and Criticism*. Cambridge: Cambridge University Press, 1997.

JAFFÉ, Michael. "*The Standard Bearer*: Van Dyck's Portrait of Sir Edmund Verney." In *Art and Patronage in the Caroline Courts: Essays in Honour of Sir Oliver Millar*, edited by David Howarth,

90–106. Cambridge: Cambridge University Press, 1993.

JOHNS, Richard. "Framing Robert Aggas: The Painter-Stainers' Company and the 'English School of Painters.'" *Art History* 31, no. 3 (2008): 322–41.

JONES, Ann Rosalind, and Peter Stallybrass. *Renaissance Clothing and the Materials of Memory*. Cambridge: Cambridge University Press, 2000.

JONES, Jonathan. "Rembrandt and Slavery: Did the Great Painter Have Links to this Abhorrent Trade?" *Guardian*, February 9, 2021, https://www.theguardian.com (accessed February 19, 2021).

JUNOD, Karen. *"Writing the Lives of Painters": Biography and Artistic Identity in Britain 1760–1810*. Oxford: Oxford University Press, 2011.

KAUFMANN, Miranda. *Black Tudors: The Untold Story*. London: Oneworld Publications, 2018.

KEBLUSEK, Marika. "Entertainment in Exile: Theatrical Performances at the Courts of Margaret Cavendish, Mary Stuart and Elizabeth of Bohemia." In *The Triumphs of the Defeated: Early Modern Festivals and Messages of Legitimacy*, edited by Peter Davidson and Jill Bepler, 173–90. Wiesbaden: Harrossowitz, 2007.

KEMMER, Claus. "In Search of Classical Form: Gerard de Lairesse's 'Groot Schilderboek' and Seventeenth-Century Dutch Genre Painting." *Simiolus: Netherlands Quarterly for the History of Art* 26, no. 1/2 (1998): 87–115.

KILLIGREW, Anne. *Poems by Mrs Anne Killigrew*. London: Samuel Lowndes, 1686.

KILLIGREW, Thomas. *Thomaso, or, the Wanderer: A Comedy, the Scene Madrid*. London: Henry Herringman, 1663.

KING, Reyahn, ed. *Ignatius Sancho: An African Man of Letters*. London: National Portrait Gallery, 1997.

KING, Reyahn. "Ignatius Sancho and Portraits of the Black Élite," In *Ignatius Sancho: An African Man of Letters*, edited by Reyahn King, 15–44. London: National Portrait Gallery, 1997.

KINNEY, Arthur F., and Linda Bradley Salamon, eds. *Nicholas Hilliard's Art of Limning*. Boston, Mass.: Northeastern University Press, 1983.

KLEEBLATT, Norman L., ed. *John Singer Sargent: Portraits of the Wertheimer Family*. New York: Jewish Museum, 1999.

KLEINERT, Katja. *Atelierdarstellungen in der niederländischen Genremalerei des 17. Jahrhunderts: Realistisches Abbild oder glaubwürdiger Schein?* Petersberg: Michael Imhof, 2006.

KOERNER, Joseph Leo. *Bosch and Bruegel: From Enemy Painting to Everyday Life*. A. W. Mellon Lectures in the Fine Arts 57. Princeton: Princeton University Press, 2016.

KOLDEWEIJ, Anna Cecilia. "Koninklijke verbeelders verbeeld? Twee recent ontdekte tekeningen van Gerard van Honthorst in perspectief." In *De Verbeelder verbeeld(t): Boekillustratie en beeldende kunst*, edited by Anna Cecilia Koldeweij and Jos Koldewij, 68–76. Nijmegen: Vantilt, 2017.

KÖLTZSCH, Georg-W. *Der Maler und sein Modell: Geschichte und Deutung eines Bildthemas*. Cologne: DuMont, 2000.

KOOS, Marianne. "Wandering Things: Agency and Embodiment in Late Sixteenth-Century English Miniature Portraits." *Art History* 37, no. 5 (2014): 836–59.

KUSCHE, Maria. "Sofonisba Anguissola: Her Life and Work." In *Sofonisba Anguissola: A Renaissance Woman*, edited by Sylvia Ferino-Pagden and Maria Kusche, 26–105. Washington, D.C.: National Museum of Women in the Arts, 1995.

LABORDUS, Jorunn. "Gerard van Honthorst en zijn prinsessen." In *Vrouwen en kunst in de Republiek: Een overzicht*, edited by Els Kloek, Catherine Peters Sengers, and Esther Tobé. Utrechtse Historische Cahiers 19. Hilversum: Verloren, 1998.

LAIRD, Mark. *A Natural History of English Gardening, 1650–1800*. New Haven and London: Yale University Press, 2015.

LAIRESSE, Gérard de. *A Treatise on the Art of Painting, in all its Branches: Accompanied by Seventy Engraved Plates, and Exemplified by Remarks on the Paintings of the Best Masters*. Edited by William Marshall Craig. London: Edward Orme, 1817.

LAMMERTSE, Friso and Alejandro Vergara, "A Portrait of Van Dyck as a Young Artist." In *The Young Van Dyck*, edited by Friso Lammertse and Alejandro Vergara, 23–74. Madrid: Museo Nacional del Prado, 2012.

Latham, Robert, and William Matthews, eds. *The Diary of Samuel Pepys*. 11 vols. Berkeley: University of California Press, 1970–83.

Leca, Benedict. "'A Favourite among the Demireps': Thomas Gainsborough and the Modern Woman." In *Thomas Gainsborough and the Modern Woman*, edited by Benedict Leca, 43–105. London: Giles Ltd for the Cincinnati Museum of Art, 2010.

Lewalski, Barbara Kiefer. *Writing Women in Jacobean England*. Cambridge, Mass.: Harvard University Press, 1993.

Lewis, W. S., ed. *The Yale Edition of Horace Walpole's Correspondence*. 48 vols. New Haven: Yale University Press, 1937–83.

Liedtke, Walter. "Van Dyck's 'Influence' in the Dutch Republic." In *Aemulatio: Imitation, Emulation and Invention in Netherlandish Art from 1500 to 1800; Essays in Honor of Eric Jan Sluijter*, edited by Anton W. A. Boschloo, Jacquelyn N. Coutré, Stephanie S. Dickey, and Nicolette C. Sluijter-Seijffert, 304–17. Zwolle: Waanders Publishers, 2011.

Lloyd, Stephen, ed. *Richard & Maria Cosway: Regency Artists of Taste and Fashion*. Edinburgh: Scottish National Portrait Gallery, 1995.

Loxley, James. "Poetry, Portraiture and Praise: Suckling and Van Dyck, Lovelace and Lely." *Seventeenth Century* 32, no. 4 (October 2017): 351–69.

McClain, Molly. *Beaufort: The Duke and His Duchess, 1657–1715*. New Haven and London: Yale University Press, 2001.

McCreery, Cindy. *The Satirical Gaze: Prints of Women in Late Eighteenth-Century England*. Oxford: Clarendon Press, 2004.

McGee, C. E. "Cupid's Banishment: A Masque Presented to Her Majesty by Young Gentlewomen of the Ladies Hall, Deptford, May 4, 1617." *Renaissance Drama* 19 (1988): 226–64.

McGrath, Elizabeth. *Jordaens, Psyche and the Abbot: Myth, Decorum and Italian Manners in Seventeenth-Century Antwerp*. Groningen: Stichting Gerson Lezingen, 2009.

McManus, Clare. *Women on the Renaissance Stage: Anna of Denmark and Female Masquing in the Stuart Court (1590–1619)*. Manchester: Manchester University Press, 2002.

McNeil, Peter. *Pretty Gentlemen: Macaroni Men and the Eighteenth-Century Fashion World*. New Haven and London: Yale University Press, 2018.

Maddicott, Hilary. "'Qualis vita, finis ita': The Life and Death of Margaret Lemon, Mistress of Van Dyck." *Burlington Magazine* 160, no. 1379 (February 2018): 92–100.

Maës, Gaetane. "Van Dyck's Anger in Kortrijk and His Decision to Paint 'Only for People and Not for Donkeys.'" In *Facts & Feelings: Retracing Emotions of Artists, 1600–1800*, edited by Hannelore Magnus and Katlijne Van der Stighelen, 187–200. Turnhout: Brepols, 2015.

Malvasia, Carlo Cesare. *The Life of Guido Reni*. Translated and edited by Catherine Enggass and Robert Enggass. University Park: Pennsylvania State University Press, 1980.

Marcus, Sharon. "Queer Theory for Everyone: A Review Essay." *Signs* 31, no. 1 (Autumn 2005): 191–218.

Messenger, Ann. "A Problem of Praise: John Dryden and Anne Killigrew." In *His and Hers: Essays in Restoration and Eighteenth-Century Literature*, 14–40. Lexington: University Press of Kentucky, 1986.

Miedema, Hessel, ed. *The Lives of the Illustrious Netherlandish and German Painters, from the First Edition of the Schilder-Boeck (1603–1604): Preceded by the Lineage, Circumstances and Place of Birth, Life and Works of Karel Van Mander, Painter and Poet and Likewise His Death and Burial, from the Second Edition of the Schilder-Boeck (1616–1618)*. 3 vols. Doornspijk: Davaco, 1994.

Millar, Oliver, ed. "Abraham van Der Doort's Catalogue of the Collections of Charles 1," *Walpole Society* 37 (1958–60): 120–21.

—, ed. "The Inventories and Valuations of the King's Goods, 1649–1651." *Walpole Society* 43 (1970–72): 1–448.

—. "Strafford and Van Dyck." In *For Veronica Wedgwood These: Studies in Seventeenth-Century History*, edited by Richard Ollard and Pamela Tudor Craig, 109–23. London: Collins, 1986.

—. *The Tudor, Stuart and Early Georgian Pictures in the Collection of Her Majesty the Queen*. 2 vols. London: Phaidon Press, 1963.

Miller, Monica L. *Slaves to Fashion: Black Dandyism and the Styling of Black Diasporic Identity*. Durham, N.C.: Duke University Press, 2009.

Miller, Shannon. "Consuming Mothers/Consuming Merchants: The Carnivalesque Economy of Jacobean City Comedy." *Modern Language Studies* 26, no. 2/3 (Spring/Summer 1996): 73–97.

Molineux, Catherine. *Faces of Perfect Ebony: Encountering Atlantic Slavery in Imperial Britain*. Harvard Historical Studies 175. Cambridge, Mass.: Harvard University Press, 2012.

Montrose, Louis. *The Subject of Elizabeth: Authority, Gender, and Representation*. Chicago: University of Chicago Press, 2006.

Moore, Peter. "Dialogues in Paint and Print: Mezzotint Portraiture and Intermedial Exchange." In *Court, Country, City: British Art and Architecture, 1660–1735*, edited by Mark Hallett, Nigel Llewellyn, and Martin Myrone, 433–56. New Haven and London: Yale University Press for the Yale Center for British Art and the Paul Mellon Centre for Studies in British Art, 2016.

Muller, Jeffrey M. "Anthony van Dyck and Flemish National Identity: A Clash of Images between the Two World Wars." In *Van Dyck, 1599–1999: Conjectures and Refutations*, edited by Hans Vlieghe, 305–12. Turnhout: Brepols, 2001.

—. "The Quality of Grace in the Art of Anthony van Dyck." In *Anthony van Dyck*, edited by Susan J. Barnes, Arthur K. Wheelock, and Julius S. Held, 27–36. Washington, D.C.: National Gallery of Art, 1990.

—, and Jim Murrell, eds. *Edward Norgate: Miniatura, or, The Art of Limning*. New Haven and London: Yale University Press, 1997.

Myrone, Martin. *Bodybuilding: Reforming Masculinities in British Art 1750–1810*. New Haven and London: Yale University Press for the Paul Mellon Centre for Studies in British Art, 2005.

—, and Alice Insley. *Hogarth and Europe*. London: Tate, 2022.

Nagel, Alexander. "Fashion and the Now-Time of Renaissance Art." *Res: Anthropology and Aesthetics*, no. 46 (2004): 32–52.

Neumeister, Mirjam, ed. *Van Dyck: Gemälde von Anthonis van Dyck; Bayerische Staatsgemäldesammlungen, München*. Munich: Alte Pinakothek/Hirmer, 2019.

Nichols, John. *Biographical Anecdotes of William Hogarth: With a Catalogue of his Works Chronologically Arranged; and Occasional Remarks*. 3rd edn. London: John Nichols, 1785.

Nigro, Jeffrey A. "'Favourable to Tenderness and Sentiment': The Many Meanings of Mary Crawford's Harp." *Persuasions On-Line* 35, no. 1 (Winter 2014), www.jasna.org/persuasions/on-line/vol35no1/nigro.html.

Nocentelli, Carmen. "Teresa Sampsonia Sherley: Amazon, Traveler, and Consort." In *Travel and Travail: Early Modern Women, English Drama, and the Wider World*, edited by Patricia Akhimie and Bernadette Diane Andrea, 81–101. Early Modern Cultural Studies. Lincoln: University of Nebraska Press, 2019.

Northcote, James. *The Life of Sir Joshua Reynolds …: Comprising Original Anecdotes of Many Distinguished Persons, his Contemporaries; and a Brief Analysis of his Discourses*. 2nd edn. 2 vols. London: Henry Colburn, 1819.

Novikova, Anastassia. "Virtuosity and Declensions of Virtue: Thomas Arundel and Aletheia Talbot Seen by Virtue of a Portrait Pair by Daniel Mytens and a Treatise by Franciscus Junius." *Netherlands Yearbook for History of Art / Nederlands Kunsthistorisch Jaarboek* 54 (2003): 308–33.

O'Day, Rosemary. "Family Galleries: Women and Art in the Seventeenth and Eighteenth Centuries." *Huntington Library Quarterly* 71, no. 2 (2008): 323–49.

Ogborn, Miles. "Locating the Macaroni: Luxury, Sexuality and Vision in Vauxhall Gardens." *Textual Practice* 11, no. 3 (December 1997): 445–61.

Orgel, Stephen. *The Illusion of Power: Political Theater in the English Renaissance*. Berkeley: University of California Press, 1975.

Ormond, Richard, and Elaine Kilmurray. *John Singer Sargent: Complete Paintings*. 9 vols. New Haven and London: Yale University Press for the Paul Mellon Centre for Studies in British Art, 1998–2014.

Osborne, Mary Tom. *Advice-to-a-Painter Poems, 1633–1856: An Annotated Finding List*. Austin: University of Texas Press, 1949.

Osborne, Toby. "A Queen Mother in Exile: Marie de Médicis in the Spanish Netherlands and England, 1631–41." In *Monarchy and Exile: The Politics of Legitimacy from Marie de Médicis to Wilhelm II*, edited by Philip Mansel and Torsten Riotte, 17–43. Houndmills, Basingstoke and New York: Palgrave Macmillan, 2011.

Pace, Claire. "'Delineated Lives': Themes and Variations in Seventeenth-Century Poems about Portraits." *Word & Image* 2, no. 1 (January 1986): 1–17.

—, and Janis Bell. "The Allegorical Engravings in Bellori's Lives." In *Art History in the Age of Bellori: Scholarship and Cultural Poetics in Seventeenth-Century Rome*, edited by Janis Bell and Thomas Willette, 191–223. Cambridge: Cambridge University Press, 2002.

Palmer, Caroline. "Brazen Cheek: Face-Painters in Late Eighteenth-Century England." *Oxford Art Journal* 31, no. 2 (2008): 197–213.

Parry, Graham. *The Golden Age Restor'd: The Culture of the Stuart Court, 1603–42*. Manchester: Manchester University Press, 1981.

—. "Van Dyck and the Caroline Court Poets." In *Van Dyck 350*, edited by Susan J. Barnes and Arthur K. Wheelock, 247–62. Studies in the History of Art 46. Washington, D.C.: National Gallery of Art, 1994.

Pasquin, Anthony [pseud. John Williams]. *The Royal Academicians, a Farce*. London: Denew and Grant, 1786.

Paulson, Ronald. *Book and Painting: Shakespeare, Milton, and the Bible; Literary Texts and the Emergence of English Painting*. The Hodges Lectures. Knoxville: University of Tennessee Press, 1982.

—. *Emblem and Expression: Meaning in English Art of the Eighteenth Century*. Cambridge, Mass.: Harvard University Press, 1975.

Pears, Iain. *The Discovery of Painting: The Growth of Interest in the Arts in England, 1680–1768*. New Haven and London: Yale University Press for the Paul Mellon Centre for Studies in British Art, 1988.

Perrinchief, Richard. *The Royal Martyr, or, The History of the Life and Death of King Charles I*. London: printed by J.M. for R. Royston, 1676.

Perry, Gillian. *Spectacular Flirtations: Viewing the Actress in British Art and Theatre, 1768–1820*. New Haven and London: Yale University Press for the Paul Mellon Centre for Studies in British Art, 2007.

Piles, Roger de. *The Art of Painting: And the Lives of the Painters; Containing, a Compleat Treatise of Painting, Designing, and the Use of Prints: ... Done from the French of Monsieur de Piles. To Which Is Added, an Essay towards an English-School, ...* London: J. Nutt, 1706.

—. *Cours de peinture par principes*. Paris: Chez Jacques Estienne, 1708.

Pointon, Marcia. *Hanging the Head: Portraiture and Social Formation in Eighteenth-Century England*. New Haven and London: Yale University Press for the Paul Mellon Centre for Studies in British Art, 1993.

—. "Material Manoeuvres: Sarah Churchill, Duchess of Marlborough and the Power of Artefacts." *Art History* 32, no. 3 (June 2009): 485–515.

—. "Portrait! Portrait!! Portrait!!!" In *Art on the Line: The Royal Academy Exhibitions at Somerset House, 1780–1836*, edited by David H. Solkin, 93–110. New Haven and London: Yale University Press for the Paul Mellon Centre for Studies in British Art and the Courtauld Institute Gallery, 2001.

—. *Strategies for Showing: Women, Possession, and Representation in English Visual Culture, 1665–1800*. Oxford and New York: Oxford University Press, 1997.

—. "'Surrounded with Brilliants': Miniature Portraits in Eighteenth-Century England." *Art Bulletin* 83, no. 1 (March 2001): 48–71.

Pommier, Edouard. *Théories du portrait: De la Renaissance aux Lumières*. Paris: Gallimard, 1998.

Porter, Roy. "The Cosways' London." In *Richard & Maria Cosway: Regency Artists of Taste and Fashion*, edited by Stephen Lloyd, 97–100. Edinburgh: Scottish National Portrait Gallery, 1995.

Posner, Donald. "The 'Duchesse de Velours' and Her Daughter: A Masterpiece by Nattier and its

Historical Context." *Metropolitan Museum Journal* 31 (1996): 131–41.

POSTLE, Martin, ed. *Johan Zoffany RA: Society Observed*. New Haven and London: Yale University Press for the Yale Center for British Art and the Royal Academy of Arts, 2011.

POTTER, Lois. *Secret Rites and Secret Writing: Royalist Literature, 1641–1660*. Cambridge: Cambridge University Press, 1989.

PRESTON, Claire. "Ekphrasis: Painting in Words." In *Renaissance Rhetorical Figures*, edited by Sylvia Adamson and Gavin Alexander, 115–30. Cambridge: Cambridge University Press, 2007.

—. "The Gallery, the Eye, and the Rhetoric of Observation in Some Seventeenth-Century Descriptions." *Seventeenth Century* 32, no. 4 (October 2017): 371–92.

PUGET DE LA SERRE, Jean. *Histoire curieuse de tout ce qui c'est passé à l'entrée de la reyne mère du roi treschrestien dans les villes des Pays Bas*. Antwerp: Imprimerie Plantinienne de Balthasar Moretus, 1632.

PUTTFARKEN, Thomas. *Roger de Piles' Theory of Art*. New Haven and London: Yale University Press, 1985.

QUINN, Vincent, and Mary Peace. "Luxurious Sexualities." *Textual Practice* 11, no. 3 (December 1997): 405–16.

RAATSCHEN, Gudrun. "Merely Ornamental? Van Dyck's Portraits of Henrietta Maria." In *Henrietta Maria: Piety, Politics and Patronage*, edited by Erin Griffey, 139–63. Aldershot: Ashgate, 2008.

RACKHAM, H., trans. *Pliny: Natural History*. 10 vols. Loeb Classical Library. Cambridge, Mass.: Harvard University Press, 1949–62.

RADCLIFFE, Sir George, ed. *The Earl of Strafforde's Letters and Dispatches, with an Essay towards his Life*, 2 vols. London: William Bowyer, 1739.

RATHER, Susan. *The American School: Artists and Status in the Late Colonial and Early National Era*. New Haven and London: Yale University Press, 2016.

REID, Lindsay Ann. "Louise Hollandine and the Art of Arachnean Critique." In *Women Artists and Patrons in the Netherlands, 1500–1700*, edited by Elizabeth Sutton, 113–42. Amsterdam: Amsterdam University Press, 2019.

RETFORD, Kate. *The Art of Domestic Life: Family Portraiture in Eighteenth-Century England*. New Haven and London: Yale University Press for the Paul Mellon Centre for Studies in British Art, 2006.

—. *The Conversation Piece: Making Modern Art in Eighteenth-Century Britain*. New Haven and London: Yale University Press for the Paul Mellon Centre for Studies in British Art, 2017.

REYNOLDS, Graham. "A Miniature Self-Portrait by Thomas Flatman, Limner and Poet." *Burlington Magazine* 89, no. 528 (March 1947): 63–67.

—, with Katharine Baetjer. *European Miniatures in the Metropolitan Museum of Art*. New York: H. N. Abrams for the Metropolitan Museum of Art, 1996.

REYNOLDS, Sir Joshua. *A Journey to Flanders and Holland*. Edited by Harry Mount. Cambridge: Cambridge University Press, 1996.

RHYS, Ernest, ed. *Margaret, Duchess of Newcastle: Life of the Duke, Memoirs of Her Own Life & Certain Sociable Letters*. London: J. M. Dent, 1915.

RIBEIRO, Aileen. *The Dress Worn at Masquerades in England, 1730 to 1790, and Its Relation to Fancy Dress in Portraiture*. Outstanding Theses from the Courtauld Institute of Art. New York: Garland, 1984.

—. "Portraying the Fashion, Romancing the Past: Dress and the Cosways." In *Richard & Maria Cosway: Regency Artists of Taste and Fashion*, edited by Stephen Lloyd, 101–5. Edinburgh: Scottish National Portrait Gallery, 1995.

RICHARDSON, Jonathan. *An Essay on the Theory of Painting: By Mr. Richardson*. London: Printed by W. Bowyer for John Churchill, 1715.

—. *An Essay on the Theory of Painting: By Mr. Richardson*. 2nd edn. London: A. Bettesworth, 1725.

—. *Two Discourses: I. An Essay on the Whole Art of Criticism, as It Relates to Painting … II. An Argument in Behalf of the Science of a Connoisseur; Wherein Is Shewn the Dignity, Certainty, Pleasure, and Advantage of It*. London: W. Churchill, 1719.

RIDING, Jacqueline. "'A Session of Painters': Legacy, Succession, and the Prospects for British Portraiture after Kneller." In *Court, Country, City: British Art and Architecture, 1660–1735*, edited by Mark Hallett, Nigel Llewellyn, and Martin Myrone, 353–79. Studies in British Art 24. New Haven and London: Yale University Press for the Yale Center for British Art and the Paul Mellon Centre for Studies in British Art, 2016.

Roach, Joseph. "Celebrity Erotics: Pepys, Performance, and Painted Ladies." In *Politics, Transgression, and Representation at the Court of Charles II*, edited by Julia Marciari Alexander and Catharine MacLeod, 233–50. Studies in British Art 18. New Haven and London: Yale University Press for the Paul Mellon Centre for Studies in British Art, 2007.

Rodger, N. A. M. *The Command of the Ocean: A Naval History of Britain, 1649–1815*. London: Allen Lane, 2004.

Rogers, Malcolm. "'Golden Houses for Shadows': Some Portraits of Thomas Killigrew and His Family." In *Art and Patronage in the Caroline Courts: Essays in Honour of Sir Oliver Millar*, edited by David Howarth, 220–42. Cambridge: Cambridge University Press, 1993.

Rohr, Alheidis von. "'Peint par Madame l'Abesse': Louise Hollandine Prinzessin von der Pfalz (1622–1709)." *Niederdeutsche Beiträge zur Kunstgeschichte* 28 (1989): 143–60.

Rooses, Max. "De vreemde reizigers Rubens of zijn huis bezoekende." *Rubens-Bulletijn* 5 (1897): 221–29.

Rosenthal, Angela. *Angelica Kauffman: Art and Sensibility*. New Haven and London: Yale University Press for the Paul Mellon Centre for Studies in British Art, 2006.

—. "She's Got the Look! Eighteenth-Century Female Portrait Painters and the Psychology of a Potentially 'Dangerous Employment.'" In *Portraiture: Facing the Subject*, edited by Joanna Woodall, 147–66. Manchester: Manchester University Press, 1997.

Ruiz Gómez, Leticia, ed. *A Tale of Two Women Painters: Sofonisba Anguissola and Lavinia Fontana*. Madrid: Museo Nacional del Prado, 2019.

Salomon, Xavier F. *Van Dyck in Sicily, 1624–1625: Painting and the Plague*. London: Dulwich Picture Gallery, 2012.

Sanders, Julie. *Caroline Drama: The Plays of Massinger, Ford, Shirley and Brome*. Plymouth: Northcote House in association with the British Council, 1999.

—. "Caroline Salon Culture and Female Agency: The Countess of Carlisle, Henrietta Maria, and Public Theatre." *Theatre Journal* 52, no. 4 (December 2000): 449–64.

Sanderson, William. *Graphice: The Use of the Pen and Pensil. Or, The Most Excellent Art of Painting*. London: Robert Crofts, 1658.

Schama, Simon. "The Domestication of Majesty: Royal Family Portraiture, 1500–1850." *Journal of Interdisciplinary History* 17, no. 1 (Summer 1986): 155–83.

Schwartz, Gary. "Love in the Kunstkamer: Additions to the Work of Guillam van Haecht (1593–1637)." *Tableau* 18 (Summer 1996): 43–52.

Scott Thomson, Gladys. *Letters of a Grandmother, 1732–1735: Being the Correspondence of Sarah, Duchess of Marlborough, with Her Granddaughter Diana, Duchess of Bedford*. London: Jonathan Cape, 1943.

Sedgwick, Eve Kosofsky. *Between Men: English Literature and Male Homosocial Desire*. New York: Columbia University Press, 1985.

Seidlitz, W. von. "Bericht eines Zeitgenossen über einen Besuch bei Rubens," *Repertorium für Kunstwissenschaft* 10 (1887): 111.

Shaftesbury, Anthony Ashley Cooper, 3rd Earl of. *Second Characters, or, The Language of Forms*. Edited by Benjamin Rand. Cambridge: Cambridge University Press, 1914.

Sheriff, Mary D. *The Exceptional Woman: Elisabeth Vigée-Lebrun and the Cultural Politics of Art*. Chicago: University of Chicago Press, 1996.

Slive, Seymour. *Rembrandt and his Critics, 1630–1730*. Utrechtse bijdragen tot de kunstgeschiedenis 2. The Hague: M. Nijhoff, 1953.

Smith, S. Birket, ed. *Dr. Med. Otto Sperlings Selvbiografi (1602–1673), oversat i uddrag efter originalhaandskriftet med saerligt hensyn til forfatterens ophold i Danmark og Norge samt fangenskab i Blaataarn*. Copenhagen: Andr. Fred. Høst & Søns Førlag, 1885.

Smith, John Thomas. *Nollekens and his Times: A Life of that Celebrated Sculptor and Memoirs of Several Contemporary Artists, from the Time of*

Roubiliac, Hogarth and Reynolds to That of Fuseli, Flaxman and Blake. London: Colburn, 1829.

Smuts, R. Malcolm. *Court Culture and the Origins of a Royalist Tradition in Early Stuart England*. Philadelphia: University of Pennsylvania Press, 1987.

Sohm, Philip. "Gendered Style in Italian Art Criticism from Michelangelo to Malvasia." *Renaissance Quarterly* 48, no. 4 (December 1995): 759–808.

Solkin, David H. *Art in Britain 1660–1815*. Pelican History of Art. New Haven and London: Yale University Press, 2015.

——. *Painting for Money: The Visual Arts and the Public Sphere in Eighteenth-Century England*. New Haven and London: Yale University Press for the Paul Mellon Centre for Studies in British Art, 1993.

——. "Private and Public Relations: Gainsborough's Family Album." In *Gainsborough's Family Album*, ed. David H. Solkin, 16–39. London: National Portrait Gallery, 2018.

Spencer, Alfred, ed. *Memoirs of William Hickey*. 4 vols. New York: Alfred A. Knopf, 1913.

Spratt, Thomas, ed. *The Poetical Works of Abraham Cowley*. 4 vols. Edinburgh: Apollo Press, 1784.

Staves, Susan. "A Few Kind Words for the Fop." *Studies in English Literature, 1500–1900* 22, no. 3 (Summer 1982): 413–28.

Steggle, Matthew. *Richard Brome: Place and Politics on the Caroline Stage*. Manchester: Manchester University Press, 2004.

Stephens, Richard. "The Palace of Westminster and the London Market for Pictures." In *Court, Country, City: British Art and Architecture, 1660–1735*, edited by Mark Hallett, Nigel Llewellyn, and Martin Myrone, 29–50. New Haven and London: Yale University Press for the Yale Center for British Art and the Paul Mellon Centre for Studies in British Art, 2016.

Stewart, J. Douglas. *Sir Godfrey Kneller and the English Baroque Portrait*. Oxford Studies in the History of Art and Architecture. Oxford: Clarendon Press, 1983.

Stoichita, Victor. *The Pygmalion Effect: From Ovid to Hitchcock*. Translated by Alison Anderson. Chicago: University of Chicago Press, 2008.

——. *The Self-Aware Image: An Insight into Early Modern Meta-Painting*. Translated by Anne-Marie Glasheen. Cambridge: Cambridge University Press, 1997.

Sumner, Ann, ed. *Death, Passion and Politics: Van Dyck's Portraits of Venetia Stanley and George Digby*. London: Dulwich Picture Gallery, 1995.

Suthor, Nicola. *Bravura: Virtuosität und Mutwilligkeit in der Malerei der Frühen Neuzeit*. Munich: W. Fink, 2010.

Talley, Mansfield Kirby. *Portrait Painting in England: Studies in the Technical Literature before 1700*. London: Paul Mellon Centre for Studies in British Art, 1981.

Tallon, Laura. "'To Vindicate Her Beauty's Cause': The Sister Arts and Women Poets, 1680–1800." PhD dissertation, Boston University, 2016.

Tassi, Marguerite A. *The Scandal of Images: Iconoclasm, Eroticism, and Painting in Early Modern English Drama*. Selinsgrove, Penn.: Susquehanna University Press, 2005.

Thorssen, Marilyn J., ed. *A Critical Edition of James Shirley's "The Lady of Pleasure."* New York: Garland, 1980.

Tobin, Beth Fowkes. *Picturing Imperial Power: Colonial Subjects in Eighteenth-Century British Painting*. Durham, N.C.: Duke University Press, 1999.

Town, Edward. "A Biographical Dictionary of London Painters, 1547–1625." *Walpole Society* 76 (2014): 1–235.

Toynbee, Margaret, and Gyles Isham. "Joan Carlile (1606?–1679) – An Identification." *Burlington Magazine* 96, no. 618 (September 1954): 273–77.

Tscherny, Nadia. "An Un-Married Woman: Mary Edwards, William Hogarth, and a Case of Eighteenth-Century British Patronage." In *The Other Hogarth: Aesthetics of Difference*, edited by Bernadette Fort and Angela Rosenthal, 212–23. Princeton: Princeton University Press, 2001.

Van der Stighelen, Katlijne. "Cornelia Pruystinck en Lynken Cuypers: Over de grootmoederlijke erfenis van Anton van Dyck." *Jaarboek Koninklijk Museum voor Schone Kunsten, Antwerpen* (1995): 243–87.

—. "Van Dyck's Character Revisited: Valentiner versus de zeventiende-eeuwse historiografische traditie." In *Van Dyck 1599–1999: Conjectures and Refutations*, edited by Hans Vlieghe, 229–52. Turnhout: Brepols, 2001.

—. "Van Dyck's First Antwerp Period: Prologue to a Baroque Life Story." In *Van Dyck 1599–1641*, edited by Christopher Brown and Hans Vlieghe, 35–48. London: Royal Academy of Arts, 1999.

—. "Young Anthony: Archival Discoveries Relating to Van Dyck's Early Career." In *Van Dyck 350*, edited by Susan J. Barnes and Arthur K. Wheelock, 17–46. Studies in the History of Art 46. Washington, D.C.: National Gallery of Art, 1994.

VALENTINER, W. R. "Van Dyck's Character." *Art Quarterly* 13 (1950): 87–105.

VEEVERS, Erica. *Images of Love and Religion: Queen Henrietta Maria and Court Entertainments*. Cambridge: Cambridge University Press, 1989.

VERNEY, Frances Parthenope. *Memoirs of the Verney Family during the Seventeenth Century*. 4 vols. London and New York: Longmans, Green, and Co., 1892.

VERTUE, George. "The Note-books of George Vertue Relating to Artists and Collections in England, vol. I." *Walpole Society* 18 (1929–30): 1–163.

—. "The Note-books of George Vertue Relating to Artists and Collections in England, vol. IV." *Walpole Society* 24 (1935–36): 1–197.

VEY, Horst. "Die Bildnisse Everhard Jabachs." *Wallraf-Richartz-Jahrbuch* 29 (1967): 157–86.

—. *Die Zeichnungen Anton van Dycks*. 2 vols. Brussels: Verlag Arcade, 1962.

VICKERS, Nancy. "The Mistress in the Masterpiece." In *The Poetics of Gender*, edited by Nancy K. Miller, 19–41. New York: Columbia University Press, 1986.

VLIEGHE, Hans. *Corpus Rubenianum Ludwig Burchard, Part XIX (2): Portraits of Identified Sitters Painted in Antwerp*. London: Harvey Miller, 1987.

WALL, Cynthia. "The English Auction: Narratives of Dismantlings." *Eighteenth-Century Studies* 31, no. 1 (Fall 1997): 1–25.

WALPOLE, Horace. *Anecdotes of Painting in England*. 4 vols. London: J. Dodsley, 1782.

—. *Anecdotes of Painting in England*. 4 vols. New York: Arno Press, 1969.

WARNER, Malcolm, and Robyn Asleson, eds. *Great British Paintings from American Collections: Holbein to Hockney*. New Haven and London: Yale University Press, 2001.

WARNER, Michael. *Publics and Counterpublics*. New York: Zone Books, 2002.

WATERHOUSE, Ellis. *Painting in Britain, 1530–1790*. Pelican History of Art. London: Penguin, 1953.

WEILER, Larissa. "'For an Assured Freende is the Medicine of Life': Van Dyck and the English Virtuoso." *Netherlands Yearbook for History of Art / Nederlands Kunsthistorisch Jaarboek* 70 (2020): 214–39.

WELLS, Juliette. "A Harpist Arrives at Mansfield Park: Music and the Moral Ambiguity of Mary Crawford." *Persuasions* 28 (2006): 101–14.

WENDORF, Richard. *The Elements of Life: Biography and Portrait-Painting in Stuart and Georgian England*. Oxford: Clarendon Press, 1990.

—. *Sir Joshua Reynolds: The Painter in Society*. Cambridge, Mass.: Harvard University Press, 2009.

WEST, Shearer. "Patronage and Power: The Role of the Portrait in Eighteenth-Century England." In *Culture, Politics, and Society in Britain, 1660–1800*, edited by Jeremy Black and Jeremy Gregory, 131–53. Manchester: Manchester University Press, 1991.

WESTERMANN, Mariët. "After Iconography and Iconoclasm: Current Research in Netherlandish Art, 1566–1700." *Art Bulletin* 84, no. 2 (June 2002): 351–72.

WEYERMAN, Jacob Campo. *De levens-beschryvingen der Nederlandsche konst-schilders en konst-schilderessen, met een uytbreyding over de schilder-konst der ouden*. 4 vols. The Hague: E. Boucquet, H. Scheurleer, F. Boucquet, and J. de Jongh, 1729.

WHEELOCK, Arthur K. "The Search for 'The Central Orb': Van Dyck and His Historical Reputation." In *Anthony van Dyck*, edited by Arthur K. Wheelock, Julius Samuel Held, and Susan J. Barnes, 11–16. Washington, D.C.: National Gallery of Art, 1990.

WHITE, Christopher. *Anthony van Dyck & the Art of Portraiture*. London: Modern Art Press, 2021.

WILKINSON, C. H. *The Poems of Richard Lovelace*. 2nd edn. Oxford: Clarendon Press, 1953.

WILLIAMSON, George Charles. *Richard Cosway, R.A.* London: G. Bell and Sons, 1905.

WITTKOWER, Rudolf. *Bernini's Bust of Louis XIV*. Oxford: Oxford University Press, 1951.

WOLFTHAL, Diane. "Household Help: Early Modern Portraits of Female Servants." *Early Modern Women* 8 (Fall 2013): 5–52.

WOLOHOJIAN, Stephan, Melinda Watt, and Michael Gallagher. "A Grand Tableau: Charles Le Brun's Portrait of the Jabach Family." *Metropolitan Museum of Art Bulletin* 75, no. 1 (Summer 2017): 5–48.

WOOD, Christopher S. "'Curious Pictures' and the Art of Description." *Word & Image* 11, no. 4 (October–December 1995): 332–52.

—. "Indoor–Outdoor: The Studio around 1500." In *Inventions of the Studio: Renaissance to Romanticism*, edited by Michael Cole and Mary Pardo, 36–72. Chapel Hill: University of North Carolina Press, 2005.

WOOD, Jeremy, ed. *Lives of Rubens*. London: Pallas Athene, 2005.

—. "Nicholas Lanier (1588–1666) and the Origins of Drawings Collecting in Stuart England." In *Collecting Prints and Drawings in Europe, c. 1500–1750*, edited by Christopher Baker, Caroline Elam and Genevieve Warwick, 85–122. Aldershot: Ashgate, 2003.

—. "Van Dyck: A Catholic Artist in Protestant England, and the Notes on Painting Compiled by Francis Russell, 4th Earl of Bedford." In *Van Dyck, 1599–1999: Conjectures and Refutations*, edited by Hans Vlieghe, 167–98. Turnhout: Brepols, 2001.

—. "Van Dyck's 'Cabinet de Titien': The Contents and Dispersal of his Collection." *Burlington Magazine* 132, no. 1051 (October 1990): 680–96.

WOODALL, Joanna. *Anthonis Mor: Art and Authority*. Studies in Netherlandish Art and Cultural History 8. Zwolle: Waanders, 2007.

—. "Don't Be Seduced." *Art History* 16, no. 4 (December 1993): 657–63.

YATES, Julian. *Error, Misuse, Failure: Object Lessons from the English Renaissance*. Minneapolis: University of Minnesota Press, 2003.

ZIEGLER, Georgianna. "'More than Feminine Boldness': The Gift Books of Esther Inglis." In *Women, Writing, and the Reproduction of Culture in Tudor and Stuart Britain*, edited by Mary E. Burke, Jane Donawerth, Linda L. Dove, and Karen Nelson, 19–37. Syracuse: Syracuse University Press, 2000.

ZIONKOWSKI, Linda, and Miriam Hart. "'Is She Musical?': Players and Nonplayers in Austen's Fiction." In *Art and Artifact in Austen*, edited by Anna Battigelli, 206–23. Newark: University of Delaware Press, 2020.

ZWICKER, Steven N. "Sites of Instruction: Andrew Marvell and the Tropes of Restoration Portraiture." In *Politics, Transgression, and Representation at the Court of Charles II*, edited by Julia Marciari Alexander and Catharine MacLeod, 123–38. Studies in British Art 18. New Haven and London: Yale University Press for the Paul Mellon Centre for Studies in British Art, 2007.

Photograph Credits

bpk Bildagentur / Alte Pinakothek, Bayerische Staatsgemäldesammlungen / Art Resource, NY: 1

© The Metropolitan Museum of Art, New York: 3, 12, 32, 34, 43, 58, 72, 77, 80, 85

KHM-Museumsverband: 6

Royal Collection Trust / © Her Majesty Queen Elizabeth II 2022: 7, 16, 19, 22, 44, 49, 57, 65, 66, 67, 69, 75, 90, 92, 98

© Mairie de Bordeaux, Musée des Beaux-Arts, photo Frédéric Deval: 8

© The Frick Collection: 9, 59, 68

© National Trust Images / John Hammond: 10, 76

Private collection / Bridgeman Images: 11

© National Trust Images: 15

© Museo Nacional del Prado: 17, 21

Fondation Custodia, Collection Frits Lugt, Paris: 18

Courtesy Sotheby's: 20, 47

© National Trust: 26

Image courtesy of the Leiden Collection, New York: 27

Gemäldegalerie, Dresden (missing since 1945) / Alinari Archives, Florence: 33

Courtesy of the Getty's Open Content Program: 35

© The Trustees of the British Museum: 36, 54, 55, 79, 82, 83, 84, 88, 93

Courtesy Lamport Hall Preservation Trust: 38

Collection of the Duke of Northumberland, Syon House, London / Bridgeman Images: 39

© Christie's Images / Bridgeman Images: 40

Courtesy of the Crocker Museum of Art, Sacramento, California; gift of Suzanne Nady in memory of her parents, Jeanne and Joseph Falk: 41

© Philip Mould Ltd, London / Bridgeman Images: 45

Courtesy of the Huntington Art Museum, San Marino, California: 46

Alloa Tower, Collection of the Earl of Mar & Kellie: 51

© RMN-Grand Palais / Art Resource, NY: 52

Collection of the Earl of Pembroke, Wilton House, Wilts. / Bridgeman Images: 53

© Coram in the care of the Foundling Museum, London / Bridgeman Images: 56

Blenheim Palace, Oxfordshire, UK / Bridgeman Images: 61, 63, 64

© Ashmolean Museum: 70

© Royal Academy of Arts, London / photo John Hammond: 73

© Royal Academy of Arts, London / photo Prudence Cuming Associates Limited: 74

The Devonshire Collections, Chatsworth. Reproduced by permission of Chatsworth Settlement Trustees / Bridgeman Images: 96

© The Fitzwilliam Museum, Cambridge: 97

Courtesy of the Lewis Walpole Library, Yale University: 99

Photo NGC: 100

© National Trust Images / Derrick E. Witty: 103

Index

Page numbers in *italics* indicate illustrations

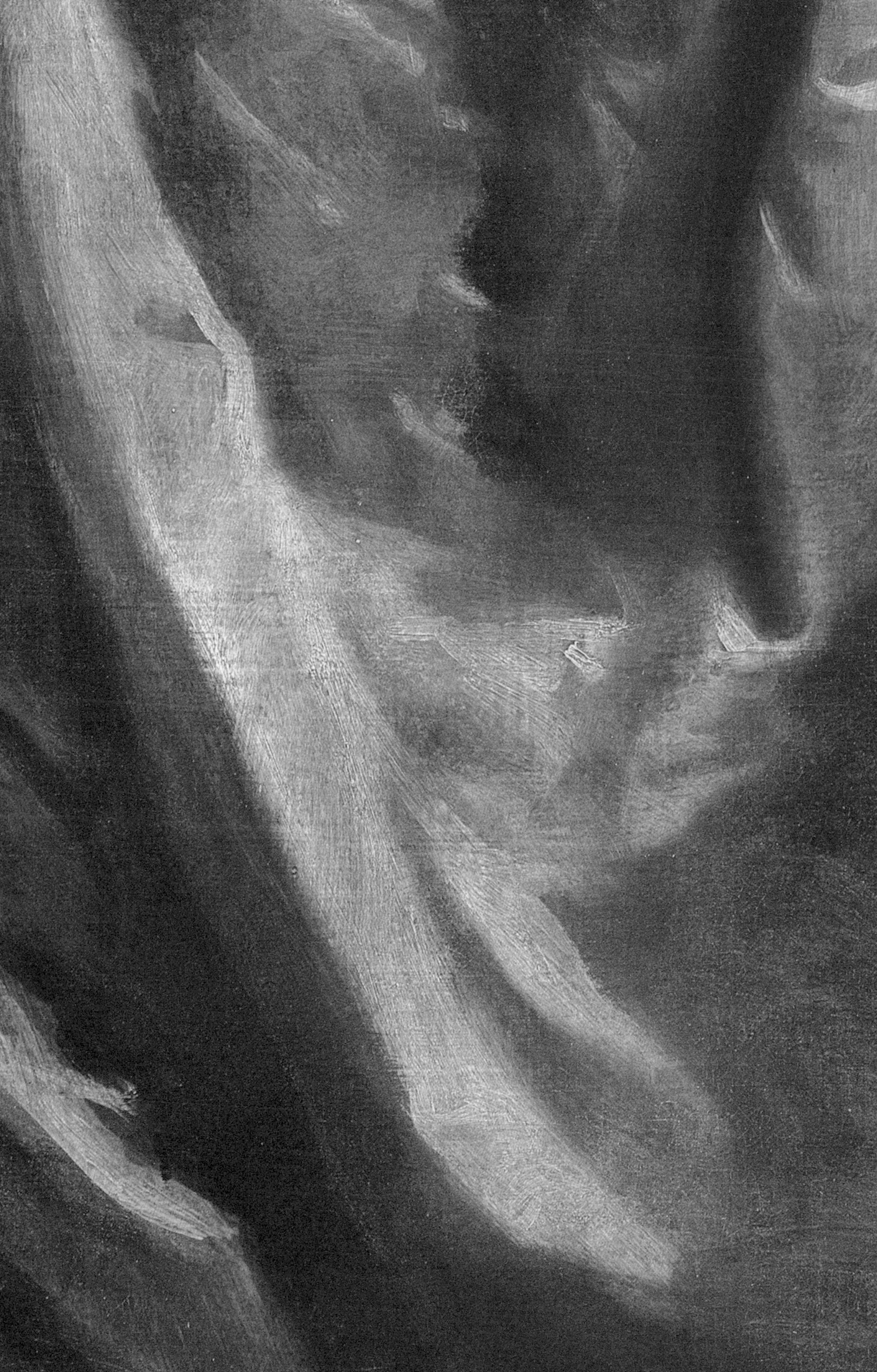

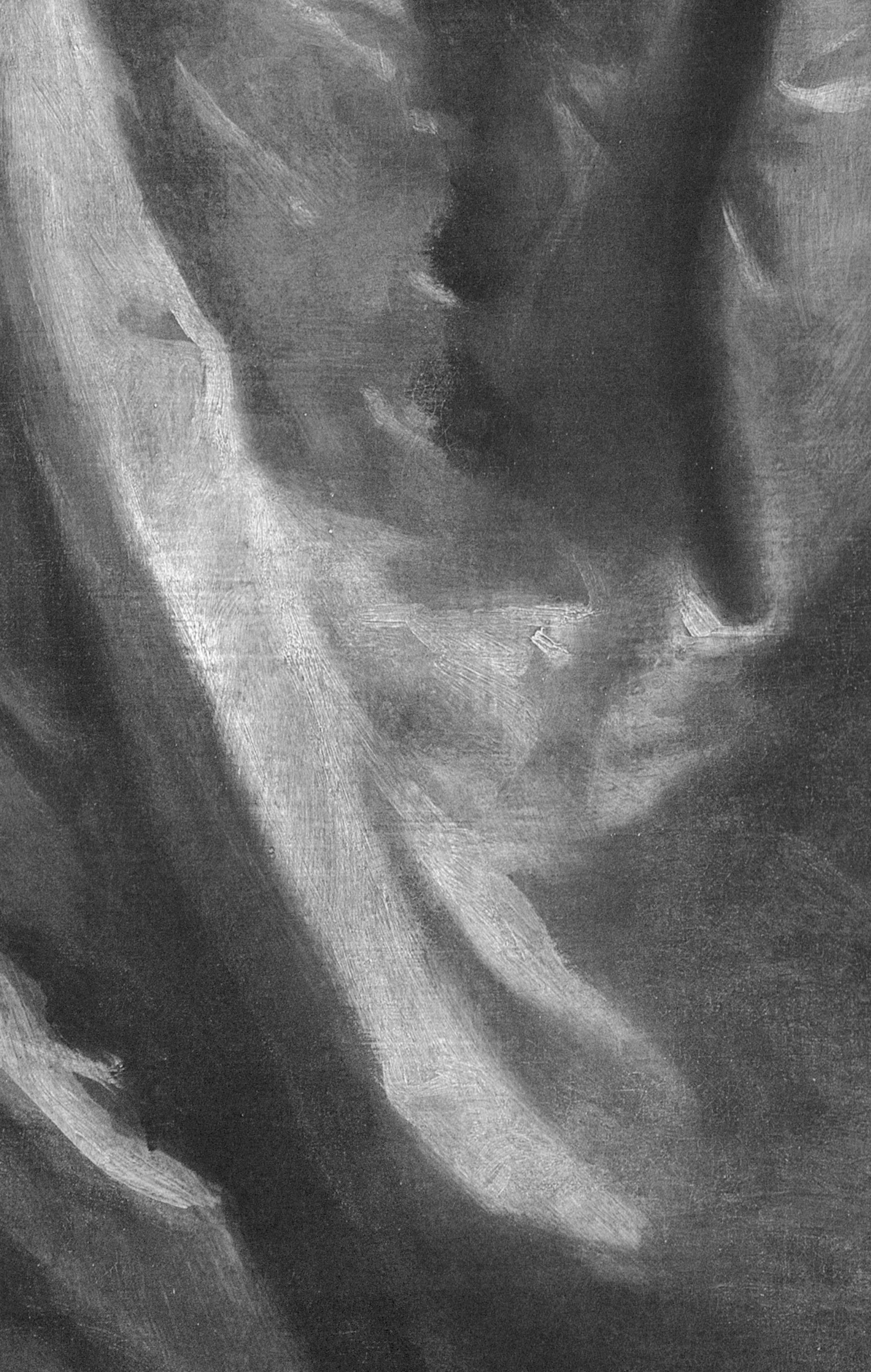